*Ris*

# Risk and Responsibility

WILLIAM LEISS AND
CHRISTINA CHOCIOLKO

McGill-Queen's University Press
Montreal & Kingston • London • Buffalo

© McGill-Queen's University Press 1994
ISBN 0-7735-1177-6 (cloth)
ISBN 0-7735-1194-6 (paper)

Legal deposit third quarter 1994
Bibliothèque nationale du Québec

This book has been published with the help of the
Canada Council through its block grant program and
Queen's University.

Printed in Canada on acid-free paper

---

**Canadian Cataloguing in Publication Data**

Leiss, William, 1939–
    Risk and responsibility
    Includes bibliographical references.
    ISBN 0-7735-1177-6 (bound). –
    ISBN 0-7735-1194-6 (pbk.)
    1. Risk – Sociological aspects. 2. Risk perception –
Sociological aspects. 3. Responsibility – Sociological
aspects. I. Chociolko, Christina, 1958–   . II. Title.
HM256.L44 1994   302′.12   C94-900249-6

---

Typeset in Baskerville 10/12
by Caractéra production graphique inc., Quebec City

# Contents

# Tables and Figures

FIGURES

# *Acknowledgments*

CHRISTINA CHOCIOLKO: My contributions to this book could not have been written without help and co-operation from many people. This is especially true with respect to my research on power frequency electric and magnetic fields health effects. Thanks to all those who over the years have given freely of their time in being interviewed or providing materials. I regret that it is not possible to thank everyone by name.

I am especially grateful to the reviewers who took the time and trouble to read and comment on earlier versions of my chapters, including Dr. David Bates (University of British Columbia), Dr. Kelly Gibney (B.C. Hydro), Dr. Andy Marino (Louisiana State University), Dr. John Marton, Richard Gallagher (B.C. Cancer Agency), Dr. Antonio Sastre (Bailey Research Associates), and Dr. Indira Nair (Carnegie Mellon University). Their informed criticism motivated several refinements and improvements. Any remaining errors are, of course, my sole responsibility.

Thanks also to Bob Anderson who first encouraged me to pursue my interest in the power frequency electric and magnetic fields health effects issue and showed me, more generally, that an academic environment within which I could pursue my interest in the relationships between science, technology, and society did indeed exist. Special thanks to Bill Leiss, who through the Centre for Policy Research on Science and Technology (CPROST) has given me the freedom to pursue my own and our mutual interests in health and environmental risk controversies, and to Liora Salter, whose pioneering work on science and public policy continues to inspire me. I look forward to continuing our work together as I pursue my research on the role of government scientists in environmental policy-making.

My more recent exploration of the use of consensus-negotiation processes in resolving environmental and natural resource disputes has benefited greatly from numerous discussions with Sarah Flynn (B.C. Commission on Resources and Environment), Alan Etkin, and Glenn Sigurdson (Sigurdson Milne) among others. I also owe thanks to the Multi-Stakeholder Working Group on Pulp Mill Effluent in B.C., especially Ann Hillyer of the West Coast Environmental Law Association, and participants in Washington State's Timber, Fish, and Wildlife agreement for giving me the opportunity to observe and for answering my questions about their processes.

Finally, I thank my friends and colleagues at CPROST and at Canadian Student Pugwash for their support. But most importantly I am indebted to my family. It is to my father's memory, my mother, and Rob that I dedicate this finished work.

The authors jointly thank two master's degree candidates in the Department of Communication at Simon Fraser University, Carolyn Liu and Alan Etkin, who made major contributions to the Alar case study reported in chapter 6, and also Ph.D. candidate Lori Walker, who provided research assistant support during the preparation of the manuscript.

Our ongoing work has benefited also from our association during 1992-93 with the members of a working group, convened under the auspices of the World Health Organization's European Centre for Environment and Health, which prepared the volume *Communicating Environment and Health Risks in Europe* (1993): Richard Stern (World Health Organization, The Netherlands), Marco Biocca (Italy), Philip Gray (U.K.), Klara Farago (Hungary), and Peter Wiedemann (Germany).

WILLIAM LEISS: Most of what I have learned about risk stems from my longstanding collaboration with Dan Krewski, Chief of Biostatistics and Computer Applications in the Environmental Health Directorate, Health and Welfare Canada, and with many of his associates in the Health Protection Branch in Ottawa, especially Len Ritter (now Executive Director of the Canadian Network of Toxicology Centres) and Manny Somers (now at the National Research Council). I have also benefited from an equally extensive mutual involvement in risk management issues with Frank Cedar and his colleagues in the Pesticides Directorate of Agriculture Canada, Ottawa, especially Wayne Ormrod and Jean Hollebone. Quite simply, the writing of this book would not have been possible without their indirect collaboration; at the same time, I must absolve all of them of any direct liability for the standpoint assumed in this book.

No less valuable has been my close collaboration with the Institute of Risk Research at the University of Waterloo, in particular with Niels Lind, John Shortreed, and Steve McColl. The Waterloo group is Canada's pioneer in the creation of an institutional framework for systematic risk research, and everyone in Canada who works in this area owes them a debt of gratitude for their service to this vitally important public policy area. I have enjoyed other long-term associations on risk management issues with the following: Bob Caton, Concord Environmental, Vancouver; Doug Chambers, SENES Consultants, Richmond Hill, Ontario; Robin Gregory, Decision Research, Eugene, Oregon; Kathryn Harrison and George Hoberg, University of British Columbia; Andy Keir, Keir Consultants, Toronto; Ed and Julia Levy, Quadra Logic Technologies, Vancouver; Carolyn Miller and Harvey Lerer, Environment Canada, Ottawa; Russ Roberts, National Research Council, Revenue Canada, and Industry, Science and Technology Canada, Ottawa; John Robinson, Director of the Sustainable Development Research Institute at the University of British Columbia; Marvin Stemeroff, management consultant, Deloitte & Touche, Guelph; Hajo Versteeg, consultant, Ottawa; Maria Paez Victor, Ontario Hydro; and Peter Victor, Ontario Ministry of Environment. I am especially grateful to Neil Collishaw (and later Murray Kaiserman), Tobacco Products Section, Health Protection Branch, Ottawa, for giving me an opportunity to participate in the Canadian government's defence of the Tobacco Products Control Act and in the difficult controversy over tobacco marketing and health protection.

The continued support from Stan Shapiro, Dean of Business Administration at Simon Fraser, and Roberta Shapiro, attorney, as well as from Arthur and Marilouise Kroker and Gaetan and Céline Tremblay of Montreal, is always a pleasure to acknowledge. My twenty-year collaboration on environmental issues, advertising, and other areas with Steve Kline, Department of Communication, Simon Fraser has been extended – courtesy of his limitless talents – to risk-perception research. More recently, new linkages have been established for me with the developing field of the management of technological change, thanks to Paul Guild, who holds the NSERC-SSHRC-Bell Northern Research-B. C. Tel chair in this area at Simon Fraser and the University of Waterloo. But, above all, it was Liora Salter, now of Osgoode Hall Law School at York University, who introduced me to risk management issues and who has collaborated with me on many projects in this area; her tireless devotion in exploring new research areas, her keen awareness of equity and ethical issues in public policy formation, and her generosity in aiding colleagues and students have set a very high standard of performance which many of us seek (usually unsuccessfully) to emulate.

Among the most enjoyable aspects of my academic work has been the mutual learning process on risk issues with my students at Simon Fraser: doctoral candidates Christina Chociolko, Roman Onufrijchuk, Pascal Milly, Richard Smith, and Lori Walker, as well as master's students Christine Massey and Miriam Levitt. Finally, members of my staff in the Office of the Vice President, Research, especially Barb Ralph and Holli Edgelow, assisted greatly in keeping my research efforts alive during my tenure in administration; Holli Edgelow expertly prepared the many drafts of the manuscript.

Robin Gregory took time from his own busy schedule to read a draft of this manuscript and provide good advice, for which we are most grateful; the readers for the Press also made many helpful suggestions, which we have incorporated. A number of individuals and institutions have furnished indispensable research materials over the years: Frank Cedar of Agriculture Canada, Diane Kirkpatrick of Health and Welfare Canada, and the staff at the Information Services Division, Office of Pesticides Programs, Environmental Protection Agency, Washington, D.C., who maintain the Public Dockets and who respond quickly and generously to requests for copies of materials from their voluminous collections, which are in themselves a tribute to the freedom of information legislation in the United States. Finally, I am pleased to acknowledge here the continuous support provided by a series of Social Sciences and Humanities Research Council grants, both under the strategic grants (Human Context of Science and Technology) and research grants programs, as well as a small grant from the Institute for Risk Research, during the entire period from 1987 to 1993 during which the research and writing for this book and the journal articles that preceded it was under way.

Marilyn Lawrence has been my companion for this book (as she has been for all of them), together with Magnus (properly: BISS Am. Can. Ch. Paquestone's Quantum Leap CD), Sappho, and Yoko, our Great Danes; my share of this project is dedicated to them.

# *Preface*

Controversies over how to manage health and environmental risks are among the most bitter disagreements in contemporary society. Trying to determine what is in the public interest is at the heart of these disagreements, but the core concerns of major sectors – industry, governments at all levels, and a wide range of voluntary associations – are also at stake. In Canada and elsewhere we have not had much success so far in seeking to defuse these controversies and to find solutions acceptable to a broad range of social actors. In this book we try to explain why this is so and what might be done about it.

In brief, our diagnosis is as follows. We cannot avoid encountering a very broad range of risks, some occurring naturally (earthquakes, disease, and so forth) and others being generated in our industrial economy (pollution and the like), many of which, at some time or other, will cause monetary and other types of losses to some persons and organizations. But, of course, our industrial activity also yields a broad range of individual and collective benefits, such as an abundance of goods, longer life, and leisure opportunities; these risks and benefits are in fact inseparable. Thus it is only to be expected that all individuals and institutions will seek to procure the benefits and avoid the losses. The best way to avoid losses is to find another party who can be tagged with the responsibility for assuming a risk from which you benefit.

For example, if we wish to enjoy the considerable advantages of products made from asbestos, a valuable mineral whose manufacture entails some risks, we can arrange to have those products made in other countries (especially where wages are lower) and simply purchase the finished goods. If we wish to indulge ourselves in the pleasures of nicotine addiction despite our awareness of the health risks, we can arrange to have a publicly funded health care system assume the responsibility for dealing with the resulting illnesses, while making no higher payments to support that system than others do. If we have sufficient investment capital and wish to make profits from underground coal mining, we can arrange to have the well-known excess occupational risk assumed by those in economically depressed regions who need the work. Or, if we and our fellows in one area have enough votes, we can make people living in areas with lower population densities deal with our garbage or see their rivers dammed to produce electricity.

In all these and myriad other ways, all of us, as individuals and organizations, have abundant opportunities to secure a benefit while off-loading the responsibility for the risk on someone else. Indeed this goes on all around us, every day. Not surprisingly, those who think that they are getting the short end of the stick in these trans-actions are inclined to become upset, sometimes seriously so, and if they can they may seek to nullify them. The outcomes of these struggles are not a trivial matter for us, because many (but not all) of the activities in question produce the stream of net benefits on which the prosperity of industrial society depends. If those who are clearly disadvantaged are not dealt with fairly – that is, if we do not establish a just allocation of responsibility for risks – one by one those activities will be curtailed by their opposition, and we shall all be the poorer.

*Note to the reader:* Those who are familiar with the risk studies liter-ature may wish to skip or skim chapter 2, which is designed primarily to introduce the previously uninitiated to this subject.

# *Abbreviations*

| | |
|---|---|
| ADI | acceptable daily intake |
| ALARA | as low as reasonably achievable |
| BATNA | best alternative to a negotiated agreement |
| BC CCA | British Columbia Cancer Control Agency |
| BC PIAC | British Columbia Public Interest Advocacy Centre |
| BCA | Benefit-Cost Analysis |
| BCFGA | British Columbia Fruit Growers Association |
| BCSF | British Columbia Stakeholder Forum |
| BCTF | B.C. Tree Fruits Ltd. |
| BCUC | British Columbia Utilities Commission |
| C-S RD | Comox-Strathcona Regional District |
| CAPCO | Canadian Association of Pesticides Control Officers |
| CEA | Cost-Effectiveness Analysis |
| CNA | Canadian Nuclear Association |
| CNS | central nervous system |
| COFI | Council of Forest Industries |
| CPFP | Canadian Pacific Forest Products |
| CVRC | Comox Valley Rerouting Committee |
| DER | Department of Environmental Regulation (U.S.) |
| EDB | ethylene dibromide |
| FDA | Food and Drug Administration |
| HPB | Health Protection Branch |
| HWC | Health and Welfare Canada |
| IWA-Canada | International Woodworkers of America – Canada |
| MOH | Ministry of Health |
| MRL | Maximum Residue Limits |
| MSF | multi-stakeholder forum |
| MW | megawatts |
| NCI | National Cancer Institute |

| | |
|---|---|
| NEP | National Environmental Protection Act (U.S.) |
| NESC | National Electric Safety Code (U.S.) |
| NOEL | no observable effect level |
| NRDC | Natural Resources Defense Council (U.S.) |
| NYS PSC | New York State Public Service Commission |
| OSHA | Occupational Safety and Health Administration (U.S.) |
| OTA | Office of Technology Assessment |
| PCP | pentachlorophenol |
| PPWC | The Pulp, Paper and Woodworkers of Canada |
| PUC | Public Utilities Commission |
| RBA | Risk-Benefit Analysis |
| ROW | Right of Way |
| SAP | Scientific Advisory Panel |
| SEIA | Socio-Economic Impact Analysis |
| TLV | threshold limit value |
| UDMH | unsymmetrical dimethylhydrazine |
| UFFI | urea formaldehyde foam insulation |
| USDA | United States Department of Agriculture |
| WCB | Workers Compensation Board |
| WCELA | West Coast Environmental Law Association |

*Risk and Responsibility*

# CHAPTER ONE

# Introduction:
# The Trouble with Risk

... the defining of risk is essentially a political act.
Roger E. Kasperson[1]

"Risk" is one of the most powerful concepts in modern society. Its power is derived from its range, for it is at the same time intuitively familiar and broadly applicable in everyday life, on the one hand, and exceedingly subtle and open to precise statement in its statistical expressions, on the other.

To the extent to which gambling has been a favourite activity since time immemorial, the meaning of risk has always been intuitively evident to people. To gamble is to incur voluntarily a certain loss (the value of the wager) in the expectation of a larger gain, with the foreknowledge that the chance of any return on the wager is in some degree less than certain. Today, anyone who plays a low-stakes game of poker with friends, buys a house, makes a borrowing decision based on expectations of interest rate changes, dabbles in the stock market, closes a purchase of a major consumer durable on the promise that the "lowest available price" has been offered, chooses a career path in the light of expected future labour market conditions, plays the lotteries or frequents the casinos – that is, almost everyone in society – engages more or less knowingly in risk-taking behaviour.

Despite the general public's familiarity with risk-taking activity, disagreements about how to manage some types of risks – specifically, those that affect our health and the condition of our natural environment – are among the most heated controversies in contemporary society. This appears to cause great vexation to many engineers and natural scientists, who are skilled in the technical description of risk (as the probability of occurrence of events), and who simply cannot comprehend what the fuss is all about. They look at the generally low probabilities of expected harm associated with most health and environmental risks, compare this to the often high levels of public concern, and conclude that the public is hopelessly confused in its thinking about risk.

Yet there is a simple explanation for the otherwise puzzling level of controversy associated with the concept of risk, one that is rooted in the *fear of falling victim unfairly to uncompensated loss*. People know from their experience with gambling of all kinds that risk involves the chance of loss. They also know that they can control their exposure to loss so long as their participation in the game is voluntary. But when their exposure is involuntary – for example, when the nuclear power industry seeks to build a plant near their community – many wonder whether, if something does happen to damage their health, things can be put right again, and who will be responsible for doing so.[2]

Individuals can make bad mistakes if their fear of uncompensated loss causes them to become excessively risk-averse, that is, to have an unreasonable level of concern about something for which there is a high degree of assurance that no harm is likely to come to them. Exposure to loss from risk-taking activity is intuitively obvious; less clear is the exposure that results from excessive risk aversion. For example, the development of a technology with the potential for enormous health benefits, such as a new drug, might be inhibited by concerns about what appear to be negligible levels of potential harm. There is an important point here: Both individuals and societies can be exposed to the chance of loss *as a result of both risk-taking and risk-averse behaviour.*

We are exposed to the chance of loss from risk-averse behaviour simply because enormous benefits to both society and individuals accrue from judicious risk-taking. This is patently obvious in such cases as the development of prescription drugs, for in most cases the side-effect risks (of varying severity, including death) are far outweighed by their palliative results. (We assume that the risks and benefits have been assessed carefully by competent regulatory authorities, as they are today in Canada.) And yet, no matter how advantageous the trade-offs between benefits and risks may be, given the complexity of the institutional, legal, economic, and personal relations that can be involved in risk-taking activity, the allocation of responsibility for the inevitable losses associated with that activity can prove to be exceedingly difficult. For example, in the case of women in the United States who had taken the drug diethylstilbestrol (DES) during pregnancy and whose daughters had suffered severe adverse health effects later in life, a complex lawsuit and an innovative legal ruling was required in order to sort out who would bear responsibility for the losses.[3]

If there is one lesson in the book we have written, it is this: *All of us in modern society have a direct and vital interest in the proper allocation of responsibility for risky activity.* On the one hand, we simply cannot maintain our attained level of material well-being without engaging in such activity. On the other hand, any failure to properly apportion responsibility for the inevitable losses, and to compensate adequately those who suffer unfairly the adverse effects of societal choices about risks, will result in a gradually rising level of popular support for risk-avoidance in evaluating new technologies or lifestyle options.

This book is about the interplay of risks and responsibilities. It utilizes the case study approach to its subject matter, looking at this interplay in the light of some major controversies about health and environmental risks that have occurred in North America and elsewhere recently, which in some instances are still very much on the agenda. Our principal cases illustrate the risks and responsibilities associated with electromagnetic fields and power line frequencies; Alar, a chemical growth-regulator for food crops; and antisapstain chemicals, which are pesticides used on softwood lumber products. We also present shorter studies on Alachlor, a herbicide used worldwide for many crops, especially corn and soybeans; formaldehyde, a widely used industrial chemical; and tobacco use. The relevant concerns centre primarily on human health risks, although environmental impacts are also important in some instances. These cases were selected for their abundant documentation and because the controversies surrounding them certainly are representative of societal debates about environmental and health risks generally.

In the social allocation of responsibility for risks, some losses incurred by individuals (such as those due to wagering at racetracks and gaming tables) are easily assignable exclusively to those who engage in the activities, and thus do not give rise to claims for compensation. On the other hand, liability for other types of losses (such as those suffered by innocent bystanders in accidents) is assumed to fall, one way or another, on the shoulders of the public or insurers. But even where a collectivity assumes liability, the apportioning of shares of responsibility among its various institutions – private sector firms (including insurance firms), governments at various levels, and a mixture of the two – is vexatious, with the resultant quarrels often ending up in the courts. For example, who is responsible for the losses incurred by tobacco product users? The individual consumers, who, it is held by some, ought to have known better than to use such dangerous products? Governments, which happily collect huge tax revenues from the sale of these goods and also require manufacturers to place specific health hazard warnings on them, and which are then arguably responsible if, due to the inadequacy of such warnings, many consumers ignore them? The manufacturers, who are legally entitled to flog their hazardous wares, and who until recently absurdly but strenuously denied the abundant evidence of epidemic adverse health effects? And if the answer is "all of the above, in some measure," what are the precise shares of liability among them? Many decades of expensive court battles will be required before a definitive answer to this last question is found.

The results of our case studies will show that neither the distinction between voluntary and involuntary risk, nor any other such straight-forward dichotomy, can offer a simple and widely acceptable formula for allocating responsibility for risks. Yet there are some useful lessons to be drawn from our society's experiences to date with health and environmental risk controversies, especially about the basis for arriving at a consensus on these matters, and we review these lessons in our concluding chapter.

## WHAT IS RISK?

Two quite different but equally fundamental aspects of the concept of risk are intertwined in all of the discussion to follow. First, risk means "exposure to the chance of loss"; and second, for many (but not all) of the risks that we in modern society encounter, our exposure is deliberately induced by some social actor in order to realize an incremental net benefit. None of the disagreements about risk that pervade our society are comprehensible unless we see the necessary connection between these two propositions. So, for example, an individual exposes herself to potential loss of health in return for the pleasures of nicotine addiction; workers using toxic chemicals to turn out consumer goods are exposed to potential loss or diminution of health in return for jobs, company profits, and an overall contribution to economic prosperity; the public is exposed to risk from the chlorine added to drinking water in return for the health benefits derived from chlorine's capacity to combat infectious agents and contaminants; and both agricultural workers and the general public are exposed to potential loss through the application of pesticides in return for a range of benefits, including improved quality of the food supply, profits and economic prosperity, and protection from disease-carrying insects.

We appear to be surrounded by risks. Indeed, we are and always have been. Risk is an inherent feature of the unpredictable variation that occurs in the repetitive events that make up the interactions of all organisms with their environments, such as, in the case of humans, the billions of separate molecular-level "events" involved in eating, sleeping, and moving about every day. To some extent what has happened recently is that we have become more aware of the riskiness present in our environment, simply because we are able (with greater or lesser degrees of assurance) to "put a number on" the effects arising from our encounters with hazards that have been around since the beginning of time, such as geological radon gas, or that have become a familiar part of everyday life, such as cigarette smoking. It may be that this has caused some people to worry more than is warranted about hazards to their health, yet it is also the case that an acquaintance with what risk means can be of substantial benefit to us.

Assuming the existence of good records, the occurrence of individual events within an overall framework of repetitive activity can be described with a high degree of accuracy, and with this knowledge we can often take sensible steps to reduce risks and avoid some losses. For example, some experts now believe that between 40 and 50 per cent of all regular cigarette smokers will die prematurely as a result of their habit, which is a risk of 1 premature death for every 2 or 2.5 cases of lifetime exposure (few other risks even come close to such a figure, at least in the industrialized world).[4] Presumably we could use this knowledge to make sensible choices about what we choose to indulge in.

Note that while a well-described risk has an air of precision about it, precision is not the same thing as certainty. Risk estimates are a composite assortment of uncertainties, stemming from an inescapable difficulty in specifying relevant parameters, especially exposure. Thus the precision that is spoken of here has to do with the random distribution of effects within populations, not the fate of particular individuals. The value of risk estimates, despite the above-noted limitations, has to be judged in relation to the alternatives available as aids in decision-making – hunches, intuitions, and sheer guesswork, all of which are greatly vulnerable to error.[5]

Risk estimates can be very valuable in controlling or modulating our exposure to hazards, including those that cannot be avoided as well as those to which we wish to expose ourselves on account of their offsetting benefits. For example:

- estimating the probability of major earthquakes in specific areas allows us to formulate appropriate building codes;
- the huge databases on automobile accidents help both individuals and societies to develop appropriate behavioural norms for wearing seatbelts and avoiding the consumption of alcohol and other

psychoactive drugs, and help manufacturers to design safety improvements;

- the epidemiological data relating tobacco use to a wide variety of severe adverse health effects, including fatal lung and heart diseases, can be useful in offsetting the intuitive discounting of risk by individuals, who are misled by the very long latency periods (twenty years or more) of tobacco-induced disease into thinking that the activity is far less hazardous than it actually is;
- the discovery of statistical associations between excessive exposure to hazardous materials, both naturally occurring and invented – asbestos, vinyl chloride, radon, mercury, lead, feldspar, uranium, pesticides, and many others – and adverse health effects, both for humans and other species, can lead to regulations that are crafted with sufficient precision so as to protect individuals against unacceptable risk while still allowing us collectively to derive huge benefits from the use of such materials.

Despite this precision, however, there is no shortage of disagreement among individuals concerning the significance of various risks.

### WHY IS RISK CONTROVERSIAL?

We believe that health and environmental risks (especially those to which people are exposed involuntarily) are controversial because people believe – with good reason, we might add – that they cannot control their exposure to the chance of unfair and uncompensated loss. This belief arises, in part, because the experts testify that there are large uncertainties in the estimates.[6]

What do we mean by "loss" in the spheres of environmental and health risks? Some but by no means all of its dimensions are:

1 In the realm of individual and family health and well-being:
  - adverse physical or physiological consequences, including death;
  - adverse psychological effects, due to stress, worry, or anxiety;
  - lack of or decline in amenities, such as a pleasant physical environment.

2 In the realm of individual and family prosperity:
  - loss or diminution of present livelihood through injury or death;
  - loss of personal equity through relative decline in home property values;
  - loss of future opportunity for career and income.

3 In the realm of societal well-being:
   • lack of or decline in the social stability brought by economic growth, both quantitative and qualitative;
   • exposure to large-scale risks, originating in nature or society, that cannot be controlled by available technologies.

In this context a question comes immediately to the fore: "Who is responsible for making recompense for the potential loss?" To say that those who engage in risky activity must be prepared to underwrite the chance of loss is irrelevant for the entire range of activities that fall under the category of "involuntary risk." Admittedly, in the not-so-distant past, unlucky individuals who were exposed to special hazards as a result of the random distribution of occupational conditions (think of the chimney-sweeps of the early modern era and their scrotal cancer[7]) were left to suffer unaided the consequences of their fate; but most of us would find such callousness unacceptable these days. Exposure to involuntary risks is often the result of accidental factors (such as the pattern of residential housing) and is very unevenly distributed among the population. Thus while "society" as a whole benefits from an activity such as toxic chemical production, for example, some fraction of the population living near the plant bears a disproportionate share of whatever excess risk exists. In such cases the questions of who ought to be responsible for the elevated level of risk, and what steps should be taken by way of mitigation or compensation for excess risk, are very lively ones indeed.

The dominant institutions in our society, which are usually the proponents of projects leading to the citizen's exposure to involuntary risks (new chemicals, power installations, hazardous-waste treatment, and the like), are all too often evasive or silent when it comes to indicating who will be responsible for resultant losses to individuals. This pervasive side-stepping of the issue of responsibility provides a perfectly simple and understandable explanation for much of the public's risk-averse attitudes with respect to involuntary risk. Moreover, even when those institutions do communicate with the citizenry, they often emphasize the inevitable uncertainties associated with risk estimates as if those unknown factors were comforting (e.g., "most probably nothing bad will happen"), not understanding that this information is more likely to increase the citizen's concern.[8] Nevertheless, opponents to risk-taking activity have been characterized as irrational, ignorant, inconsistent, overzealous, mentally ill, and victims of a host of other infirmities. In a superb early chapter of her book *Risk and Rationality*, K.S. Shrader-Frechette has assembled and dissected a nice selection of this nonsense, exposing its fallacies as well as the right-wing political agenda that motivates much of it. As an antidote one cannot do better than to keep in mind the wisdom of Paul Slovic:

... although one may legitimately disagree with public perceptions of risk, they are clearly not irrational. More generally, psychometric research demonstrates that, whereas experts define risk in a narrow, technical way, the public has a richer, more complex view that incorporates value-laden considerations such as equity, catastrophic potential, and controllability.[9]

It is easy to see why risk-assessment experts who have a sophisticated understanding of probability theory might assume that the general public will always be hopelessly confused about risk. It has been pointed out that citizens can threaten their own long-term prosperity by being excessively risk-averse and by overestimating the health and environmental risks to which they are involuntarily exposed. Indeed, such public attitudes can most certainly be self-defeating, for example, if they lead to calls for the removal of toxic substances (asbestos in buildings, hazardous wastes already buried in relatively stable land formations) when this act is more likely to increase rather than decrease the overall level of risk.

Asbestos removal is a good example. The charge has been laid that there is a huge difference in the health risks associated with different forms of this mineral (chrysotile vs. amphibole crocidolite); that most of the asbestos in place in buildings is the chrysotile form, which has relatively low risk associated with it; and that many billions of dollars will be wasted in removing chrysotile asbestos from buildings for no good reason. An editorial in the magazine *Science* concludes: "Asbestos in buildings, unless damaged, does not shed fibers. The removal process releases asbestos fibers which could result in more cancer in the workmen than would have resulted in the usual occupants had the asbestos been left in place." Very persuasive arguments have been advanced in support of this charge.[10]

What are the various sources of the public's pervasive risk-averse attitudes? Many have been detailed nicely in Paul Slovic's risk-perception research (there is a brief section in chapter 2 about this). Yet in our opinion one of the chief sources of citizens' overestimation of risk is a vague, intuitive familiarity with the long history – stretching back to the origins of the Industrial Revolution – of the *calculated under-assessment of risk by our dominant institutions* (industry and governments), in particular the wilful neglect involved in the exposure of workers to hazardous substances and processes. We shall return to this topic at greater length in chapter 3.[11]

Even where voluntary risks, such as an individual's consuming of hazardous substances or engaging in hazardous sports, are concerned the matter of responsibility for risk-taking is far from uncontroversial. This is especially true in societies such as Canada, where the collectivity, through a publicly funded health care program, assumes general responsibility for health care for all individuals. Under these circumstances the fraction of the population who use tobacco products or other psychoactive drugs (legal or illegal); who drive automobiles recklessly; who choose skiing, motorcyle-riding or other relatively hazardous recreations; or who expose themselves thoughtlessly to sexually transmitted diseases – in other words, those who voluntarily expose themselves to an elevated level of risk – in effect do not take responsibility for the excessive health-care costs of their individual choices, but rather spread the responsibility for the effects of their risk-taking behaviour across the entire population, including of course those individual taxpayers who abstain from all of the above. As the financial burden of collective health care escalates remorselessly, this allocation of risks and responsibilities by individuals likely will be challenged at some point.

### THE NATURE OF RISK-TAKING ACTIVITY

The *chance of loss* and the *expectation of net benefit* are inescapably linked in risk activity. The reasons for this become clearer with the aid of a useful matrix worked out by Kenneth MacCrimmon and Donald Wehrung. In it they identify three basic determinants of risk – lack of control, lack of information, and lack of time – and describe them as follows:[12]

If we had complete control over the situation, we could determine the best outcome and there would be no risk. If we had complete information about which event would occur, we could select the best alternative based on this knowledge and again there would be no risk. If we had unlimited time in which to decide which alternative to choose, we could wait until the outcome of the uncertain event was resolved and then choose the best alternative after the fact. This scenario also involves no risk.

The determinants fold into and compound each other. Thus, lack of control, which may result from either natural or human forces, can

Table 1-1
Relation Between Components and Determinants of Risk

| Determinants of Risk | Components of Risk | | |
|---|---|---|---|
| | Magnitude of Potential Loss | Chances of Potential Loss | Exposure to Potential Loss |
| Lack of Control<br>Natural forces<br>Human forces<br>Insufficient resources<br>Insufficient information<br>Insufficient time | Cannot effect size of potential loss | Cannot effect chances of potential loss | Cannot effect exposure to potential loss |
| Lack of Information<br>Inadequate<br>Unreliable<br>Unfamiliar<br>Unpredictable<br>Insufficient time | Do now know size of potential loss | Do not know chances of potential loss | Do not know exposure to potential loss |
| Lack of time<br>Must choose before uncertain event occurs | Insufficient time to understand or reduce magnitude of potential loss | Insufficient time to understand or reduce chance of potential loss | Insufficient time to understand or reduce exposure to potential loss |

Source: MacCrimmon & Wehrung 1986, Table 1.1; reprinted with permission of The Free Press (a division of Macmillan, Inc.) from Kenneth R. MacCrimmon and Donald A. Wehrung, *Taking Risks: The Management of Uncertainty*, ©1986, Kenneth R. MacCrimmon and Donald A. Wehrung.

stem from insufficient resources but also from insufficient information or time. Lack of information can be caused by inadequate or unreliable data, but also from lack of time. Lack of time is simply a reflection of the fact that we must make a choice before an uncertain event plays itself out (thus bets must be placed at the racetrack before the horses leave the gate).

MacCrimmon and Wehrung then array these determinants of risk against what they call the components of risk: the magnitude of potential loss, the chances of potential loss, and the exposure to potential loss. The resultant matrix is shown in Table 1-1.[13]

When we engage in risky activity all three of the determinants are usually operative. However, the degree or extent of the risk to which we are exposed is often controllable, and this is easiest to see in the case of a voluntary risk. Thus in a decision to wager on a horse race we can limit our exposure to loss by deciding to put down just a small bet; we can also seek to limit the chance of loss by gaining information about the event, including the comparative records of the horses, jockeys, and trainers; finally, we can seek to gain greater control over the circumstances – specifically, avoiding a race that has been "fixed" by unscrupulous actors – by only frequenting those establishments that have a good reputation.

Where involuntary risks such as exposure to loss from earthquakes or floods are concerned, both individuals and societies will seek to reduce risks to some level that may be thought to be "acceptable" by gaining time (advance planning for emergencies), gaining information (doing scientific research on patterns of occurrence), and gaining control by reducing exposure (regulating building construction on fault lines and flood plains). Normally some risk will remain simply because the costs of eliminating it – say, by changing the entire course of a river – are simply too great, especially when we realize that devoting excessively large resources to eliminating one area of risk may yield an overall net loss in well-being, because we have been unable to address other areas where reducing risk would be relatively more cost-effective. This is largely a function of the huge range of risks to which we are exposed, and under these circumstances it might be wise to compare the value of an additional investment of public resources in flood control with an equal investment in an entirely different area altogether, such as a media campaign to encourage seatbelt use while driving. Allocation of private and public resources in the light of comparative risk reduction, however, is a most contentious issue, largely because the responsibilities for risk control in different domains tend to fall on quite different shoulders, and we do not yet have a good mechanism for amalgamating those responsibilities.

We first introduce the reader in chapter 2 to basic risk terminology and to the approaches that have evolved for managing health and environmental risks,[14] before setting out on our exploration of the main theme in our book, namely, the interplay between risk and responsibility. We conclude this chapter with a brief look at Canada's risk-management process in the case of formaldehyde, which shows how institutions approach the matter of trade-offs between risks and benefits for industrial chemicals.

In chapter 3 we then seek to explain more fully why, despite our abundance of talented risk managers and the elaborate procedures devised to date for managing risks in the public interest, so many environment- and health-risk issues remain controversial. We elaborate some of the specific ways in which both institutions and individuals seek to avoid assuming full responsibility for the risks they initiate by seeking to off-load the potential losses on other parties. This theme is pursued through a discussion of how both experts and the general public calculate the types of trade-offs between risks and benefits, and the resultant net benefits or losses, that appear to reside in the hazardous activities they propose to engage in. These sometimes elaborately calculated trade-offs are full of estimates and assumptions that, upon scrutiny by others, often turn out to have highly unstable foundations, typically leading to an exaggeration of benefits and an understated or incomplete description of risks. Charges of attempted manipulation and deception and of a casual trifling with the lives or well-being of innocent persons are often the result. The charges and counter-charges are not infrequently couched in extreme terms, and in the United States, where a fondness for paying lawyers' bills prevails, are fought out in the courts, sometimes over a period of a decade or more of continuous litigation.[15] We conclude this chapter with a quick look at tobacco use, a case in which many individuals continue to make trade-offs for themselves in a very risky domain.

In Part Two, "Obstacles to Consensus: Two Seemingly Intractable Controversies," we present a pair of extensive and original case studies drawn from very different arenas in which long and bitter controversies have occurred. The first (recounted in chapters 4 and 5) has to do with concerns over the possible health effects from the electrical and magnetic fields associated with power lines and the use of electrical equipment in homes, offices, and factories. The second, described in chapter 6, deals with Alar, a chemical used as a plant growth-regulator (classified as a pesticide) on apple and other fruit and vegetable crops from 1968 to 1989; after simmering for many years the controversy over Alar came to a head in a blaze of media publicity in the first half of 1989 and ended with the manufacturer's withdrawal of its product from the marketplace.

In both cases we have a similar objective: to track the interplay between, on the one hand, the highly technical assessment of risks and benefits and the trade-offs between the two made by hosts of experts working for a variety of institutions, and, on the other, the public perception of these same elements. These types of controversies cannot be understood unless one is willing to delve deeply into the rival processes of reasoning and accumulation of evidence that the various parties submit for the public record and fight over in administrative hearings, courts, the offices of public officials, citizens' forums, and the media. We have taken the trouble to supply a full record of these processes in the two cases. But we have also sought not to dump a jumble of convoluted and conflicting testimony onto the reader's table, so to speak, but rather to sort through and array the material with a purpose in mind: namely, to pinpoint the key zones of disagreement so as to be able to say what might have been the grounds of a possible consensus among the contending parties.

In the past thirty years or so, risks associated with industrial chemicals have given rise to the most hard-fought battles, and within this category pesticides occupy a place of special prominence, largely because they are substances deliberately engineered to destroy organisms. The fight over Alar was typical of these battles, and there is much to learn from that record that is applicable to others now being waged (over chlorine, for example) and still others yet to come.[16]

When the outcome of a pesticide battle has been to withdraw a chemical from the market, often other chemicals – which may or may not be structurally related to each other – have been substituted for the offending one. This is what makes our other case study about electric and magnetic fields (EMF) so important, because here no substitution is possible in principle, a fact that will limit severely society's range of risk-management options if at some point an irresistible public demand for action – based upon a perception of unreasonable adverse health effects from exposure to power line EMF – is demanded. Given the absolutely indispensable nature of electricity supply in a modern economy, everyone has an interest in arriving at a reasonable, consensual, and cost-effective set of decisions about how to manage this issue.

Part Three, "Towards Consensus," returns to the Alar case, in order to ask whether a consensus among interested parties might have been achieved if the actors had had the will to do so. (This topic is in fact suggested by the public confession made by some of those parties that it might have been desirable and possible to seek to achieve a mutually agreed-upon resolution to their differences – alas, a confession made too late at the ceremonies held after it was all over.) We then go on to explore what has been achieved in other areas when interested parties have indeed chosen to try to negotiate their differences and arrive at a voluntary agreement, and we try to distill from these experiences, still in their infancy, some lessons and guidelines that may be generally applicable to controversies over environment and health risks.

This discussion sets the stage for our final elaborated case study, which deals with another protracted dispute, this one over the chemicals called antisapstains, which have been used in the wood products industry for a long time. This dispute, however, ended with a voluntary agreement that has many remarkable aspects, from which we seek to draw more precise guidance applicable to other situations.

Our concluding chapter, entitled "Useful Lessons," argues that our society must find a way to develop broad popular support for appropriate risk-taking activity if we are to avoid the prospect of paralysing our mechanisms of government and jeopardizing our future well-being by indulging in zero-sum disputes. We go on to ask all of the contending parties to conduct themselves in ways that will further this end. We ask individuals and groups to abandon all unreasonably risk-averse stances and to recognize that our well-being as a society depends upon continuous risk-taking activity, so long as it is responsibly and equitably managed in the public interest; we ask institutions to take responsibility for conducting full and honest risk assessments in a timely fashion, so as to provide a credible basis for all parties to confront the onerous tasks of balancing benefits and risks with the best possible information base and of arriving at acceptable trade-offs between them. And we ask all parties to face each other directly across the table, at every opportunity that presents itself, and to negotiate their differences in frank and open exchanges.

If and when they do so, they will find that the inherent difficulties in risk assessments will represent one of the chief and enduring obstacles to negotiating consensus, no matter how high the level of goodwill among the parties. The outcomes of scientific risk assessments that describe possible adverse effects (serious illness or death) are at the centre of most controversies about health and environmental risks. This is simply because the potential losses appear to so outweigh any possible benefits (say, in employment income or "better products") that the very notion of calmly acquiescing in "rational" trade-offs seems obscene. In other words, an adverse effect that threatens to diminish an already achieved quality of life appears more ominous than does the surrendering of a future stream of benefits, even if it were the case that without those benefits the attained standard of living must decline, for good health is perceived to be a necessary presupposition for the enjoyment of any level of other benefits whatsoever.

This should be confronted as a challenge, not as an excuse for abandoning the effort. We hope that the explorations of risk-assessment problems in the cases considered in this book, as well as the valuable contributions along the same lines of other authors referred to in our notes, will be received in this spirit. And because this is such a core element in all of the discussion to follow, we thought it appropriate to close this chapter with a sample of what is involved when the assessment of risks erupts into controversy.

### ALACHLOR: A RISK-ASSESSMENT CONTROVERSY

There is a case in Canada in which conflicting scientific health-risk assessments squared off against each other in a quasi-legal setting, and fortunately a full verbatim transcript of the proceedings was kept.[17]

The case involved Alachlor, a herbicide made by the Monsanto Corporation under the trade name Lasso® and widely used around the world on a variety of crops, especially corn and soybeans. It was registered for use in Canada in 1969. Like Alar, Alachlor became the subject of an EPA Special Review and of separate but concurrent regulatory proceedings in Canada; like Alar, it was classified by the EPA in category $B_2$, "probable human carcinogen," against the strong objections of the registrant company. Unlike Alar, at the end of the regulatory proceedings Alachlor was allowed by the EPA to stay on the American market, while in Canada its registration was cancelled by the federal government based on the judgment of Health and Welfare Canada (HWC) that it presented an unacceptable health risk.

The reason we know so much about the conflicting risk assessments is that in Canada the registrant forced the government to defend its decision before a quasi-judicial tribunal, including cross-examination of officials by lawyers, and the resulting five-thousand-page transcript of proceedings offers a glimpse into this corner of "mandated science" that is ordinarily closed to public view.[18] The events leading up to the formation of the tribunal can be described briefly.

The controversy began in the United States and Canada when authorities in both countries realized, in 1976, that the original toxicology studies submitted by Monsanto in support of its registration application were possibly worthless. The studies involving Alachlor were among over a thousand done under contract during the 1960s and 1970s in the United States by Industrial Bio-Test Laboratories, a private scientific testing firm. Many hundreds of these tests were subsequently found to be fraudulent (the company was prosecuted and convicted). In both countries registrants were required to submit new and valid studies. Monsanto submitted its replacement toxicology studies on Alachlor in 1982.

Having evaluated Monsanto's replacement studies, Health and Welfare Canada's scientists concluded their assessment with a finding that the product's use represented unacceptable risk to human health. This judgment was passed on to Agriculture Canada, which has statutory authority over pesticides in Canada and which notified Monsanto in 1985 that it was proceeding to cancel the registration for Alachlor. The company exercised its right of appeal under Canada's Pest Control Products Act, and the federal Minister of Agriculture appointed a five-member tribunal to hear the arguments. The tribunal agreed unanimously that the cancellation decision was unjustified and in 1987 advised overturning it, but the Minister refused to accept this advice.[19]

Monsanto went to court later that year (not a common step in Canada) arguing before the Federal Court of Appeal that since the

Minister was bound by the act to establish the tribunal he was similarly bound to accept its findings, certainly where the members were unanimous. The court declined to so circumscribe the Minister's discretionary authority, the Supreme Court of Canada refused to grant leave to appeal, and thus the cancellation was allowed to stand.

In the United States, the EPA initiated a Special Review of Alachlor at the end of 1984 with a "Position Document." The "Technical Support Document," containing downward revisions of the assessed risk, appeared in September 1986, and in that same month the EPA's Scientific Advisory Panel (SAP) conducted hearings on this document, grilling the agency scientists on their toxicology data evaluations and questioning sharply (but, unlike with Alar, not explicitly rejecting) the $B_2$ classification. Dietary risk was assessed by EPA staff in 1984 to be in the range of $1 \times 10^{-4}$ to $1 \times 10^{-5}$, but in 1986 this had been reduced to the range of $2 \times 10^{-5}$ to $2 \times 10^{-6}$ because of revised estimates for residue levels.[20] In 1986 total losses to farmers were figured at \$500–\$750 million and reduction in net social benefits at \$300–\$500 million. The agency concluded its risk/benefit analysis by saying that the dietary risks were "reasonable given the benefits of continued use," but it required occupational exposure to be reduced by placing Alachlor in a "restricted" category, meaning that only certified applicators could apply it, and by other provisions.

The official notice of this set of regulatory actions, as finally published in the *Federal Register* on 31 December 1987, contains an extended "dialogue" between EPA staff and the report of its Scientific Advisory Panel, with the former stating clearly where it remained in disagreement with the latter.[21]

The transcript of hearings before the Alachlor Review Board in Canada has been dissected by Brunk, Haworth, and Lee in their 1991 book *Value Assumptions in Risk Assessment*.[22] They compare in detail three different scientific risk assessments – by Monsanto, Health and Welfare Canada, and the Alachlor Review Board – dealing with (1) the minute particulars of the toxicology data (nature, type, and significance of the tumours in test animals[23] as well as the dose-response interpretation); and (2) the methodology of exposure studies, including what assumptions to make regarding the applicator's compliance with recommended safety procedures and how best to "amortize" short-term exposures occurring in the act of application over a farmer's lifetime. The "bottom line" results were as follows:[24]

• MONSANTO: "There is no reasonable probability that Alachlor presents a risk to humans."

- HEALTH AND WELFARE CANADA: There is unacceptable carcinogenic risk to humans.
- REVIEW BOARD: A "reasonable" estimate falls about midway between the first two. HWC's risk estimates are an "unreasonable worst-case scenario," and a preferable risk estimate would place human exposure at a level one to ten thousand times lower than the lowest dose at which carcinogenic response was observed in the rat, which is a "reasonable margin of safety"; when this correction is done, and risk is balanced against benefits, continued use of Alachlor represents an acceptable trade-off.

For the most part, the discussion in Canada used qualitative criteria, not the quantitative estimates so much in favour in the United States.

Brunk, Haworth, and Lee go on to analyse in minute detail the way in which each of these positions (especially the first two) was defended in the course of the extended hearings, which included formal cross-examination of government officials and expert witnesses by lawyers for both Monsanto and the Government of Canada. Because the transcript is so rich they are able to show clearly how, for both Monsanto and HWC, interpretive differences based on qualitative judgments – which are to some extent arbitrary on both sides, or at least open to rebuttal from an equally good dissenting argument – when they are factored step by step into the building blocks of a completed risk assessment, can lead from the same data to diametrically opposed conclusions. Moreover, these interpretive differences range from quite broad issues (how to amortize exposure) to incredibly detailed ones (the intricate pathology of animal tissue indicators).

To some extent the Review Board tried to side-step the impasse between Monsanto and the Canadian government by admitting into evidence new data (not previously submitted by the registrant) and new expert witnesses. Using this new evidence to reduce HWC's risk estimate, the Board then found that the risk/benefit trade-off was tipped in Monsanto's favour. But Brunk, Haworth, and Lee expose as a mere self-delusion the Board's explicit statement that its judgment was purely "scientific." They demonstrate convincingly that the Board arrived at its position on an acceptable trade-off in effect by *double-counting the benefits,* and in seeking to explain why the Board might have been led to do this, they uncover the relevant set of operative assumptions about technology and social policy that lay behind their conclusions.[25]

A wide range of interest groups participated in the latter stages of the regulatory proceedings on Alachlor both in the United States and in Canada, but the general public never got involved in the

Alachlor controversy in the same way it did in the Alar case. Had it done so, the sense of despair and frustration over conflicting scientific risk assessments that can be detected in the Alar case (as we shall see in chapter 6) would have been amplified in this one.[26]

Going one step further, we know that there are between 60,000 and 70,000 industrial chemicals in common use, about 3,000 of which account for most of the use volume by weight.[27] On how many of them do we have general agreement among major interested parties on a risk assessment? Far too few. In the United States during the last decade there have been bitter and sometimes downright dirty bureaucratic struggles over the risk assessments for formaldehyde, lead, cadmium, benzene, pesticides generally, asbestos, and many other substances – struggles that all too often have been dragged into the courtroom or the congressional hearing room, where judges and politicians appear to get a special thrill out of hearing paid experts give conflicting testimony on scientific reasoning and then expostulating on why one side or another "won" this gladitorial combat.

How is the general public to determine its own stance? In many of these cases the public has been given a good view of this clash of experts, which might explain why so many people are completely confused as to how risk-taking or risk-averse they should be in dealing with such substances. On the other hand, in cases involving such hazards as nuclear power, PCBs, dioxins and furans (as a class of compounds), and pesticides generally, for a variety of reasons the public's "assessment" of risk appears to deviate markedly from an expert consensus for no good reason, in other words, to be unreasonably risk-averse as judged from the experts' standpoint.[28] With respect to environmental risks, all too often governments, in their desperate search for economic development megaprojects that have marginally positive bottom lines, appear to be compromised with respect to their manipulations of environmental and socio-economic impact assessments. Small wonder, therefore, if citizens are inclined to disbelieve anything they hear from these sources. Finally, in many domains of voluntary risk (automobile use, legal and illegal drug use, exposure to sunlight, and many others), where the databases are large and the expert risk assessments quite reliable, many citizens appear to be insufficiently risk-averse, from a public policy standpoint, with respect to both individual health effects and social costs.

In all such settings our sophisticated, quantitative risk assessments (where they exist) too often do not seem to serve fully or adequately their essential purpose – namely, to provide a sound basis for reasonable, humane, and cost-effective choices for both institutions and individuals. Given the great time, trouble, and money it takes for our skilled scientists to produce them (not to mention the vexations imposed on the laboratory animal subjects), with difficulties inherent in every step – the interpretation of test animal tissue pathology, the models for extrapolation from animal data to human health effects, the collection of reliable human exposure data, with all of the foregoing assembled by one group and then reviewed and often re-reviewed by others, and so on – it is a shame if, at the end of all this, there is no agreement among major interested parties on either the reliability or the usefulness of these endeavours.

What is to be done? Could we simply dispense with scientific risk assessment entirely and seek to resolve controversies over environmental and health risks without them? Or, if we cannot do without them, can we "insulate" them from the zones of contention and so protect the neutrality and objectivity that ought to belong to them intrinsically (or so many would claim) as the offspring of scientific research?

There are many reasons why we should not think that we can do without scientific risk assessments, however flawed or incomplete they might be in practice. On the one hand, institutions are unlikely to be able to do without them, because decisions based on evaluations of risks involve the actual or potential accumulation of substantial liabilities for compensation as a result of occupational exposure (there are billions of dollars of outstanding claims for asbestos-related diseases alone), catastrophic accidents, or changing morbidity and mortality patterns. Neither the shareholders of private firms nor the citizens who elect governments are likely to tolerate the making of such decisions on purely subjective or intuitive grounds. On the other hand, individuals cannot do without guidance from risk assessments either. We often underestimate risks associated with familiar activities and thus become over-confident of our ability to avoid harm. As the risk-perception studies have shown so well, our purely intuitive judgments about risk often mislead us badly and cause us inadvertently to undermine the basis of our own well-being.

Can we insulate risk assessment, thus preserving its neutrality and objectivity? Numerous well-argued studies have concluded that there  is no hope of insulating science and its idealized neutrality with respect to social interests once it enters the realm of economic and public policy choices where interests do contend.[29] Risk assessments that are designed to assist private firms and governments to make judgments about the probability of harm to others flowing from their choices, no matter how finely outfitted they may be in the elaborate costumes of science, will inevitably be stripped of those protective garments and made to serve the simpler ends of self-interest. Brunk, Haworth, and Lee come to the same conclusion after reviewing exhaustively the Alachlor Review Board's reasoning. They go on to argue that risk acceptability is an "intrinsically *political* debate among the various value communities (e.g., industry, farmers, environmentalists, farm-wives, etc.)" and that such debates ought to be refereed not by scientists but by "the traditional *political* institutions where questions of social value are typically hammered out, whether these be the legislatures or the government agencies beholden to them."[30]

This is where we must part company with them, however. We can only think that they may have arrived at this conclusion by considering too limited a sample of such controversies. If one looks further, even no further than the cases involving Alar and antisapstains reviewed later in this book, one could not fail to conclude that "government agencies" are incapable of "hammering out" matters of conflicting social values. The same could be said for political institutions, if by them is meant legislative bodies. The thing that most terrifies sensible politicians, and rightly so, leaving aside those that seek to profit by the manipulation of single-issue fanaticism, is a value conflict.

Government regulatory agencies routinely settled matters of risk acceptability in the past behind closed doors, all by themselves, quietly and without fuss. They were able to do so because the constituencies they served were limited in scope and operated on the basis of similar values and assumptions. In agriculture, for example, those constituencies were the suppliers and users of new chemicals and associated technological solutions that transformed the entire basis of farming practices in a few short decades after the Second World War. Unintended side effects, such as the impact of DDT on bird populations or of excessive chemical fertilizer use on soil productivity, for a long time were beyond the pale of contemplation.

The beginning of the end for the ability of those agencies to "solve" matters such as acceptable risk occurred when a wider spectrum of constituencies, including labour, consumer, and environmental interests, forced themselves into the meeting rooms and began demanding an equal say in the outcomes. For a while some agencies, like the EPA, tried to respond with a high-wire act of extraordinary agility, juggling the competing demands of myriad special interests while also using a balancing-bar at which Congress and the White House tugged intermittently. Despite their valiant efforts, however, the final results were not pretty.

We do not disagree that democratically elected legislatures are the ultimate authorities on acceptable risk, as they are on most items of civic business. Yet the compromises that rightly mark all legislative action tend to blur the solutions they encapsulate, certainly so far as complex technical matters are concerned. To illustrate, citizens can understand the political trade-offs that result in benefits flowing to specific regions when military contracts are directed to local districts, and they can judge for themselves the appropriateness of the distribution. But who in his or her right mind would expect a palatable result from a debate among legislators as to whether the upper limit of acceptable risk for any and every case of health or environmental risk should be set at $1 \times 10^{-5}$ as opposed to $1 \times 10^{-6}$? Or whether or not either Alar or Alachlor, or both, should be banned from a jurisdiction?

This may be regarded as a poor attempt at a *reductio ad absurdum* on the views quoted just above: what Brunk and his co-authors meant is that the "government agencies beholden to" those legislators should decide such matters, subject to the legislators' ultimate concurrence. And yet we believe that our case studies, as well as many others, show that the risk assessment judgments in all such instances could have and indeed have had all kinds of different outcomes, every one of them passionately justified by appeals to proper science, depending on the agency, the prevailing political winds in the national jurisdiction, the economic forces bearing upon the users, the year, and even the identities of the particular civil servants involved. No experienced politician would wade willingly into this swamp.

We suggest therefore that neither government agencies nor the political masters they serve are in any position to make judgments for the rest of us on acceptable risk. So how are such judgments to be made? Brunk, Haworth, and Lee say (in a passage cited earlier) that risk acceptability is properly the subject of an "intrinsically *political* debate among the various value communities." A nice idea, in principle, but in truth such a debate almost never occurs, largely because ordinarily there is no venue in which it can take place; for the most part the interactions among such parties amount to a pseudo-conversation in which each speaks but none listens. This absence of a venue in which interested parties regularly could meet face to face is useful to all of them, in a perverse way: it helps them to avoid taking responsibility for the full consequences of the positions they each hold on what are acceptable risks and acceptable risk/benefit trade-offs.

# PART ONE

# The Roots of Disagreement

# CHAPTER TWO

# Managing Risks

There is no such thing as "real risk" or "objective risk."
Paul Slovic[1]

In a number of important senses, managing the process of technological innovation in modern industrial societies is nothing but the assessment, communication, and management of risks. Through an understanding of the nature and consequences of risks, governments, businesses, and the public seek to monitor and control those industrial products and practices that are potentially harmful to human health, the well-being of other species, and ecosystem functions.

In practice, managing the risks associated with technological innovations means making difficult choices on highly complex matters. Industries, regulatory authorities, and citizens must determine levels of acceptable risk for environmental and health hazards – for instance, those caused by toxic chemicals. There are often widely differing judgments on what levels of risk are acceptable and on who is entitled make the call. All parties must also make choices about how to balance estimated health and environmental risks against the estimated economic and social benefits to be derived from using toxic chemicals, in full knowledge of the likelihood that new information accumulated in the future will show that certain earlier choices were incorrect.

For members of the public, managing the process of technological innovation means making choices about the truly bewildering array of risks present in industrial societies, both voluntary (such as smoking or skiing) and involuntary (such as airborne lead or occupational hazards). This means, among many other things, deciding how to regulate one's exposure to voluntary risks, how to rank risks in relation to each other, and deciding to what extent governments should regulate hazardous products and processes and how much they should spend on reducing risks associated with them.

## HEALTH AND ENVIRONMENTAL RISKS

Health and environmental hazards share the dimensions of risk summarized by MacCrimmon and Wehrung (Table 1-1). They also illustrate the interrelation of the two aspects mentioned earlier: exposure to potential loss is the source of our concern, and (except for natural hazards) our exposure to potential loss originates in a social decision to seek some overriding net benefit.

In order to understand better the nature of the frequent disagreements about these types of risks, we must spend a bit more time on defining the key terms in the debate. The definitions quoted below are from a useful handbook compiled by the Environmental Health Directorate of Health and Welfare Canada's Health Protection Branch.[2] The reader will note that the main thrust of these definitions is towards arriving at, first, a quantifiable estimate (risk assessment) of the potential loss, and second, an institutional decision (risk management) on how best to control the assessed risk by specifying boundary conditions for actions and allocating responsibility for consequences.

In this context risk itself is defined as "a measure of both the hazard to health (or the environment) from exposure to a substance and the probability of its occurrence." The key word here is "measure": *how great* are both the consequences and the likelihood of the unwelcome event? Risk is also multi-dimensional. It is a function of both the nature of a particular hazard arising from a product, process, or natural occurrence (for example, the fire that can result from a flammable substance) and of the chance that any person or group will encounter that hazard and suffer an adverse effect. Chance or probability is primarily a function of exposure, although it is also dependent on the intensity of exposure as well as on the susceptibility of particular organisms to specific substances. Both acute and chronic effects are investigated through studies in toxicology, epidemiology, and molecular chemistry.

Thus risk is a function of hazard plus exposure. Hazard has been defined as "the adverse impact on health that can result from exposure to a substance"; exposure as "contact between a substance and an individual or a population." (Note that we may refer to hazards to the environment as well, that is, to ecosystems and to plant and animal species.) The threat posed by a hazard depends not only on the severity of its effect but also on whether or not the effect is reversible. Sometimes the substance itself is regarded as the hazard, and sometimes it is the adverse impact that is highlighted. For example, if a quantity of gasoline is stored in your basement in a poorly sealed container, is the hazard represented by the gasoline itself or by the possible fire caused by the ignition of its vapours? In practical terms the difference is usually irrelevant.

The main subcategories for the risk approach to health and environmental issues are: risk assessment or risk analysis; risk perception and acceptable risk; risk communication; and risk management. Each will be discussed briefly.

### Risk Assessment

Risk assessment or risk analysis attempts to provide scientific estimates of health and environmental risks, and to identify sources of uncertainty inherent in scientific data. A comprehensive summary of approaches in this area prepared by the United States National Science Foundation presents the components of risk assessment as follows:[3]

- Risk-Source Characterization: A description of the characteristics of the risk source that have a potential for creating risk (e.g., types, amounts, timing, and probabilities of release of toxic substances, energies, etc.).
- Exposure Assessment: Measurement or estimation of the intensity, frequency, and duration of human or other exposures to the risk agents produced by a source of risk.
- Dose-Response Assessment: Characterization of the relationship between the dose of the risk agent received and the health and other consequences to exposed populations.
- Risk Estimation: The process of integrating a risk-source characterization with an exposure assessment with a dose-response assessment to produce overall summary measures of the level of the health, safety, or environmental risk being assessed.

The resulting risk analysis and assessment is supposed to reveal fully the nature and significance of each of the components, as well as that of the overall judgment; the methods used to make dose-response extrapolations; the assumptions used in arriving at estimates of effects and degrees of uncertainties in those estimates; and the distribution of risk across various sectors of the population.[4] The "bottom line" for a risk assessment often presents the possible adverse effect in the form of a certain (numerical) probability that there will be an increased risk, based on all the assumptions made in the analysis, for each segment of an exposed population and for each type of exposure, summed up as total risk.

*Risk Perception*

Another dimension entirely is represented by perceived risk. In the final analysis, regulatory, legislative, and legal authorities all must respond to the way in which the citizens in each country understand the nature and variety of risks in the environment, how they "rank" each type of risk in relation to others, and how they expect public authorities to manage or control risks. This understanding is conveyed in electoral platforms (for example, George Bush's posturing in 1988 as the candidate who would be the "environmental president"), in lobbying by pressure groups, in public reactions to media coverage of catastrophic accidents, and in many other ways. There is no doubt that the prevailing public idea of acceptable risk does affect the outcomes of risk-management processes. Disagreements between "expert" and "public" evaluations in risk assessments present a great challenge to attempts to arrive at a reasoned consensus on the management of risks in contemporary industrial societies.

Perceived risk has been defined as "an impression or intuitive judgement about the nature and magnitude of a health risk. Perceptions of risk involve the judgements people make when they are asked to characterize and evaluate hazardous substances and activities." It is still possible to encounter the view that the public perception of risk is largely "irrational," despite the fact that a great deal of innovative research has been done in this area during the last fifteen years, the results of which show clearly that in many cases there is a distinct underlying pattern in intuitive judgments about risk.[5]

Risk perception research has been heavily influenced by psychological studies examining how people make judgments under conditions of uncertainty.[6] These studies have shown that most people experience difficulties in understanding probabilistic expressions, and also that people tend to overestimate the frequency of rare events and underestimate the frequency of common events. Perceptions of risk are also known to change markedly over time as new information becomes available. These characteristics, as well as others associated with them in the processes of everyday decision-making, frequently lead individuals to deny uncertainty, misjudge risks, and maintain unwarranted confidence in judgments of fact. In general, our information processing is hindered by biases and limitations that affect our subjective evaluation of probabilities.

Certain characteristics of risk are also known to influence risk perception. For example, individuals tend to voluntarily accept higher risk levels for themselves than for society as a whole, frequently because they feel that the benefits are worthwhile and that they have autonomy over their lives.  In general, three main factors have been shown to influence perceived risk: the degree to which the hazard is understood, the degree to which it involves feelings of dread (including fatalities), and the size and type of the population at risk (especially if children are singled out).

In addition, we all tend to simplify complex and uncertain information, relying on rules of thumb and tradition to shape our perceptions. Further, there are difficulties in detecting omissions in information received, in evaluating opinions, and in detecting inconsistencies in debates about risk. Despite these difficulties in assessing risk, people may utilize existing information to form strong views about risks, and such perceptions are often resistant to change: new evidence that is consistent with initial perceptions is accepted, while that which is contrary is dismissed.

Finally, most people do not perceive all lives to be of equal value, nor do they perceive all forms of death as equal. Frequently, nonfatal health impairment such as permanent brain damage is seen as more serious than death itself. Oftentimes in the public's view, the significance of an event's *probability* tends to decrease as conceivable *consequences* increase, until what is possible becomes more feared than what is probable.

The judgments made by "the general public" about hazards and risks are often contrasted unfavourably with those made by experts who have professional training in engineering or natural-science disciplines and who use quantitative methods for assessing and comparing risks. Such experts are wont to contrast "real risk" with "perceived risk," using "real risk" as a code phrase for expert (quantitative) risk assessment. The former is implicitly "correct" while the latter is "incorrect."

This is most unfortunate for a number of reasons. First, it assumes a level of certainty and finality about quantitative risk assessments that is patently unjustified. Expert assessments change regularly (as they must) with the arrival of new information, just as they did within the last few years in the area of thresholds for maximum permissible exposure to radiation sources. Second, it overlooks the fact that in the majority of cases where industrial chemicals or processes are concerned, reliable quantitative risk assessments have never been carried out, usually due to lack of good exposure data, but in many instances also because the basic hazard identification profile is incomplete.[7] When hazards are underassessed by experts, as they have been all too often in the history of industrial society, people have no choice but to rely upon their intuitions. Third, in a series of insightful studies Paul Slovic and his colleagues have explored the many vagaries in the expert assessment of risk, including such factors as over-confidence, use of essentially different measures for the same activity or technology, and inability to make risk judgments in areas outside the expert's own field that are qualitatively different from the judgments about risk made by a cross-section of the general population.[8] Researchers have also shown that there are wide variations in judgments on fundamental matters of scientific interpretation among professional toxicologists, which are related to their primary institutional affiliation (industry, government, or university). In general there is now widespread agreement that until recently the capacity of scientific risk assessment to render definitive verdicts for the non-expert public on the scope and magnitude of most hazards was "oversold" by experts, and that lower expectations would be more fitting.[9]

The most up-to-date research has confirmed these findings, telling us that "the controversies over chemical risks in our society may be fueled as much by weaknesses in the science of risk assessment as by misconceptions of the public."[10] Thus the only safe guideline when dealing with disagreements about risk is to eschew any presupposition about who may be right or wrong, or "rational" as opposed to "irrational," and to regard all statements about risk as having equal standing, subject to the findings of a rigorous examination of the logical and factual basis of those statements.

### Acceptable Risk

In an attempt to develop risk policies that will be satisfactory to the public, decision-makers have utilized the notion of "acceptable risk."[11] This concept is based on the assumption that there exists a small but non-zero probability of an untoward event of some sort occurring, below which level the general population is willing, tacitly or explicitly, to accept a risk. The increasing sophistication of analytical methodology has resulted in the detection of environmental contaminants in ever-decreasing levels of concentration, with concentrations at the parts per trillion or quadrillion level now being measured. Unless exposure is unusually great (as it is sometimes) or the substance is unusually potent (as in the case of chemical and biological warfare materials, which are designed for just this effect), or there is bioaccumulation of toxic substances over time, the level of risk associated with environmental toxicants at such concentration levels is probably relatively small – but it is not zero. The difficulty for society is, once again, rooted in comparative risk. Would it be wise to seek to eliminate altogether some technologically created hazards, such as dioxins, when the assessed level of probable adverse effect at some non-zero level appears to be far less – by many orders of magnitude – than are other existing risks in our environment arising from common natural hazards or voluntary human activities?[12] It is important to consider what level of risk should be considered socially acceptable.

There are no well-marked paths in this forest, however. In a very real sense only the tacit acquiescence by the general public of any country in its government's regulatory policy illumines, by default, that nation's sense of acceptable risk. To be sure, when controversies over specific substances flare up (see the cases discussed in later chapters), that acquiescence can vanish overnight, and a new threshold for acceptable risk can emerge – *usually for that substance alone*! A kind of tacit conspiracy between the public and its government keeps the loss of acquiescence from spreading to the entire realm of regulated substances, which is a very good thing, because it would be impossible to re-evaluate everything that has gone through the system previously in the light of changing standards for acceptable risk.[13]

What follows is our guess about what lies hidden in this forest, that is, the largely unarticulated, composite judgment about the basis for what passes as acceptable risk. Our hunch is that all of the following conditions have to be met for a level of risk to be judged acceptable:

- the level of risk itself is below some threshold (NOEL), or on a risk-risk comparison a risk is incurred to avoid another risk of greater magnitude;
- benefits clearly appear to outweigh risks, ultimately just on the intuitive level (e.g., "our industry needs to use this risky product or process in order to remain competitive in world markets");
- there is no manifestly unjust distribution of risks and benefits, in particular, the lives or health of some specific and identifiable individuals are not being sacrificed in the name of the "general good."

A few comments by way of amplification are necessary. First, NOEL is the "no observable effect level" (more fully, "no observable adverse effect level"), which refers to the dose of a potentially toxic material that does not produce evidence of illness when administered to a sample of test animals in laboratory studies. When a safety factor is added and some statistical manipulations are carried out, the NOEL can be translated into an "acceptable daily intake" (ADI) of that material for humans, expressed in quantitative terms: so many micrograms per kilogram of body weight. (All food additives are regulated in this way, for example.) However, in the specific case of medical treatment for life-threatening illness, we will voluntarily incur a risk that is known to have a high probability of actually doing us harm (such as a bone-marrow transplant with its attendant risk of fatal infection) if the intention is to avoid the even greater risk that would ensue if the treatment were not administered. This is what is known as a risk-risk comparison.[14]

The second element in the composite judgment of acceptable risk is that benefits must outweigh risks. In some types of regulatory decision-making, a great effort is made to estimate these benefits in quantitative terms, but the general public rarely sees such calculations; rather, for the most part there is only the broad statement that some level of potential benefit exists and that it is vital for our economic well-being to seek to realize that benefit.[15] The third element deals with distributive justice: everyone knows (or at least suspects) that some individuals incur certain types of risks – usually in occupational settings – that are not imposed on the general public, and that this is acceptable so long as both the first and second requirements (the determination of a quantitatively estimated threshold by a regulatory authority, and the existence of net benefits) have been respected. But there are other limits as well, especially the principle that no humans will be exposed to any level of risk purely for the sake of benefiting other persons, as so-called "guinea pigs," again with the exception of medical procedures (where terminally ill patients may be given experimental drugs with their consent).[16]

Governments, which are mandated to make decisions on public health issues, are compelled by the sheer numbers of risks that must be managed to take a broad perspective on the totality of risks and the means of reducing them. Policies that are directed primarily at alleviating public anxieties, particularly in response to well-publicized accidents, can result in large expenditures having low relative effectiveness. Conversely, serious risks may also be neglected due to public indifference or lack of awareness.

## RISK COMMUNICATION

Relevant to dilemmas of risk perception and acceptable risk is a growing interest in "risk communication." By this phrase is meant the flow of information and risk evaluations back and forth among academic experts, regulatory practitioners, interest groups, and the general public. The sharp disagreements that can occur among members of these constituencies over the best ways to assess or manage risks are sometimes based on disagreements over principles or approaches, sometimes on differences in the information base available to various parties, and sometimes on a failure to consider carefully each other's position. At least some portion of those disagreements can be expected to disappear when due attention is paid to the need for better risk communication. In particular, it is important that risk data be expressed in understandable terms, that uncertainties surrounding estimates of risk be understood, that perceived risks be taken into account, and that effective channels of communication be established among individuals, advocacy groups, governments, and corporate actors involved in decisions about risks.[17]

The term risk communication has been formally defined by Covello and his associates as "any purposeful exchange of information about health or environmental risks between interested parties." More specifically, they state that

risk communication is the act of conveying or transmitting information between interested parties about (a) levels of health or environmental risks; (b) the significance or meaning of health or environmental risks; or (c) decisions, actions, or policies aimed at managing or controlling health or environmental risks. Interested parties include government agencies, corporations and industry groups, unions, the media, scientists, professional organizations, public interest groups, and individual citizens.[18]

With this broad definition, risk communication encompasses most forms of communication within the process of risk assessment and risk management, including information flows among academic experts, regulatory authorities, special interest groups, and the general public. However, it also focuses on the communicative processes through which individuals and institutional actors negotiate their interests and concerns about the assessment and management of risks in contemporary society. Thus, risk communication is what all participants in the risk assessment process engage in by virtue of their public involvement. This includes their attempts to inform, persuade, or warn others, to analyse problems and circulate findings on new knowledge, to change attitudes or behaviour, to set charges or rates for costs, or to carry out legally mandated responsibilities. We represent risk communication flows schematically in Figure 2-1.[19]

The risk communication process itself can often become an explicit focus of controversy. Charges of media bias or sensationalism, of

Figure 2-1
The Communications Processes Model of Risk Communication

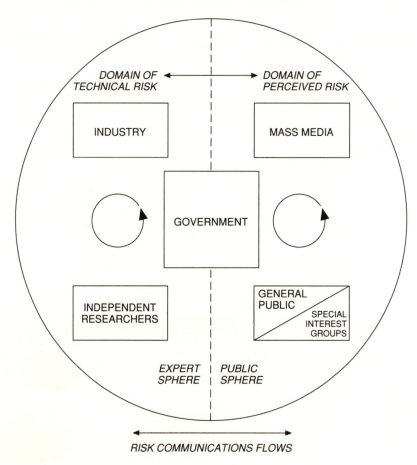

RISK COMMUNICATIONS FLOWS

Reproduced with permission from Leiss and Krewski, p. 100

distorted or selective use of information by advocates, of hidden
agendas or irrational standpoints, and of the inability or unwillingness of regulatory agencies to communicate vital information in a
language the public can understand, are common. Such charges are
traded frequently at public hearings, judicial proceedings, and conferences, expressing the general and pervasive sense of mistrust felt
by many participants towards others. Of course there are also general
differences of principle, outlook, and values among the citizenry;

disagreements will persist even with the most complete and dispassionate knowledge of others' views.

Note especially that this model presents the essential structure of risk communication flows as a two-part process:

1 The interchanges within either of two zones, represented by the arrows that are curved into a circle. The zones illustrate a "domain of technical risk" (risk as assessed by experts) and a "domain of perceived risk" (risk as assessed by all those who do not have technical expertise in the specific area of concern, some of whom may have technical expertise in another area, of course). In these interchanges, what happens in each zone often does not impinge on what is happening in the other;
2 The interchanges between the two zones, represented by the two-way arrows crossing the dotted centre line, with the parties speaking fundamentally different "languages" in the process of communicating their assessments of risk.

It can be seen readily that this model incorporates risk perception as an integral feature of risk communication flows themselves.

The language of technical risk is found in formal risk assessments by regulatory agencies, for example, and often includes complex mathematical statements. The language of perceived risk is that spoken by the ordinary citizen. The "parties" to risk communication flows (industry, researchers, governments, media, public) are situated within the whole sphere in the place determined by which "language" each normally speaks; governments straddle the line because their responsibilities require them to speak both languages in many different settings. However, any party can occupy either side of the line; the sole criterion is what language it chooses to speak on a specific occasion.

The inherent difficulties in communicating research findings from experts to lay audiences are based on incomplete data; on the complexity of theories that necessarily incorporate probabilities, ranges of uncertainties, and choices of extrapolation models; on the unwillingness of many experts to make a genuine effort to understand public concerns; and on many other factors. These factors foster mistrust of experts on the part of the general public. Public understanding can be limited because, for example: the public's perception of risk is often inconsistent; risk information by its very nature often frightens the public; strongly held beliefs are hard to modify; and views are easily influenced by the ways in which information is presented. These limitations in turn foster mistrust of the general public on the part of experts. The practice of appropriate risk communication seeks to improve the workings of these processes described above, and in so doing to reduce the level of mistrust among participants.[20]

To improve risk communication practices, for example with respect to information presentation, there is a strong need for delivering quantitative risk estimates in intuitively meaningful terms that do not oversimplify problems of uncertainty. We need to know more about how to present the consequences of risk, as well as the probabilities of occurrence, in order to make the appropriate impact at the individual level at which people evaluate how they should respond personally to risk information. We need to know more about the bases of informed consent with respect to establishing an acceptable risk for the public, evaluating both the public's information needs on risk and also the adequacy of information presentations. And we also need to know more about the ways in which messages about risk are received by the public; to this end, we might launch tests for measuring the "comprehensibility" of different types of messages.[21] These results would assist us in making progress towards the ultimate practical objective for risk communication, namely, the formation of a reasonable consensus in contemporary society on how to assess and manage risks.

## MANAGING RISKS: AN OVERVIEW

About a decade ago there was an attempt to win widespread acceptance for a qualitative distinction between risk assessment and risk management, where the former would be seen as a scientific process and the latter as a bureaucratic or "political" one.[22] In this perspective, risk assessment would strive for a strictly "objective" characterization (normally in quantitative terms) of the types and severity of potential harm, to be arrived at by using the most up-to-date research methods that had the confidence of the scientific community. Thus hazards would be identified, for example, in controlled laboratory experiments or in environmental monitoring with the aid of well-established scientific protocols, and presumably the results of such investigations thereafter would be available for critical review through an independent peer-review process. Furthermore, the ongoing methodological debate on the adequacy of the types of extrapolations that are made from animal test data to presumed human health effects, as well as the techniques and mathematical models used in such extrapolations, would be refined continuously and openly in peer-reviewed journals. The overriding criterion for acceptability of results is whether the procedures of risk assessment do or do not meet the current standards of good scientific practice.

With the benefit of further experience we can now say with confidence that this attempted distinction has collapsed, largely because most people now recognize the weight of the *qualitative judgments* that are built into the process of risk assessment, judgments over which spirited disagreements inevitably arise.[23] Indeed, a recent article refers to "a substantial literature documenting the strong influence of the social and political context of risk assessment."[24]

Whereas an ultimately futile attempt was made to "insulate" risk assessment – seen ideally as partaking of the "disinterested" spirit of science – from the play of societal disputes, from the outset it was apparent that risk management decisions inevitably would be heavily influenced by factors arising out of contentious political and social processes.[25] Political or legal authorities in one jurisdiction, responding to a wide spectrum of interest group pressures, ban (or permit) use of a substance that is permitted (or banned) elsewhere, or regulate its uses according to quite different standards, although all are operating with similar databases and risk assessment methods. Variations in conceptions of acceptable risk and perceived risk in various societies, or even in different regions and subpopulations within a society, also result in risk management decisions that are substantially different from place to place.[26] The impact of societal controversies about risks on the practice of both assessing and managing these risks, as detailed in cases reviewed in succeeding chapters of this volume, show that there cannot be an authoritative resolution to them by scientific experts or government agencies alone if no attempt is made also to explore paths towards consensus among the interested parties.

And yet risk management as practised by government agencies goes on daily amidst the controversies, working according to procedures designed to confer some regularity on the decision-making process. Part of the need for such regularity lies in the bewildering array of responsibilities such agencies have for overseeing the uses of industrial technologies, the safety of our food supply and consumer products, prescription drugs and medical devices, thousands of chemicals, naturally occurring hazards of all kinds, and so on. Two main presuppositions govern this process: first, that risk is acceptable only in the light of demonstrable benefits; and second, that there ought to be a continuous striving to reduce the level of risk associated with hazardous materials or practices to a point that is "as low as reasonably achievable." We shall give a brief overview here of those established procedures.

## RISK MANAGEMENT PROCEDURES

Governments and industries have developed a set of administrative procedures for making their own choices about how to manage the risks associated with technologies. There is a range of risk management approaches that have been worked out in Canadian practice. They are: Cost-Effectiveness Analysis (CEA), Risk-Benefit Analysis (RBA), Benefit-Cost Analysis (BCA), and Socio-Economic Impact Analysis (SEIA).[27]

Cost-Effectiveness Analysis is the most restricted of the four. CEA takes a predetermined goal as its objective (e.g., a 50 percent reduction in the level of allowable applicator exposure to a pesticide) and seeks the means of achieving that objective with the least monetary cost. In the example given, this might be achieved through better protective gear, changes in the formula mix, or a different method of application. In a CEA, the costs of each of these ways of meeting the risk management objective would be estimated, so that the least-cost means could be identified. These costs normally would include costs, for the administration of the regulation, to the farmer, to the pesticide producer, and to the taxpayer. (We shall follow our pesticide example throughout this discussion, but the same procedures are meant to apply to all of the risk management responsibilities listed above.)

The main difference between a CEA and a Risk-Benefit Analysis (RBA), using this illustration, is that in RBA there is no predetermined health or other objective specified. Instead, the potential risks to health and anticipated (net) benefits derived from the use of the product must be weighed against each other. Net benefit is the benefit to the consumer from the use of the pesticide minus the sum of the costs, as above.

In a completed RBA, the health and environmental risks are sometimes stated as the probability of the occurrence of some incremental adverse impact – for example, three cases of a certain type of cancer per one million lifetime exposures – that would be avoided if the product were not used. Net benefits can be expressed entirely in monetary terms, but qualitative judgments are also made. The overall evaluation of this information is a two-step consideration. First, whether the levels of risks indicated fall within the guidelines for acceptable risks to health established by the relevant scientific authorities (this is the domain of risk assessment specialists). Second, if the first criterion is met, whether the risks appear to "outweigh" the benefits, or vice versa, including an explanation of why that judgment should be accepted (this is the domain of the risk managers).

Approaching the same issue with Benefit-Cost Analysis (BCA), health effects would be incorporated directly into the evaluation of the benefits and costs and not kept separate, as in a RBA. If a new pesticide posed a certain type of additional health risk to applicators, then the estimated monetary cost for incremental medical expenditures would be added to any other costs of using it. Alternatively, the new pesticide might be a substitute for a more hazardous chemical already in use, in which case the reduction in health risk would be counted as a benefit. BCA requires that all costs and benefits of all relevant alternatives (including health effects) be evaluated in monetary units. Benefits are estimated in terms of a person's willingness to pay for them, whether or not they actually have to make the payment (if relevant data is lacking, various techniques are used to arrive at these estimates).[28] Costs are figured in terms of a person's likely demands to be compensated for encountering additional health risks. The basic objective of BCA is to simulate the workings of a perfectly competitive market situation, and to ask how the market would decide an issue (in this case, whether to register a new pesticide) if it were perfectly competitive and all effects were taken into account.

A Socio-Economic Impact Analysis (SEIA) is the most comprehensive of the four techniques in that it seeks to incorporate the widest range of probable impacts. Thus, whereas a BCA will be concerned with only one type of market-based effects (so-called "allocative effects," those concerned with changes in production and consumption), a SEIA takes into account so-called "non-allocative effects" as well: changes in international trade, rate of inflation, employment, regional impacts, and so forth. Although few regulatory decisions in themselves will have significant non-allocative impacts, this cannot be ruled out entirely. There are a number of agricultural chemical products with significant extent of use or market predominance for a specific commodity, and major regulatory actions affecting them could bring into play the kinds of effects for which a SEIA might be appropriate.

Risk management has been defined in the Environmental Health Directorate handbook as "the selection and implementation of a strategy for control of a risk, followed by monitoring and evaluation of the effectiveness of that strategy." In one sense risk management consists simply in putting together the elements of risk already described into an "orderly" framework, so that a reasonable and responsible decision can be reached by an agency that has authority to manage risk.

Given the clear importance to society of managing risks responsibly and effectively, it is not surprising that efforts are being made now to bring some procedural discipline and commonality to this process. A good deal of work has been done, for example, towards establishing a "protocol" or standard for risk analysis.[29] This protocol sets out the steps that must be followed in order that a risk assessment performed by any agency will meet minimum criteria widely recognized by professionals in Canada and elsewhere.

For some time now, the risk management process has been represented in the form of a step-by-step decision-making model; one example of such a model is shown in Figure 2-2.[30] In Canada, risk management models were pioneered by Daniel Krewski and Emmanuel Somers at Health and Welfare Canada's Health Protection Branch. In these health risk management models, the entire process is triggered by the need to begin with a hazard identification (for example, of formaldehyde) and move directly to a risk assessment; the consideration of what industrial benefits may be derived from the substance in question, and how to manage the regulatory process in light of them, occurs later and separately.[31] But in most cases of regulatory risk management, for example evaluation of prescription drugs or pesticides, separate pathways are marked out for the simultaneous consideration of hazards and benefits (or value), with hazard identification and risk assessment on one side and benefit identification and net benefit assessment on the other. The presumptive judgment rule is that only if benefits clearly "outweigh" risks will the product be allowed to be introduced to or remain on the market.

As we have seen, risk management decisions are composed of many and diverse inputs, ranging from the intricacies of toxicological science to the farmer's elementary profit-and-loss calculations. The basic purpose of all such models is to enable the originators of those decisions, as well as all those who are or may be affected by them, to identify the inputs that are of particular interest and to get a sense of how specific inputs figured in the final outcome. In the absence of this information the outcome itself – to allow or to ban a substance or to restrict its uses in various ways – may appear to be purely arbitrary, whether or not any affected party happens to agree with the decision itself. This may seem to be a trivial point, but those who can remember a time, not so long ago, when no enlightenment was offered to the public by regulatory agencies on how risk management decisions were arrived at will not so regard it. (Only ten

Figure 2-2
The Risk Management Process

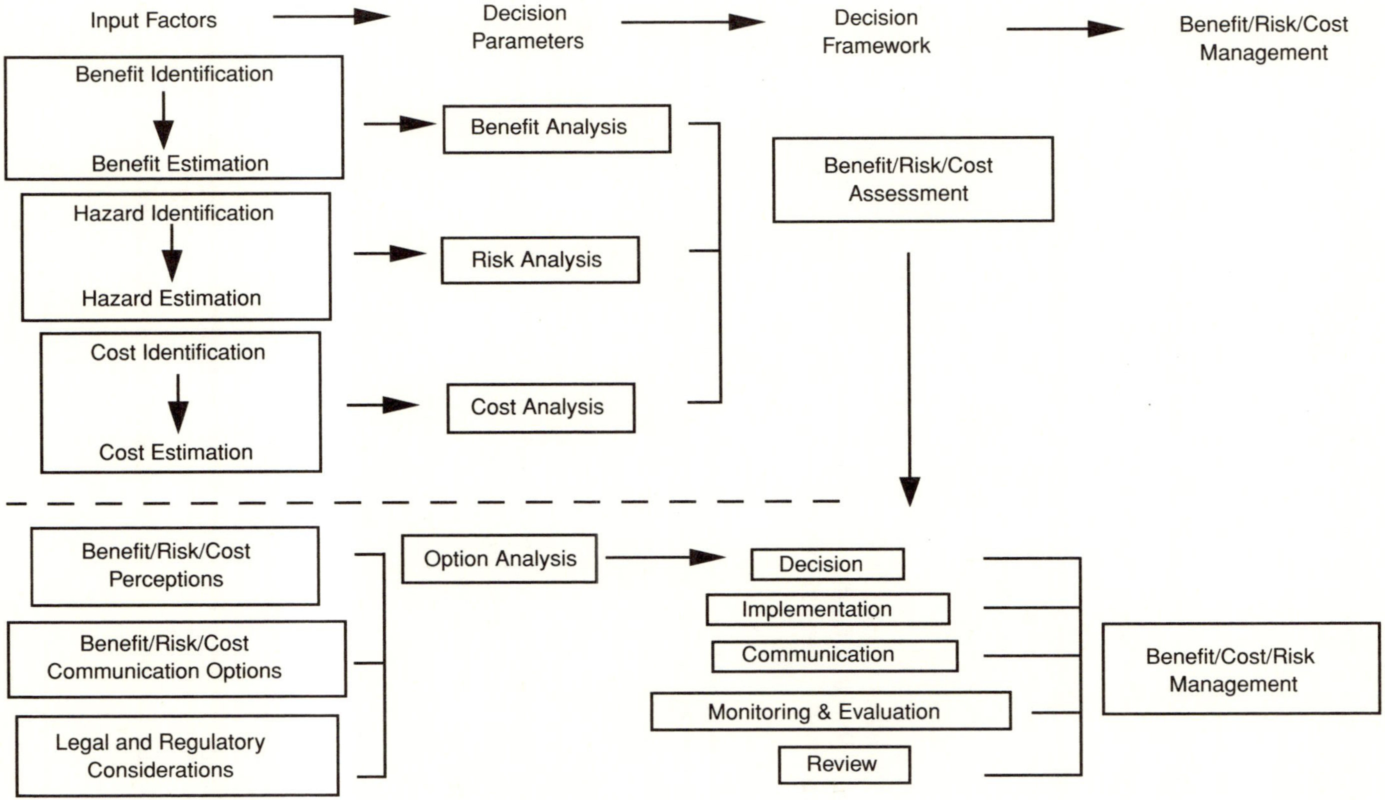

*Source:* Report of the CPHA National Advisory Panel on Risk/Benefit Management of Drugs (1993), Figure 4.1 (modified).

years ago a public interest group in the United States had to take the Environmental Protection Agency to court in order to gain access to the materials that made up key decision-making inputs.) Knowledge about what the risk management decision inputs consist of and how each of them is entered and weighed in relation to all others is an indispensable prerequisite for both public participation and public consent.

We have already reviewed the key inputs on the hazard identification and risk assessment side of the first column in Figure 2-2. Benefit identification and assessment has been mentioned previously in connection with risk/benefit analysis (RBA) and cost/benefit analysis. Briefly put, these are the summation of the net economic gains – or other gains, such as health benefits, which may or may not be converted into monetary terms – to all parties, including consumers, manufacturers, and producers.

The box labelled here "Option Analysis," in the second column, is very important, and in fact may be regarded as the key element in risk management decision-making. Here the agency explores all the means available to it under existing legislation, regulations, and accepted practices to maximize benefits and minimize losses. This almost always ends up as an attempt to reduce risks by modifying the approved patterns of use for a hazardous substance or process. The simplest illustration has been given earlier in our discussion of the cost-effectiveness analysis: if human exposure can be reduced by requiring more adequate safety equipment, then by definition the risk will be reduced as well, and if the change is significant, then the decision balance can be tipped. In other words, a significant risk reduction can bring an activity within the bounds of acceptable risk, and so can be permitted, whereas in its absence the activity would be banned on the grounds of unacceptable risk. The same applies to the "balancing" of benefits and risks, although in most cases even a very positive excess of benefits over risks will not produce approval for an activity if the levels of risks considered purely in isolation are unacceptable in themselves.

Figure 2-2 is drawn from the area of prescription drugs, where Canada and other countries have stringent regulatory procedures in place to control the flow of new medications into the marketplace. The following is an extract from the document used as a guide by regulatory officials at Health and Welfare Canada's Drugs Directorate:

*Overall Conclusions from Clinical Studies:* This section should provide a discussion of the benefits and risk of the drug under the conditions of use recommended, based on an evaluation of the research data available. Compare the expected clinical benefits with the possible adverse effects. Determine risk acceptability. Assess and compare the benefit/risk ratio of the drug in relation to related drugs or others used as standards in controlled clinical trials.[32]

An example of how these guidelines are used in practice is provided by regulatory action on Accutane™, which is the trade name for the only available drug for the treatment of severely disfiguring acne. This drug has immense personal benefit to those who suffer from this condition, but it also entails a most serious side-effect risk, for in women who become pregnant while taking the drug it can lead to thalidomide-like deformities in the fetus. After regulatory review in the United States and Canada, the risk management decision was to leave Accutane on the market while increasing dramatically the risk communication messages to both doctors and patients in order to reduce the risk to fetuses.[33]

What most models of this type chiefly lack is any indication as to where and how communication flows – especially communication between the agency and the public – are supposed to occur during the risk management process. Increasingly, agencies are recognizing the principle that all documentation making up the risk and benefit assessments ought to be available as public resources for examination by interested parties. Where confidential business information is at stake (for example, in the chemical formulas and analyses of anticipated market penetration for new technologies), government organizations such as the U.S. Environmental Protection Agency have instituted special procedures to guard that confidentiality while still ensuring access to properly accredited interested parties. Most importantly, agencies increasingly are recognizing the need to articulate the rationale underlying regulatory decisions, especially the basis for their judgment that "benefits outweigh risks" (or vice versa).[34]

## TWO SOLUTIONS FOR RISK MANAGEMENT CONTROVERSIES

It will be apparent by now that among other things, the risk management process is a domain in which two major institutional forces in modern society meet and interact: science and technology, on the one hand, and our economic and political institutions, on the other.[35] More than this, the early risk management models clearly were predicated upon the now-discredited distinction between assessment and management, with the idea that the former could yield a perfectly neutral and objective assessment of hazard identification, risk estimation, and the specification of technical solutions to exposure, as well as comparisons of relative risks. In short, the operative presupposition was that, in principle, everyone who wished to take the trouble to understand the scientific basis of risk assessment, and who was starting from the same knowledge base, would agree on the nature of risks and their consequences. We may label this the "technical solution."

From the standpoint of someone adopting the technical solution, the tasks of social institutions charged with the responsibility for managing risks (industry and governments) were seen largely as follows: (1) to set policies and adopt specific solutions in accord with scientific findings, and (2) to challenge and overcome the "irrational" responses that are widespread in the public perception of risk. From this perspective, risk communicators had the special mission of translating the scientific understanding of risk into common-sense terms and of cajoling the mass media into transmitting this understanding accurately to the public.

The best example of this solution is provided by the case of nuclear power generation. The engineering assessment of hazards and risks associated with this activity ranks it very low on the overall set of risks for individuals in contemporary society, and on this basis it is judged by many in the scientific community to be a very attractive option for energy policy. On the other hand, this attitude meets strong resistance in the general public, which consistently has perceived these risks to be much more serious than the engineers will concede. This case illustrates well the weakness of the technical solution, for the great number of public information campaigns from industry and governments to date has failed to change the public's perception of risks arising from the use of nuclear power.[36]

By now most specialists in the field recognize the inherent weaknesses in the technical solution. In the first place, there is simply no basis for assuming that the scientific assessment of risk can be characterized as a "neutral" or purely objective process. Among other things, there are too many unresolved (and perhaps unresolvable) uncertainties in risk estimation, requiring too many assumptions that rest on problematic grounds and are subject to challenge and to honest disagreement. As Krewski and Birkwood put it:

During the risk assessment process, analysts may overlook hazards, deem them unimportant, or ignore them because they are difficult to assess. Decisions are often influenced by judgements or policy due to gaps in scientific information. Assumptions must frequently be used in order to fill in gaps in the underlying scientific data base, and to allow for timely decision making. In order to maintain scientific credibility, the inferences and judgments used in such assumptions should be supported by scientific data and the assumptions and their likely impact on the risk assessment outcome be identified and communicated to the public.[37]

Furthermore, there are very considerable social and economic interests in the outcomes of managing risks, and each interested party can be expected to select for itself, out of the sea of uncertainties, those assumptions and methods of analysis that put the best face on the problem at hand.

These weaknesses have led to the increasing interest in another approach, which may be labelled the "process solution." This does not start from the science/policy contrast, but rather assumes that either or both scientific and policy considerations may emerge at any time, and in any setting, where risk management issues are at stake. In the process solution approach it is assumed that all who intervene in disagreements about risk are interested parties who bring a set of presuppositions and values to the dialogue – in other words, none is "neutral" or disinterested. The process solution still presupposes that health and environmental risk problems are inherently complex and can only be described adequately in the first instance in scientific languages, using theories of the physical world, findings based on the technical instrumentation of laboratories, and probabilistic mathematics.[38] But it gives equal weight to the fact that it is in the last instance the perception of risks by members of the public *within the entire context of broader social and economic conditions* that is the decisive criterion for public policy decision-making. Thus, it should be expected that at various times and places societies will manage the same types of risks – as assessed by the science of the day – quite differently.

In this perspective, science and policy are (ideally) not two solitudes, but rather two continuously evolving sets of understanding of the world, understandings that are mediated by the dominant institutional structures of society: "The impotency of quantitative risk assessment in adversarial settings has important implications for the way that we manage risk in our society. One implication is that those who assess and manage risks need to relate to their constituents over the long term in ways that establish trust, credibility, and mutual respect."[39] The task of assessing and managing health and environmental risks in modern society thus becomes the search for possible bases of consensus in controversies about those risks, including the

evolution of special forums designed for dispute resolution and negotiation among interested parties. We shall have much to say about
this alternative approach later in this volume.[40]

In bringing this chapter to a close, we offer an illustration of the
principles of risk assessment and risk management as applied in
Canada during the 1980s to the case of a specific substance.

## A RISK MANAGEMENT CASE: FORMALDEHYDE[41]

Formaldehyde, one of the most widely used chemicals in industrial
society, is an essential ingredient in the resins that go to make up a
wide variety of plastics and glues, which are in turn used in a huge
array of common consumer products such as plywood. It also has
other well-known uses in embalming and the preservation of animal
tissue, and it is released into the environment during the combustion
of many organic materials, such as tobacco.[42]

In the late 1970s formaldehyde began to be widely used in homes
as a component in urea formaldehyde foam insulation (UFFI); almost
immediately a rash of complaints surfaced from the residents of
homes where UFFI had been placed, including eye, skin, and upper
respiratory tract irritations. Preliminary analysis showed that UFFI
was breaking down and releasing formaldehyde gas into the interiors
of homes, whereupon several different regulatory agencies in Canada
and the United States initiated a risk assessment procedure.

In January 1980 a major scientific study was published with experimental evidence linking formaldehyde to the induction of nasal
cancer in laboratory rats. The risk assessment procedure triggered
by these findings, which could lead to the designation of formaldehyde as a suspected, possible, or probable carcinogen according to
a classification scheme promulgated by the International Agency for
Research on Cancer, then looked for supporting evidence in the
available toxicological data. Such evidence was found: formaldehyde
is genotoxic (induces cell mutations) in a variety of cultured cells;
there is a strong dose-response relation in the nasal carcinomas in
the rat study; and structure-activity analysis (where evidence is
sought in the toxicity profiles of chemically related compounds,
which in this case are aldehydes) also yielded positive results. In the
laboratory study the dose-response curve was found to be notably
non-linear – that is, the observed effect (induction of nasal carci-
noma) rises sharply at doses between 6 and 15 parts per million
(ppm) and then levels off, indicating the likelihood of a threshold
effect. Next, epidemiological evidence was surveyed, based on studies

of workers exposed to high levels of formaldehyde over many years, but this was not conclusive. Nevertheless, the database as a whole was regarded as sufficient justification for classifying formaldehyde as "probably carcinogenic to humans." This represents the hazard identification phase.

For the risk estimation phase, the mechanisms for exposure must be studied, beginning with the dose-response analysis. If the means of exposure is inhalation via the nasal passages, what does the analysis of the pharmacokinetic mechanism (the relation between the concentration of formaldehyde in ambient air and the dose delivered at the tissue site) show? Further, what is the mechanism of biological action in nasal tissue that leads to genotoxic effects (for example, reaction with DNA)? And is it the duration or the intensity (or both) of the dose that produces the cellular impacts? Next, the interspecies extrapolation exercise is undertaken, which adjusts for differences in the pharmacokinetic mechanisms of rats and humans as well as differences in the types of exposure experienced by the laboratory rats in the scientific study, on the one hand, and the typical kinds of actual human exposure in both occupational and residential settings, on the other.

Taking all such factors into account, the risk estimation concluded as follows: for humans, lifetime exposure at the level of 0.1 ppm in air may result in an excess cancer risk for exposed persons, induced by formaldehyde, of somewhere between 3.1 cases in every 10,000 and 1.3 cases in every 1,000. Within the set of scientifically assessed health and environmental risks, this is relatively high.

Sampling of formaldehyde concentrations in Canadian UFFI-insulated homes led to the conclusion that in 10 percent of those homes the 0.1 ppm level was exceeded; it was also estimated that in occupational settings the level could reach as high as 1 ppm. Finally, it is well established that a significant fraction of the human population has a hypersensitivity (allergic) reaction to formaldehyde that is triggered at very low doses.

The 0.1 ppm level was initially set as an "upper limit" for exposure, meaning that this was the level that would trigger an effort, initiated by government agencies, to reduce the formaldehyde concentrations down to or below that level. In Canada at least two significant programs followed from this regulatory stance. First, UFFI was banned under the authority of the Hazardous Products Act and financial assistance was offered to homeowners, in cases where the 0.1 ppm level was exceeded, for removing the UFFI (later the same offer of assistance was extended to the owners of all UFFI-insulated homes). Second, two federal government departments worked with the

Canadian Particle Board Association, on a consensual basis, to promote technological change in the plywood and particle board industries that resulted in an eight-fold reduction in formaldehyde emissions in the manufacturing process.

In retrospect, the upper limit of 0.1 ppm, set for the removal of UFFI from homes, turns out to have been an arbitrary choice and by no means a determination of acceptable risk. Once UFFI was banned, the long-term concerns about formaldehyde exposure reverted to the areas of occupational settings (involuntary risk) and smoking (voluntary risk). In Canada, provincial governments are responsible for regulating occupational exposure. In the late 1980s, what is called the "threshold limit value" or TLV – the allowable concentration of a substance (formaldehyde, in this case) in ambient air in occupational settings – for at least some provinces was 2 ppm, twenty times the so-called upper limit of 0.1 ppm. This was so despite the fact that in 1988 the Federal-Provincial Advisory Committee on Environmental and Occupational Health recommended that the target level for any measures taken to reduce formaldehyde concentrations in air should be 0.05 ppm – half of the existing "upper limit."

The essential reason for this seemingly arbitrary play with numbers is quite straightforward. Formaldehyde is an extremely useful industrial chemical and as such contributes significant, long-term economic benefits. Furthermore, the numbers that have been utilized as exposure targets reflect what can be achieved by industries using the guideline known as ALARA ("as low as reasonably achievable"). ALARA is a perfect illustration of a risk/benefit trade-off, where the determination of a socially acceptable level of health risk for some people is made in the light of some estimate about how great a financial burden firms are likely to be able to bear in changing production technologies so as to control the amount of formaldehyde emissions in their plants. In other words, an upper limit of exposure for workers in industries using products containing formaldehyde or any other toxic substance is a function of someone's calculation that, at a particular time, there is an upper limit to a firm's capacity to invest in risk-reducing technology, given the need to preserve the firm's viability (including its ability to employ those workers) under current market conditions. Such calculations, which are pervasive in modern society, are for the most part tacit and informal and are made under circumstances as yet poorly understood by the general public. It is only when controversies erupt over health and environmental risks that they become explicit, leading us to raise questions about the allocation of responsibilities for the balancing of benefits and risks.

# CHAPTER THREE

# Apportioning Responsibility

... "zero risk" demands should perhaps be interpreted
as expressions of "zero trust."

Brian Wynne[1]

The uncertainties that burden the management of risks are magnified
when risks are arrayed against potential benefits – that is, when both
individuals and institutions (particularly government agencies) are
asked to accept a case for the existence of net benefits based on a
calculated trade-off. To the inescapable uncertainties about risk are
added a bundle of suspicions among interested parties about each
other's motives in advocating the acceptability of trade-offs: that benefits are overstated by the proponents of risky technologies; that too
many individuals who personally indulge themselves in quite risky
activities also demand an absurd level of protection from involuntary
risks; that the long latency of many adverse health effects will eventually make a mockery of the initially rosy picture of net benefits;
that if actual losses for involuntary risks are incurred, those who will
bear the greatest portion of those losses will not be the same persons
to whom the lion's share of benefits accrue; and finally, that when the
bills for real losses finally are totted up, which presumably could be
paid out of the fund of net benefits in society's accounts, no one will
step forward to take responsibility for ensuring that anything at all
will actually be paid in the way of mitigation or compensation.

Still, neither the acknowledged difficulty in estimating and managing both risks and risk/benefit trade-offs nor the widespread feelings of suspicion and mistrust that envelope social exchanges on risk
issues can explain the intensity of the disagreements among persons
representing different interest groups. Why do risk management
decisions give rise to such profound disagreements among social
interests? The answer turns out to be an exceedingly simple one,
and it also provides the inner connection between the terms that
make up the title of this book: both institutions and the experts that
serve them, on the one hand, and individuals among the general

public, on the other, *have a direct interest in under-assessing and under-estimating risks so as to maximize net benefits for themselves.* In other words, all have an interest in denying responsibility for the frequency and magnitude of the potential losses associated with risk-taking behaviour.

## THE PROCLIVITY FOR UNDER-ASSESSING RISK

Lest we be misunderstood here, we hasten to add that a habit of routinely under-assessing risk constitutes perfectly "reasonable" utility-maximizing behaviour for both institutions and individuals in a market-oriented society. A moment's reflection will reveal why this is so. Remember that uncertainty – the compounded effect of lack of time, lack of information, and lack of control – is the very hallmark of risk as such. Moreover, a great many risks of a similar kind, involving overlapping health and environmental impacts introduced by new industrial technologies, are being undertaken simultaneously. The combined result of these factors is to make the ascription of particular effects to particular causes nearly impossible. Furthermore, in the majority of cases, when knowledge about the discrete causes of specific types of losses is finally in hand, it is too late to compensate those who suffered losses; or the technologies and practices that occasioned the losses have been superseded; or those who might have been held accountable are no longer around (the firm is no longer in business and the government has long since been discredited politically); or liability and proof *de jure* cannot be established to the satisfaction of a court.

In this setting, all players – institutions and individuals alike – have an interest in seeking to realize the potential net gains to themselves from initiating risk-taking activity (which in the aggregate during the history of industrial society have proved to be enormous) *by offloading some or all of the negative consequences onto others who do not stand to benefit to the same degree as the initiator does.* The obvious example is those captains of industry who accumulated enormous personal wealth during the first phases of industrialism while also exposing the working class to great risk of death or crippling injury in mines and factories. The irony is, however, that the system of socially managed capitalism we now enjoy, which has limited that arbitrary class power and spread the benefits of economic growth far more equitably, enables a much larger segment of society to engage (albeit on a much more modest scale for the most part) in this type of utility-maximizing behaviour.[2]

*Trade-offs Mediated by Institutions and Experts*

Let us look at this interest in under-assessing risk – or, what is functionally equivalent, an interest in avoiding disputes about risk by failing to conduct disinterested scientific assessments – from the standpoint first of modern institutions and the experts who serve them. Both private-sector business firms and public-sector government agencies play this game.[3] What allows them to play it is both the technological complexity of advanced industrial societies and the inherent complexity in the chemical and biological structures of natural systems. With so many interacting elements at work, to isolate single cause-and-effect relationships in any subset of those systems is terribly difficult and often impossible; in many cases the evidence arrives after the fact, when the damage has already been done, as mortality and morbidity statistics reveal their patterns in retrospective epidemiological studies. In the meantime, the case is made that the risks have been estimated by experts to the best of our scientific ability and that there is a large net benefit (in jobs and economic growth) to be gained for society as a whole by initiating a new technology; both businesses and governments in today's sociopolitical structure have a keen interest in making a convincing argument for this scenario. And on the whole, we believe, they are right.

When the initial reassurances prove to be vacuous, however, the unseemly rush to deny responsibility for losses is painful to observe. We have in mind not so much the more general inability to forecast losses accurately through inadequate knowledge, but rather the all too numerous cases of deliberate concealment of knowledge and culpable deception. A sample of some well-known cases in the preceding generation would include the following:[4]

- the mind-numbing efforts of the tobacco industry to deny the causative link between smoking and a wide range of fatal diseases;
- the concealment for thirty years by the Johns-Manville Corporation and other firms of good evidence associating occupational exposure to asbestos with lung disease;
- the frenetic response of the chemical industry to Rachel Carson's exposé of the environmental effects of DDT;
- the "IBT scandal," a notorious case of fraudulent toxicological testing of pesticides (which systematically understated cancer cases in laboratory animals) in the United States in the 1970s;
- the concealing by A.H. Robins Corporation of evidence of large-scale adverse health effects in women using the "Dalkon Shield" intrauterine device for contraception;

- most recently, failure to assess with due rigour the risk of a methane gas explosion in the Westray mine in Nova Scotia;
- and generally, the systematic underestimation by federal and provincial governments of the environmental risks associated with the "megaprojects" of which they are so fond.

However, what is more telling is the attempt by the perpetrators of these actions to deny the existence of disinterested scientific evidence, and even of generally accepted scientific methodologies themselves, when it serves their purposes to do so – usually in courts of law where they are seeking to deflect liability claims against themselves. The tobacco industry provides the most outrageous example, but there are plenty of others.[5] On the other hand, when what is required is only the generation of sufficient doubt about suspected cause-and-effect relations, rather than a defence against actual liability for losses, the very nature of risky activity itself – founded as it is on probabilites rather than certainties – makes this requirement easy to meet.

Let us be clear: in all of the above-mentioned cases, the industrial products and processes at stake delivered significant social, economic, and personal benefits; and also in all of the specific cases mentioned risk was systematically underestimated, sometimes with culpable deceit. On the other hand, in the overwhelming majority of cases, such as the use of formaldehyde in manufacturing processes, *the occupational health risk was not assessed by competent public authorities*, at least for a very long time. In the case of formaldehyde, even after an assessment was done and the risk was shown to be relatively high, the norm for occupational exposure in Canadian provinces was allowed to exceed by a wide margin the level at which the Canadian government was subsidizing its removal from homes.

For the most part, institutions and their resident experts underestimate risk by failing to take responsibility for mounting a sufficient effort to estimate risks using the best scientific methods available at the time. In most cases, the monetary costs involved in deploying the requisite scientific expertise would be a trivial fraction of the expected direct benefits to the proponent or initiator of a risk-taking activity. Quite simply, *it is preferable not to know*.

### EXCURSUS ON CADMIUM

Cadmium is a very useful industrial metal, and there is an long-running controversy in the United States about how to regulate worker exposure to it:

The U.S. Occupational Safety and Health Administration [OSHA] estimates 14 workers a year will die of lung cancer and dozens more will develop kidney disease unless factories reduce cadmium dust and fumes. A White House office is fighting proposed regulatory change as unnecessary, as are the cadmium industry and the Vice-President's Council on Competitiveness. Each side claims that science supports its view and accuses the other side of playing politics. And each side uses the same studies of the health risks of cadmium to justify its conclusions. This is the bizarre world of risk analysis ... .[6]

The latest chapter alone in the regulatory management of cadmium in the United States stretches over a period of five years.

The bureaucratic struggle emerged into open view in late 1989 when economists at the White House's Office of Information and Regulatory Affairs launched an attack on OSHA's health risk estimates, a calculated move that was clearly part of a conservative political agenda for "deregulation." So bitter did the ensuing interagency warfare become that a medical specialist working for OSHA sought and won the protection of Congress in order to keep from being fired!

The first sallies were over the interpretation of toxicology data and extrapolations from animal studies to assumed adverse human health effects (a theme that will return throughout this book). Then industry lobbyists got involved, flooding other government agencies with analyses of cadmium's economic benefits, and even claiming that the regulation of cadmium might harm national security (it is used in nuclear weapons). As of the time of writing, OSHA – which had been instructed by the Bush administration to consider the impact of its regulatory standard on the "international competitiveness" of American industry – had not yet promulgated a safety standard for occupational exposure to cadmium.

The cadmium struggle was just one episode in the overt politicization of risk assessment in the United States during the Reagan and Bush administrations. In its latter stages, the political agenda was masterminded in the offices of the President's Council on Competitiveness (chaired by the vice-president), which proposed to set up a group of scientists under its bureaucratic control to oversee the assessment of risk by all other government agencies. A plan drafted by the President's Council also called for "changes in the basic scientific assumptions and mathematical models that agencies now use to determine the risk of a compound to human health."[7] Few experts would disagree that those assumptions and models ought to be rigorously reviewed and challenged by scientific authorities and revised where necessary; equally, few experts ought to be under the mis-apprehension that any such exercise conducted under the above-mentioned auspices would have very much to do with the disinterested pursuit of truth.

In general, institutions have an interest in under-assessing risk, largely because, given the complexity of the interlocking system of chemical, biological, technological, political, and above all legal processes,[8] they are protected (in all save the most egregious cases) from having to accept responsibility and liability for actual losses – which for the most part are suffered by specific individuals, who do not receive anything like adequate compensation for the excess risk to which they unwittingly exposed themselves. For the most part this does not involve criminal intent, merely a discreet avoidance of their obligation to assess risks adequately. But it also reflects a noticeable lack of pressure to discharge that obligation on the part of the public, which after all is empowered with sufficient authority in our democracy to compel more responsible behaviour on the part of the dominant institutions. Why is this so?

### Trade-offs Mediated by Individuals

Perhaps the most salient reason for this apparent inability of the public to have an effect on the process is that many individuals, too, have a direct interest in the game of underestimating risks. They do so for exactly the same end that institutions pursue, namely, to maximize direct benefits to themselves by off-loading some or all of the consequences from their choices onto institutions that can be held responsible for part or all of the losses, should they occur.

Many individuals voluntarily engage in a number of different kinds of relatively high-risk activity; the quantitative risk assessment for those activities, which is based on very reliable evidence, shows that the level of risk is far higher than what many people find acceptable for involuntary risks.[9] Among the better known are: use of tobacco and other types of psychoactive drugs, both legal and illegal; immoderate use of alcoholic beverages or their misuse under particular unsafe conditions (pregnancy, combined with other drugs, etc.); drinking and driving, as well as driving cars at excessive speed and driving motorcycles and off-road "sport-utility" vehicles; listening to popular music at high decibel levels, with the resultant permanent hearing impairment; engaging in (or failing to take sufficient precautions with) familiar risky recreations such as bicycling, skiing, rock-climbing, and water sports, as well as oddities such as "bungee-jumping"; unnecessary exposure to sexually transmitted diseases by the failure to take elementary safety precautions; ignoring warnings about protecting skin from excessive ultraviolet rays in sunlight; keeping loaded firearms in the home; careless use of domestic and backyard machinery and appliances; and, generally speaking, indulging in unhealthy lifestyles through poor diet and exercise regimes.[10]

Due to the longstanding demand for personal insurance, firms in that business have accumulated extensive and reliable databases for actuarial purposes, and so the level of risk associated with many of these activities is known with a high degree of precision. Such databases tell us that in the ordinary routines of everyday life there are serious risks in the following domains:[11]

- injury in household accidents (670,000 annually in Canada);
- injury in sports and recreation accidents (1,200,000 annually in Canada);
- injury and death in automobile accidents (over 700,000 injuries and 4,000 deaths annually in Canada);
- illness and death in tobacco and alcohol consumption (according to the federal Department of Health, about 38,000 smoking-related deaths annually in Canada);
- injury and death in high-risk occupations such as fishing, logging, mining, piloting aircraft, and fire-fighting.

What do individuals hope to accomplish by underestimating the frequency and magnitude of such risks in everyday life?[12] Obviously, to maximize personal benefits while also shifting responsibility onto others for whatever losses might occur. Since most such losses would take the form of adverse health effects – death, illness, or injury – this is a rather serious matter for nations with universal health care systems funded largely by general tax revenues.[13] On the individual level, what it means is that the risk-averse segment of the population is compelled to share the losses of the risk-prone, without deriving any of the offsetting benefits. On the institutional level, it means that both governments and businesses (at least large employers, which often include some health coverage in benefits packages) find health care costs rising continuously, in part from the types of individual risk-taking described above. Such costs reduce the amount of public resources available for investment in risk-reduction technologies in other areas, and, to the extent that they render that nation's business sector less competitive in global markets, they also reduce the sum total of economic benefits available for other types of consumption. We suspect that this situation will not be allowed to go on indefinitely in the face of remorseless increases in health care budgets, and that at some point governments wishing to uphold universal programs will compel risk-prone individuals to purchase supplementary insurance (publicly or privately underwritten) for their sins.

To summarize, the direct interest that both institutions and individuals have in underestimating risks is manifested in attempts by risk-takers to shift responsibility for potential losses onto others' shoulders. Quite naturally the others resent this brazen act. Institutions and their hired experts denounce individuals for demanding unacceptable levels of protection against involuntary risks inherent in the technologies that also bring impressive net benefits. Individuals reply by denouncing those same institutions for failing to even try to assess most such risks with the abundant scientific expertise at their disposal, and thus to saddle unjustly a random segment of the population, who may never even know the source of their troubles, with losses that will never be compensated.[14]

The main point is this: both sides are correct. These bitter accusations, setting the parties to risk disputes at each other's throats, serve the function for each side (subconsciously, no doubt) of deflecting attention away from its own manifest inadequacies in risk management. The remainder of this chapter, the case studies in our chapters that follow, and similar material published elsewhere all should be read with this explanation in mind; the nature of the intense controversies about these matters is incomprehensible in its absence.

## HOW EXPERTS MAKE RISK/BENEFIT TRADE-OFFS

Intuitive trade-offs among risks and benefits play a large role in the formation of public opinion and personal choices where "risky" activities and controversial technologies are concerned. We suggest that the nature of these intuitive trade-offs may be inferred from the public's tacit acquiescence in the prevailing set of risk management decisions. Some important presuppositions are wrapped up in this suggestion. First among them is our belief that our democratic institutions are sufficiently robust to allow the citizenry as a whole to exercise ultimate control over political events, including our society's risk management agenda. Thus, risk management decisions by agencies can be challenged and sometimes changed; and a wide variety of interest groups, with varying levels of influence on events, can influence the outcome of decision-making processes.[15] For the most part those decisions are not challenged, however, and we go about our daily business under their authority, usually without ever thinking about the reasoning on which they are based. Some examples are: prescription drugs, our food and drinking-water supply, transportation safety, building construction, electricity and other forms of energy supply, occupational health and safety – in other words, virtually every aspect of our lives. In a number of these domains, an elaborate set of calculations has been made by duly authorized representatives of various agencies, balancing benefits and risks and assessing the appropriateness of trade-offs between them.

As individuals we incorporate (tacitly) these innumerable judgments into our daily routines, along with those we make ourselves, more or less consciously – whether or not to use psychoactive drugs, to drive with due care and attention, or to incur or avoid innumerable other risks. The most important point of all is that we have the right to try to persuade our fellow citizens that one or more of those judgments made by others, exercising legitimate authority through public agencies, is wrong and ought to be changed. Or the right to try to persuade them that at least some of the risk judgments they make spontaneously, which are reflected in their attitudes towards risks such as smoking or pesticides, are fundamentally wrongheaded.

Like the determinants of perceived risk, which as we have seen are basically qualitative in nature, intuitive risk/benefit trade-offs are largely structured by qualitative distinctions among human health, environmental, and socio-economic factors. Whether a particular trade-off will be regarded as appropriate is largely a function of two considerations: (1) what the types of risks and benefits in question are, and (2) how those sets of risks and benefits are distributed among the population.

The types of benefits we encounter typically in the health and environmental protection spheres may be summarized as follows: (1) health benefits to individuals (HB-I); health benefits to society (HB-S); and economic benefits, both to individuals and society generally (EcB).[16] All individual health benefits are also, in a derivative sense, social and economic benefits; and social health benefits are also economic benefits. Looked at from another angle, economic benefits also may become, in a derivative sense, both collective and individual health benefits – e.g., through healthier living conditions resulting from improvements to the built environment. Finally, the two dimensions (benefits and risks) are not commensurate: there are definite risks to "the environment" *per se* resulting from human activity (i.e., where "the environment" is considered to be non-human nature rather than the built environment), whereas, strictly speaking, no benefits accrue to at least the undomesticated portion of non-human nature as a result of human activity.

Risks may be classified as follows: (1) health-individuals (HR-I); (2) health-social (HR-S); and (3) environmental (EnR). In most cases, health risks to society are just the sum total of health risks facing individuals, but a widely distributed health risk, such as an epidemic, may also have secondary consequences in social disruption, and therefore we classify these separately.

## A TYPOLOGY OF RISK/BENEFIT SCENARIOS

Our hypothesis is that there are fundamentally different types of applied risk management situations, falling into the following six categories:

Type A: Natural Hazards
Type B: Prescription Drugs & Medical Procedures
Type C: Control of Infectious Disease
Type D: Industrial Hazards
Type E: Nuclear Energy
Type F: Large-Scale Environmental Manipulations

Each type will be illustrated briefly. We propose that the distinctions among them are dependent on the two factors mentioned above: (1) the types of benefits and risks pertaining to each, and (2) the distribution of benefits and risks among the population in each case.

*Type A: Natural Hazards.* Example, geological radon gas. Benefits: none. Risks: HR-I, HR-S (thus risk/benefit approach not relevant). The distribution of benefits and risks is not an issue from a risk management standpoint. There is a secondary issue in the adequacy of compensation by society to victims of natural hazards, who are usually randomly distributed among the population.

*Type B: Prescription Drugs and Medical Procedures.* Example: cancer therapy. Benefits: HB-I. Risks: HR-I. The distribution of risks and benefits is not an issue, because it is the same individual to whom both apply. In extreme cases, such as in some forms of cancer therapy, great risks will be voluntarily assumed, including the risk of death, because the potential benefits are commensurable. Thus, so far as most therapeutic measures are concerned, risk/benefit trade-offs do not become controversial. However, there are exceptions, two of which may be mentioned: (1) Allegations are sometimes made that there are forms of medical procedures, such as unnecessary surgery, that are carried out by doctors for their economic benefit; if so, then there is a distributional issue here, because there is always some risk to the patient attendant upon surgery; (2) Elective surgical procedures such as fat removal and consumer demand for medical devices such as breast implants can lead to controversy if it can be shown that consumers had insufficient warning with respect to the known hazards associated with such procedures and devices.

*Type C: Control of Infectious Disease.* Example: vaccination. Benefits: HB-I, HB-S. Risks: HR-I, HR-S. Individuals must "weigh" the risk of contracting the disease against the small but not insignificant risk of a serious adverse reaction to the vaccination itself. Such risks are randomly distributed in the population. From the standpoint of society, there is a clear net health benefit to universal acceptance of vaccination programs. Also, where voluntary action is concerned (the individual's desire to visit foreign countries where certain diseases are prevalent), society will impose the vaccination risk. Both benefits and risks are computed in commensurable terms, that is, in health protection; the distribution of risk does not seem to be a matter of justice or fairness in this case.

*Type D: Industrial Hazards.* Examples: toxic chemicals; mining or processing of hazardous minerals; workplace accidents. Benefits: EcB, (HB-I). Risks: HR-I, EnR. We have in mind here a class of industrial activities in which the primary health risks are imposed upon individual workers and their families, with secondary health risks for the general population, as well as broad categories of environmental risks (for example, the entire dispersed mix of air and water pollutants, constituting risks to non-human species and long-established ecosystems in addition to humans).

For what is called here the primary level of risk, there is a direct risk/benefit trade-off, where the two sides are incommensurable. Both benefits and risks pertain in the first instance to the same persons (exposed workers). There are also considerable benefits, potentially some business risks, and some medical costs (but no health risks) for other individuals, firms, and society in general. Some would say that there is no distributive issue here, since workers who expose themselves to such risks do so voluntarily or receive excess compensation to offset excess risks. However, in our view, both the fairness of the conditions under which such risks are assumed and the adequacy of the excess compensation (where it is actually paid) are debatable.

In the United States, risk/benefit analysis has been explicitly the traditional (and legally mandated) approach to regulatory decision-making for pesticides and other toxic chemicals. In Canada, Agriculture Canada has had a *de facto* risk/benefit approach in the case of pesticides for some time.[17] Economic benefits arising from the manufacture and use of toxic chemicals have conventionally been thought to accrue to producers, users, and society in general. Certain risks, however, pertain both to users, who are deriving benefits, and also to other persons, such as agricultural and factory workers, who bear an excess risk in comparison to the rest of the population; thus distribution is definitely an issue. The designation HB-I is put in brackets here because it appears odd that health benefits should be attributed to industrial hazards, but such benefits do exist, and it is most unfortunate if they are overlooked. Clear health benefits are derived from certain toxic chemicals, such as those used in medicines and in pesticide products like insecticides and fungicides, especially those used against bacteria, fungi, and moulds that directly affect human health (e.g., chlorine in drinking water and swimming pools), for the control of infectious diseases carried by insects, for the suppression of pests that attack or contaminate stored foods, and so forth.[18]

*Type E: Nuclear Energy.* Benefits: EcB. Risks: HR-I, HR-S. This is assigned its own place in the typology because we have abundant evidence to show that most people regard it as a qualitatively distinct case. It is otherwise a classic risk/benefit trade-off situation (industrial hazard). There are risks to individuals from an ongoing hazard – radioactivity from spent fuel and reactor components – as well as a general social and environmental risk attendant upon a potential catastrophic event (reactor accident). It is often considered to be a special case because of the inter-generational risk represented by radiation-induced genetic damage. The workplace hazards stemming from uranium mining and reactor operation fall under Type D. The distributional issue here lies in the excess risk assumed by the portion of the population living in proximity to the power generation or waste-storage facilities.

*Type F: Large-Scale Environmental Manipulations.* Benefits: EcB. Risks: EnR. We have in mind environmental impacts where human action is a significant or the sole contributing factor, recognizing that major ecosystem alterations also result from natural causes. Examples are

Table 3-1
Risk Management Typology (Risk/Benefit Analysis)

| Type | Benefits | Risks |
|---|---|---|
| A: Natural Hazards | None | HR-I/S |
| B: Drugs/Medical | HB-I | HR-I |
| C: Infectious Disease | HB-I/S | HR-I/S |
| D: Industrial Hazards | EcB, {HB-I} | HR-I, EnR |
| E: Nuclear Energy | EcB | HR-I/S, EnR |
| F: Environmental | EcB | EnR |

hydroelectric projects and other water system diversions, removal of forest cover, desertification or soil deterioration, ozone depletion, and so forth. The notion that there are trade-offs made here seems obscure and sometimes even offensive to some people, who regard the natural environment and its wild inhabitants as having no value or rightful "interests" in themselves and as having meaning only as a resource for the satisfaction of human need, or who dismiss out of hand the notion of aboriginal title vested in indigenous peoples. Thus it is instructive to see how the possibility that we shall lose access to as-yet-undiscovered, naturally occurring therapeutic agents that may exist in the tropical forests has become a cogent argument for their better preservation. Controversies usually erupt when indigenous peoples claim that large-scale environmental alterations will destroy their traditional "way of life," by which they mean not just the land's sustaining economic resources but also their "spiritual" relation to a portion of the earth and its non-human inhabitants.

## A RISK MANAGEMENT TYPOLOGY

See Table 3-1. The basic point about this typology is that there are important *qualitative* differences among the six types of risk management situations, differences that are governed either by the special character of the risk (nuclear power) or by the kinds of trade-offs that are conventionally made with respect to each. Our supposition is that such qualitative differences demand clear variations in approaches to managing risks. Risk managers and risk experts stumble into grievous errors, especially when dealing with the public, if they overlook or forget this – as they often do.

With some exceptions, risk/benefit trade-offs are usually unproblematic with respect to Types B and C, where (1) the types of benefits and risks are commensurable, and (2) there are no known

or significant distributive issues. Such trade-offs are inherently problematic where these two conditions do not obtain (Types D, E, and F).[19]
For Types D and E, risk/benefit trade-offs are inherently problematic
because of the ways in which benefits and risks are distributed in
society: there is no clear match between those who reap the benefits
and those who take the risks. Type F is a special case, where the
proponents of development often charge that its opponents are motivated by an irrational concept of "preservation for its own sake" and
furthermore have no valid interest in the territory in question.

To say that something is "inherently problematic" is not to say that
it is wrong or useless. We make use of many things that are inherently
problematic, because despite their faults they are, on balance, the
best available means for realizing our common objectives. Rather,
that expression means only that there are contentious aspects to
something which are part of its nature and thus cannot be easily
removed. This serves or should serve as a warning to the risk manager not to try to ignore the issue of distributive justice in these types
of controversies.

It is especially important to confront the issue of distributive justice
directly and openly, because in cases where risk/benefit trade-offs
are inherently problematic (Types D, E, F) a distributional unfairness
may be hidden in the risk management decision. This can occur
because, in using the conventional expression for net benefit ("benefits outweigh risks"), the risk manager may not make explicit the
basis of the judgment for *each of the affected interests separately.* Thus
in the case of formaldehyde, which is used in a broad range of
different industries, some manufacturing applications may have
incorporated far better risk-reducing technologies than others; if the
worker exposure to formaldehyde is averaged over all industries, an
overall net benefit calculation for the uses of this hazardous substance
may conceal cases of clearly unacceptable risk.

Achieving public trust in such cases thus depends on the ability
and willingness of the risk manager to explain clearly the risk management approach that has been adopted. This means, among other
things, accepting the obligation to state explicitly, and to defend
against challenge:

- a rationale for the judgment that the course of action being advocated or permitted represents acceptable risk;
- an explanation of how the distribution of risks and benefits has
  been taken into account;
- a specification of the decision-making steps, including points where
  inputs from interested parties has been recognized;

• an explanation for how benefits and risks have been "balanced" against each other, couched in terms that are readily understandable by the general public.

## HOW INDIVIDUALS MAKE
## RISK/BENEFIT TRADE-OFFS

Difficult, and sometimes intractable, problems arise – for example, in attempts to change public attitudes towards controversial technologies or to change individual behaviour in risky activities such as smoking – because at bottom what we are trying to deal with is a fundamental disagreement over the types of risk/benefit trade-offs, explicit or implicit, that are embodied in those cases. We shall try to show that this is largely because there is a hidden dimension in these applied problems, with two components: first, the elusive perception of benefits by individuals, and second, the intuitive (and indeed often subconscious) risk/benefit trade-offs that individuals make in everyday life and which are reflected in their attitudinal and behavioural orientation to risk issues.

We describe two paradigmatic situations, one in which intuitive risk estimations are significantly lower than are formalized risk estimations by experts, and another in which the former are significantly higher than the latter. The hidden dimension can become visible when our attention is focused on applied problems in the areas of risk communication and risk perception – for example, during attempts to affect individual behaviour on public health issues, such as smoking; to change firmly held public attitudes (on nuclear power, for example); to enhance industry's hazard communication abilities at the community level; and to find acceptable solutions for the siting of waste management and hazardous-waste treatment facilities.

At the purely intuitive and often subconscious level, we all make innumerable judgments about risk/benefit trade-offs every day: when we decide what "personal rules" to use in driving a car or crossing streets as a pedestrian; when participating in sports and recreational activities; when choosing a diet and exercise regimen in light of what doctors have told us about our exposure to health risks; when using electrical appliances and tools; when using tobacco, alcohol, or other drugs; and so forth. It is quite possible that the general framework of these intuitive risk/benefit judgments for everyday personal activities are the foundations of the opinions that individuals hold on what are acceptable risks in any activity, including the "big" social issues (nuclear power, toxic chemicals, and the rest). We concede that all of the personal, everyday activities mentioned above fall into the category of voluntary risk, and most of the social issues into involuntary risk, and that the public's different attitudes with respect to each explains most of the difference in the risk estimations made by individuals. But there is more to this story.

By now the "risk tables" from risk perception research, where people from various constituencies have been asked to rank the risks represented by heterogeneous activities and technologies, are quite well known. Until recently, however, we had no complementary insight with respect to perceived benefits. Now the work of Paul Slovic and his colleagues on the perception of risks associated with prescription drugs has finally begun to address this lack. We have reproduced here (Figure 3-1) their two tables, on perceived risk and perceived benefit, for the same set of twenty-nine activities and technologies; the respondents were a representative sample of the adult population of Sweden surveyed in March 1988.[20]

In their commentary, Slovic and his colleagues report that the perceived risks and benefits are not positively related (correlation = −.23); judging the tables from a rougher intuitive stance, we might say that they are almost a mirror image of each other. On the assumption that the seven-point scales for the two tables were commensurable, Slovic *et al.* then subtracted the benefit mean from the risk mean for each item and produced a scale of mean net benefits.[21] The six items at the bottom of the scale for perceived net benefit (starting with the lowest) are: cigarette smoking, alcohol, pesticides, food additives, sleeping pills, and nuclear power. What is interesting about this list is that three of the items (cigarettes, alcohol, sleeping pills) would fall into the category of voluntary risk, and the other three (pesticides, food additives, nuclear power) are among those normally consigned to involuntary risk. Yet in terms of perceived risk/benefit trade-offs or net benefits, they are thoroughly mixed together.

This suggests to us that there are major gaps in our understanding of how risk/benefit trade-offs are thought about by the whole spectrum of individuals and interest groups (including experts) that take part in debates about risk.[22] In a study published some time ago we find the following comment:

Psychological research also indicates that people have great difficulty in making decisions among risky options where the person could experience either a gain or a loss. This difficulty in trading off risks against benefits is increased to the extent that information about comparative risks and benefits is not readily available to the consumer and/or is not in a form he or she can easily use.[23]

Figure 3-1
Perceived Net Benefit and Perceived Risk

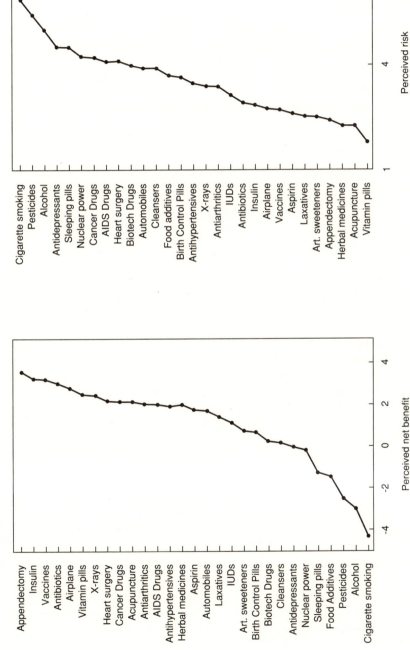

Generally speaking, there are two forms of intuitive risk/benefit trade-offs whereby individuals underestimate voluntary risks and overestimate involuntary risks. They are:

- where individuals and groups are motivated to downplay risk and to perceive significant benefits, and where the intuitive risk estimates vary considerably from expert risk estimates;
- where individuals and groups downplay or ignore benefits, and also perceive risks to be significantly greater than do experts who are working from formal risk estimation protocols.

Each of the two will be discussed briefly and illustrated with examples. It should be noted that, where references are made in the discussion to the difference between what are called "intuitive" and "expert" assessments, no inference should be made that one or another party is "right" or "wrong."

### Downplaying Risks

In the first form of intuitive risk/benefit trade-offs, individuals and groups seem to be motivated to downplay risk and to perceive significant benefits; these intuitive risk estimates vary considerably from expert risk estimates. Here the trade-off is driven primarily by the individual's perception of real benefits; thus the corresponding downplaying of risk is primarily a function of the magnitude of the perceived benefits. From the standpoint of a formalized risk estimation, it is as if the perceived benefits "cloud" the person's judgment. A good example is driving. In surveys, up to 95 percent of drivers rate their road performance as "above average"; this and other evidence indicates that driving risks are significantly downplayed as a result of overconfidence. Other examples include various participation sports, especially high-risk sports such as skiing, where relatively high and persistent injury rates appear to indicate that individuals underestimate risks. In all of these cases there may be a number of important factors involved in the downplaying of risk; what is suggested here is that the individual's perception of the benefits to be derived from the activity is one of those factors.

All of the examples listed above fall into the category of voluntary risk. But others that can be offered do not. In what we could call an "intermediate" kind of risk (on the voluntary-involuntary spectrum) are many workplace hazards. Here, as is well known, hazard warnings are often ignored and safety equipment is under-utilized. Again, there are a number of salient factors in this behaviour, but it seems clear that the individual's perception of benefits (adequate job performance and peer approval) is one of the factors involved in the intuitive underestimation of risk.

Examples in this case can also be cited from the involuntary risk category. First, exposure to air pollution, particularly where automobile exhausts are a significant factor: the lack of sufficient public pressure on governments (a lack that is widely shared around the world, including Canada) to take adequate remedial action on this environmental problem is, hypothetically, a function of the high perceived benefits derived from private automobile ownership. Second, exposure to geological radon gas in the United States: according to Peter Sandman's analysis, there is considerable apathy in potentially affected households, and Sandman interprets this, at least in part, as reflecting inadequate media attention to a risk that does not cause "outrage."[24] But one other factor could be that the home is perceived as a "safe place," and that this perception of the benefits of being at home (i.e., protection from the dangers of the outside world) also leads to the downplaying of risk.

In all cases of the first form of intuitive risk/benefit trade-offs, from the perspective of expert risk assessors the objective of risk communication efforts would be to shift the individual's perceived net benefit "calculation." Assuming for the sake of argument that either a government agency or an interest group assumed responsibility to do such a thing in the cases described above, how could this be done? Two suggestions are:

1  Identify the structure of perceived benefits: having discovered the population subgroups at special risk (e.g., young women who are smoking), undertake a research program to uncover the attitudinal and behavioral factors involved in the users' understanding of the personal benefits associated with the activity, so that counteracting risk information can be directly relevant to the strongest motivations that support the activity.
2  Identify the attitudinal barriers to hazard warnings: again, having discovered the population subgroups at special risk, investigate how to increase the behaviour-modifying impact of existing warnings, and how to devise more effective ones, to undermine the downplaying of risk.[25]

The operative assumption behind this strategy is a simple one: one cannot "reach" individuals who are thought to be at risk, in relation to familiar activities, unless one knows how they perceive on a very personal level the benefits they associate with those activities.

*Downplaying Benefits*

In the second form of intuitive risk/benefit trade-offs, individuals and groups downplay or ignore benefits and also perceive risks to be significantly greater than do most (but not necessarily all) experts who are working from formal risk estimation protocols. Here benefits are counted largely in social (economic) terms, and, hypothetically, the downplaying of perceived benefits is a function of the perception of risk. Specifically, it may be that the "remoteness" of benefits from the everyday lives of individuals leads in part to an amplification of risk.[26] As we shall see, this type of situation also typically involves large-scale technologies, and the diminution of perceived benefits may also be a function of the feeling of "powerlessness" in relation to those technologies.

The best example of this type is energy generation from nuclear power. Nothing is more familiar from the "risk tables" than the enormous and persistent gap between the public and the expert estimation of the risks associated with nuclear energy generation. In one of the tables used frequently by Paul Slovic, in a ranking of perceived risk associated with thirty activities and technologies, where number one represents the most risky, the experts ranked nuclear power at number twenty, whereas both college students and the League of Women Voters ranked it number one.[27] The hypothesis here would be that at least a part of this difference in risk estimation is due to a very pronounced difference in benefits estimation between experts and the public. The downplaying of benefits by the public almost certainly is a function of the perceived availability of energy from other (presumably "safer") sources. Therefore it would be interesting to test this hypothesis, especially in relation to a growing public awareness of environmental and health risks associated with the use of fossil fuel energy, including public perception of the hypothesized long-term global "greenhouse effect."[28]

There can be no doubt that nuclear energy is and will remain for the foreseeable future an inherently controversial technology. In 1987 the Canadian Nuclear Association (CNA) developed a five-year communications plan, backed with an initial $4-million budget, "to increase public support for the peaceful use of nuclear technology to the level where those in favour of further nuclear development are at least equal to those opposed."[29] Two of the four strategy components in the communications plan were to "broaden the public (individual) appreciation of the benefits of uranium and nuclear technology" and to "focus on the regional and local benefits derived from uranium, nuclear industry and technology." (Another was to "respond to public concerns," but the word "risk" is never used, and therefore the public is not encouraged to think about nuclear power in terms of risk/benefit trade-offs.)

This strategy has been carried out by means of an advertising campaign in both print media and on television. Elaborate audience targeting research was done. One consultant's report advised the industry to target its messages at married women with children at the lower end of the income and education distributions, for these individuals appear to be especially resistant to approving nuclear power.[30] Nevertheless, after two years of effort and expenditure under the communications plan, an opinion survey poll showed that only 14 percent of Canadians strongly favoured using nuclear energy to generate electricity, a drop of 3 percent in this category from the preceding year.[31]

Another example is pesticides, where the disagreements among interest groups have been fierce and protracted.[32] For the most part, pest management issues, both in the agricultural and forestry sectors, have been considered by the public almost exclusively in terms of perceived risk. When benefits have been considered at all, they have been thought to accrue only to those who manufacture the products and those who use them on farms and forests; benefits thus have the characteristic of "remoteness" described above. But many persons are also what might be called "casual" consumers of domestic pesticides, using them rather freely in their homes, gardens, swimming pools, and so on. Especially where localized outbreaks of severe insect infestations are concerned, many persons find immediate and tangible benefits in pesticide use (including quite careless use at times), and thus make intuitive and, for the most part, undoubtedly unwitting risk/benefit trade-offs in using pesticides in domestic situations.

When experts are faced with this second form of intuitive risk/benefit trade-offs, they often resort to risk comparisons, seeking to deflate a perceived risk estimation by comparing the expert risk assessment of the technology at issue (nuclear power, pesticides) with the expert risk assessment of some familiar activity such as smoking. This approach, despite its natural appeal to experts, is almost always met with scorn by the public, and experts have been advised to eschew it or at least use it with extreme caution. Still, many of those who sit on the expert side of disagreements over such technologies as nuclear power and pesticides would like to shift the intuitive net benefits (or risk/benefit trade-off) "calculation" that is made by other interest groups and many members of the public at large.

As we have seen, the communications strategy deployed by the Canadian Nuclear Association has this objective, albeit in a tacit form.

But the Association does not seem to realize that this tacit form of the strategy is precisely its problematic aspect. When private industry, governments, and quasi-public industries or Crown corporations attempt to change public attitudes about controversial technologies, and especially when they choose media advertising campaigns for this purpose, they run the risk of being perceived as seeking to manipulate public opinion. This perception arises for a number of reasons – for example, unequal resources and access to mass media outlets and, more importantly, failing to tell the whole story.[33] It also arises in large part simply because the specific nature and objectives of the strategy, as well as the market research that results in audience targeting (e.g., the women in the CNA strategy), are not public documents; rather, they are regarded, like all marketing campaigns, as proprietary or confidential information. We submit that this approach is both wrong in principle and likely to be self-defeating in practice since, due to the perceived manipulative intent, it runs a very high risk of "backfiring" on its proponents.

It would be more prudent for the pro-technology interests not to attempt to shift the intuitive net benefits calculations, but rather simply to play a part in clarifying for members of the public the nature of the risk/benefit trade-off components in decision-making about controversial technologies, specifically: (1) clarifying the attitudinal basis of thinking about the benefits associated with controversial technologies; (2) clarifying the types of implicit judgments people make within their sense of intuitive risk/benefit trade-offs with respect to controversial technologies.

The two types of situations described here are fundamentally different in nature. In the first (downplaying risks), the attempt to shift the net benefits calculations of individuals rests primarily on public health objectives, and there is no reason why the strategy of seeking to influence public attitudes and behaviour, as well as all the research and planning on which it is based, should not be completely accessible to public inspection and critique. Here the "interest" behind the strategy is simply one of the public good, and thus in principle it requires no other justification. Even so, in a democratic society the public has a right to expect that the proponent will "declare" publicly both that interest itself and the nature of the campaign through which the desired attitudinal and behavioural shift is being sought. This reasoning applies even more strongly in the case of the second situation (downplaying benefits), where an attitudinal shift is being sought on behalf of a controversial technology. We submit that the interested party (whether private, public, or quasi-public agency) should declare itself and its strategic objectives clearly to the public, so as to remove the taint of attempted manipulation. Furthermore, the research and documentation on which the strategy is based ought to be available to the public for inspection and critique.

To return to the nuclear power example, the message proponent, in this case the Canadian Nuclear Association, ought to have stated quite openly, at the outset of its campaign, that it hoped to bring about a shift in the way many members of the public think about risk/benefit trade-offs with respect to this technology. (Fairness demands that other interest groups be able to have their messages heard as well; if those with the greater resources at their disposal were to assist the others in this regard, their own credibility might be enhanced significantly.) This is certainly a case of "letting the chips fall where they may." In the end, many among the public could decide to opt for rigorous energy-conservation measures, entailing profound lifestyle changes, in order to reduce the perceived risks associated with maintaining major energy-generating technologies of all sorts, including nuclear power. Or, as a result of a greater exposure to the debate among interested parties, some of them might very well change the nature of their sense of appropriate risk/benefit trade-off calculations with respect to nuclear energy. In general, the primary objective for new initiatives undertaken by organizations in the areas of risk communication and public risk perception should be, quite simply, to enhance the ability of interested parties to reflect on the adequacy of their own judgments in the intuitive risk/benefit trade-offs that we are all required to make in everyday life.

RISK MANAGEMENT BY
INDIVIDUALS: THE CASE OF
TOBACCO USE

At the end of chapter 2 we offered a brief case study on involuntary risk and its management by institutions and experts, using the example of occupational exposure to formaldehyde. Here we offer a complementary abbreviated case study of voluntary risk and the management of such risks by individuals, citing the most notorious example, that of tobacco use.

The health effects of tobacco use constitute a worldwide epidemic of massive proportions. Over four thousand different chemical compounds have been identified in tobacco to date, and of these, several hundred are classified as toxic and over fifty are known carcinogens.[34] In addition, the nicotine present in tobacco smoke is a powerful psychoactive agent. A review of the medical evidence by a committee established by the Royal Society of Canada in 1989 concluded:

"Cigarette smoking can, and frequently does, meet the criteria for the definition of drug addiction."[35]

The major known health consequences of smoking, confirmed in scientific evidence that is accepted by everyone not associated with the tobacco industry, are:[36]

- damage to the lungs (chronic bronchitis and emphysema);
- cancers in organs exposed directly to tobacco smoke (mouth, throat, larynx, lung) as well as other organs derivatively exposed to its carcinogens (esophagus, pancreas, renal pelvis, bladder);
- arterial damage resulting in coronary heart disease and other forms of arterial disease, including stroke.

For all such diseases, the relative risk attributable to tobacco use is calculated by dividing the risk for smokers by the risk for never-smokers. The relative risks from smoking for the diseases listed above, according to the evidence available in 1989, are:

- Coronary heart disease: 2 to 4 times for sudden cardiac death[37]; over 30 percent of all coronary heart deaths and over 50 percent of all cardiovascular deaths (mainly coronary heart disease and stroke) are caused by smoking.
- Stroke: about 2.5 times.
- Overall cancer mortality: 2 times (30 percent of all cancer deaths are attributable to smoking).
- Lung cancer: 15 to 20 times (smoking is the major cause of lung cancer – over 80 percent of lung cancer deaths are attributable to smoking).
- Emphysema/Chronic Bronchitis: between 10 and 20 times (impact similar to that of lung cancer).

Given the hypersensitivity of North Americans to anything labelled a "cancer-causing substance," the following presents a particularly telling set of statistics:

Lung cancer *alone* is responsible for the fact that this nation's [U.S.] age-adjusted cancer mortality rate has been increasing (by 9 percent from 1950 through 1985). Excluding lung cancer, age-adjusted cancer mortality has actually been *falling* – by fully 13 percent.[38]

About 400,000 Americans and 40,000 Canadians die prematurely each year as a result of smoking, making it by far the largest single

Table 3-2
Smoking Prevalence, Age 20 and Older

|  | United States | Great Britain | Canada | Norway |
|---|---|---|---|---|
| *Males 20+* | | | | |
| 1974/5 | 43.4 | 52 | 45.6 | 49.6 |
| 1986/7 | 31.7 | 35 | 32.3 | 43.8 |
| *Females 20+* | | | | |
| 1974/75 | 31.4 | 41 | 32 | 31.4 |
| 1986/7 | 26.8 | 31 | 26.6 | 33.3 |

preventable cause of premature death. Yet in the late 1980s over 50 million Americans and almost 7 million Canadians were still smoking.

Smoking rates in North America and western Europe peaked in the early 1970s and have been declining at a constant rate ever since, for every group in the population except young women (and women generally in Norway). A sample of the data on smoking prevalence among males and females age twenty years and older is given in Table 3-2.[39] The least amount of decrease is among females, and smoking rates in the under-twenty-five population of all these countries is now roughly equal for males and females. The declines are by no means evenly distributed throughout the population, however. On the contrary, smoking is much more prevalent in the lower socio-economic groups in all these countries, and the rate of decline over time differs very sharply by educational level. In the United States, from 1974 to 1987, smoking prevalence for the highest educational category dropped from 28.3 to 16.3, but for the lowest it was virtually unchanged (36.5 to 35.7); in Canada, the corresponding figures for 1975–86 were 31.2 to 19.9 for the highest and 37.6 to 31.6 for the lowest educational category. Projections suggest that by the year 2000 in the United States only 10 percent of college graduates will be smokers, whereas the figure for those who have only a high school education will be 30 percent.[40]

The serious campaign by governments to reduce smoking prevalence began with the U.S. Surgeon General's 1964 report, "Smoking and Health." Later reports from the same source have been able to rely upon increasingly well-established data about causative links between smoking and health effects, and the tone of the reports has become more forceful.[41] The health hazard warnings that are required to be placed on tobacco packages and in the text of print advertisements (where advertising is permitted) were useless until the mid to late 1980s, when the warning texts finally began to specify the type of adverse effects attributable to tobacco use. However, all governments have failed dismally to discharge their responsibilities by insisting (in law and regulation) that these messages be designed effectively so as to counteract the known impediments to effective communication, such as the mechanisms of "screening out" and "discounting" used by smokers to avoid the force of the message, and the clever strategies of the ad designers, which subtly draw attention away from the warning message.[42] This is particularly discouraging since these same governments are well aware that nicotine is one of the most powerful addictive drugs known to medical science, and are equally well aware – given how many smokers attempt repeatedly and unsuccessfully to quit – how much smokers need fresh rounds of strident hazard warnings, as well as other types of encouragement and assistance, in their efforts to kick their habit.

In any case, no hazard warnings can compete with the limitless creativity of ad designers. In a notorious recent instance, a new U.S. ad campaign image known as "Joe Camel" achieved within an astonishingly short time a recognition factor (percentage of respondents who correctly identified the "Joe Camel" image with cigarettes) of 30 percent of three-year-old children and over 90 percent of six-year-olds![43] The same campaign had an almost 100 percent recognition factor among nine-to-twelve-year-olds, the crucial age at which many of those who end up as smokers take up their habit – good news for an industry that regularly kills large numbers of its best customers and therefore must recruit replacements without fail.[44] Only a complete ban on all forms of advertising and publicity is suitable for a consumer product which, if it were proposed for sale today, certainly would not be allowed into general circulation, and if available at all in a country such as Canada would be scheduled under either the Hazardous Products Act or the Food and Drugs Act, with its sale and circulation tightly restricted.

Kenneth E. Warner estimates that the broad campaign against smoking during the last twenty-five years has resulted in producing (in the United States) 35 million fewer smokers and almost 800,000 fewer smoking-related deaths.[45] And still, in the United States today, each year about one million people – three thousand every day – are added to the rolls of regular smokers; comparable or higher rates of recruitment are occurring in many other countries in the world. Those who so indulge themselves for the attendant pleasures of nicotine addiction voluntarily incur a risk of serious adverse health effects which has no equal, by a very wide margin, in the everyday life of modern society.

Almost certainly, for the group of tobacco users among us – still a significant fraction of our whole population – the chance of loss from the entire set of involuntary environmental risks to which they are also exposed, taken together, would not begin to approach the potential losses they so casually inflict upon themselves. Their irresponsibility in the face of the excess risk they run is a nice match for the equivalent irresponsibility of our dominant institutions, which – especially in the area of occupational exposure – all too often find every excuse imaginable in order to avoid doing the detailed risk assessments that they are perfectly capable of carrying out.[46] The fact that both many individuals and most institutions are busily trying to offload the consequences of their risk-taking choices onto others – in other words, to avoid taking full responsibility for their choices – explains why so many disputes about risk in our society are so bitter.

# PART TWO

# Obstacles to Consensus: Two Seemingly Intractable Controversies

# CHAPTER FOUR

# Power Frequency Electric and Magnetic Fields Part One: Expert Assessment

## INTRODUCTION

This chapter and the next deal with controversies over possible health effects of power frequency electric and magnetic fields (PF E/MF). In chapter 5, we will examine the use of technical expertise by parties involved in a dispute in British Columbia over the proposed routing of a power line; in this chapter, we will set the scene by reviewing the state of the science and the history of the PF E/MF and human health issue in general.[1]

PF E/MF are invisible lines of force surrounding any wire carrying electricity. They are produced not only by electric power generation, transmission, and distribution systems (see Figure 4-1) but also wherever electric energy is used, whether in domestic activities, transportation, or in industry. These fields are prevalent throughout industrialized society. In much of the Americas, PF alternating-current (AC) fields reverse polarity with a frequency of 60 cycles per second (60 Hz), and in most of the rest of the world with a frequency of 50 Hz. (Although both AC and direct-current DC technologies are used to transport the world's electric energy, the bulk of it is transported by AC. Direct current PF E/MF are not discussed here.)

Industrialized society is utterly dependent on the benefits provided by electric power: electric energy provides lighting, refrigeration, heat, motor drive, and countless other services that promote human health and welfare. With increasing industrialization and constant advances in technology, the demand for electric energy continues to rise; in recent years it has doubled about once every ten years in highly industrialized countries.[2] These demands have resulted in an increase in total transmission line mileage and in voltages. In 1892,

Figure 4-1
Simplified Electric Power System

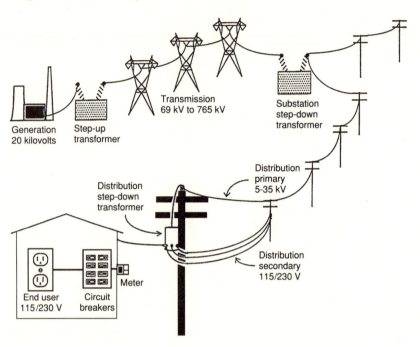

Reproduced with permission from U.S., Congress, OTA, *Biological Effects*, 5

the highest voltage utilized in North America was 10 kilovolts (kV);[3] today, the most efficient and economical long-distance transmission lines are rated at 765 kV. As a result of this increase in use and delivery, exposure to PF E/MF has increased considerably in the last few decades and will likely continue to do so in the future. The demand for electric energy is expected to increase by about 40 percent in the United States by the year 2000.[4]

Acute effects of exposures to very intense PF electric fields have been recognized for many years. These include perception of the field (for example, from hair vibration), discomfort due to spark discharges, discomfort and muscular contractions due to contact currents from touching ungrounded conducting objects (such as vehicles), and interference with some cardiac pacemakers. (Interference with cardiac pacemakers can be eliminated through modifications in product design.) Exposure to very intense magnetic fields can produce visual phenomena called magnetophosphenes. Short-term shocks and perception distortions are not presently the subject of interest, however. They occur above fairly high and well-known intensity thresholds and are quite well understood; regulations are in place to ensure public and worker safety in this respect. Concerns have been raised, however, over possible health effects from long-term sub-acute exposure to PF E/MF.

PF E/MF do not involve a significant propagation of energy through space, and, because the energy they contain is far too low to break chemical or molecular bonds or heat tissue significantly, most scientists have assumed that the fields are biologically innocuous. However, beginning in the late 1960s and early 1970s, a growing body of research has demonstrated that under certain circumstances PF E/MF can produce effects in biological systems. There is also epidemiological evidence of an association between certain cancers and residential and occupational environments with elevated (or above average) fields. It is not yet clear if exposure can give rise to significant human health problems because scientific research is incomplete and results of existing studies are contradictory.

The issue of the effect of PF E/MF on human health issues has become the subject of serious scientific study and heated debate in Canada, the United States, and around the world, and has been addressed by the World Health Organization (WHO) and the International Radiation Protection Association (IRPA). This debate has not been restricted to the scientific forum. The controversy has made people more aware of their proximity to power lines, and siting new lines has become much more difficult. Government has been called upon to take regulatory action. Litigation has been initiated against the utility industry by plaintiffs claiming that exposure to the fields has caused health effects or poses a risk to public health, or that property values have decreased due to such concerns. Because of the scientific uncertainty and the complex nature of the topic, media reports have been uneven and unclear in their presentations. The controversy and concern over PF E/MF health effects have given impetus to the research effort.

### STATE OF THE SCIENCE (TO DECEMBER 1988)[5]

Research results on PF E/MF health effects are complex and inconclusive. Many experiments have looked for effects and found no difference between biological systems that were and were not exposed. However, a number of positive findings demonstrate that, under certain circumstances, even relatively weak fields can produce changes at the cellular level. It is not possible to demonstrate that health hazards from PF E/MF exposure do exist, and they may not. However, the emerging evidence no longer allows one to categorically assert that there are no risks.[6]

## Cell and Tissue Laboratory Studies

The cell membrane appears to be the primary site of interaction between "extremely low frequency"[7] (ELF) fields and the cell.[8] The cell membrane is responsible for transmitting information arriving at its surface to the cell interior so that life processes can occur. ELF experiments have focused on how exposure might be changing processes governed by the membrane. Changes included: modulation of calcium ion flows;[9] interference with DNA synthesis and RNA transcription;[10] interaction with the response of normal cells to hormones and neurotransmitters; and interaction with the biochemical kinetics of cancer cells.

Research has demonstrated that, under certain circumstances, cell membranes are sensitive to externally imposed "low-frequency" (LF) electromagnetic fields (EMF), even when the fields' intensity is much weaker than the cell membrane's natural fields.[11] Therefore, processes governed by the cell membrane (such as a cell's capacity to recognize other cells) may be disrupted by exposure. ELF fields do not have enough energy to disrupt the structure of DNA. However, research has shown that exposure may interfere with RNA transcription patterns, resulting in the production of structurally changed proteins. (Protein synthesis is a very complicated; experiments yield no simple interpretation about potential ELF effects on organisms.) Experiments have demonstrated that ELF exerts an effect on endocrine tissue and endocrine processes *in vitro*, and that the effects show windows (biological effects seen in specific narrow ranges of field intensity and frequency). It is not possible to draw further inferences. ELF experiments on interaction with the immune response of cells showed that exposure had no significant effects on normal or immunized cell immunological functions. However, cells already stimulated by mutagens (agents that provoke an immune response) may be affected. Experiments have examined the effect of ELF fields on cancer cells. One hypothesis is that fields promote cancer formation or growth rather than initiate cancer. (Any potential relationship between field intensity and degree of promotion may be highly complex.)

It is difficult to predict whether and how effects demonstrated at the cellular level will affect the whole organism. When an external agent such as an ELF field perturbs a cellular process, other processes may compensate for the perturbation. The lack of a theoretical model to explain and understand potential cellular-level effects presents another problem in deductions about possible health concerns. Until recently, cell membrane biology (still in its infancy) was not well enough understood to advance hypotheses (still at a speculative stage) about potential mechanisms of action; several decades of carefully designed experiments may be required before all current evidence can be placed in a coherent framework. Furthermore, there appears to be no analog among known environmental hazards. ELF cellular effects are complex and dependent on a number of factors, including frequency and field strength, time pattern of exposure to the field, and direction of the applied field. They may also depend on whether the field is a simple alternating or pulsed field.

*Whole Animal (and Human) Laboratory Studies*

Whole animal experiments have involved many different subjects, including rats, mice, miniature swine, cows, guinea pigs, and chicken eggs. The subjects have been examined under a range of electric and magnetic field intensities and for various exposures and durations.

Experiments on detection, behaviour, learning, and avoidance responses in animals have shown that there are central nervous system (CNS) effects that may be windowed, but no general conclusions can be drawn. Studies of effects on reproduction, growth, and development have measured a wide range of factors (such as reproductive behaviour, prenatal viability, alterations in physical parameters, gross malformations, and CNS development). Most studies examining developmental effects have concluded that no overt defects and malformations resulted from exposure. However, because some studies have seen subtle effects, the possibility of an effect remains. Overall, studies examining the effects of 60 Hz fields on bone growth and repair have shown that high-intensity electric fields do not have a strong effect in rodents. Animal studies of CNS effects from ELF exposure have indicated that interactions may vary with the background static fields present, the time of day, and exposure duration. Studies have found that developing nervous systems may be particularly susceptible, and effects may be latent, manifested only in certain situations or later in time. Research also shows that ELF fields are specific with respect to affected regions of brain tissue. (Public health implications, if any, remain unclear.)

Experiments conducted on blood and immune system chemistry indicate no general or overall immune system performance changes or short-term endocrine system changes from several months' exposure to high-intensity electric fields. However, ELF experiments on the effects of electric and magnetic fields on circadian systems of man, primates, and lower animals indicate a definite effect on the periodicity of physiological functioning.[12] (Whether such effects are deleterious or long-lasting is not clear.) Physiological and psychological disorders have been associated with circadian system dyssynchrony, including altered drug and toxins sensitivity, internal conflicts between the timing of sleep physiological processes, and psychiatric disorders such as chronic depression.

### Epidemiological Studies

Epidemiological studies have investigated the association between residential (for both adults and children) and occupational (for adults) ELF field exposure and cancer; the focus has been on cancer because of historical observation, not because cancer is the most likely effect. Cancer promotion (versus initiation) is most often cited as the role ELF fields play in carcinogenesis, but no experiment or theory proves that ELF fields promote cancer or growth of tumours.

All studies are based on proxy exposure measures: in other words, in occupational studies, job titles are assumed to indicate actual exposure, and in residential studies spot measurements and/or electric-supply system wiring configuration code are assumed to indicate the amount of exposure. The validity of these measures as indices of historic field exposure has not been determined.[13] Furthermore, because most people are normally exposed to PF E/MF, it is not practical to hope to conduct an epidemiological study involving unexposed people. A basic assumption is that the use of electrical appliances and exposure to household or office wiring represents the normal or background exposure level. The studies are done to determine whether people who are exposed to field levels above background show any measurable difference in disease rates. People living close to power lines, workers in various "electrical occupations," and people who use electrically heated beds are assumed to have higher exposures.[14]

### Childhood Cancer

Three of the five studies that investigated the association between ELF field exposure and childhood cancer found positive results. The most recent study (by the New York State Power Line Project) found:

- A 30 percent increase in risk (with an odds ratio of 1.31) for all cancers was observed at high magnetic fields (2.50+ mG). Higher field ranges did not always give a higher cancer risk.
- Lymphoma, brain tumours, soft tumours, and "other cancers" showed an odds ratio (OR) of 1.3 to 1.6 at high field exposures (2.5 mG+). Leukemia showed an OR of 2.11 for the high field exposures and 1.23 for the 1.00–2.49 mG field range.
- Cancer risk was not associated with magnetic field values at residence of birth.
- Higher electric fields did not show higher cancer risk.
- Results on the relationship of childhood cancer to use of appliances, electric blankets, heated water beds, and electric heat were mixed but suggested a few trends. Electric blanket and isolette exposures were associated with increased risk of all cancers, especially brain and soft tissue for isolette exposure.

### Residential Exposure and Adult Cancer

Two of the three studies that examined the association between adult cancer and residential exposure to ELF fields found positive results. One study (by Wertheimer and Leeper) found an association between nervous system, uterus, and breast cancers, with an increasing risk for higher current configurations. Another study, by the New York State Power Line Project (NYSPLP), found no association between acute nonlymphocytic leukemia and residential wiring configuration and field exposure. The studies do not provide enough evidence that residential field exposure increases cancer risk.

### Occupational Exposures and Adult Cancer

About twenty studies have examined the association between cancer – in particular, leukemia and brain cancer – and occupational ELF field exposure. Electrical worker populations or ham radio operators in the United States, England, Sweden, and New Zealand have been used. Together, the studies indicate a small positive association or no association.

Studies of the association of ELF exposure and leukemia show electrical equipment assemblers and aluminum workers have the highest relative risk (RR) of all "electrical" occupations. However, uncertainties exist because, for example, job classification does not clearly indicate actual occupational field exposure, and studies did not consider confounding variables and other exposures. Studies show that telegraph, radio, and radar operators – the third-highest RR group – consistently exhibit increased risk. They do not provide sufficient evidence that occupational PF E/MF exposures increase leukemia or brain cancer risk.

The association between brain and CNS tumours and occupational ELF field exposure has been examined in several studies, including some general cancer studies. Because adult brain cancer is rare, it is difficult to establish a causal association.[15] Also, because the brain is a favoured site for metastasis,[16] cases counted as primary brain cancer may actually be secondaries from a different organ where the cancer actually initiated. Furthermore, exposure is estimated from job titles or general occupation codes: the code "electrical occupations" may include workers such as electrical and telecommunications engineers who are no more exposed to ELF than the average individual.[17]

### GENERAL HISTORY (TO DECEMBER 1988)[18]

When electricity was first introduced in the 1800s, the public was apprehensive. Only when it became clear that there was no threat of fire or electrocution, and that enormous benefits could be derived, did fears abate. By the 1930s transmission lines had become symbols of industrial development and modernization, and in the 1940s, with the introduction of the U.S. Rural Electrification Administration, high-voltage transmission lines came to represent democracy in action.

Public attention initially focused on the aesthetic impact of large towers, on the aesthetic and ecological impacts of their right of way (ROWS), and on nuisance effects (e.g., audible noise, radio and television interference, and induced shocks from their strong electric fields). Provincial and state regulatory agencies adopted standards insuring that the lines did not produce gross effects, such as shock and burns.[19]

By the late 1960s and early 1970s, individuals, citizen groups, governments, the scientific and public health communities, and the electric utility industry began to express increasing concern about the effects of PF E/MF exposure on human health. This concern was occasionally reflected and influenced by the media.[20] Most scientists assumed that PF E/MF levels commonly present in the environment were biologically innocuous, since they did not cause shock or heat body tissue significantly. Furthermore, field strengths were very small, well below the threshold of physical perception.[21]

Many scientists associated with the discovery of electricity and the formulation of its laws, including Hertz, Faraday, Tesla, and Volta, were deeply concerned with the effect of electricity on animals and the electrical fields that originate within animals. However, by 1900 the early connections thought to exist between electricity and biology were broken. The search for answers to biological processes such as disease, growth, and reproduction increasingly employed the concepts and framework of solution chemistry. Biologists generally did not incorporate electricity in either their theories or the conduct of their experiments during the first two-thirds of the twentieth century. During this same period, the study of electricity evolved into a highly specialized set of disciplines aimed at understanding the interaction of electricity with non-living matter. Virtually the only knowledge produced by their combination was the determination of the current required to stimulate nerves, or cause shock, or kill or burn an organism.

In the mid-1960s, scientists began to conduct laboratory experiments dealing with the effects of very minute amounts of electricity on both humans and animals. Their individual research aims were diverse: to alter growth patterns, stimulate regeneration, treat tumours, alter the course of specific diseases, and so on. The focus of their research was either therapeutic or purely speculative. It grew out of some scientists' dissatisfaction with the failure of the chemical approach to furnish insights into the way that living things functioned, and their desire to utilize the methods and concepts of newly emergent areas of thought, such as solid-state physics and information theory. In some instances the electric environment to which the investigator exposed the biological systems under study was similar to that created by high-voltage transmission lines.[22]

By the 1970s the utility industry had grown from many small companies into several large companies. However, by that time transmission lines had become negative social symbols for the environmental movement, which emerged in the 1960s as a vehicle for social concerns about central authority and control.[23]

Not only has a shift occurred in the last twenty-five years in attitudes towards technology in general, but there has also been a growing preoccupation with technologically induced risk.[24] The perceived importance of efficiency and productivity has decreased, while the importance of aesthetics, pollution control, safety, and health has increased. The establishment of the U.S. National Environmental Protection (NEP) Act in 1969 institutionalized the change by requiring that non-economic impacts be considered in decisions affecting the environment.[25]

Increasing demand for power and the economies that could be realized when electricity was transmitted at high voltage led to increasingly higher-transmission voltages. Transmission at 345 kV began in the mid-1950s, followed by 500 kV and 765 kV in the late 1960s. Environmental groups, government agencies, and some members of the scientific community began to question if past biological effects research and experience with lower-voltage lines provided an adequate basis for determining the possible health and environmental effects of higher-voltage lines. Only a small amount of research had been conducted to explore the possible effects, especially long-term, on biological systems from transmission line electric fields. Almost no research had been conducted investigating magnetic field effects.[26]

The utility industry was not well prepared to address claimed health effects from PF E/MF. Previous industry research had focused on corona, the primary environmental issue prior to the mid-1960s.[27] Audible noise and "let-go" current considerations had also been investigated, usually by engineers and physicists, with end-points definable in familiar engineering terms. Scientifically defensible research was limited to the development of computation methods and measurement techniques based on well-founded analytical and experimental procedures. Even on this subject there was considerable debate as to correct procedures, adequacy of instruments, and the ability to trace electric field measurements.[28]

Interest in the possible long-term health effects from PF E/MF was largely prompted by Soviet reports in the 1960s (first given wide distribution at an international conference in 1972) regarding health problems experienced by men working in 400 kV and 500 kV switchyards.[29] By the early 1970s a number of projects involving both humans and animals were reported in the scientific literature by groups in the United States, West Germany, France, Spain, Sweden, and Japan. With the exception of Spain, researchers in western Europe and the United States did not identify any prompt or acute effects other than from spark and electric discharge, and no permanent effects.[30] However, of the seven studies that were directly related to effects on humans, only two were based on long-term exposure to PF E/MF.[31]

None of the early studies received wide acceptance from the scientific community. They were criticized for poor exposure assessment, lack of control groups, and multiple methodological weaknesses. The research results indicated the need for further research to resolve inconclusive or contradictory research findings.[32] The need for an interdisciplinary effort was only starting to be recognized. Those projects based on sound engineering principles had little merit as biological studies; the few studies by groups qualified to conduct biological experiments were flawed by improper or untraceable electrical characteristics. In particular, electric shock could not ruled out as a confounding factor.[33]

Two events in particular made it clear that existing data was insufficient to determine if there were human health effects from PF E/MF: literature reviews conducted by the U.S. National Academy of Science (NAS) for Project ELF, and both literature reviews and a research program conducted by the New York State Public Service Commission (NYS PSC) to assess the effects of 765 kV transmission lines.[34] In the late 1960s, the U.S. Navy first proposed construction of Project Sanguine, an ELF magnetic field submarine communications system;[35] the electric and magnetic fields produced would be similar in several respects to those created by high-voltage transmission lines. In response to public concern, and to comply with the recently enacted NEP Act, a laboratory research program investigating exposure effects on animals and plants was conducted. Some of the early studies reported effects while others were inconclusive.[36] The U.S. Navy then commissioned the National Research Council (NRC) to conduct a literature review; published in 1977, the review concluded that the E/MF produced by Project ELF would not cause any significant biological effects other than shocks.[37] In 1973, the New York Power Authority (NYPA) announced plans to build two 765 kV transmission lines from the Canadian border to Central New York State to carry hydroelectric power from Quebec.[38] The licensing proceeding held by the NYS PSC from 1975 until 1977 involved the first lengthy hearing on the subject of PF E/MF health effects. Although there was considerable opposition for several reasons, the potential for health risks became the dominant issue.[39] In addition to the Soviet reports, some scientists had come forward with reports of effects on small animals.[40]

During the mid 1970s, slight improvements were made in the conduct of research, incorporating control groups with improved exposure assignment. Research focused primarily on trying to prove that the (electric) fields had no biological effects. Although the null hypothesis is a valid scientific tool, it cannot be proven in any general sense.[41] Consequently, the studies received limited public acceptance. The U.S. Department of Energy (DOE) and the Electric Power Research Institute (EPRI) also realized that spending millions of dollars trying to prove that there were no effects would elicit little support from the scientific community.[42] Therefore, they developed laboratory research programs that would focus on broad-based screening studies. Large numbers of rats, mice, and various individual cells were exposed to high levels of PF E/MF to see if there were any general effects, because there was no indication what system or function, if any, was most likely affected.[43] (The use of screening studies rather than specific hypothesis-testing caused some concern. If scientists looked deep enough and hard enough, they were likely to find some level of interaction.)[44]

The research programs initiated by the U.S. DOE and EPRI explored areas that were considered most likely to produce effects. From an engineering point of view, this required a focus on electric fields. There was a long history of public exposure to weak magnetic fields with few accepted claims of effects. Also, the Soviet studies claimed effects based on strong electric fields. Concurrently, rigorous research on exposure assessment was instituted to provide the link for engineering changes if significant health effects were found. Most of the studies found no differences between exposed and unexposed groups. The few studies that did find effects were followed up with more detailed experiments, using a range of field intensities and varied exposure conditions and durations to look for mechanisms to explain the effects that had developed and determine their significance.[45]

In addition to the substantial U.S. DOE and EPRI research programs, the Bonneville Power Administration (BPA) and Southern California Edison began significant programs.[46] (BPA primarily funded environmental and livestock studies.)[47] Diverse end-points were examined, often with good experimental protocols. However, although many studies showed no effects, there were rarely enough numbers of subjects to detect low-level effects.[48] The possibility of biological effects from non-ionizing radiation (NIR), other than tissue heating, was gaining acceptance by some scientists. A number of U.S. federal agencies and international agencies called for more research.

In 1976, scientists Bawin and Adey made a controversial discovery: low intensity radio frequency (RF) carrier waves modulated by certain ELF elicited biological effects. Further research showed the calcium efflux effect in nerve tissue cells at 60 Hz but not at 55 Hz or 65 Hz. (The unusual behaviour of calcium flow from cell membranes in brain tissue *in vitro* was the first clear, reproducible effect of ELF fields observed in biological tissue.)[49] Due to these "frequency windows," it appeared that a threshold below which exposures were without effect might not exist. The U.S. Environmental Protection Agency (EPA) basic science research program initially focused on the biological effects of RF electromagetic radiation (EMR).[50] By 1982, after confirming the existence of frequency windows, a modest program of work with ELF, including PF, was begun in an effort to isolate cause and effect relationships. "Intensity windows" were discovered, where no enhancement of effects occurred at either higher or lower intensities. There was also increasing evidence that the earth's geomagnetic field influenced effects.

Until the late 1970s, researchers had concentrated most of their efforts on the effects of electric fields around transmission lines. By the early 1980s, an increasing number of epidemiological studies were reporting associations between cancer and residential and occupational environments where the PF magnetic field was thought to be elevated. As a result, the focus of investigations began to shift to magnetic field effects, especially cancer, and to other sources of PF fields, such as distribution lines and electric blankets.[51] In 1979, the first (case-control) study to link magnetic fields and cancer was published by Wertheimer and Leeper. They reported a possible association between childhood cancer and proximity to "high current configuration" distribution lines in Denver, Colorado.[52] Wertheimer and Leeper were also the first to report, in 1982, an association between adult cancers and residential wiring configurations.[53] In 1982, a study by Milham reported that power station operators had 2.5 times the death rate from leukemia in Washington State, the first report of an association between cancer and PF E/MF exposure in the workplace.[54]

Two of the three subsequent epidemiological studies of PF magnetic fields and childhood cancer, conducted by researchers in the United States and in Sweden, also suggested an association. The four studies of PF E/MF and cancer among electrical workers that followed in the United States and Britain were also positive.[55] In 1986, Wertheimer and Leeper reported a link between magnetic field exposure from electric blankets and electrically heated waterbeds to miscarriages, and to reduced birth weights and lengthening of the gestation period for infants born to exposed mothers. However, all findings were considered highly uncertain because of the many theoretical concerns and methodological questions raised, particularly the problem of long-term exposure assessment.[56]

Although some investigators speculated that a causative association might exist, others, given the lack of convincing evidence, were more tentative and considered causation as only one of several possible hypotheses. Promotion was a possibility, but most known chemical promoters were characterized by a degree of tissue specificity. Furthermore, if the association was causal, an increase in exposure over time would be followed by an increase in disease. Many believed that a temporal relationship had not been shown because a concomitant overall increase in cancers had not followed the rapid growth of electrification and use of electrical devices in the United States during the past century.[57]

By 1979, concern among the public, as well as in regulatory and technical circles, about possible health effects from PF E/MF had increased. Numerous studies in the early 1980s further increased public concern, precipitating additional research efforts and regulatory activity. Although many of the weaknesses and limitations of the pioneering epidemiology were expected to be overcome by ongoing studies, the existing studies were still inconclusive and inconsistent.[58] Mounting fear and public activism were already causing delays in the licensing and construction of major transmission facilities and promoting the formation of regulatory policy.[59] For example, a series of events precipitated by the Florida Power Corporation's attempt to gain certification for a 500 kV transmission line culminated with the Florida Siting Board's order that the Department of Environmental Regulation (DER) promulgate a PF E/MF standard.[60] In 1985, a Texas County civil court ruled that Houston Lighting and Power, in building a 345 kV transmission line within sixty metres of a school, had acted "with callous disregard for the safety, health, and well-being" of the children. The jury ordered Houston Lighting and Power to pay $25 million in punitive damages and to move either the line or nearby school buildings.[61]

In an effort to address these problems, the U.S. DOE sponsored a three-year study on risk assessment at Carnegie Mellon University (CMU) in 1982, broadening the already multi-disciplinary nature of the PF E/MF and human health controversy. By 1985, researchers concluded that the limits in scientific knowledge precluded conducting a meaningful 60 Hz field risk assessment or bounding analyses for developmental abnormalities and cancer end-points.[62] By 1983 EPRI had expanded and reoriented their research focus to magnetic field effects. Similarly, by 1985 the U.S. DOE had determined magnetic field effects to be of higher priority, although in several DOE programs research on both electric and magnetic fields continued.[63] DOE laboratory screening studies mostly concentrated on physiological systems considered highly sensitive to external stimuli, or to follow-up on earlier clinical reports of health problems.[64]

Reflecting the increasing interest in PF E/MF and higher frequency EMR health effects research, the Bioelectromagnetics Society (BEMS) grew into a substantial professional society. BEMS is the only scientific society that deals exclusively with bioelectromagnetics research and questions related to the biological effects and uses of electromagnetic energy. Its refereed scientific journal, now published six times a year, is the single most important EMF/EMR scientific journal in the world.[65] Similarly, two commercial newsletters – *Transmission/Distribution Health & Safety Report* (TDHSR) (now called *EMF Health & Safety Digest*) and *Microwave News* – began publishing by 1983. They carry reports on the latest scientific, regulatory, and other developments in the field.

By the mid 1980s, results of several major research projects were available, with an increasing number of studies indicating a small but possible risk.[66] Numerous literature reviews had been conducted by private contractors, universities, electric utilities, and government organizations throughout the United States and other countries, and by international organizations such as the WHO and the IRPA. With few exceptions there was general agreement that electric fields such as those produced by transmission lines had not been shown to cause harmful effects (other than shocks) in people or animals. However, because of effects reported in some studies, most reviewers pointed out the need for further research.[67] Although significant methodological advances had been made and there had been an accumulation of effects data, there was still a lack of experimental and epidemiological data on human exposures, insufficient data from animal experiments, and a lack of understanding of basic mechanisms by which low-intensity fields could interact with biological systems, especially magnetic fields.[68]

A few reviews included the specific recommendation of "prudent avoidance."[69] As a result of work done for the Florida DER on practical policy options for the siting of transmission lines, which addressed the potential for PF E/MF health risks, researchers at CMU proposed a policy of prudent field avoidance in which utilities would be given incentives to choose transmission line corridors that minimized the number of people who lived nearby.[70] Although the concept of "more is worse" did not necessarily apply to PF field exposure, one thing was known for certain: if the fields posed a hazard to human health, the impact would be proportional to the number of persons exposed. In the case of distribution systems and appliances only, fields could be eliminated at a modest cost; however, the costs of entirely eliminating fields from most sources was larger than society seemed willing to pay.[72]

Although individually flawed, collectively the studies could not be ignored. Many scientists were not convinced of health effects and wanted more substantial evidence. However, by 1986, budgets within various U.S. federal agencies for research on the health effects of NIR were being slashed, reflecting the Reagan administration's civilian budget-trimming. Most of the EPA's projects dealing with ELF fields were shut down in 1986.[73] The U.S. DOE's ELF budget dropped from a high in 1985 of $4.7 million to $2.7 million in 1986. (Even so, DOE continued to be the major source of PF field effects funding. EPRI was second, with $1.7 million budgeted in 1986.)[74] These cuts occurred after scientists had determined that the fields did have effects but before they could characterize and quantify the risks, if any, that were involved.

The NYSPLP Scientific Advisory Panel (SAP) Final Report, published in 1987, marked the first time that an impartial group of scientists had concluded that E/MF associated with transmission lines, especially magnetic fields, may be a hazard to human health and a factor in the cause of cancer and nervous system dysfunction.[75] In addition to evaluating previous scientific work, sixteen biological and health-related studies on transmission line E/MF had been conducted.[76] The majority of the studies were negative, with no effects on reproduction, growth, or development in isolated cells; a few did find effects, including the possibility that magnetic fields might affect body rhythms. One epidemiological study (by Savitz) was considered especially convincing. The case-control study reported a modest statistical association between proximity to household wiring and distribution lines and childhood cancer in Denver.[77] The study replicated and improved on Wertheimer and Leeper's 1979 study and avoided most of the design flaws of earlier studies.[78] Although the relative risk (1.5) was lower, the thoroughness of the study gave the findings greater weight. Still, exposure assessment, while improved, was criticized as a major weakness, and the number of cases involved in the study was small.[79]

According to the SAP final report, magnetic fields from power lines, mainly distribution lines, could account for 10 to 15 per cent of all cases of childhood cancers;[80] however, a causal link had not been established and information on population exposures was incomplete.[81] The link between adult cancer and power lines was left out because it was even more uncertain. (Another NYSPLP study found no association between adult non-lymphocytic leukemia and residential wiring configuration or residential field exposure.)[82] As a result of the NYSPLP, transmission line PF E/MF levels of new high voltage lines in New York State were limited to those produced by 345 kV lines that had already been in operation for many years.

The NYSPLP findings generated headlines in newspapers all over the world. Public concern escalated, and a flurry of regulatory and scientific activity began internationally. In the United States, congressional hearings were held in 1987; these constituted the first federal forum to specifically address the issue of possible health effects from transmission line E/MF. Although the hearings were held too late in the Washington budget cycle to increase federal levels of spending in 1988, DOE and EPRI would continue to be the major sources of funding for research in North America, with EPRI substantially increasing its research budget, from $1.7 million to $5 million. DOE spending would dip from a high in 1985 of $4.7 million to a low of $2.1 million in 1988.[83] In the fall of 1986, when rumours began to circulate that Savitz's study would support Wertheimer and Leeper's earlier work,[84] the Canadian government set up a working group and made $50,000 available to Health and Welfare Canada (HWC) for research.[85] Ontario Hydro also expanded its research efforts.[86]

In addition, by 1987 several reports, based primarily on census data, had suggested that electrical occupations might carry an elevated risk of leukemia and brain cancer. However, a large and comprehensive epidemiological study on occupational exposure had not yet been done.[87] These same cancers were specifically elevated in the childhood studies.[88]

The NYSPLP lent credibility to those few "dissenting" scientists who were outspoken about the possible health effects of PF E/MF. Throughout the history of the controversy, highly visible disagreements among experts, coupled with accusations of biased research agendas, had fuelled concerns, particularly those of the public. These concerns were occasionally reflected and influenced by the media. Expert disagreement was most often on display at public hearings and court cases concerning power line sitings. Less adversarial debate was also carried out, as usual, in scientific journals and at the two large scientific conferences where many scientists presented their latest research findings – the annual BEMS meeting and the annual U.S. DOE/EPRI Contractors' Review.[89]

Some scientists continued to state that, on the basis of all the evidence, there were no health hazards or risk from PF E/MF exposure.[90] Conventional wisdom held that PF E/MF could pose no threat to human health because there was no substantial transfer of energy from PF fields to biological systems and because all cells in the body maintained large natural electric fields across their outer membranes. Furthermore, there was no large-scale and obvious public health effect associated with electrification.[91] Another problem in deducing possible health effects from cellular effects was the lack of a theoretical model to explain and understand the detailed mechanism of interaction. This led some scientists to believe that a confounding factor was involved. Researchers began calling for whole animal experiments examining magnetic field exposure/cancer promotion to support or refute the epidemiology. An animal model was needed because of questions of dose-response relations, effects of frequency of field, and possible questions of interaction between 60 Hz and Earth's DC magnetic fields were not easily studied.[92]

By December 1988, several residential and occupational epidemiologic and laboratory studies, sponsored by industry and government, were planned or under way around the world to determine the mechanisms of interaction and effects, if any, of potential significance in terms of human health.[93] For example, Hydro Québec, Electricité de France, and Ontario Hydro were co-sponsoring a $3-million epidemiological case-control study of electrical utility workers.[94] PF E/MF would be one of the risk factors examined in a $2.5-million U.S. National Cancer Institute (NCI) study of the causes of childhood leukemia.[95] The New York State Department of Health (DOH) was considering undertaking a major research program similar to the NYSPLP. (The question of who would provide funding was not resolved.)[96]

Work had begun on standardizing study designs and methodologies. The more recent studies had larger sample populations to account for low-level effects, and most were devoted to testing hypotheses. Exposure was measured more accurately, with recently available instrumentation for personal dosimetry of E/MF allowing examination of the assumptions made regarding exposure sources and improvement of the quality of surrogate measures.[97] The pattern of lower or no risk reported by the better-designed and -executed studies continued, providing additional support for the possible role of PF E/MF in the etiology of cancer. For example, there was a consistent lack of evidence of adult acute leukemia risk from residential E/MF sources, including electric blankets, but a rather consistent suggestion of excess acute myelogenous leukemia and brain cancer from occupational exposures of electrical workers.[98] Yet, even with a diversity of end-points, the epidemiological studies were considered to be of questionable quality. Taken together, the results of the "hundreds" of studies conducted over the previous two decades throughout the world were inconclusive, and few replications had been conducted. Several scientific reviews of the literature concluded that no link had been established between E/MF such as those produced by transmission lines and adverse health effects. However, they pointed out that some studies suggested the possibility of adverse effects, and the need for long-term research to resolve the issue was universally acknowledged.[99]

Intensifying public opposition to new power line sitings in (for example) New York, Montana, and Florida, and, to a much lesser degree, increasing concern about PF E/MF health effects in general from various other sources, including existing power lines, had placed pressure on government and industry. Public concerns had already stalled some transmission line projects and, in several states, health effects had become the central issue in transmission line site hearings.[100] Several court cases against utilities had been initiated in several states by the public based on potential and claimed health effects, and, by landowners in particular, based on perceived transmission line health effects.[101] Other, less dramatic incidents were occurring all over the United States.[102] Although there had not been extensive media coverage, articles about PF E/MF health effects were appearing with increasing regularity in reputable national publications and, more recently, on radio and television programs.

In response to these actions and public concerns, regulatory agencies, standard-setting bodies, utilities, and school boards were struggling to make policies. (Neither the American nor Canadian federal governments had taken the lead.) There were two opposing views: one, that enough evidence of potential health effects existed to caution limited exposure, and two, that research must present proof of harmful effects before practical limits were determined.[103] Some governments, legislatures, and agencies were simply asking for literature reviews. Others were taking action by holding hearings, allocating or requiring funds from industry for further research, and issuing limits for power line ROWs.[104] A number of American states (including New York, California, Washington, Virginia, and Florida) and at least one Canadian province (Ontario) were considering regulation of general public and occupational exposures to E/MF associated with power lines.

By December 1988 seven states had already set limits on power line electric field intensity (see Table 4-1). New York was the first state to consider restricting distribution line E/MF, but no state has yet considered regulating appliance fields.[105] U.S. federal activity was directed towards possible power line standards through the EPA. The final report was due in 1987, but they were still grappling with whether or not to recommend exposure limits[106]; Canadian provincial and federal governments had not set any standards.

After the 1985 court case brought by a school against Houston Lighting and Power, increasingly parents and school boards expressed concern about the siting of power lines near schools and vice versa. Concern continued to increase following the report of the

Table 4-1
Summary of U.S. Standards for Transmission Line E/MF Strength

| State/BPA | Electric Field | | Magnetic Field | |
|---|---|---|---|---|
| | On Right-of-Way | Edge of Right-of-Way | On Right-of-Way | Edge of Right-of-Way |
| Florida | 8  kV/m[1]<br>10  kV/m[2] | 2  kV/m | – | 150 mG (max. load)[1]<br>200 mG (max. load)[2]<br>250 mG (max. load)[3] |
| Minnesota | 8  kV/m | – | – | – |
| Montana | 7  kV/m[4] | 1  kV/m | – | – |
| New Jersey | – | 3  kV/m | – | – |
| New York | 11.8 kV/m | 1.6 kV/m | – | 100 mG[5] |
| North Dakota | 9  kV/m | – | – | – |
| Oregon | 9  kV/m | – | – | – |
| BPA | 9  kV/m<br>5  kV/m[4]<br>3.5 kV/m[6]<br>2.5 kV/m[7] | 5  kV/m | – | – |

1. For 230-kV or smaller lines
2. For 500-kV lines.
3. For 500-kV double-circuit lines.
4. Maximum for highway crossings.
5. Proposed interim standard.
6. Maximum for shopping centre parking lots.
7. Maximum for commercial/ industrial parking lots.

Reproduced with permission from U.S., BPA, DOE, *Electric and Biological Effects*, June 1989, 58

NYSPLP: by 1988, disputes had occurred in (for example) Arizona, Ontario, Alberta, New York, and Florida.[107] In addition, concern continued to be raised by some members of the public, by governments, and by the scientific community over the credibility of health-effects research conducted by electric utilities (most American research was supported by the EPRI and DOE).[108]

Furthermore, calls were being made for participation by U.S. federal agencies whose missions concerned public health. The EPA Office of Radiation Programs had begun phasing out their entire non-ionizing radiation (NIR) program[109]; yet according to some, without the EPA most of the work would be done by agencies with a stake in downplaying risks. There was disagreement over which federal agencies (EPA or the National Institutes of Health) should take over the major role.[110]

Little or no research had been done exploring the technical and economic feasibility of reducing or eliminating PF E/MF exposure due to health concerns, whether from power lines or other sources. A small amount of work had been done at CMU in 1984 and EPRI in 1988 on design strategies to reduce exposure.[111] One CMU researcher had explored the issue of product liability risk to manufacturers and how to motivate manufacturers to act.[112] Most utilities and manufacturers had not acted to decrease power line fields on their own because no human health risk had been established.[113] However, a few utilities began to look for ways to mitigate fields in designing and siting of power lines.[114] For example, the Bonneville Power Administration began to consider adopting a policy of "prudent avoidance" in 1987. At least one waterbed-heater and one electric-blanket manufacturer had also taken steps to reduce their products' E/MF.

By mid 1988, risk communication projects were underway to gain a better understanding of public perception of PF E/MF health effects and to develop communication tools to address those concerns. For example, the public's focus on high-voltage transmission lines was felt to be misplaced, because more recent studies had implicated an association with distribution lines and appliances. However, arguments that exposure from sources other than high-voltage transmission lines was greater were not well accepted because of the conscious and voluntary nature of such exposure.[115] By late 1988, CMU's Centre for Risk Perception and Communication was testing an experimental public information document.[116] (In 1987, CMU researchers concluded that risk managers had a moral obligation to communicate to the public the possible risks of PF E/MF, but in the absence of clear evidence of health problems, such communication should occur only if people asked for information.)[117] Work sponsored by the U.S. DOE and by the EPRI was also underway at CMU and private consulting firms to help utilities factor PF E/MF considerations into the decision-making process.[118]

# CHAPTER FIVE

# Power Frequency Electric and Magnetic Fields Part Two: A Public Controversy

## INTRODUCTION

The PF E/MF and human health issue first received wide public recognition in British Columbia during the summer of 1989.[1] The B.C. Hydro and Power Authority was constructing a transmission line to supply power to an expanded Canadian Pacific Forest Products (CPFP) pulp mill at Gold River on Vancouver Island. Unsatisfied with the response of B.C. Hydro to their concerns about health effects from the PF E/MF associated with the transmission line, residents along the right of way (ROW) filed complaints with the provincial ombudsman, who turned the matter over to the B.C. Utilities Commission (BCUC). After being inundated with requests to reroute the new transmission line, the BCUC ordered that a public inquiry be held July 11–12 in Courtenay, B.C.

  B.C. Hydro's experts testified that the transmission line E/MF posed no health risk. The residents' expert testified that they were a health risk. Although the main purpose of the inquiry was to gather information on PF E/MF health effects, several scientific issues commonly raised by experts in the area were not addressed by either "side." Instead, the inquiry more resembled a court of law. The lawyers for B.C. Hydro, the residents, and the BCUC spent much of their time contesting the credibility of the other side's expert witnesses, questioning their strength of opinion and expertise in the PF E/MF health effects area. Expert witnesses from both sides spoke with a legally inspired caution. A chronology of events before, during, and after the Courtenay inquiry is shown in Table 5-1, and a list of people involved in the controversy follows at the end of this chapter.

### PRE-INQUIRY EVENTS

Canadian Pacific Forest Products (CPFP) owns and operates pulp and paper mills throughout Canada, including a bleach kraft pulp mill near the village of Gold River, B.C. CPFP, along with its partners in Gold River Newsprint Ltd. Partnership, wished to expand the Gold River operation at a projected capital cost of $323 million by adding a chemi-thermo mechanical pulp mill and a newsprint mill.[2] A feasibility study conducted by B.C. Hydro in 1987 determined that a 230 kV transmission line should be built along an existing ROW from Qualicum to Campbell River to provide power to the expanded operation.[3] Three 138 kV transmission lines were already on the ROW. The existing transmission line to the mill was capable of providing 40 megawatts (MW) of the 90 MW of power required by the mill.[4] The proposed line was included in the Resource Plan submitted by B.C. Hydro to the BCUC in April 1988.[5]

B.C. Hydro and CPFP concluded their discussions in the summer of 1987 and B.C. Hydro was committed to provide power by approximately July 31, 1989. The newsprint mill was scheduled to commence production September 1, 1989, for shipments in October 1989; the mill required the power by August 15 to meet break-in, production, and shipment schedules. There was no time allowance for possible delays.[6] In September 1987, Premier Bill Vander Zalm publicly announced the project, stating, "It's a great day for British Columbia and Gold River. Now the pulp and chips produced won't have to be shipped elsewhere to be processed. They will do it here and utilize B.C. labour and products." No government concessions or incentives were given to the company to encourage the development of the mill. CPFP proceeded with the mill expansion in the fall, using a "fast track" approach.[7]

B.C. Hydro used the approval granted for the existing 138 kV lines ROW to begin the 230 kV project. They followed the normal review process, communicating with the appropriate federal and provincial government resource agencies, seeking the necessary government (including regional districts and municipalities) approval, and advising them of the proposed construction.[8] None of the responses received raised health concerns.[9] Construction of the line proceeded as planned.

### EMERGING CONCERNS

All but 30 kilometres of the 145-kilometre Dunsmuir/Gold River transmission line passed through unpopulated areas. The most contentious portion of the seven-kilometre corridor through the Courtenay-Cumberland-Merville area would prove to be near Royston and Marsden Road.[10]

John Marton, Ph.D., a Courtenay psychologist, was advised by B.C. Hydro in September 1987 of the need to clear standing trees on his property. At this time, and in correspondence continuing through the middle of 1988, Marton raised concerns with B.C. Hydro about the possible health risks, of childhood cancer in particular, from the increased PF E/MF levels resulting from the new transmission line.[11] Lorne March, Ph.D., Director of Environmental Services for B.C. Hydro, told Marton that there was no proof of a causal relationship between PF E/MF and childhood cancers and therefore no action was required by B.C. Hydro.[12] He provided Marton with a 1987 literature review by the Ontario Ministry of Health (MOH) and the executive summary and table of contents from a 1985 literature review by the Bonneville Power Administration (BPA). Both reviews concluded that there was no convincing evidence of a human health risk from PF E/MF.[13]

Marton disputed this conclusion and, in a letter to Larry Bell, Chairman of B.C. Hydro, requested compensation for the cost of moving.[14] In response, Frank Klassen, Vice President of Administration for B.C. Hydro, refused Marton's request for compensation and stated that, in the absence of proof, they were "faced with perception of risk rather than known risk." He included a copy of an "open letter" to the public from David Savitz, Ph.D.[15] In the letter, Savitz stated that his study did not prove that PF magnetic fields caused childhood leukemia and that the question of a possible hazard had yet to be resolved. Interest or concern might be justified, but the study was "not sufficiently convincing to warrant drastic action by homeowners."[16]

Marton wrote Klassen on May 4 and cited a paragraph from the New York State Power Line Project Scientific Advisory Panel (NYSPLP SAP) Final Report stating that, although there was no conclusive proof of a causal relationship between residential magnetic fields and certain childhood cancers, there was cause for concern. Marton asked on whom the burden of proof fell (the citizens or B.C. Hydro) and, if risk could not be assessed accurately, on whom the cost of minimizing risk fell (those close to the lines or all users). On June 10, Klassen wrote Marton stating that he saw "little merit" in continuing their correspondence and rejected Marton's assertion that B.C. Hydro was introducing fields of a potentially dangerous level.[17] In reply, Marton requested up to $20,000 in compensation – but not necessarily on the basis of health risks – if B.C. Hydro wished to avoid setting a precedent.

On February 5, 1989, Marton wrote to the provincial ombudsman seeking assistance in dealing with the matter. After discussion with the British Columbia Utilities Commission (BCUC), the ombudsman decided to defer the handling of the matter and similar complaints to the BCUC.[18] The ombudsman also referred Marton to Richard Gathercole, Executive Director and General Counsel for the B.C. Public Interest Advocacy Centre (BC PIAC).[19]

### Increasing Concerns

By the end of January 1989, all but one property owner along the ROW had signed compensation agreements for timber and damages.[20]

Frank Kavka first learned about the new transmission line in February 1988 when he received a phone call from Pat Beavan, Land Representative, B.C. Hydro, who had informed him that his property would be surveyed. Beavan was unable to "guarantee" Kavka that the line would not pose a health risk to his family and, as a result, Kavka refused to give his consent for the line. Kavka "knew," having grown up in Eastern Europe, that high-voltage transmission lines were a health risk.[21] On January 31, a B.C. Hydro crew began work at Frank Kavka's property, despite his verbal objections. For health reasons, Kavka wanted a buffer zone of trees between his home on Marsden Road and the transmission line.

Frank Kavka also wanted more than the $2,000 compensation for timber and damages offered by B.C. Hydro.[22] Kavka wanted $10,000 to cover lost future yields of mushrooms and berry bushes.[23] On February 8, the Kavkas filed a formal complaint with the BCUC regarding their dispute with B.C. Hydro over compensation and raised concerns about PF E/MF health effects from the new line.[24]

By February, Darlene Kavka had begun to search for information on EMF health effects at local libraries and found very little. After locating a ten-year-old article by Robert Becker and Andrew Marino reporting adverse effects on mice exposed to PF E/MF, she contacted Robert Becker, Ph.D., an orthopaedic surgeon and pioneer in the treatment of difficult bone fractures with electric currents to promote healing. According to Kavka, the first thing Becker said to her was "You've got a real problem on your hands." He also told her that "electromagnetic fields around high-voltage transmission lines might be the most serious source of pollution in the world," gave her the names of scientists whose research supported his position, and suggested where she could locate relevant literature, including a transcript of the 1987 U.S. House of Representatives subcommittee hearing on health effects of transmission lines.[25]

Darlene Kavka made her first public presentation to the Comox-Strathcona Regional District (C-S RD) board on March 28, stating that numerous health effects had been associated with high-voltage power lines, including an "indisputable link" between "ELF electromagnetic radiation" and childhood cancer.[26] Kavka stated that, according to B.C. Hydro, homes within 90 to 120 metres from the existing and planned lines would have magnetic field readings of about 6 mG. The increased levels from the new line "could result in the Royston/Courtenay area seeing a childhood cancer incidence of between 2 and 5 children per thousand, as opposed to a *1-child-per-1000* incidence in the overall population. This means that within 2 years 2 to 5 children per 1000 could develop potentially fatal and avoidable cancers [emphasis added]." According to Kavka, the researchers she had contacted by phone were "adamant that people take action to protect themselves." She also said that, in Europe, there were magnetic field exposure guidelines and people were not allowed to work under the lines.[27]

The C-S RD board voted 17 to 1 to write to B.C. Hydro requesting that new high-voltage overhead transmission lines, including the new 230 kV line, not be routed through densely populated residential areas or near schools within the district, largely because of the suspected link between EMF and childhood cancer.[28]

Darlene Kavka had begun to organize a committee (later known as the Comox Valley Rerouting Committee, or CVRC) to "force" B.C. Hydro to reroute the new line. She made presentations, on behalf of the CVRC, to the Arden Parents' Group and Comox Valley Teachers' Association. As a result, both groups and the board of School District 71 requested that B.C. Hydro and the BCUC reroute the line. In particular, the board of School District 71 wanted the line routed away from Arden Elementary School, which was 400 metres from the ROW.[29] By early May, Gathercole had contacted the Kavkas after Thom Thompson, Manager of Government and Public Affairs for B.C. Hydro, informed him that they planned to forward a second formal complaint to the BCUC requesting that the EMF health effects issue be examined in depth before B.C. Hydro be allowed to finish constructing the line. As Gathercole was preparing the Kavkas' complaint, Chris Boatman, Vice-President of Corporate and Environmental Affairs for B.C. Hydro, suggested a meeting within a week with a group of residents in Courtenay.[30]

In early May, B.C. Hydro indicated that it was prepared to bring in experts to speak with the residents. The two experts would be B.C. Hydro's Lorne March and William Bailey, Ph.D., of Environmental Research Information (ERI) Inc.[31] ERI is a New York-based consulting firm that specializes in reviewing, analysing, and conducting research on environmental health issues such as occupational health, microwave, radio frequency, video display terminals, and, infrequently, chemicals. ERI had conducted some research on the biological effects of PF E/MF and had already been retained by utilities, public service commissions, public utility commissions, and other state advisory bodies.[32]

### Buy-out Offer

On May 8, an informal meeting was held at B.C. Hydro's office in Courtenay between B.C. Hydro's Chris Boatman, Thom Thompson, and Ken Curley (Area Manager), and the Kavkas, John Marton, and their lawyer, Richard Gathercole. B.C. Hydro maintained its position that there was no scientific evidence to indicate a conclusive relationship between PF E/MF and an increase in childhood leukemia, and offered to provide people living adjacent to the ROW with relevant scientific literature that could be used as a basis for their decisions regarding the possible risks. They would also, on request, provide further information and take field measurements, and have an expert available for discussions. If concern persisted about PF E/MF health risks, B.C. Hydro would negotiate the purchase of property at a "fair market value" determined by independent appraisers, one selected by the property owner and one selected by B.C. Hydro. Interested owners had until May 31 to register their requests.[33] The buy-out offer was made to Marton and to the Kavkas on the condition that they not pursue their complaint to the BCUC. Marton immediately accepted the offer. However, the Kavkas had already (tentatively) accepted a private offer on their property. Frank Kavka insisted that the offer be extended to other residents.[34]

The C-S RD was informed about the offer to purchase the following day at a meeting with Boatman, March, Thompson, and Jeff Barker, Project Manager, Transmission Projects, B.C. Hydro. March made a presentation on the PF E/MF health effects issue. Elizabeth Shannon, school board trustee, maintained School District 71's position that the line be rerouted away from Arden Elementary School.[35] B.C. Hydro stated that the line was being "pushed" through for economic reasons and that the line would not be moved because there was no substantial evidence that children had increased risk of cancer from elevated PF E/MF levels. B.C. Hydro's argument that people took risks when using a microwave oven was countered with the statement that people did so by choice. Kavka told the Comox *Free Press* that B.C. Hydro made some "very inaccurate statements" at the meeting.[36]

On May 9 and 12, B.C. Hydro delivered or mailed letters to approximately 144 property owners adjacent to the ROW.[37] The letter stated that the New York State Public Service Commission (NYS PSC) report "summarized the findings of the wealth of scientific research conducted throughout the world over the past two decades. This research demonstrated that there [was] no reason to believe that exposures to electric and magnetic fields [posed] a risk to human health." The letter reiterated the agreement made at the meeting of May 8 and closed with, "To repeat, we believe that the enclosed material should allay concerns and alleviate the necessity for exercising this [buy-out] option. However, we are sensitive to the feelings of owners when issues such as this are raised and wish to leave the decision up to each person."[38] A "background report" on the PF E/MF health effects issue prepared by ERI and the executive summary of BPA's literature review were included with the letter.[39]

### ERI Background Report

The "Background Report on Health Issues Associated with Exposure to Power Frequency Electric and Magnetic Fields" was prepared on "very short notice" in response to one of B.C. Hydro's first requests for information. The report cited the findings of six "non-adversarial" panels: the 1987 NYSPLP panel; the 1985 Florida E/MF Scientific Advisory Commission (a "blue ribbon" panel) on PF E/MF health effects; the 1979 American Institute of Biological Sciences and 1985 National Academy of Sciences panels on project ELF; and the 1984 and 1987 World Health Organization panels on the generic question of EMF. A number of studies on "community epidemiology" were reviewed. In particular, the results of Wertheimer and Leeper's 1979 and Savitz's 1988 studies were questioned because of surrogate exposure measurements. Several other studies were cited which failed to find PF E/MF health effects. The ERI report then concluded, "The New York [PSC's] statement succinctly [summarized] the findings of the wealth of scientific research conducted throughout the world over the past two decades. This research demonstrated there [was] no reason to believe that exposure to electric and magnetic fields [posed] a risk to human health. These data should reassure the public that transmission lines [did] not jeopardize the health of those who reside in their vicinity."[40]

The Kavkas were elated over B.C. Hydro's buy-out offer. An editorial in the *Courtenay Comox Valley Record* commended B.C. Hydro for their action.[41] The utility industry had never made such an offer before. Darlene Kavka received calls from citizen groups with similar concerns in New York and Ontario.[42] The *Transmission/Distribution Health & Safety Report* (TDHSR) contacted several utility representatives for reactions to the buy-out offer. Most had heard of the offer; of those who agreed to comment, most expressed reservations about the wisdom of the move. Neither Ontario Hydro (the offer was impractical) nor TransAlta Utilities Corporation (the offer was unjustified) intended to follow a similar course of action.[43] Boatman told TDHSR that the offer was "a reaction to a situation that had gotten out of hand." It "defused ... a very emotional issue." In the future, B.C. Hydro would be more aware of "public perceptions." They had not determined whether such an offer would be made in other cases. According to Peter McMullan, Corporate Communications, it "certainly" did not apply to existing lines.[44]

### Extreme Concern

Although the buy-out proposal was designed to defuse the situation, it was interpreted by many people as clear evidence that B.C. Hydro recognized a PF E/MF health risk. The media highlighted the unusual proposal and it drew substantial publicity. The majority of property owners to whom the proposal was made were confused about the health effects issue and were forced to make important decisions on short notice using conflicting information and hearsay. They were also confused about the eligibility criteria[45] and conditions of the buy-out offer, including its deadline.

Not all owners whose property was adjacent to the ROW received the letter. Some owners who were not adjacent to the ROW (and did not receive a letter) were closer to the ROW than their neighbors who did receive letters. A few owners who did not receive letters contacted B.C. Hydro regarding the proposal and received no reply. Many owners thought they had to decide to accept the buy-out offer by May 31, rather than simply register their interest. A number of residents approached the BCUC and expressed their concerns.[46]

B.C. Hydro placed a notice in local papers stating, "If you own property adjacent to or near the transmission line right-of-way, and you wish to know more about the effects of the line on your property, please call Ken Curley ... toll free."[47] Residents, unable to reach Curley, contacted Darlene Kavka for more information. She was inundated with calls up until a few days past the deadline and again after a headline article appeared in the *Free Press*. Kavka assisted residents by composing and typing letters in reply to B.C. Hydro's offer.[48]

On May 16, the school board voted unanimously to delay a $1-million expansion at Arden Elementary School until more PF E/MF health effects information (concerning both children and employees) had been received.[49] Darlene Kavka told the board that B.C. Hydro had taken a reading at the school forty times higher than the any of the figures subsequently released. However, she conceded that a number of readings must be taken over a period of time to obtain accurate results.[50] Shannon stated that she would not accept B.C. Hydro's self-monitoring of "its own pollution." The board also agreed that B.C. Hydro should fund an independent study to monitor PF E/MF levels within the school.[51]

Darlene Kavka had contacted Marino, who agreed to meet with residents for a one-day seminar in mid-June, provided his $1,500 (US) per day "travelling expenses" were covered.[52] By the end of May, Gathercole, now also representing the CVRC, was negotiating with B.C. Hydro to bring in Marino, an "authority on EMR" (according to the *Record*), to speak at Arden Elementary School. B.C. Hydro would decide after all the buy-out requests had been examined.[53] According to Kavka, B.C. Hydro had offered at the May 8 and 9 meetings to pay for an expert chosen by the residents. Marton, aware of the disagreement among scientists on the issue, was against bringing in Marino because, if the discussion "got into scientific expertise," the residents' "point of view" would be "muddled." Marton preferred to focus the discussion on "what form of risk was acceptable" and "whether B.C. Hydro had any responsibility, given that the risk was unknown." According to Kavka, Gathercole was also not in favour of bringing in an expert.[54]

Andrew Marino, a biophysicist, has his B.Sc. in physics, M.Sc. and Ph.D. in biophysics, and J.D. in law. He is a professor in the Department of Orthopedic Surgery and Department of Cellular Biology and Anatomy, Louisiana State University (LSU) Medical Centre. Marino is the chairman of the Louisiana State Medical School Institutional Review Board for Human Research and an associate professor in the Department of Bio-Engineering, Louisiana Technical University. He is also the president of the International Society for Bioelectricity, a member of three other bioelectricity-oriented scientific groups, and editor of the *Journal of Bioelectricity*.[55]

Marino was an associate of Becker's at the Veteran's Administration Medical Center in Syracruse, New York, from 1964 to 1981. He has investigated the use of electrical energy to treat or cause disease in animals and conducted clinical studies in which electricity is applied to humans for therapeutic purposes. His studies have linked PF E/MF exposure to abnormal growth in laboratory rats and mice and linked living near power lines to suicide in humans. Marino has published two books, as well as approximately sixty papers and twenty abstracts, editorials, and rejoinders on the subject of EMF health effects. Marino has testified as an expert witness on the EMF health effects issue numerous times, beginning in 1977 when he testified, along with Becker, on behalf of the NYS PSC, that PF E/MF was a health risk and industry-sponsored research was tainted. Since then, he has testified several times for PSCs (including those in New York State and California), but generally he speaks on behalf of the people themselves. Marino has also published a third book which deals with the politics, particularly in New York State, of the EMF health effects issue.[56]

By May 31, B.C. Hydro had sent out 144 buy-out letters and received 153 responses. Ninety per cent of the responses indicated an interest in the purchase offer.[57]

*Public Inquiry Ordered*

On June 12, the BCUC ordered that a public inquiry be held in Courtenay on July 11 and 12 because of public concern over EMF health effects. Particular concern focused on the possibility of long-term health risks, including cancer, especially in children. This was the first time the BCUC had received such a large number of complaints, in the form of "many" letters and more than forty phone calls, including several inquiries made by the BC PIAC on behalf of the Kavkas. The BCUC felt that many of the people's concerns were fuelled by misinformation and lack of information, and wanted to ensure that the issue was "out in the open" so people could judge for themselves.[58]

The BCUC also ordered that construction halt on the section of the line through the Courtenay-Cumberland area until the BCUC resolved the complaints. For the first time in Birtish Columbia, a major utilities project had been put on hold because of public pressure. B.C. Hydro's buy-out offer was also put on hold.[59]

The terms of reference of the inquiry were:

• determine the need, routing, and timing for the project;

- review the process followed with respect to the environmental assessment of the project and identify any appropriate mitigation measures;
- determine the levels of electric and magnetic fields associated with the new line, and assess the impact of these on the current fields created by the existing 138 kV line; and
- address the health-related concerns as expressed by property owners impacted by the new line, respecting biological effects of the electrical and magnetic fields generated by the line.

John McIntyre, Chairman of the BCUC, was appointed to chair the inquiry with the assistance of Commissioner Milt Swanson, QC, and staff members Bill Grant, Director of Engineering and Accounting, and Neptune Smith, Manager, Engineering and Project Review–Electrical.[60] Karl Gustafson, of Lane, Mitchener, Lawrence, and Shaw, was appointed as BCUC counsel. McIntyre would work with BCUC staff and develop decisions and/or recommendations, and present the inquiry findings and recommendations to the BCUC "as a whole" for approval. Swanson and the other two full-time commissioners would have "some" input while McIntyre defended his report.[61]

Darlene Kavka asked the BCUC how the costs of expert witnesses would be covered, and pointed out that B.C. Hydro could better afford to bring such witnesses to the inquiry. The BCUC responded that they were aware B.C. Hydro could "overwhelm them with technical studies," but also pointed out that the experts could submit written evidence rather than testify in person. Frustrated with B.C. Hydro's "stalling tactics," CVRC members had pooled their money and begun raising funds to bring in Marino for four days. Some members believed that B.C Hydro had reneged on their offer to bring in an expert selected by the residents specifically because Marino had been chosen. Over $5,000 of the $10,000 that the CVRC needed to pay for legal and travel expenses was raised through methods such as bottle drives, neighbourhood canvassing (about 120 families had made donations), and a telephone blitz of local businesses (which raised $1,000). A flea market would be held the following weekend. Donors would be assured of a seat at the free lecture.[62]

B.C. Hydro was requested by the BCUC to provide the following information:

- Was the EMF concern discussed with the B.C. MOH?
- Demonstrate that the best possible route was selected. Describe the "next best route" if the disputed segment was bypassed, and include a capital cost breakdown.

- State B.C. Hydro's policy with respect to EMF considerations adjacent to a ROW.
- Was B.C. Hydro contributing to any ongoing EMF research?
- Provide a synopsis of meetings and discussions B.C. Hydro or its agents conducted with residents along the proposed route on EMF health-related concerns.
- File all technical or other information on which B.C. Hydro based its assessment of the EMF issue, with special focus on biological effects.[63]
- What selection criteria were used by B.C. Hydro to determine residents' eligibility for the buy-out offer? If any residents less than twenty metres from the ROW were not sent a letter, explain why.
- Provide an example of a typical ROW agreement for property owners and identify any existing anomalies.
- Describe how B.C. Hydro would provide arbitration and resolution of land disputes (clearing and compensation) outside of the Utility Commission Act.
- Provide a list of all residents in the area who had contacted B.C. Hydro on EMF-related health concerns associated with this line.
- Identify personnel to be used in the inquiry, including external consultants.[64]

After Paul Brodeur's series of articles titled "Annals of Radiation: The Hazards of Electromagnetic Fields" appeared in *The New Yorker*,[65] the CVRC decided to approach the press. According to Karen Walsh, the CVRC's Treasurer, "None of us wanted to, but it helped, and, during the inquiry, we felt the public's support." Gathercole disagreed with bringing in the press.[66]

At a July 4 local press conference in the home of a CVRC member, Darlene Kavka presented the results of a health survey the CVRC had conducted of 120 adults and 103 children (representing 62 of 257 families) whose illnesses had started or worsened since moving to the Marsden Road area. Residents had a "significant number" of physical ailments, including migraines, Crohn's disease, allergies, miscarriages and abnormal births, menstrual cycle irregularities, and cancer. Kavka admitted that the survey was not "scientific."[67]

The CVRC also told the press that B.C. Hydro had been less than forthright in explaining the potential health hazards of the transmission line's magnetic field. B.C. Hydro's own literature hinted at the possibility of an increased incidence of leukemia in people living within 300 metres of such lines. The CVRC said that although studies had not necessarily confirmed Wertheimer and Leeper's 1979 study, neither had they shown conclusively that exposure would not harm one's health. Darlene Kavka stated, "We are not radical people, and we're not trying to hurt anyone. But we feel as if we're part of a massive experiment, and we choose not to be experimented on." Walsh said, "From May 12 to June 15, I repeatedly tried to get B.C. Hydro to answer questions about the effects of the electromagnetic field. I wanted to know if it was safe. I wanted reassurance. They couldn't give it."[68]

By July 8, the BCUC had engaged "expert adviser" Richard Gallagher, M.A., B.C. Cancer Control Agency (BC CCA), to "assist the public" in the review of the technical information and studies relating to PF E/MF. Gallagher, a "well-known" scientist and epidemiologist active in the PF E/MF field,[69] would advise on the strengths and weaknesses of the various epidemiological studies, in comparison with the "pronouncements from both sides."[70] An "independent expert" was hired because, although the BCUC was fairly sure that the inquiry would be "balanced," they were "not sure enough."[71] (Marino's position had been anticipated on the basis of transcripts of his testimony in other situations. The position of B.C. Hydro's experts was anticipated on the basis of their pre-filed evidence and conversations with B.C. Hydro's counsel, Ken MacKenzie of Guild, Yule, and Co.) Gallagher would only "take the stand" if the testimonies were "terribly out of balance." In addition, because much of the evidence was technical, he would help analyse the information and help the BCUC ask the right questions so that the "record would be complete."[72] Linda Erdreich and Antonio Sastre, both of ERI, would act as expert witnesses for B.C. Hydro at the inquiry. Neither had testified as an expert witness before.[73]

More than 150 people attended Marino's two-and-a-half-hour lecture. According to the *Free Press* and the *Record*, Marino stated that transmission line EMF played a significant role in causing illness and could cause genetic damage. EMF acted as a stressor on the body and disease occurred when the system was "overloaded." Numerous studies, including Marino's, had shown that constant exposure to high EMF, such as those from transmission lines, produced birth abnormalities in laboratory animals, changes in blood protein, and changes in brain activity. He cited studies reporting greater incidence of leukemia among workers exposed to EMF and linking spontaneous abortions to electric blanket use. Marino said that B.C. Hydro's proposed line would generate an EMF 100 metres wide on each side of the ROW. "An EMF will go through everything. There is a health risk." In addition, Marino said that experts had already proven that EMF increased the likelihood of illness, but utilities and the military didn't want people to know. Utility companies compounded the problem because they wanted to put their lines in as cheaply as possible.

Representatives of B.C. Hydro who attended the lecture (described by one as a "love-in") did not participate in the discussion that followed Marino's lecture.[74]

The inquiry began on the evening of July 11, included the evening of July 12, and lasted until July 14. Attendance by the public was unusually high for a BCUC hearing and varied from about 125 to 180 people.[75] The inquiry had been preceded by the submission of written evidence from Linda Erdreich and Antonio Sastre for B.C. Hydro, and by Andrew Marino for the CVRC. The former concluded: "The research conducted to date fails to substantiate the suggestion that exposure to electric and magnetic fields from power transmission lines poses a risk to human health."[76] Marino, on the other hand, arguing from the premise that chronic exposure to biological stress has been shown to be a risk factor for disease, noted that laboratory studies had shown EMF to be a biological stressor; therefore, such fields, when present in the environment, act as biological stressors and are thus risk factors for disease.[77]

The BCUC's panel included John McIntyre, Milt Swanson, Bill Grant, Neptune Smith, Karl Gustafson, and Richard Gallagher. B.C. Hydro's first panel included Linda Erdreich, Antonio Sastre, and counsel Ken MacKenzie. Their second panel included Chris Boatman, Jeff Barker, Pat Beavan, Paul Wong (an electrical engineer with Powertech Labs, a B.C. Hydro subsidiary), and MacKenzie. The CVRC's panel included Marino, Darlene Kavka, counsel Richard Gathercole, and Joan Vance, a lawyer for the BC PIAC. CPFP's panel included R.J. Bauman, counsel. There were twenty-two individual witnesses, including Ann Edwards, MLA (Kootenay) and Opposition critic for Energy, Mines and Petroleum Resources; Bob Skelly, MP (Comox/Alberni); Marton; and representatives of School District 71, C-S RD, the Merville Environmental Committee, and Friends of Strathcona Park.[78] Randy Ross, Radiation Protection Services, B.C. MOH, attended the inquiry as an observer on behalf of the B.C. MOH.[79]

*Summary of Oral Testimony:*
*Health-Related Issues*

What follows are summaries of selected parts of the oral testimony, based on the published transcripts of the hearings.

*1. B.C. Hydro (I).* Ken MacKenzie stated that B.C. Hydro did not wish to be adversarial. The problem was "one arising out of the basic nature of scientific inquiry. Scientific inquiry is empirical and the facts should speak for themselves. And the conclusions in any empirical study should be capable of confirmation by repetition or replication."

The biological effects of electromagnetic fields was "a relatively new area of scientific enquiry .... The results to date are not so consistent that conclusions can be stated in an unqualified manner. Most ... support the conclusion that EMF, particularly at the levels involved here, do not present a risk to health." Some studies did suggest an association and should not be dismissed. Some results were inconsistent and had not been adequately explained. Some inconsistencies "may be due to the normal statistical variations between different samples, and then again, they may not." B.C. Hydro could not give "unqualified assurance or a definite statement that there [was] no health risk involved in EMF. More scientific research needs to be done. All that B.C. Hydro [could] do [was] retain qualified and independent experts to provide their best judgment on the evidence to date and be guided by their advice."[80]

2. *Erdreich and Sastre*. Linda Erdreich and Antonio Sastre provided a review and evaluation of the studies related to PF E/MF health effects. Sastre said that the conclusion of a laboratory study by Marino (designed to improve on the methodology of his 1977 study) was justified when published in 1980, but a number of subsequent attempts at replication had failed. He had "heard" that Marino was attempting a third study. "If clarification on ... the mouse studies, or any of the other places in which the bulk of the scientific community has failed to replicate Dr. Marino's studies, if any light is shed on that by this inquiry, not only would this commission have done a tremendous service to the people of B.C., but to scientists throughout the world."[81]

Richard Gathercole asked Sastre if an exact replication of Marino's studies had been attempted. Sastre replied that some attempts had been made. That was "generally the case in science" and that had "never impeded consensus on reproducible findings." In the case of an inexact replication, "one determines whether, on the basis of all available scientific knowledge and judgment," the changed variable was likely to have been a "critical" one. It was important not to dismiss a study because of "failure of reproduction when, in fact, things were wildly non-comparable." It was also "irresponsible as a scientist" to say that unless a study was an exact replication, its relevance to anything else was "questionable." Sastre stated that he had not conducted a study similar to Marino's 1977 study but he did have related experience, hence his "judgment that the method was inappropriate."[82]

Sastre stated that investigators should be consulted to supplement reviews of published studies. ERI consulted Charles Graham regarding his studies on human performance, physiology, and subjective state and found he had replicated his own studies (testing the stressor hypothesis) with slight variations "several times," essentially finding nothing. Sastre commented that that was a "scientist's nightmare." "Negative data seldom see the light of day" and the peer review system was interested only in positive effects unless there was "controversy." This was "part of the reason" why Graham had published only three articles on his work.[83]

Erdreich and Sastre criticized the methodology and conclusions of a 1981 study by Perry, Marino, et al. that reported people living near power lines had a higher rate of suicide. Sastre told Gathercole that by the time he'd discussed the study with Erdreich (he had discussed it earlier with others), they had been notified that they might be involved in an adversarial proceeding and thought it "grossly improper to contact Dr. Marino."[84]

Gustafson, after reading an excerpt from an article in *Public Utilities Fortnightly*,[85] asked Sastre to comment on the amplification of weak electromagnetic signals at the cell surface. Sastre was familiar with this theory but stated that it had received "very little if any experimental support that would be considered convincing." Another theory suggesting the earth's static geomagnetic field (or an artificially adjusted field) determined whether 60 Hz E/MF produced biological effects he judged "absolutely fantastic." However, none of the related studies actually measured the field across the cell membrane. In addition, the effects could be reproduced in the lab but it was "very difficult to extrapolate to anyone being under a transmission line."[86]

Sastre gave a lengthy explanation delineating the difference between a stressor and a stress reaction. Major variables determining the impact of a stressor on the body were its intensity and duration. An acute stressor became a chronic stressor through prolonged exposure. A chronic stressor must first be acute. Sastre had seen no evidence that PF E/MF was a stressor.[87]

Erdreich told Gathercole that the Savitz study that reported an association between proximity to household wiring and distribution lines and childhood cancer was internally inconsistent because it showed a greater risk at low power than high, "which is the reverse of what you would logically expect." In response to the Chairman's question about why it was logical to expect that, Erdreich said, "Most agents act that way ... and we have insufficient data to think [otherwise]." Toxicologists, she said, use as a "rule of thumb" the statement "toxicity is dose."[88]

Gustafson again read from the *Public Utilities Fortnightly* article stating that several parameters, including field strength, frequency, and time of exposure, "may be necessary to define dose," and that the simple assumption that "more is worse" may not apply to some of these parameters. Sastre replied that, based on his background in pharmacology and toxicology, the exceptions he knew of fell into "one category," where there was an increase in effect with dose to a plateau and then a decrease.[89]

Gustafson noted that Erdreich and Sastre, in their written evidence, had assumed that magnetic field measurements more directly reflected exposure than wiring codes. Erdreich responded that Savitz made the same assumption and it seemed "fair" to her. She agreed that if measurements were taken long after diagnosis, they may not reflect dosage or exposure, but "then again, they may." Sastre stated that a study was only as good or as bad as the proxy exposure measure used by the researcher. In an ongoing study, Kaune and Savitz were attempting to validate wiring codes as a proxy exposure measure. An earlier study by Kaune found a low correlation (16 percent) between measured magnetic fields and wiring codes; most scientists and epidemiologists would prefer a 70 to 80 percent correlation. Sastre said that it would be some time before good and accurate dosimetric measures became available. Portable monitors had been available only for the past year or two.[90]

Gustafson said that of ten studies randomly selected by Gallagher from the thirty-odd occupational studies concerning PF E/MF health effects, six or seven showed relative risks (RRs) that were of reasonable significance (1.4, 1.3, 1.9). Although the other three or four were much lower, "we found it rather startling." When Erdreich suggested that their selection was "not quite random," Gustafson assured her it was. She then said that the limitations of the type of study conducted should be kept in mind. However, she thought that the "occupational issue merits further study."[91]

Sastre stated that laboratory study of PF E/MF effects involved difficulties not ordinarily encountered in other fields, in terms of exposure facility design and PF E/MF measurement. In addition, all aspects of human epidemiology were complex, especially when associations were very weak. The odds ratios were very low and, at least some of the time, failed to reach statistical significance, "which is the scientist's cornerstone of saying, is this due to chance or is this a real reflection of the world?"[92] Gustafson read from a journal article in which Savitz stated that an elevated odds ratio could be expected if magnetic field measurements were more complete. Erdreich replied that his hypothesis was possible, "but it's only speculation because this is the appropriate approach for the analysis of this kind of data." Sastre reminded Gustafson of the ongoing work by Savitz *et al.* on surrogate exposure measures: "It's certainly not something that he ignores and certainly not something that we ignore."[93]

Erdreich, in response to a question from Gathercole, stated that agents usually caused a specific disease, not a number of different cancers. This was one of the reasons she had "difficulty" with Wertheimer and Leeper's 1979 study, which reported a link between magnetic field exposure from electric blankets and electrically heated waterbeds to miscarriages, and to reduced birth weights and a longer gestation period for infants born to exposed mothers.[94] In response to Gathercole's comment that Wertheimer and Leeper (and Erdreich) had published in the *American Journal of Epidemiology*, a "well-respected" and "prestigious" journal, Erdreich said that publication was "evidence of merit, [but] not of perfection." It was "important for the people to understand that publishing articles allows other scientists to see them and evaluate them ... . If an article is considered to have some merit, or to address an important issue, it gets published ... . All of us who consider ourselves scientists have critiqued other people's studies and have listened to critiques of our own studies and have taken those critiques to go design better studies. It's fair game and it's [the] nature of the science. I think it's very hard for people who aren't in science to understand this business. But it's very difficult to do a perfect study, and studies are published to allow other people – you were all here for the cold fusion discussion." The peer-review process involved in publishing "says a lot about the individual studies. But my experience on health risk assessment tells me that decisions of major [import] are made after evaluations of all of the data and weighing the evidence. And it's not only the United States, it's international. All scientists do it that way and all major decisions are made with an evaluation of all of the evidence."[95]

Sastre elaborated on Erdreich's comments, stating that they were correct but incomplete, based on his experience on the editorial board of two journals. He found papers in which neither he nor his reviewers could find any flaws. "Our collective scientific experience says this can't possibly be right but we know that we can be wrong ... And we collectively decide with the senior editor and reviewers ... [that] science will be best served by publishing the paper." This could mean that the paper was "wonderful and flawless," "competent," or that science would be "best served by publication and the attempts at replication and discussion that [would] ensue."[96]

In response to Gathercole's query of whether any of the panel members were employed by or did research on behalf of the utility industry, Erdreich stated that she did not think any were. She said, "Research funding is not considered to be a bias in science because people have to publish their papers with their source of funding annotated at the bottom so that it behooves people to be objective." Recalling her experience with the U.S. EPA, Erdreich stated, "We had the confidence that academic people could be independent, especially under the peer review process ... . There's a general feeling that it is useful to have these studies funded by industries. Unfortunately, it's just the nature of our funding in the Western world." Later, Sastre, under cross-examination by Bauman, stated that there may have been one participant on the Florida panel from a utility, but otherwise the members were from outside industry.[97]

Gathercole noted that there was "some disagreement among reputable scientists" regarding the health risks associated with power lines. Erdreich responded, "There is disagreement [and] there is some consensus among reputable scientists ... I get the impression that there are more people who feel ... there is no health risk than there are scientists who feel there is a health risk .... I'm not sure whether I should make that statement, but that's the impression I get from reading the literature." She agreed with Gathercole that an assessment should not be based on counting up "the numbers on one side and the numbers on the other."[98]

In reply to Gathercole's asking if the proposed B.C. Hydro 230 kV line was safe, Erdreich responded, "'Safe' is a very broad term. I'm providing information that says from my reading of the data, there is no indication of potential health risks of concern. 'Safe' becomes a value judgment." Erdreich agreed with Gathercole that her opinion was based on the work and readings she had done. She added, "And I expressed my credentials and I don't have credentials in seventy-five different fields."[99] Gathercole asked Erdreich if, in her opinion, there were health risks associated with the new 230 kV and the three existing 138 kV lines running through the Comox Valley. Erdreich replied that there were no health risks and that no hazard had been shown from those kinds of exposures.[100]

When asked if the addition of a fifth line would change her opinion, Erdreich stated, "That would be unlikely to change my opinion ... One of the kind of guiding lights of health risk assessment is that you have to understand some very basic points. Most people recognize that almost anything could be dangerous if you give enough dose ... But, if something is not generally a hazard and is not associated with a hazard under normal circumstances ... small changes in a dose don't make a difference." If a sixth or seventh line were added, it became speculative; nor had she seen "any measurements." Gathercole said that he understood Erdreich to be saying that at some point there might well be a health hazard. Erdreich replied, "As a scientist I just don't like to make sweeping generalizations ... Health risk is usually related to the amount of exposure only if something is proven to be a potential hazard to begin with."[101]

Erdreich agreed with Gathercole's suggestion that it was "fair to say" the causes of various health effects were unknown. "We have different amounts of information on different diseases, but there are very few where we know all of the factors." When Gathercole asked how Erdreich could say the line was safe if the causes or potential causes of various health effects were unknown, she replied, "How can you jump from a – you can introduce anything for that argument. If we don't know what causes leukemia, we don't know what causes it. It doesn't mean this line causes it ... unless we have evidence. I'm here to provide information on evidence."[102]

Gathercole asked Erdreich if there was any evidence that the line was safe. Erdreich replied, "One usually doesn't have that kind of evidence in that they've studied everybody ever exposed and looked at the incidence of cancer and compared it to people who weren't exposed. There's rarely an opportunity to do such a study." Gathercole asked if she could "point us to any study that meets the standards which you've set out that conclusively determines that ... this line or a line similar to this poses no health risk." She replied, "One wouldn't really in a scientific world expect to find any one study that conclusively gives such a global statement. I can't find that for anything ... What we really feel is that the weight of evidence strongly suggests that the line is safe" based on the "weight of the evidence that is available and that we have reviewed."[103]

Erdreich did not agree with Gathercole's suggestion that, given the state of the scientific evidence, exposing people to the increased levels was human experimentation. "I recognize that whenever you have a positive study it becomes very difficult to ... address the health risks because, in people's minds, positive studies weigh more than negative studies. And negative studies and replication are very important, and really very scientifically challenging to evaluate ... When something poses a potential hazard ... then it is important to look at it and see at what level it's safe, [at] what level it poses infinitesimally little risk, and [at] what level it poses a risk ... In my experience, when some chemical does not pose a hazard [it] is not associated with adverse health effect[s] ... When something does not pose a hazard, then it really isn't important in these narrow ranges to talk about ... the amount of exposure."[104]

Erdreich said that although future studies might change her opinion, she based it on the "level of possibility, because we're talking about drastic changes here, and if the possibility is very low, and my uncertainty is very low, I feel it doesn't support a conclusion that there is a hazard." Questioned further by Gathercole, Erdreich stated that she was "uncomfortable" with the whole concept of human experimentation: "Of course, I'm against it. It just doesn't seem to be an applicable term here. I mean, we allow people to smoke. Is that human experimentation? People do it willingly." Gathercole said that choice was the issue. Erdreich replied, "But when there's no risk, what's the issue?"[105]

In response to the Chairman's comments about whether there would "ever be total consensus" regarding the issue of health effects, Erdreich said, "That's why we're stuck with that term 'weight of the evidence' ... It's a regulator's nightmare."[106] Later, the Chairman commented on "the division that exists in the scientific community ... the 'competition,'" and asked Sastre if there was a "more universal approach ... that could possibly address this issue in a way which could ... eliminate the negative and have a scientific community that's more united on the issue as it addressed the public concern, and their perception of reality." Sastre replied, "I'm afraid there are no quick fixes." More "reliable scientific data" was needed, "which takes time." "Believe me, if there were quick fixes we would have been using them ... I'm not aware of any ... and, believe me, people have tried."[107]

Erdreich told Gustafson it was useful to pursue the PF E/MF health effects issue: "I know that this audience finds the ambiguities frustrating ... It's very hard to impart my experience with epidemiological studies that have really low [strengths of] associations, less than two, because so many of them have later proved to be unfounded. You all were around for coffee and pancreatic cancer." A major investigator, author of the first and one of the "foremost" epidemiology texts, had conducted a study with "some design flaws." Some members of the scientific community thought his subsequent publicizing of the results (a "statistically significant risk of 1.5") on television was "irresponsible" because the public became "inflamed." Media reports were "biased" because "journalists have a short amount of time. Experiences like that make me very wary of over-interpreting data."[108]

Erdreich told the Chairman that several studies were already planned that would help generate the information required to resolve the PF E/MF health effects issue: "We have to keep an open mind and see what the results are." However, the two studies by the U.S. National Cancer Institute and the BC CCA (involving large populations of children) were case-control studies; the ideal prospective study was unlikely. Also very important was the determination of individual PF E/MF exposures. Earlier studies were not necessarily "flawed by incompetence" but "by not having the experience to work on." Sastre told the Chairman that "seldom if ever is there one study ... that clears the air." His "utopia ... would be an accumulation of good laboratory and epidemiology studies which together ... make it very clear" if there is a hazard. The tools of risk analysis would then be applied to indicate what should be done. Erdreich, using the increasing concern about hazardous waste sites in the United States as an analogy, added that perhaps a study comparing the health status of the community to another could be "useful and reassuring" (as Marton had suggested), but such studies sometimes lacked strength.[109]

*3. Marino.* After being sworn in, Andrew Marino said that the literature on PF E/MF health effects could not be reviewed in a short period of time, "certainly not over six weeks," and that it had taken him twenty-seven years.[110]

Marino described how he calculated the level of PF E/MF before and after the addition of the 230 kV line to the existing 138 kV lines. The technique was based on an article published in an engineering journal about ten years ago which he co-authored. Measurements were "impractical." For people not using electric blankets and not living next to high-voltage power lines, the average electric and magnetic field levels were 1–3 V/m and .3-.5 mG, respectively. During cross-examination, Ken MacKenzie suggested that, due to the approximations made, Marino overstated the magnetic field level close to the line and understated the level further away. Marino replied that the assumptions were practical and routine for the method used. Later (after Marino had returned home), Paul Wong testified that the results of his magnetic field calculations were higher than Marino's. The Chairman suggested that the assumptions made by Marino were suitable for Marino's purposes. Wong replied that he would not make such assumptions as an engineer and could not accept the 300 percent error that resulted.[111]

Marino stated that, based on the literature, the existing and proposed Dunsmuir/Gold River power lines were a health risk.

Exposures from PF E/MF levels off the ROW were many times above average and produced changes in the bodies of animals and humans: "If you look at the many hundreds of studies and you discount the ones that lead nowhere, like the industry-funded ones, you are led to the conclusion that the fields are biological stressors." It was "well-established" that chronic exposure to stressors promoted disease because the body's adaptive capacity was reduced. EMF did not "'cause' disease. That's a red herring of a word in a hearing like this. No factor causes any chronic human disease." Rather, magnetic fields were risk factors for some cancers in the same way that smoking was a risk factor for lung cancer.[112]

In response to Gathercole's comment, "We have a situation where there are conflicting opinions, and that's not surprising in scientific situations," Marino interjected, "It's not the scientific situation that is the cause of the conflict, it's money ... Every study that they [Erdreich and Sastre] point to as supporting their side is paid for and run by the utility companies, and it's been my experience since 1973 that if the utility industry has anything to do with the study ... if it designs it, pays for it, analyses it, pays to have it analysed, touches it in any way, it's tainted and not worthwhile." In response to the Chairman's question of what then was worthwhile, Marino replied, "Studies that are done ... by honest scientists who don't have to sign a contract in advance to produce data that the industry wants. All the studies that they point to are done in secret. The protocol isn't available ... and the data that's obtained is held in secret ... and the industry releases only data that it chooses. That's a form of extreme bias, and it makes any result that they produce worthless. The only [studies] in science that are worthwhile ... are done in an open way, as is traditional in American science. For example, funding from NIH [National Institutes of Health] ... is the traditional way of getting competitive funds in the United States. You send the government a proposal to do a study and that proposal is public knowledge. You can't hide anything. You've got to report to the government what your data is every year ... It's been clear over the years that many of the studies that showed adverse effects, that were bad for the corporations, never saw the light of day."[113]

Marino stated that exposing humans involuntarily to power line E/MF constituted human experimentation, based on American "rules." If a proposal were made to expose humans to increased levels without consent, it would not be approved by any American medical school: "It wouldn't pass muster in any place. Maybe in Nazi Germany, but not in America."[114]

Disagreeing with Erdreich and Sastre's views about "blue-ribbon" panels, Marino said, "She [Erdreich] is new to this field. When she's here a little longer, she'll realize that virtually nobody would say that. It's simply untrue." Marino clarified for the Chairman that he was not talking about the panel members as individuals but in their roles as contractees, consultants, or advisers to the utility industry: "They have a well-known attitude about health risks, and it was because of the attitude that they were put on the panel." The Chairman questioned whether even one panel member, as a research scientist, might have produced work of value. Marino replied, "There's a contradiction in terms ... The way the game works is that you go to them, and you say, I would like some money to do research. That's what, for example, H.B. Graves did. He's the Chairman of the Florida Advisory Committee that she called a blue-ribbon panel. He's now a full-time consultant for [one of] the biggest law firms in the country that represents utility companies." At that time, Graves was an Electric Power Research Institute (EPRI) research scientist and wanted to conduct research. EPRI agreed and told Graves, "'Here's what you do.' Now, if H.B. had his choice, he would have done other things. I've talked to him and I know it."[115]

By this time, the atmosphere in the inquiry room was very tense. The Chairman stated, "I may demonstrate some sensitivity ... because it's difficult to dissociate the B.C. Utility Commission from this ... My paycheque and that of the other commissioners comes from the provincial government ... B.C. Hydro is a Crown corporation; there is some potential incestuous arrangement here because of the way we're both funded. I'm sorry, I don't wish to be argumentative, but ... I fail to see the syllogistic value ... In relation to the people's concern this is an important point ... There would seem to be two sides in terms of the expert witnesses and therefore it's important to me to be able to recognize" if there is any bias on either or both panels. Marino responded, "There really aren't [two sides] with the exception of people like these folks who have no background in this field ... They're hired to come in and to pass off the same testimony that their bosses gave in other places ... That doesn't elevate what they've said to any logical syllogistic ... meaning. What they're hoping to do is to count on the relative informality of this forum and not let you see the underlying substratum."[116]

Marino was asked, under cross-examination by MacKenzie, if an "honest and objective scientist" could conclude, based on the evidence to date, that power line E/MF exposure did not pose a health risk. Marino replied, "That would clearly be against the weight of the evidence ... If you want to reach that conclusion, what you do is ignore parts of the data." MacKenzie then asked Marino whether it was his view "that a fair-minded scientist reviewing all the data could not reach that conclusion." Marino replied, "It's not a question of being fair-minded, it's a question of including all the data ... It would be independent of the nefarious subjective state of the individual, whether he was right-minded or not is irrelevant. It would simply be against the weight of the evidence."[117]

Marino told MacKenzie that although David Savitz was a competent scientist, his opinion was "not unbiased ... If David says that there are no health effects at all ... then the EPRI would ... pull his grant because ... why should they give him $500,000 if there is no problem ... If he says there is a problem then the EPRI would [also] pull his grant because they never fund anybody who takes such a controversial view ... So David walks a fence in which he never appears at a formal hearing, and his name is always thrown about but [he] never speaks himself." After MacKenzie commented that Savitz had testified at an U.S. congressional hearing, Marino replied that Savitz also "spoke" at a Florida hearing, but what Marino was referring to was cross-examination, "the hot-seat type of testimony."[118]

Marino, responding to MacKenzie's question of whether Savitz's research was tainted by its industry association, stated that "on the contrary, David did nothing more than was done by Nancy Wertheimer" and, "to his everlasting credit," reached the same conclusion. Wertheimer originated the hypothesis and funded the study herself. "David's $330,000 was for essentially a re-examination of the same data ... . He's now doing a $500,000 study but the protocol ... is secret." Savitz, because of his "contractual relationship" with EPRI, and EPRI both refused to give Marino the protocol.[119] MacKenzie, reading from Savitz's open letter, asked Marino if the paragraph including the statement "we have not proven that magnetic fields cause cancer" was "fair comment." Marino replied, "It's a good example, Mr. Chairman, of the way words can be used to create great confusion." The "classic laboratory science definition of cause" was that there was an effect when the cause was present and no effect when the cause was not present. With regard to any chronic human disease, such as cancer, "we only speak of factors that predispose because there's no factor which when it is present always produces a certain disease in people. So this statement is a slippery-eel way of stating the obvious. We don't have a proof that magnetic fields cause cancer, and we never shall because such a thing is impossible. All we'll ever do is make plausible the link between field exposure and cancer. And the more such studies that we have, the more plausible is that link."[120]

MacKenzie asked if Marino was suggesting that the misleading statement by Savitz was biased by his source of funding. Marino answered that the statement was misleading for the reasons he had just given: "Why David acts is inside his brain. Get him here and talk to him about these studies instead of bandying his name around and we'll find out." MacKenzie then asked Marino if he was implying that Savitz's motive was improper in publishing the open letter, and whether he could have made the statement as an "honest and unbiased" scientist. Marino said he had "no comment about David's motives." When MacKenzie questioned him further, Marino stated that he was not interested in Savitz's opinion of whether power lines were a health risk because Savitz had an interest in the answer: "I think it's a bad way to make decisions."[121]

MacKenzie referred to the World Health Organization's (WHO's) Environmental Health Criteria 69, which stated that induced current densities less than 10 milliamperes per metre$^2$ (mA/m$^2$) had not been shown to produce any significant biological effects. Marino said that the statement had no relationship to the issue at hand: "No one here has been presumptive enough to testify about currents induced in people." Induced currents could not be measured. Marino also said that the report represented the collective views of an international group of experts and did not necessarily represent the position of the United Nations Environment Program, the International Labour Organization, or the WHO, and that it contained a disclaimer indicating this. The delegates included power company representatives from "many" countries, including the Philippines, Australia, and the United Kingdom. Marino added, "There was a dispute on this panel between the Western ... and the Russian scientists, and the Russian scientists walked off." Their names were not listed on all drafts of the report. MacKenzie replied that his copy of the published report included their names. Under further questioning, Marino stated that the three Soviets on the panel were with the Maraziev Research Institute in Kiev but added that their concerns were with electric field health effects. He did not know the basis of their opinions.[122]

The Chairman asked Marino if, in some circumstances, people living near a power line might be getting exposures from appliances and wiring configurations within their homes that were higher than those from the power line. Marino concurred that this might be true. Because living standards and patterns varied, individual circumstances must be placed in context. He was using .4 mG as an example of an average magnetic field level.[123] In response to a question from Gustafson, Marino stated that he did not know if there had indeed been a seven-fold increase in residential energy consumption from 1950 through to 1985. Gustafson then asked if a large increase in residential energy consumption in North America were to be shown, would Marino expect to find a corresponding increase in disease generally. Marino replied that there was "no direct correlation; disease is multifactorial."[124]

Gustafson then asked why the BCUC should accept Marino's "hypothesis over the weight of the evidence reported by others in the scientific community." Marino stated that he knew of no one in the scientific community who had "sustained the position" of the ERI panel: "The only people who take [that] position ... are people who directly work for power companies." He knew of no scientist working in bioelectricity in North America, Europe, Japan, the Soviet Union, or China who "would take the position that there is no risk from power lines ... . So your characterization of the literature is just way off base ... Now, in a sane, reasonable world where money isn't determinative, and where legal arguments don't rule, [studies] indicate that there's some risk associated with being exposed to those fields." The only common factor that the subjects were exposed to was EMF.[125]

The following exchange brought the BCUC's cross-examination of Marino to an abrupt halt.

GUSTAFSON: Your evidence as presented here has been extremely interesting, entertaining, and ... provocative and I have absolutely no doubt that you hold your views seriously and sincerely. During the course of your evidence, you've made a number of what can only be characterized ... even in the most conservative terms, as highly controversial statements, and ... some would characterize them as inflammatory and potentially slanderous or libellous. You've made allusions to Nazi Germany, ... branded a host of scientists as little more than dishonest prostitutes ... made allegations regarding international –

MARINO: Now wait a minute, wait a minute –

GUSTAFSON: Allow me to finish my question and I'll let you –

MARINO: This is ridiculous, this is ridiculous. Now, I didn't make any slanderous statements, and the evidence I gave was evidence that I'm prepared to back up if you want to go into it. Now if you want to take these one by one and ask me questions, then ask me questions. Don't give me a speech. I didn't come here to listen to that business.

GUSTAFSON: I want to ask you a serious question.

MARINO: I appreciate you do. Let's leave off the comments about my behaviour. Let the Chairman decide about that.

GUSTAFSON: You've made allegations concerning a conspiracy to suppress information. You said that certain studies had been kept secret and couldn't be accessed.

MARINO: What, for example? Are you referring to Dr. Donald Gan's study ... [or] Dick Phillip's?

GUSTAFSON: Well, you tell me. You're the one that said that certain studies –

MARINO: Well, they're the two I remember speaking about, and I wouldn't characterize them as a conspiracy. What Dick Phillips did made a lot of sense if he wanted to do his research ...

GUSTAFSON: Did you not say that power companies and scientists had worked together to suppress certain scientific data?

MARINO: No. No, you're fabricating my testimony.

GUSTAFSON: Did you not say that –

MARINO: I didn't say that at all.

GUSTAFSON: – certain studies had been kept secret?

MARINO: Certainly they're kept secret, and EPRI will tell you they keep them secret ... Ask the Chairman of the Public Service Commission in New York ... He wrote and asked them for studies and copies of their protocols and they told him no. And I've written and they've told me no. You just don't know the territory or you wouldn't make such outrageous statements.

GUSTAFSON: Well, what I'm concerned about ... is ... that many of the statements that you've made have been cast in extremely strong terms ... Have you given any consideration to the effect of that kind of statement on your position [as] a research scientist and to the weight that people will attach to the results of your research, given the strength of your convictions and the way ... you ... phrase them in this kind of forum?

MARINO: Yes, I think it would be inappropriate for me not to tell the truth, and that's what I've done. You simply find it hard to believe that some of the things I've said are true ... The issue is not whether I said them. The issue is whether they're true ... I have spent many years investigating, so far as the information is available under American process, the nature of the studies performed by industry. And although there are some exceptions, the general rule ... is that the data is rigged to support the industry conclusion ... If you're relying on that data, you're not thinking right. Now, that's simply an analysis of the data. That's not something I sucked out of my thumb.[126]

GUSTAFSON: I find the suggestion ... that data has been rigged to be a strong statement ...

MARINO: No ... I said the studies were rigged ...

GUSTAFSON: All right ...

MARINO: There's a big difference. Do you understand what the difference is?

GUSTAFSON: Yes, I do …

MARINO: Are you sure?

GUSTAFSON: Yes. And, Dr. Marino, if the studies –

MARINO: Well, why don't you explain it to me and we'll make sure it's right.

CHAIRMAN: Just a minute, Dr. Marino.

GUSTAFSON: – are rigged it implies … that people are deliberately seeking to disguise … or to hide the truth, or to falsify results?

MARINO: You just don't know the territory and you're just taking too simple a view. I don't think Dick Phillips … was thinking anything more than the $5-million contract and the thirty employees that the money would give. That's what the sponsor wanted. His job was to do that study. In and of itself there's nothing wrong with that. It becomes wrong when out of the mouth of … utility company witnesses, that's held as evidence that lines are safe, because that field didn't cause an effect. That's where the undesirability, the impropriety of it comes from, and if it offends your ears I apologize, but it's the truth.[127]

Using an oil-drilling analogy from Marino's written testimony, the Chairman suggested that perhaps some of the studies with utility involvement were simply "dry holes." Marino commented that no one would tell the Chairman they only considered part of the data, whether they had or not: "I considered all the data, Your Honour, Mr. Chairman. The negative data and the positive data." Marino said that the difficulty with the negative data was not whether it was considered or not but how it was used for argument. The industry used the negative studies to negate the positive studies: "It's only lawyer's argument that would allow you to juxtapose them. There's no scientific juxtaposition. [The] negative study scientifically only has value when it reasonably duplicates the positive study and finds an opposite result."[128]

The Chairman was troubled by Marino's position that industry-funded research was invalid even if replicated: "We're talking about millions of dollars." He asked Marino if it wasn't the case that industry paid for "everything." Marino agreed, stating that he did not know "how honourable people" were going to be in the future. He could only relate what had happened in the past: "There's a documented litany of dishonourable things that have been done with regard to the interpretation and the production of data. That leads me not to have faith in industry. If the industry produces a study which says my children are not at risk for cancer, it has a low credibility in my judgment, based on their past production." Marino estimated that since funding began with Gan's study in 1972, about $100 million

(US) had been spent by industry. He told the Chairman that, of that sum, no study had been produced "that is going to be useful for you to make a decision. They have put their money in other places."[129]

The Chairman asked Marino how people who accepted his position should respond: "Should they take you absolutely literally or ... literally in context?" Marino replied, "I'd like to be perceived as giving advice that attempts to stake out the middle ground ... . It's extreme to say it doesn't make any difference how many power lines you put on that right of way [because] there's no risk ... It's also extreme to ... attribute every disease, every clinical syndrome ... to the line. There is a middle position which amounts to a recognition that there is some health-impacting aspect of being chronically exposed to electromagnetic fields. But ... these fields don't cause disease, ... they are factors associated with disease like many other factors ... . One strategy for coping, if it's undesirable to exclude the fields from your living area, if it's impractical, or impossible, [is to] ... assess the other factors in your life that similarly produce or orient to a disease, and reduce those factors. There doesn't need to be an excessive reaction. There needs to be a total integrated view of the factors reasonably suspected to predispose to a disease, and a judgment made then."[130]

*4. Testimony by various residents.* Several residents gave anecdotal evidence on PF E/MF health effects. Clifford Thate, a rabbit breeder, attributed a decrease in conception rate and increased rate of abnormality in his rabbits to PF E/MF from the lines. He told MacKenzie that he had not consulted a veterinarian.

Herb Robertson stated that electric blankets had been found to "affect the immune system." He also stated that "electromagnetic radiation" had been used to heal bone and cause bone growth. Robertson's wife developed thickening of the bone in her leg and migraines when they moved into their house. Both his wife's migraines and his three-year-old son's speaking problems and belligerent behaviour disappeared when the family moved into town while their house was being renovated. Since moving back, his son had developed thickening of his collarbone. Robertson believed that he and his daughter were not affected because they were at work or school during the day.[131]

One local resident stated that she was on adrenal and thyroid medication, and suffered from frequent and severe headaches, muscle weakness, dizzy spells, allergies, constant fatigue, and heart palpitations. Both she and her daughter experienced dramatic changes in their birthmarks. She lost her first child due to birth defects which could not be attributed to heredity. The health problems had surfaced since she resided in her home near the lines.[132] Another resident attributed her headaches, loss of hair, vomiting, and insomnia to stress from the lines. One man stated that his family was using more Tylenol.[133]

5. *B.C. Hydro (II)*. After being sworn in, B.C. Hydro's second panel recounted their involvement in the Courtenay controversy, focusing in particular on how the PF E/MF health effects issue had been handled. During cross-examination, the panel was asked if they would live near transmission lines. Beavan said that he was not concerned about possible health effects and lived within 100 metres of a double 230 kV circuit. Both Wong and Barker said they would not live nearby for aesthetic reasons. Boatman said that health concerns would be one of the factors he would consider (along with aesthetics, property value, and personal needs), but it would not be the deciding factor.[134]

Boatman told the Chairman that the Chairman's decision would have a considerable effect on the whole of society. He told Joan Vance, a lawyer representing the CVRC, that if a definitive link between power line E/MF and health effects were to be found in the future, that B.C. Hydro would not have a contingency plan. However, if that were to be the case, the whole of society would have a "major problem," not just B.C. Hydro.[135]

### BCUC REPORT AND RECOMMENDATIONS

On July 26, John McIntyre submitted his Report and Recommendations to the BCUC. The following day, the BCUC adopted the Report in full and ordered that:

- the stop-work order be lifted;
- the citizens' request for re-routing be denied;
- B.C. Hydro extend the buy-out offer to residents immediately adjacent to the ROW to September 15, 1989;
- B.C. Hydro exclude the (net) cost of the buy-out program from the cost of service;
- B.C. Hydro collaborate with the B.C. MOH in devising and funding EMF research programs; and
- B.C. Hydro apply to the BCUC for a "Certificate of Public Convenience and Necessity" for all future 138 kV and above transmission lines.[136]

The following section summarizes the BCUC's Report and Recommendations.

### Electromagnetic Fields and Health

Over the past few years, there had been increasing concern about PF E/MF health effects. The public might have been focusing on high-voltage transmission lines rather than other sources because of their high visibility. Other sources of PF E/MF included electric distribution wiring (fields similar to transmission line fields but of lower intensity), electric home appliances (significant levels of magnetic fields while in use), and electric blankets and water-beds (probably the strongest sources of magnetic fields). The health issues surrounding B.C. Hydro's proposed 230 kV transmission line were examined in the context of overall human exposure and health effects, in addition to the particular exposure resulting from the power line.[137]

### Health Effects – General

• there is "insufficient evidence to support a presumption of actual health risk";
• a "blanket condemnation" of published studies based simply on their source of funding is unacceptable;
• more research is needed, and B.C. Hydro, other Canadian utilities, and the Canadian Electrical Association should sponsor such research, in an arm's-length relationship;
• the fears expressed by residents do not appear to be well-founded and, in addition, "there may well be motives for the action of a few which transcend the EMF issue";
• there is no reason to delay expansion of the local elementary school as a result of EMF concerns.

### Recommendations

"Electric distribution lines, household wiring, and electric appliances [created] the greatest preponderance of EMF radiation." Scientists from Carnegie Mellon University, in a June 1989 report to the U.S. Congressional Office of Technology Assessment, advocated "prudent avoidance," e.g., the avoidance of continuous close contact with electric blankets and alarm clocks. An extension of their views "could be that some [might] view it as 'prudent avoidance' that young children be discouraged from continuous play on the ROW itself ... Simple actions could substantially reduce overall exposure" because magnetic fields fell off sharply with distance.[138]

The magnetic field from the proposed 230 kV line would also fall off rapidly with distance. Magnetic fields from the existing lines at residences near the ROW were not "substantially different" from the ambient magnetic fields from household wiring and appliances. In some cases, in fact, the field from the distribution lines was "more significant" than that from the transmission lines. It was important that EMF health risks from both transmission lines and other sources be determined. "The Commission must not gloss over this issue as a result of the inconclusive nature of the current scientific literature. The matter [deserved] attention and coordinated scientific study." There was "much work ongoing throughout the world."[139]

*Re-routing issue.* There was no "compelling reason" to re-route the line (through the Courtenay, Cumberland, or Merville areas). B.C. Hydro might "find it advantageous to consider re-routing of its transmission lines at a future date when the final routing of the Island Highway is complete." B.C. Hydro should reconsider the routing of its transmission lines in conjunction with the appropriate agencies to determine if there were any "socio-economic advantages" in locating the utility and transportation corridors adjacent to each other (in keeping with the B.C. government's "Guidelines for Linear Developments").[140]

*B.C. Hydro's buy-out proposal.* Neither B.C. Hydro nor the BCUC "[perceived] an actual health risk from EMF emissions, however, it [was] clear that the good intentions of B.C. Hydro in making the buy-out offer [had] resulted in heightened public concern with respect to both the EMF health issue and land values."[141] B.C. Hydro should continue to honour its commitment to purchase properties because: the offer had created expectations, leading some recipients to make financial commitments; and also "in fairness to those who failed or were unable to respond" by the deadline, those who qualified but were unaware, and "those who were unable to reach an informed and reasoned decision because of the continuation of uncertainty caused by the inquiry process." The offer should be continued with a deadline for response of September 15, 1989.

"The appraised purchase price should reflect the market value of the property as of May 8, 1989. In addition, B.C. Hydro should ensure that all those involved in the buy-out scheme are given a clear understanding of their options. Purchases should be completed expeditiously." If property values in the Courtenay area had "appreciated significantly from May 8 to the date of individual binding agreements to sell, the property values [were] to be adjusted by a percentage value to account for the upward market movement" (using the District Real Estate Board as a reference). Valuations should be based on the three existing transmission lines in the corridor and exclude any impact the proposed new 230 kV line might have on the property values. Given the purpose of the buy-out offer, eligibility of properties for the buy-out should be based on a "consistent rationale," that is, on proximity to the lines.[142]

*Treatment of buy-out costs.* "B.C. Hydro acted imprudently in its decision to make the buy-out offer ... The scientific evidence with respect to health hazards from EMF [was] such that no identified risk to human health [had] as yet been substantiated." The BCUC should "exclude the cost of the buy-out program from any determination of B.C. Hydro's revenue requirements or 'cost of service.'" By doing so, the BCUC could "ensure" that the buy-out costs would not affect "the rates of consumers generally" within British Columbia. The action would also "ensure there [was] no precedent established or emanating" with respect to other transmission lines in British Columbia.[143] The inquiry did not pursue "on this occasion" the question of whether the buy-out offers fell within the provisions of the Utilities Commission Act as "constituting unduly preferential conduct," although the issue might have "potential significance."

Because there was "no reliable evidence" that power-lines posed a human health risk, "it [could] be expected that any impact on land values [would] be alleviated as a result of the conclusions of this Inquiry."[144]

*B.C. Hydro research into EMF.* B.C. Hydro should collaborate with the B.C. MOH "to devise and fund research programs which [would] complement research elsewhere in North America on EMF-related issues." B.C. Hydro should also develop "public awareness information programs ... and seek a leadership role" for the B.C. MOH. The BCUC should request that the provincial government "clearly state its objectives and priorities with respect to the EMF issue so as to facilitate an appropriate environment for the implementation of B.C. Hydro's programs and those of other government agencies and public bodies." "It [was] very important that research be done in a co-ordinated manner so as to maximize the capability to resolve the EMF issue ... B.C. Hydro should investigate ways to assist in the co-ordination of studies and funding through the Canadian Electrical Association, other government agencies, or perhaps a new independent agency funded from many sources."[145]

*Future transmission line extensions of 138 kV and greater.* Until scientific research provided sufficient evidence "to make reasonably certain determinations" about EMF health hazards, the BCUC might receive complaints whenever B.C. Hydro proposed to build a high-voltage transmission line in new or existing corridors. Because the current evidence did not support "the establishment of specific standards with respect to EMF emissions and ROW widths," the BCUC should require B.C. Hydro to seek a Certificate of Public Convenience and Necessity (CPCN) for lines 138 kV and greater. The BCUC, in considering whether to issue a CPCN and whether to hold a hearing, would assess the scientific, environmental, and socio-economic evidence available at that time, and the specific physical considerations related to the proposed line. "In making application for a CPCN, B.C. Hydro should allow sufficient lead time to ensure adequate input from all parties is obtained."[146]

*Application for costs of intervenors.* Residents made an "Application" to have the BCUC pay the costs of Dr. Marino. The BCUC recognized that the costs of hiring Dr. Marino would be "onerous for the public participants and that the evidence of Dr. Marino ensured that *all sides* of the EMF scientific literature and positions of experts were brought to the attention of the Inquiry Officer." However, under the Utilities Commission Act, the BCUC could not absorb the costs of Dr. Marino, nor could it order that B.C. Hydro pay those costs.[147]

### POST-BCUC RULING

For about a month following the BCUC ruling, there occurred episodes of civil disobedience, largely in the form of blocking access to B.C. Hydro work crews, resulting in court proceedings. An editorial in the *North Island News* on August 20 commented that civil disobedience was "back in vogue" but "unfortunately" was unsuccessful. "Private enterprise and big government [had] become too wise to protest tactics. They [held] public hearings to appease the masses ... under the guise that they [were] doing something." Thus, "no one was surprised that Hydro was allowed to continue despite no conclusive evidence about the safety of electromagnetic fields." Private citizens needed to "come up with some new tactic." Civil disobedience worked in the past because government and big business were not "wise to it." Environmentalists needed to "organize en masse ... and find a spokesperson" with a "few new ideas." Someone "high profile," in a "position of authority," and respected by all: "Perhaps Dr. David Suzuki would like the job."[148]

On August 26, 1989, the $30-million Dunsmuir/Gold River 230 kV transmission line was energized at 2:55 p.m. No difficulties were encountered. According to Barker, the contractor delay "cost lots of money."[149]

By late September, of the 140 eligible properties, a total of 64 home owners, including the Kavkas, had officially asked B.C. Hydro to buy them out. B.C. Hydro had purchased its first home and would soon close on five more. B.C. Hydro did not plan to make buy-out programs a standard practice, but neither were they ruled out in the future. They knew the issue would not "go away."[150] By November 17, owners of about 71 properties had accepted the buy-out offer and 21 properties had been purchased. (B.C. Hydro had also received requests from an additional 150 ineligible property owners.) According to Barker, B.C. Hydro "might even make money" after resale. (By February 14, 4 of the 21 properties had been sold for a profit.)[151]

### Scientific Uncertainty

By December 1989, cumulative research had clearly established that, at least under some circumstances, PF E/MF could interact with and produce effects in biological systems. However, there was no definitive evidence that such effects could in turn give rise to significant health consequences. On the other hand, the possibility of significant health consequences could not be convincingly negated by high-quality research. Research was under way in an attempt to provide more definitive answers; results were not likely for a number of years.

It should be noted that uncertainties are not unusual in a scientific context; it is uncertainty that drives all of science. In fact, all scientific results are only provisional, subject to better data, better methods, and better frameworks. In the face of scientific uncertainty, political, economic, and social decisions must still be made to address the concerns of all interested parties, decisions that are beyond the formal bounds of science. Risk managers call upon experts to assist them in this process.

### Technical Expertise

The term "expert" can be used to refer to individuals who, by virtue of their being technically trained within an academic discipline, have "technical expertise." In this sense, most experts draw heavily on the authority and/or prestige of science in general or their individual fields in particular.[152] The principal experts on PF E/MF health effects who participated directly in the Courtenay controversy were Marino, Erdreich, Sastre, and Gallagher. They were engaged in risk analysis, while the BCUC (and B.C. Hydro) were engaged in option evaluation and risk management. There were a number of other experts who played a less direct, but by no means less important, role in the controversy, for example, David Savitz and the NYSPLP SAP. Technical expertise was used by all parties throughout the controversy to form, support, and alter their own and others' views on the PF E/MF health effects issue.

According to some participants, technical expertise was simply a resource exploited by all parties in the Courtenay controversy to justify their views, to create legitimacy, and to control the terms of the debate. Influence depended on the ability to manipulate knowledge or challenge evidence presented to support a particular position.[153] Because of the state of scientific understanding about the issue, it did appear that studies were lined up on either side of the public debate about regulations, or, at least, that evidence could be found to support any value position in the regulatory debate. The credibility of the experts was questioned, in both their roles as researchers (because studies were "rigged") and as expert witnesses or advisers (because of "selective" use of studies). Furthermore, it appeared that the results of the experts' work reflected the views of their sponsoring agencies. It was often observed that "science could be bought."[154]

While some scientific work is indeed influenced by interests, to consider all science and scientists as "interested" or "biased" discredits the scientific enterprise. Research "need not always reflect the economic or political interests of the researchers or those who fund them." Science is a strategy for seeking knowledge and, at its best, it is a particularly useful strategy, whatever its other limitations.[155] For specialized knowledge, society must depend on experts. There are certain technical issues relevant to policy decisions that the average citizen is not capable of understanding in depth.[156]

The following discussion takes as its premise the notion that there was at least some scientific basis for expert disagreement on the PF E/MF and human health issue and, as a result, there was a legitimate basis both for concern and for a lack of concern about possible health effects.

*BCUC Report and Recommendations*

Marino, Erdreich, and Sastre, although agreeing on the need for more research, differed in their analyses as to whether the PF E/MF associated with the Dunsmuir/Gold River lines posed a risk to human health. The BCUC considered them "interested"; Gallagher was a "neutral arbiter." It should be kept in mind that Gallagher was only in an advisory position. McIntyre, a layperson, made the final decision about the "correct" risk analysis.

In the BCUC's (that is, McIntyre's) final report, the uncertain state of the science concerning PF E/MF health effects was given as the rationale for its risk assessment. The scientific evidence was "insufficient," "inconclusive," and "unreliable." Yet scientific uncertainty provided the basis for risk management decisions made elsewhere in Canada and the United States, ranging from limiting transmission line E/MF levels to restricting school playground use by children to "business as usual."[157] None of those decision-makers concluded that PF E/MF were a definite health risk. It was not made clear in the BCUC's final report why its risk analysis was more "correct" than any other, especially Marino's. Furthermore, Gallagher's analysis was hidden. The BCUC had a public obligation to give a full explanation for its decision in the final report; the rationale given was especially inadequate for an informed public.

Each expert based his or her risk analysis on the standard scientific paradigm of their respective fields. For example, Erdreich and Sastre considered PF E/MF as the only relevant exposure, while Marino included PF, RF, and microwave exposures. Even if industry-associated research were included in Marino's analysis, he was not using the same body of data as Erdreich and Sastre. Furthermore, many experts had considered the same body of data as Erdreich and Sastre but concluded that there was enough evidence to indicate that PF E/MF was at the least a hazard, and possibly a risk, to human health. (Marton raised a number of the issues during the inquiry that were routinely debated by experts who, while limiting relevant exposures to PF E/MF, differed in their conclusions regarding health effects.) Not only was the BCUC unclear in its final report about the reasons for their choice of risk analysis, they did not acknowledge the broad range of risk analyses that existed among the experts.[158]

Science is used to support public policy. A government body must justify its actions in the political process and consequently seeks a science it can justify and explain to a wide variety of publics and interest groups. This science must be intelligible to non-scientists and facilitate clear choices. It must represent a body of evidence on which decisions can rest and be seen as rational. Only an ideal science could serve these non-scientific intentions.[159] The BCUC's final report was framed in an ideal picture of the scientific enterprise. Throughout the Courtenay controversy, science was used by the BCUC, Gallagher, B.C. Hydro, Erdreich, and Sastre (among others) as a source of legitimacy and credibility. However, they presented a picture of the scientific process, and of the relationship between science and policy decisions, that was exclusively "rationalist" in form. On the other hand, Marino (and others) presented a picture of science that emphasized what were, in his view, its irrational dimensions. Yet, after discounting all industry-associated research, he too relied on an ideal picture of the scientific enterprise to support his position.[160]

Presenting the scientific enterprise as such was not always an easy task. There were some obvious contradictions during the inquiry. Why did Becker and Savitz refuse to testify? Why did B.C. Hydro not talk to the public once the inquiry was called?[161] Why did B.C. Hydro refuse to bring in an expert chosen by the public? Why was it "inappropriate" for Erdreich and Sastre to contact Marino? If Marino and Erdreich and Sastre were considered "interested," why was Gallagher not?

## MANDATED SCIENCE

Risk analysis – whether it is deriving a quantitative analysis of risk or concluding that there is not enough information to do so – is not a "neutral process." There are many uncertainties and assumptions, and considerable social and economic interests involved. Indeed, "either or both scientific and policy considerations may emerge at any time and in any setting where risk management issues are at stake."[162]

In analysing risks, choices must be made concerning which studies to commission, how extensively to review the scientific literature, and how to interpret the findings of studies if they are conflicting, uncertain, ambiguous, or not directly applicable to the decision being made. Choices are also made concerning the bringing together of scientific material from different disciplines to reach a single decision, and the decision as to where the burden of proof lies (e.g. is the material or process in question considered safe or hazardous until proven otherwise). These choices must all be made within the constraints imposed by the time and resources available.[163]

The "scientific activity of an expert committee, of the scientists who testify for regulators, of the regulators or courts that assess scientific information, and the studies used for purposes of making public policy," whether commissioned by government officials and regulators to aid in their decision-making or produced in more conventional scientific settings, are all examples of "mandated science."[164] Mandated science alters the relationships between science, values, and public policy in significant ways.[165] Liona Salter, in a case study investigating the setting of chemical standards, argues that "a mandate to develop recommendations or decisions for public policy exerts a pressure reflected both in the activities of scientists and in their work or its interpretation." Four characteristics of mandated science distinguish it from science as it is conventionally viewed.[166]

*The idealization of science.* Mandated science relies upon an image of science as value-free, as producing invariably credible results, and, most importantly, as an inherently public enterprise. However, mandated science conforms to none of these ideals. The "moral dilemmas posed by scientific knowledge are made explicit, and few assume that science is fully independent." The conventional methodologies of science "often produce conflicting reports that cannot be resolved by further properly conducted studies." A proportion of mandated science is neither peer-reviewed, published, nor part of the open literature.[168]

*The legal substratum of scientific debates.* The decisions made in the context of mandated science are influenced by economic and social interests. More notably, the decisions, and therefore the debates leading up to them, are "deeply infused with legal issues that compound their economic and social implications many times over." They result from "discussions about liability for harm, and about measures that might be taken to restrict both harm and limit liability for it." They determine to what degree court action can be taken for possible negligence or damage to human health and the environment. The reports and conclusions of mandated scientists are used as legal evidence and therefore are "subject to the standard of proof required by the courts."[168]

Salter found that "to be considered as good science, scientific information must be developed and presented without regard for its legal implications." However, testimony of experienced participants in mandated science is "shaped by an awareness of legal standards of proof and by knowledge about how to use scientific information effectively in a court or regulatory setting." "Scientists compromise their claim to independence to the extent that they openly recognize the legal constraints," yet they must function in a legally informed manner "if their work is to be valuable to the legally oriented bodies that mandate or use their scientific work."[169]

*The peculiar nature of the debate itself.* The nature of discussion and debate within mandated science is unique. Scientific debate is neither scientific, legal, nor public policy debate. It has its "own style, methods of argumentation, and uses of language." For example, scientific information is presented "as if it were evidence in a public policy debate infused with interest group considerations," and emphasis is placed on closure. "Scientific conclusions will often be justified as reflecting a consensus of interested parties or a democratic process of decision-making." Finally, emphasis is on "the evaluation of science rather than its conduct."[170]

The unusual character of the debate in mandated science is reflected in the use of particular words and phrases. The words and phrases "lend themselves to being battlegrounds for conflicting interpretations of science that benefit some political or interest groups and not others." For example, in a scientific context, the term "scientific uncertainty" is unexceptional; the existence of contrary scientific views is not sufficient to call research into question. However, by referring to scientific uncertainty, a lawyer in cross-examination can challenge the credibility and usefulness of a study, or a regulator can justify action or inaction.[171]

Salter found that to maintain their credibility, scientists participating in mandated science "must adhere closely to conventions of scientific debate that are acceptable to other scientists." However, to be effective in the policy arena they must also speak with an awareness that others "will use what they say to further goals that are unrelated to science." "Scientists who regularly give expert testimony for regulators or for expert committees speak to at least two different audiences simultaneously, and know that their words can be subject to conflicting interpretations by each."[172]

*The manifest interplay of science and values.* Mandated science makes explicit the moral dilemmas posed by science. For example, members of an expert committee are chosen "because they can rely upon their scientific training to render themselves relatively free of interest group and moral constraints." However, because they are working in the sphere of mandated science, "they conduct assessments that are only partly scientific, and make decisions that have direct political and moral consequences." In accepting their task, they "agree to recognize constraints that scientists seldom recognize or acknowledge explicitly, and to relax constraints that scientists publicly claim to abide by." Salter argues that the knowledge that "a statement about scientific issues is inherently also a statement which privileges some interests and not others" affects the expert committee's recommendations "as much as does their knowledge about the characteristics of the natural phenomenon."[173]

Salter makes several observations that are particularly relevant when considering the use of technical expertise in disputes between parties. First, the nature of mandated science discourages participation by conventional scientists, and for those who do participate, the experience is frustrating. Research is likely to be conducted in a highly conservative manner because scientific conclusions must be justified to many different audiences or in a courtroom.[174] Participation is also frustrating because scientific statements could have significantly different meanings in scientific, regulatory, and legal discourse. Information is presented in different ways in each, and arguments effective in one discourse are often not effective in another. Only scientists experienced in mandated science could withstand the scrutiny applied in an expert hearing and court.[175]

In addition, conventional scientists are committed to conducting relatively dispassionate inquiries. However, as citizens, and as a result of their research, they are often compelled to "take a position" or to make recommendations for regulators. They observe government or regulatory scientists offering their opinions about regulation freely and company expert witnesses reaching favourable yet scientific conclusions. "At the same time, any association with advocate or interest groups, or attempts to make regulatory recommendations is seen to corrupt their own science and threaten its scientific credibility." It is easiest for conventional scientists to simply refuse to become involved in any aspect of mandated science. (Salter observed that advocacy and science can clash in the public presentation of research to a nonscientific community, not in the conduct of research.)[176]

Second, a cursory review of the academic literature is often made by policy-makers and regulators. Studies designed for regulatory purposes that yield the types of conclusions required are submitted for review to regulators. Limited resources are available for detailed examination of the wide-ranging academic literature, and there is little scope for discussion of the implications of studies not lending themselves to suitable conclusions for regulators. As a result, questions remain unaddressed and unanswered.[177]

Third, scientists adopt an "unusually critical perspective" on the studies reviewed because they are used to support legal actions and to evaluate regulations. When faced with inconclusive data or conflicting interpretations of it, scientists "often chose to identify problems in the conduct of the research, or to refer to scientific uncertainty." (If this is true and advocate groups view science and scientists as conservative and unsupportive of stringent regulation, Salter observes that it is perhaps because "statements about scientific uncertainty could be easily used in mandated science as a reason for government inaction.")[178]

In conclusion, Salter found that mandated science is "not well understood, and that it is characterized by an ideal picture of the scientific enterprise, by reliance upon overly rational procedures of risk assessment, by insufficient understanding of the difficulties in resolving mixed disputes [involving both scientific and legal issues], and by an almost naive perception that scientific statements have the same meaning, regardless of who interprets them." In addition, "the discussion of the relationship between science and values is too limited, and the reliance on institutional procedures to handle economic, trade, and interest group issues in mandated science is highly problematic." Mandated science has some norms quite different from either those of the scientific or legal process "that should be extended and articulated to deal with the constraints imposed by a policy mandate upon scientists and scientific work." It is important to distinguish when the conditions on practising mandated science are so constrained as to make it impossible.[179]

## RECOMMENDATIONS –
## PUBLIC INQUIRY

Risk managers and their publics are increasingly dependent on science and technology, and yet there is growing concern or scepticism about the answers that science can provide, at least at the time when regulatory decisions are required. If the public is to have full confidence in decisions, it needs to know how the pressures and constraints to reach conclusions that can lead to public policy or government regulation are felt by decision-makers and experts alike. These realities must be understood by all parties and taken into account when evaluating "the adequacy of scientific assessments and their fairness in both procedural and substantive terms."[180]

Risk managers should ensure that the inherent limitations of the risk assessment process (beginning with the limitations of science itself) are acknowledged explicitly by all parties and, as far as possible, compensated for. Certainly, all parties could and should contribute to this process – including the media, the public, politicians, and lawyers – but it is the risk managers who have the major responsibility and the resources to fulfil this obligation. In particular, the BCUC had an obligation to provide a comprehensive rationale for its decision in its final report. The broad range of scientific opinion on the PF E/MF and human health issue should have been acknowledged, and the basis for the differences of opinion explained. (Because it is likely that more time than was available would be required to do this, a detailed report could have followed a preliminary report outlining the decision in more general terms. A detailed report would provide the opportunity to explain adequately the state of the science on PF E/MF health effects and its many uncertainties, which may or may not have been the focus of expert disagreement. Furthermore, Gallagher's contribution to the decision-making process should have been visible throughout the inquiry.

B.C. Hydro should not have simply let the "facts" speak for themselves. The PF E/MF issue is complex and the "facts" supported a number of possible "truths." Although a wide range of information was made available to the public on request, a much more active role should have been played by B.C. Hydro in communicating with the public and the media about the disagreement among experts on the issue.[181] In particular, they should have brought their own experts in earlier and made them accessible to the residents.[182] In addition, the B.C. MOH should have been more directly involved in the Courtenay controversy, especially given its public health mandate.[183] They also had some expertise in the area.

The expert witnesses and advisers were also responsible for recognizing and compensating for the inherent limitations of the risk assessment process. In particular, although Marino advised concerned residents that if they were unsuccessful in their bid to reroute the new transmission line an "excessive" reaction was not called for and that other, perhaps more significant, risk factors in their lives should be reduced, he waited until the end of his testimony to offer this advice. Furthermore, the experts should have shared their knowledge about those aspects of the PF E/MF health effects issue over which scientists were not in agreement, and they should have made no more claim for their knowledge than was warranted.

In addition, risk managers should ensure that all parties, especially the public, are involved in the decision-making process, not only for reasons of fairness but because of the very nature of mandated science. Technical choices are inherently value-laden. In particular, the CVRC should have been provided with funds by the BCUC to cover Marino's expenses. His presence was necessary, especially during cross-examination (of both B.C. Hydro's experts and of himself), to allow for full disclosure of information.[184] Disclosure of the fees paid by BCUC and B.C. Hydro for their expert witnesses should also have been required, especially since B.C. Hydro and BCUC are provincial agencies.

The BCUC should have recognized that informed public opinion, such as that given by Marton, had much to contribute to the discussion of PF E/MF health effects. The issues that Marton raised should have been addressed further, or at least acknowledged in the BCUC's final report, even though he was not an "expert"; several other residents also put forth knowledgeable questions and arguments that were not acknowledged. It was difficult for an informed public to accept, as stated by the final report, that "all sides" of the debate were heard. Marino, Erdreich, and Sastre did not represent "all sides"; Gallagher's contribution was essentially unknown.

Furthermore, and perhaps most importantly, the public perception of risk from PF E/MF (in contrast to the technical assessment of risk) should not have so easily been dismissed by B.C. Hydro, the BCUC, and others as "irrational" or "unscientific." The two determinations of risk should have been given equal respect because, in mandated science, it is difficult, if not impossible, to separate the scientific and non-scientific components of risk assessment. Experts will include and exclude their own values. Furthermore, the public is capable of understanding the limitations and trade-offs involved in balancing health benefits with health risks.

Finally, with all parties participating and therefore responsible for the decisions made, there is a higher probability for acceptance of the decisions by a broad segment of the public.[185]

## OUTLOOK

The BCUC's ruling on the Dunsmuir/Gold River line alleviated, or at least suppressed, much of the public concern about PF E/MF health effects in the Courtenay area and elsewhere in British Columbia. Still, concerns continue to be raised – for example, at public meetings held by B.C. Hydro regarding the planned routing of several transmission lines.[186] (B.C. Hydro's EMF Issues Manager now receives 500 to 600 queries about the health effects issue each year.) B.C. Hydro refused to buy the homes of residents along the proposed route of a 138 kV line in the Duncan area, citing the BCUC's criticism that they had acted "imprudently" in the Courtenay controversy. One area resident, reacting to the proposed routing, threatened to shoot anyone from B.C. Hydro setting foot on his property.[187]

Certainly, some of the public concern during the Courtenay inquiry was influenced by factors not directly related to the PF E/MF health effects issue: for example, inaccurate and unbalanced information; the lack of trust and credibility of the BCUC, B.C. Hydro, and their experts; and the residents' lack of understanding of the associated science, and of science in general. It was also possible that some of the participants used the health risk debate as a surrogate for debate about more general social, economic, and political issues and concerns.[188] However, improved risk management and risk communication should help reduce concerns related to these aspects of the issue.[189]

The 1989 U.S. Office of Technology Assessment (OTA) report (summarized in chapter 4) is one of the most recent reviews of the PF E/MF health effects literature by a North American federal government agency.[190] The state of the science has advanced from that described in the report following several carefully performed experiments. Furthermore, some work has been done on re-evaluating the assumptions and adequacy of the methodologies used to study the PF E/MF health effects issue.[191] However, it is still not possible to conduct a formal quantitative risk analysis because a dose-response relationship has not been established and the dose-response mechanism(s) are not understood.[192]

Although most scientists now think that exposure to PF E/MF can produce biological effects, there continues to be a broad range of scientific opinion on the question of whether or not exposure poses a hazard, let alone a risk, to human health.[193] Most scientists agree that more and better research is necessary to provide confident answers to the question. Expert disagreement continues to be most visible in the public policy arena. For example, a 1990 review by the U.S. EPA on the possible carcinogenic effects of PF and RF fields initially proposed classifying PF E/MF as a probable carcinogen. Amid some controversy, including strong objections from the White House, the report was withdrawn and revised.[194] The EPA's Science Advisory Board (as well as several other federal departments and agencies) subsequently reviewed the report and concluded in 1991 that such a classification was inappropriate and that substantial revisions were required.[195] Completion of a revised draft (updated and expanded) is expected in 1994.[196]

On the other hand, a report released in March 1992 by a U.K. National Radiological Protection Board advisory group (set up to review the EPA report) concluded that "in the absence of any unambiguous experimental evidence to suggest that exposure to these electromagnetic fields is likely to be carcinogenic, the findings to date can be regarded only as sufficient to justify formulating a hypothesis for testing by further investigation." At frequencies lower than 100 kHz, the experimental evidence provides no reason to suggest a carcinogenic effect except for a small risk attributable to an effect on the secretion of melatonin. The epidemiological findings reviewed provide "no firm evidence" of a carcinogenic hazard from exposure to ELF residential and workplace electromagnetic fields.

Much of the evidence cited is inconsistent, or from inadequately controlled studies; some is likely distorted by bias against the reporting or publishing of negative results. The only "notable" finding is the consistency with which the least weak evidence relates to a small risk of brain tumours. However, the consistency is less impressive because brain tumours in children and adults are different in origin. The panel recommended more research with an emphasis on fundamental biophysical interactions and on possible promotional/ co-carcinogenic effects of electromagnetic fields. In addition, more emphasis is needed on consolidating "positive" findings and formulating testable hypotheses.[197]

The prevalence and integral role of electric energy in industrialized society makes the potential health effects issue a matter of serious scientific and public health policy concern. Furthermore, in contrast to specific chemicals, there is no alternative to electricity, the source of PF E/MF. As long as scientific uncertainty and the accompanying expert disagreement remain unresolved, the concern will persist and grow as more power lines are constructed and the public becomes better informed. In the United States and increasingly in Canada, vigorous public intervention and litigation have continued to significantly impede the private and public construction of new power lines due to concerns about health effects and potential decreased property values from perceived health effects. According to a 1990 EPRI poll of 100 utility CEOs, customer inquiries and press calls had tripled and employee concerns were up 50 percent. A CEA survey placed the issue as number one with utilities across Canada.[198]

Results of international research now under way – including several large occupational studies, several large studies of childhood leukemia, animal studies testing various cancer models, laboratory studies on interaction mechanisms, and exposure assessment studies – are unlikely to alleviate public concern. For example, two recent Swedish epidemiological studies suggest for the first time a dose-response relationship between cancer and 50 Hz magnetic field exposure.[199] In response to the Swedish studies, Sweden's National Board for Industrial and Technical Development announced that it would "act on the assumption that there is a connection between exposure to power frequency magnetic fields and cancer, in particular childhood cancer." This marked the first time a national government has recognized a PF E/MF-cancer link.[200] Risk management precedents are also being set in North American jurisdictions. The U.S. DOE's BPA voluntary adoption of a "prudent avoidance" approach to siting new transmission lines in 1989 has led to at least one state and a few utility companies following suit.

Yet, even if adopted as policy for the siting of new transmission lines, "prudent avoidance" of all populated areas is nearly impossible. And what should be done with existing lines? Furthermore, research has indicated that distribution lines may be a more significant source of exposure.[201] Better scientific understanding is the only possible way to resolve the issue in the long term. In the short term, an understanding of where the experts agree and disagree is critical to making informed risk management decisions.

A number of proposals, both specific to PF E/MF health effects and general to mandated science, have been made to help clarify and even resolve expert disagreement.[202] In this final section of the chapter, we provide a brief overview of three of these proposals.

### Science Court

The science court proposed by Arthur Kantrowitz and others extends the adversarial nature of the American legal system to involve scientists. One or more especially qualified scientists listens to prepared arguments of opposing "advocate scientists," and the "judges" then come to conclusions on the basis of their own expertise. The court's findings derive their authority primarily from the scientific reputations of the judges.[203] One of the most common concerns is that the adversarial character and formalistic nature of the science court proceedings are in opposition to the conduct of "good science."[204]

According to Allan Mazur, the science court can be realized because only a separation of "blatant evaluative or normative statements from statements of fact" is required. Mazur attempted to promote such an exchange between technical experts involved in a 1979 controversy over the health effects of high-voltage transmission lines in Minnesota. Mazur acted as an independent mediator between Becker and Marino (who considered transmission line E/MF hazardous) and four experts who were, based on hearings and published accounts, "closely associated" with the position that transmission line E/MF was not hazardous. Mazur provided a list of alleged statements of facts which was revised by Becker and Marino based on critiques received from the involved experts. The revised list was sent to the four pro-line experts for comments; three responded.

A somewhat better understanding of the technical differences between the positions was achieved. Subsequently, however, the pro-line experts did not want any involvement in a science court procedure. Mazur speculated that proponents of technological development did not want to debate scientific differences because the debate would publicize and perhaps legitimize criticism of the lines. He concluded that the controversy was primarily a dispute over political goals and only secondarily concerned with the veracity of scientific issues. Mazur also speculated that although the science court final report would probably not alter the position of the adversaries and their interest groups, it could have an important impact on that portion of the public that had not yet taken a side in the controversy, but whose interests were at stake.[205] (Marino has been an active proponent of the science court.)[206]

### Scientific Panels

Scientific panels are less formally structured than science courts. They are like other appointed committees with members who are highly regarded in their fields. After reviewing all available scientific evidence pertinent to a dispute, the panel issues a report and recommendations. Usually, the reports of scientific panels reflect at least a limited consensus among the members. However, expert panels often lack credibility because of a suspicion that "the deck has been stacked."[207]

In 1988 Robert S. Banks observed that membership on the five panels of scientific, medical, and engineering expertise assembled since 1977 to examine the issue of PF E/MF health effects was quite resticted, limiting the scope and depth of scientific expertise that could be applied. With the exception of the NYSPLP SAP, membership on these panels was drawn almost exclusively from the very small bioelectromagnetics research community. As a result, there was an increasing polarization of views without sufficient depth and diversity, especially with respect to the 60 Hz magnetic field/cancer hypothesis, making the exchange of views increasingly difficult. In an effort to address some of these problems, Banks recommended a major interdisciplinary peer-review project of the state of the science, conducted by an academic institution not presently active in the area. The project would then be published by the institution in an archival scientific journal.[208]

The U.S. National Research Council recommends independent scientific review of risk analyses because "one cannot assume that experts are significantly more self-conscious about the subtle distinction between value judgment and scientific consensus in complex analyses than non-experts are."[209] In particular, Jasanoff and others have suggested that all risk assessments made by regulatory agencies should be subject to peer review.[210]

## Scientific Consensus-Finding Conference

Milton Wessel proposed the scientific consensus-finding conference to help resolve the interim scientific issues of a socio-scientific dispute. Such a conference would function on the local, regional, national, and international levels, as appropriate. The conference would attempt to limit itself exclusively to scientific issues and seek only to identify consensus regarding scientific issues, i.e., not attempt to create agreement through negotiation. It would be procedurally fair, with a skilled, non-scientist chair and an independent secretariat and administration. The conference would encourage the widest reasonable scientific participation and solicit the largest reasonable participation of all segments of the public and of the media. No invitation or special permission would be required for attendance. The conclusions of the conference would be factored into public policy dispute-resolution mechanisms – e.g., a court, an administrative agency, a legislature, and, ultimately, the public at large. Because consensus-finding conferences lack authority, whatever effect they have is by virtue of the credibility and persuasive influence of their findings.[211] Therefore they may achieve little more than setting the stage for a court battle.[212]

In chapter 9, we will return to the question of whether or not any of these proposals can help clarify or resolve some of the expert disagreement over the PF E/MF health effects issue in general.

Table 5-1
Chronology of Key Events in the Courtenay Controversy

| 1987 | Summer | • B.C. Hydro begins construction of 230 kV transmission line along existing ROW from Dunsmuir to Gold River to provide power for CPFP pulp mill expansion. |
|------|--------|---|
| 1988 | March | • B.C. Hydro receives formal notice of health concerns about the PF E/MF associated with the new line from Marton. |
| 1989 | February | • Unsatisfied with B.C. Hydro's response, Marton writes to Provincial Ombudsman. Ombudsman defers matter to BCUC and refers Marton to BC PIAC.<br>• Kavkas file formal complaint with BCUC against B.C. Hydro regarding compensation for trees cut and PF E/MF health concerns. |
| 1989 | April | • After Darlene Kavka makes presentation about EMF health effects, C-S RD requests that B.C. Hydro reroute line.<br>• CVRC formed.<br>• Kavka makes presentations to Arden Elementary School Parents Group and Comox Valley Teachers Association. Both request that B.C. Hydro reroute line because of possible health effects. |
| 1989 | May 8 | • At meeting with Kavka, Marton, and BC PIAC, B.C. Hydro offers to provide information on PF E/MF health effects. If concerns persist, B.C. Hydro will purchase the property of residents along the ROW. |
| | May 16 | • School District 71 delays expansion of Arden Elementary School until more information is received on health effects. |
| | May 31 | • Marino agrees to conduct a seminar for residents on EMF health effects.<br>• 140 people indicate interest in B.C. Hydro's buy-out offer. |
| | June 12 | • BCUC orders that a public inquiry be held because of the amount of public concern about possible health effects. Line construction on hold. |
| | July 11–14 | • Public inquiry held. |
| | July 27 | • BCUC releases final report. Inconclusive evidence concerning PF E/MF health effects. Line not to be rerouted. Line construction to resume. B.C. Hydro to continue to honour buy-out offer but acted "imprudently" in making it. |
| | July 31 | • CVRC blocks line construction on several properties. |
| | August 9 | • B.C. Hydro granted Supreme Court injunction. |
| | August 12 | • Darlene Kavka, only remaining protester, camps out on ROW adjacent to her property. |
| | August 15 | • Wording of B.C. Hydro court injunction revised so RCMP can enforce. |
| | August 16 | • Kavka arrested. |
| | August 19 | • B.C. Supreme Court informs Kavka nothing can be done unless new evidence on health effects. |
| | August 20 | • Kavka ends protest and construction proceeds on her property. |
| | August 26 | • Dunsmuir/Gold River 230 kV transmission line energized. |
| | November 17 | • 71 property owners accepted buy-out offer. |

Table 5-2
People Involved in the Courtenay Controversy

| | |
|---|---|
| Barker, Jeff | Project Manager, Transmission Projects, B.C. Hydro |
| Bauman, R.J. | Lawyer, representing CPFP |
| Beavan, Pat | Land Representative, B.C. Hydro |
| Becker, Robert | Physician, orthopedic surgeon |
| Bell, Larry | Chair, B.C. Hydro |
| Boatman, Chris | V.P., Corporate and Environmental Affairs, B.C. Hydro |
| Carpenter, David | M.D., Office of Public Health, New York State DOH; Head, School of Public Health Sciences, State University of New York; Executive Secretary, NYSPLP |
| Curley, Ken | Area Manager, B.C. Hydro |
| Erdreich, Linda | Epidemiologist, ERI; B.C. Hydro expert witness |
| Gallagher, Richard | Epidemiologist, BC CCA; BCUC expert adviser |
| Gathercole, Richard | Executive Director and General Counsel, BC PIAC, representing CVRC and John Marton |
| Grant, W.J. | Director, Engineering and Accounting, BCUC |
| Gustafson, Carl | Lawyer, representing BCUC |
| Kavka, Darlene | Courtenay resident; Chair, CVRC |
| Kavka, Frank | Courtenay resident |
| Klassen, Frank | V.P., Administration, B.C. Hydro |
| MacKenzie, Ken | Lawyer, representing B.C. Hydro |
| March, Lorne | Director, Environmental Service, B.C. Hydro |
| Marino, Andrew | Biophysicist; CVRC expert witness |
| Marton, John | Courtenay resident; psychologist |
| McIntyre, John | Chair and CEO, BCUC; Inquiry Chair |
| McMullan, Peter | Manager, Corporate Communications, B.C. Hydro |
| Ross, Randy | Radiation Protection Services, B.C. MOH |
| Sastre, Antonio | Laboratory Scientist, ERI; B.C. Hydro expert witness |
| Savitz, David | Epidemiologist, University of North Carolina |
| Shannon, Elizabeth | Trustee, School District 71 |
| Smith, Neptune | Manager, Engineering and Project Review–Electrical, BCUC |
| Swanson, Milt | Lawyer; Commissioner, BCUC; Inquiry Commissioner |
| Thompson, Thom | Manager, Government and Public Affairs, B.C. Hydro |
| Vance, Joan | Lawyer, BC PIAC, representing CVRC |
| Walsh, Karen | Courtenay resident; Treasurer, CVRC |
| Wertheimer, Nancy | Epidemiologist, University of Colorado |
| Wong, Paul | Electrical Engineer, PowerTech Labs, B.C. Hydro |

# CHAPTER SIX

# Alar, or Who Benefits?

## INTRODUCTION

In the spring of 1989 millions of consumers stopped buying apples and apple products. The sudden action was prompted by fears about Alar®, the trade name for a chemical (daminozide) made by the Uniroyal Chemical Company and widely used since 1968 in North America and elsewhere by apple growers to prevent pre-harvest fruit drop, promote colour development, and increase storage life.[1] Those fears stemmed largely from a segment of the CBS television show "60 Minutes," which opened with reporter Ed Bradley speaking against a backdrop composed of a skull-and-crossbones motif superimposed upon an apple. The show announced that, according to allegations in Intolerable Risk, a report prepared by the Natural Resources Defense Council (NRDC), a U.S. environmental group, Alar and its associated chemical products involved a relatively high risk of cancer, with children at particularly high risk due to their above-average consumption of apples and their products, especially apple juice. In the days that followed, worried parents took their children off apple products and many school boards removed them from their lunch menus; apple sales plummeted across the United States.

Consumers in North America, who have been taught to rely upon their government regulatory authorities for a guaranteed healthy food supply, received mixed messages from those authorities in response to the allegations. In an interview shown on the "60 Minutes" segment, Jack Moore, the Deputy Director of the U.S. Environmental Protection Agency (EPA), stated that he would like to order the removal of Alar from the marketplace immediately (at least for food uses), but that his agency did not have the legal authority to do so, thus adding the element of anger to the public's fears. (On other occasions he also said that if Alar were being newly proposed for registration it would not be accepted.) This comment was followed by a camera shot of a furious U.S. congressman exclaiming that those who thought they could delay such decisions should visit a children's cancer ward. On the other hand, Canada's Department of National Health and Welfare insisted at the same time that consumers were not at any risk from apple products treated with Alar, and that the Department had no intention of ordering its removal from the marketplace! This unsatisfactory situation dragged on until, in response to sagging sales of its product and pressure from some other industry sources, Uniroyal "voluntarily" withdrew Alar from circulation on June 2, 1989.

Representatives of every interested party to this controversy were left feeling bitter and unsatisfied by its outcome. Many consumers felt that their governments had let them down, having sacrificed their children's health merely to avoid a legal battle with a large company, or at least having been unaccountably slow to act on information that had been in their possession for over fifteen years. The chemical industry felt equally wronged, since all along it had disputed vigorously the scientific validity of the studies on which the alleged cancer risk had been based: wronged by the U.S. government, which had bowed to public opinion founded on misinformation; wronged by the specific environmental group that had chosen to launch a crusade against its product on the basis of flawed science; wronged by the mass media, which had been a willing tool of the environmental group's agenda. Some prominent scientists announced their disappointment with the fact that the public was allowing itself to be misled by groups that did not hesitate to manipulate and distort scientific studies to suit their private agendas. Many apple growers felt wronged, not only in being denied access to a useful product, but specifically in suffering hundreds of millions of dollars in financial losses due to the consumer boycotts. Environmental groups felt wronged in that one government agency (the U.S. EPA) delayed so long in taking action against a chemical about which there was abundant evidence of excess risk to consumers, especially children, and in that others (the EPA's counterparts in Canada and Britain) refused to echo the EPA's announced determination to get Alar off the market. The media felt wronged in being criticized for reporting on a newsworthy event. And some government agencies, notably those in Canada and Britain, felt wronged in that many consumers and environmental groups appeared not trust their expert judgments about health risks, preferring instead to trust the views of a private group.

The controversy over Alar was not resolved; it simply dissipated after Uniroyal stopped marketing its product. The residue of that controversy can still be detected today in the lingering bitterness evident in comments scattered throughout industry trade publications, and in the lawsuit, now being heard in a U.S. federal court, filed in 1990 by the apple growers in the State of Washington against the Natural Resources Defense Council and CBS Television.[2] Bitterness also lingers in the text of an "Act Concerning the Creation of a Cause of Action for the Disparagement of Perishable Agricultural Food Products" – known to its detractors as "the fruit and vegetable Bill of Rights" – which was passed by both legislative houses in the state of Colorado in March 1991. This act proposed to allow farmers to sue for triple damages anyone whose disparaging acts caused financial losses to them, and it defined disparagement as "dissemination to the public in any manner of any false information which is not based on reliable scientific facts and scientific data, which the disseminator knows or should have known to be false, and which casts doubt on the safety of any perishable agricultural food." Much to the chagrin of the act's backers, the Governor vetoed the bill.[3]

Is there a better way for us to deal with such controversies? Curiously, despite the fact that in the Alar issue just about every stakeholder wound up feeling wronged, and many claimed substantial economic injury as well, no institutional stakeholder stepped forward to take responsibility for seeking an answer to this question. One cannot hope to answer it, however, unless the full complexity of the issue itself – in this case, what was at stake for each interested party and what events had unfolded in the twenty-one years between the time Alar was first registered for food uses (1968) and the time when its manufacturer surrendered those registrations (1989) – is known.

We have undertaken to examine this information as a prelude to constructing an imaginary event, namely, a "consensus exercise" that might have been held. This exercise includes questions that might have been posed, both to the group of invited participants as a whole and to particular stakeholders. They are hard questions, to which there are neither easy nor certain answers. Our supposition in fashioning this imaginary event is that, despite the onerous nature of the questions and the lack of ready answers to them, the stakeholders may have been more fully satisfied *by virtue of their involvement in this process itself* than they were by what actually unfolded in 1989. This imaginary event is described at the beginning of chapter 7 and in chapter 8 we provide a more adequate proof of the plausibility of our supposition in the form of a case study on a related issue.

In recounting the Alar story we have drawn upon the rich documentation that exists in the EPA's "Special Review Public Docket on Daminozide," consisting of thousands of individual items filed between 1980 and 1992.[4] This includes a huge volume of material on the risk assessment of daminozide and on the contaminant chemical UDMH (under certain conditions, daminozide decomposes to UDMH), prepared by a host of scientific experts working for governments, the industry, public interest groups, and others; a substantial amount of material that quantifies the benefits of daminozide in economic terms to users; interventions by a variety of public interest groups; position papers, correspondence, and technical analyses by EPA staff; voluminous correspondence from the public and politicians both for and against the continued use of Alar; records of meetings between EPA staff and Uniroyal; verbatim transcripts of the Scientific Advisory Panel (SAP) hearings; and other material.[5]

Among all those who took part in the controversy over Alar, relatively few – Uniroyal and its lawyers, some EPA personnel, the outside scientists who acted in one role or another, and the NRDC staff assigned to this project – would have taken the trouble to peruse more than a fraction of these documents. What most citizens had to go on was a few snippets of contradictory advice from various "experts" filtered through a television or newspaper report. If we maintain the position – as we wish to do – that in a democracy the citizens are the court of last resort on what consititutes acceptable risk, we appear to be left with two equally unpalatable choices: (1) citizens must accept whatever their government experts tell them, or (2) citizens must make up their own minds, despite the fact that they can never hope to be aware of, nor understand, more than a minuscule fraction of the technical documentation on which a well-informed decision might be made. (In the Alar case, the first choice was not even available, since equally well-placed government experts in two neighbouring countries, the United States and Canada, were taking virtually opposite positions.)

In our imaginary consensus exercise on Alar (chapter 7) we try to make a plausible case for the proposition that there may be a better way.[6] In so doing, we strike out on a quite different path of analysis than the one taken by other recent commentators on the Alar case. For Harrison and Hoberg, an important consideration is to what degree a regulatory action is "stringent" (i.e., enforces a relatively risk-averse standard for acceptability of a chemical), although this criterion could never tell us whether or not such an action was "reasonable" or "fair" considering the interests of all parties; also, they say that the more conservative Canadian approach to communicating with the public about the risk of Alar entailed "potentially misleading the public concerning the nature of the risk," although they offer no evidence to suggest that Health and Welfare Canada's risk assessment was inferior to any other on scientific grounds.[7] Our own evaluation of what is important in the Alar controversy is much closer to Jasanoff's:

For better or worse, the last twenty years of broadly participatory agency decisionmaking have created a nation of experts. Not all are equally competent in every aspect of assessing risk, but the views of a well-informed citizenry and their expectations regarding the legitimacy of the administrative process are nonetheless entitled to respect. Thus the traditional concerns of democratic societies – the effectiveness of participation, the procedural correlates of fairness – cannot be forgotten in the search for improved communication of technical uncertainty. The multiple characterizations of risk that hold some claim to legitimacy in this society have to be accommodated through genuine dialogue. Only when the regulatory process develops mechanisms for achieving this result will there be a framework of communication that facilitates understanding and even leads to consensus.

Jasanoff's proposition – "the most promising way to foster communication among the actors [in the risk debate] is to have them acknowledge their stakes explicitly and to negotiate their differences openly"[8] – will serve as a good motto for our imaginary consensus exercise on Alar.

Table 6-1 offers an overview of the main events in this developing controversy. We shall begin with the multiple components of the expert risk/benefit analysis of daminozide: first, a detailed review of the risk assessments (composed of two elements: hazard profile and exposure estimates) made by the different parties as various scientific studies were completed and evaluated; next, the economic benefits assessments; finally, the consideration of risk/benefit trade-offs. Next, we shall try to guess what elements of the aforementioned expert analysis the "general public" might have been aware of at various points, or at least what elements of the debates among experts might be judged relevant to public concerns. In all this we shall be following faithfully the record of what actually transpired. But we shall end up with a long series of (unanswered) questions, which will form the program for our imaginary consensus exercise.

Before we begin, a word of warning to the reader. Like all other major disputes over health and environmental risks, the fight about

Table 6-1
Chronology of Key Events – Daminozide and UDMH

| Date | Actor | Event |
|---|---|---|
| 1963 | Uniroyal | Daminozide registration for ornamentals |
| 1967 | EPA, HWC | Initial toxicology reviews |
| | | Initial U.S. tolerances (e.g., 30 ppm for apples) |
| 1968 | Uniroyal | Daminozide registration for fruit crops (1973 in Canada) |
| 1973 | B. Toth | Study: UDMH causes cancers in mice |
| 1977 | B. Toth | Study: Damonizode causes cancers in mice |
| 1978 | NCI | Daminozide causes cancers in rats and mice |
| 1980 | HWC | Daminozide residues break down into UDMH; new regulatory restrictions and studies |
| 1980 | EPA | Considers Special Review, later retreats under unfavourable political climate |
| 1982–89 | HWC | Further reviews of complete toxicology database; replacement studies ordered |
| July 1984 | EPA | Special Review announced, including many new studies required of registrant |
| 12/09/85 | EPA | Position document announces "expedited cancellation" for food uses of daminozide |
| 04/10/85 | EPA | Science Advisory Panel fails to support EPA staff; criticizes lack of pertinent data |
| 22/01/86 | EPA | Proposed cancellation revoked; new studies ordered; measures to reduce exposure; tolerances lowered (e.g., 20 ppm for apples) |
| 31/01/89 | EPA | Intention to ban food uses for Alar |
| 26/02/89 | NRDC/CBS | Wide coverage of *Intolerable Risk* |
| 02/06/89 | Uniroyal | Withdraws product from market |

Alar drew upon an information base (scientific and non-scientific) that spanned more than twenty years and became extraordinarily complex over time. In order to give a plausible account of the positions assumed by each of the parties, including the information base on which each was operating at different times, we must delve into much detail. Only in this way can we describe realistically what might have been the basis for a social consensus – the consensus that eluded the parties in this case – or perhaps, at least, what specific problems would have confronted the parties individually and collectively had they attempted to sit down together and seek a consensus position. We believe this is worth the effort. We hope too that the contrast between the Alar case and the one that follows in chapter 8, in which, after much feuding, a consensus was reached, will be much more instructive, especially in terms of its applicability to other situations, as a result of the detail we have supplied here.

ALAR: "WHAT DID THE
EXPERTS KNOW, AND WHEN
DID THEY KNOW IT?"

Daminozide is an amino acid derivative that was first registered in the United States for use on ornamental plants (potted chrysanthemums) in 1963 and for use on food crops beginning in 1968. It is classified as a type of pesticide called a "plant growth regulator," that is, it controls the growth (including reproductive growth) of various plants and their flowers and fruits.[9] It affects flower-bud initiation, fruit set and maturity, and pre-harvest fruit drop. More specifically, it helps bring young trees into the fruit-bearing stage early by promoting the development of fruit buds; it overcomes the tendency for biennial bearing so that the grower gets a uniform, annual harvest for a constant annual return; it controls excessive vegetative growth by up to 30 percent, which is important since high-density plantations are more economical; it overcomes pre-harvest drop (i.e., keeps fruits on the tree longer until the farmer is ready to pick them); it increases fruit firmness; it controls fruit size, preventing the Spartan apples from growing too large for efficient storage; and it helps improve the colour of some varieties.

Alar was always used primarily on apples, primarily on McIntosh, Spartan, and Delicious varieties: apples grown with Alar are firmer and less subject to bruising, thus they store and travel better. Taken together, Alar's effects on the market quality of fruit crops both at time of harvest and during storage were substantial. Over the years after 1968 it was registered for use on a variety of orchard crops such as apples (the main use pattern), sweet and sour cherries, nectarines, peaches, prunes, and pears; on peanuts (the next largest use after apples), to modify the growth of vines; and on brussel sprouts, peas, grapes, cantaloupes, and tomatoes.

Daminozide is translocated throughout the plant, being rapidly absorbed through the leaves, roots, and stems – thus its residues cannot be washed off the surfaces of fruits, for example. It is also rapidly excreted in the urine and feces of animals that produce milk. It has low acute toxicity to fish and terrestrial wildlife, does not persist in soil, and does not bioaccumulate; thus there was never a major concern about environmental impacts on non-target organisms. One of the major non-economic benefits claimed for daminozide was that, in strengthening the bond between the plant and the stem of its fruit, it made the plant less susceptible to the effects of a pest known as the "leaf miner." Plants attacked by the leaf miner must be treated with other pesticides; thus it was claimed that using daminozide under these circumstances substituted for other pesticides that would have been applied to the crop in its absence. In any case, the manufacturer's applications for use of Alar on ornamentals and food crops required the preparation of a toxicological database for review by regulatory agencies.

### EXPERT JUDGMENT (A): RISK ASSESSMENT

EPA's "Special Review Public Docket on Daminozide" is very thin on materials from the pre-1980 period. However, it does contain a summary evaluation of the initial toxicological data, written by EPA staff member Robert Coberly and dated June 21, 1967. The summary is quoted here in full:

The toxicological data on Succinic acid 2,2–dimethylhydrazide [daminozide; often abbreviated SADH] indicates the material has a very low degree of lethal toxicity by the oral, dermal, and inhalation routes to laboratory animals. This applies to the acute, subacute, and chronic exposure periods. Additional support for this reasoning is in evidence when one considers the high dosage levels used in the subacute studies and the length of time, as shown by the metabolism study, required for elimination of the material from the body. However, the material does exhibit slight to moderate irritating effect to the skin and eyes. This does not appear significant.[10]

Of great significance to the later controversy is the fact that the rodent studies were done only with rats (both of the later Toth studies used mice); the other test animals used, according to Coberly's summary, were rabbits and dogs. Separate evaluations of the toxicological database were also carried out by Health and Welfare Canada (HWC) in 1967, prior to the granting of Canadian registration for daminozide.[11] Beginning in 1967, tolerances, or MRLs (Maximum Residue Limits), representing maximum amounts of the pesticide that are allowed to be detected at the point where the food reaches the consumer, were established for residues of daminozide on a wide variety of food products, varying in the United States from 0.2 parts per million (ppm) for eggs to 600ppm for dried tomato pomace (an ingredient in animal feed).

The EPA Public Docket does not list any other toxicological evaluation of daminozide before 1977.[12] Similarly, the list of expert evaluations done within Health and Welfare Canada on this chemical has no entry between the period 18 August 1969 and 29 September 1977.[13] Yet in 1973 Bela Toth, of the Eppley Institute for Research in Cancer at the University of Nebraska, had published the results of a study in which mice supplied with UDMH in their drinking water subsequently developed cancers of the blood vessels, lung, kidney, and liver. (Toth's research group was concerned with the carcinogenic properties of a group of chemicals known as hydrazines.) As indicated above, no notice was taken of this study by regulatory authorities with respect to their daminozide files. The reason is that not until 1980 – as a result of a published study by an official at Health and Welfare Canada – did regulatory personnel become aware of the fact that daminozide could decompose to UDMH under certain conditions, specifically when heat was applied, as in cooking.[14] This study cited a 1967 paper as first indicating that the chemical compound 1,1–dimethylhydrazine (UDMH) itself was "a carcinogen in mice." In apple juices and sauces, heat-processing converts approximately 5 percent of daminozide to UDMH; sometime later, the EPA estimated that the human body converts approximately 1 percent of ingested daminozide into UDMH.[15]

The publication of a 1977 Toth study on daminozide triggered immediate reviews by regulatory scientists, since Toth reported finding that mice that had ingested drinking water treated with daminozide developed rare blood vessel tumours in both sexes, lung tumours in both sexes, and kidney and liver tumours in males. Two aspects of the study are especially relevant to the later controversy. First, Toth hypothesized that UDMH could have contributed to the observed genesis of tumours; second, Toth ended his article with a recommendation that, based on his findings, all uses of daminozide in agriculture should be stopped!

Within months of the study's appearance, scientists at Health and Welfare Canada's Food Directorate had completed two detailed reviews of its findings. The initial review raised a series of questions about the study methodology, similar to those that were raised repeatedly in the United States later on, but it did not call into question (as some American reviewers did subsequently) the entire basis of Toth's scientific methodology. Interestingly, the HWC reviewer went further than Toth had and opined that UDMH was "very probably the causative agent" of the cancers; however, he also remarked, while acknowledging the inadequacy of the existing set of relevant studies, "it seems likely that there is a no effect level for DMH." The reviewer then did a *theoretical* calculation of the (hypothetical) exposure of Canadian consumers to daminozide residues, by multiplying the MRL numbers (e.g., 30ppm for apples) by the average daily consumption of a dozen types of treated foods. The resultant figure (0.038/mg/

kg/day), it was said, yielded a safety factor of 100,000 – that is, the daily average human intake was 100,000 times less than the intake of the laboratory animals in which tumours were found.[16] The reviewer concluded: "The author's [Toth's] suggestion, the discontinuation of SADH [daminozide] use in agriculture, can not be accepted. Therefore no regulatory action is recommended."

The second review was done about two months later and was much more cautious in tone, pointing out that no sampling or residue analysis was being done by HWC either for daminozide or UDMH, so that exposure could not be estimated reliably. It also recommended a regulatory response. No fewer than six separate actions were suggested:

1 Inquire whether there are substitutes for daminozide [the answer was no].
2 Require industry to monitor and report on 1,1–DMH [UDMH] levels in SADH [daminozide].
3 Develop a method for detecting residues of both compounds in foods.
4 Study effects of cooking on conversion of SADH to 1,1–DMH.
5 Request industry carcinogenicity study with SADH in mouse and hamster.
6 Compare metabolism of SADH in rat and mouse.

We know that at least some of these actions were taken, since number four led to the Newsome study referred to earlier. The findings of the Newsome study were a very significant part of the later controversy over Alar; Health and Welfare Canada can take credit for initiating this part of the solution to a scientific puzzle. And the entire tone of this list suggests that the Canadian regulatory authorities would take seriously the issues raised by the Toth article.

Shortly thereafter, another study, commissioned by the U.S. National Cancer Institute (NCI) and published in 1978, found that daminozide triggered uterine cancer in female rats, liver tumours in male mice, and lung tumours in male and female mice. The HWC staff reviewed this study in January 1979 and reported that, since the "no effect levels" were relatively high (3000ppm), and given the marked discrepancies in the whole set of studies (those reviewed by HWC in 1967, Toth, NCI) there was no cause for action, thus concurring with the conclusions of the first, 1977.[17] The next HWC review is dated 18 June 1980 and thus follows the publication of the Newsome study. It refers for the first time to a report on UDMH by an

International Agency for Research on Cancer (IARC) working group in 1973, and concludes that "there is little doubt that 1,1–DMH [UDMH] is a carcinogen in mice ... ." It concluded:

In terms of possible food residues of 1,1–DMH, following cooking of Daminozide residues on food crops, it is not possible to assess hazard. Prudence would indicate that Daminozide residues should be kept as low as possible. Further extensions of use should be opposed, until adequate data on 1,1–DMH carcinogenic potential are available. It would also be advisable to delete all non-essential tolerances.

We can safely assume that the accumulation of these same studies and the EPA staff's own internal reviews of them were the proximate cause of the EPA's announced plans in 1980 to conduct a "special review" of Alar.[18] (The proposed review was subsequently cancelled, following private discussions between the EPA and Uniroyal, and action was limited to a request for the completion of additional scientific studies; this was one of many events that were widely interpreted as reflecting the new Reagan administration's undermining of regulatory agendas.)[19]

The first quantitative risk assessment in the EPA files is a "draft" report dated June 6, 1981 and initially marked "Confidential – not to be released." By this time, the agency was taking into account the new information on UDMH as a breakdown product of daminozide; it assessed the dietary risk for lifetime exposure for the two substances combined as $5.9 \times 10^{-5}$ – that is, about six cases of excess risk for every 100,000 exposed persons (using average residue levels and assuming that both were carcinogens) – and on this basis drew the conclusion that "the risks calculated are significant and constitute an unreasonable adverse effect."[20] In August 1983 the EPA issued yet another data call-in for daminozide and UDMH. Following outside pressure, such as the litigation launched by the NRDC and other groups, and subsequently a new political agenda in Washington, the Special Review was formally (and finally) announced in the *Federal Register* on July 18, 1984.

During this same period Canada's health-risk evaluators continued their "watching brief" on these chemicals. By the end of 1982 they had a host of new studies done by the registrant to evaluate – metabolism, mutagenicity, environmental, and chronic toxicity studies, among others. All of the acute-toxicity studies, involving both laboratory animals and a variety of wildlife species, confirmed the earlier findings of low toxicity for daminozide. That chemical also was not found to be mutagenic, but UDMH (probably) was; the results on the whole seemed to confirm the carcinogenicity of UDMH. This review, dated December 20, 1982, concluded as follows: "Therefore, it is recommended that exposure to 1,1–dimethylhydrazine [UDMH] be *eliminated* or reduced to the lowest possible level" (emphasis added). The Canadian MRLs for daminozide were not changed, however; Alar continued to be used, and no further toxicology evaluation was undertaken for almost two years.

On August 2, 1984 further studies submitted by the registrant were reviewed, with the following recommendation at the end: "Considering the carcinogenic nature of UDMH no further uses of daminozide should be approved and its present use should be restricted as much as possible." Once again the MRLs remained unchanged; apparently the only use to which these conclusions were put was to defend HWC's position that no *extensions* of the previously approved use patterns should be allowed. Unlike the situation in the United States, in the Canadian regulatory system at that time there was no public discussion of expert health-risk evaluations.

The U.S. *Federal Register* notice of July 1984 may be regarded as the first "official" public statement by any governmental regulatory body that the use of daminozide on food crops might pose "unreasonable risks" to consumers. This risk assessment was said to be based on the following findings, resulting from EPA staff evaluations of scientific studies:[21]

1 "daminozide and UDMH cause oncogenic effects in laboratory animals and ... dietary exposure and oncogenic risk are high";
2 "daminozide is oncogenic in laboratory rats and mice";
3 "UDMH ... is oncogenic in laboratory mice and hamsters";
4 "UDMH ... has demonstrated mutagenic activity in both the presence and absence of metabolic activation";
5 UDMH is "a potent animal carcinogen";
6 "The Agency is particularly concerned about UDMH and daminozide dietary exposure to special groups of individuals (especially young children) who consume large quantities of apple products."
7 "The Agency estimates that the dietary risk from daminozide residues is high. Additionally, the Agency estimates that dietary risk from UDMH residues will also be significant."

Of course, it should be noted immediately that under procedures then in force the EPA framed these statements not as conclusive findings but rather as "presumptions" that could be "rebutted" (by the registrant, Uniroyal) through other evidence or arguments.

The quantitative risk assessment is not given in the *Federal Register* notice; instead it appeared one month earlier in "Daminozide: Pesticide Registration Standard and Guidance Document": for dietary exposure to daminozide the risk was given as $3 \times 10^{-4}$, that is, an excess risk for lifetime exposure of three cases in every 10,000 persons (the risk to those applying the chemical was estimated to be in the range of $7.5 \times 10^{-6}$ to $8.4 \times 10^{-5}$). Also in that document the EPA said that it could not quantify the risk from UDMH due to inadequacy of available data; note that this statement appears eleven years after the IARC working group concluded that UDMH is carcinogenic in mice.[22] Three cases in 10,000 is indeed a "relatively high risk"; and yet if, as the Canadian reviewers noted many years earlier, the presumptive tumour-generating effect was based primarily on UDMH, the possible risk level from exposure to the combined effect of SADH and UDMH could be much higher still.

In early 1985 the EPA received new data from Uniroyal including residue data showing that daminozide was present "at significant levels" in both fresh produce and processed foods, and evidence for the first time that daminozide could be converted to UDMH in the human body. By the late summer of that year the EPA had prepared a summary evaluation of daminozide, consisting of its risk assessment, benefits assessment, and risk/benefit analysis, thus concluding the Special Review that was first mooted in 1980. In a press release dated 28 August 1985, EPA announced that it would seek to ban food crop uses of Alar and therefore submitted its summary evaluation, along with a draft notice of intent to cancel the registration of daminozide, to its Scientific Advisory Panel (SAP), an expert group of outside advisers. The SAP was established by the U.S. Congress in 1975 within the terms of the enabling legislation for pesticides (the Federal Insecticide, Fungicide, and Rodenticide Act), and the EPA is required by law to submit its scientific analyses to this body to ascertain that those analyses have been performed according to the accepted canons of science.[23]

The hazard profile of SADH and UDMH as assembled by EPA staff, which would form one of the pillars of the final health-risk assessment, had already been subjected to detailed scrutiny by an in-house group of experts. The Health Effects Division of the EPA's Office of Pesticides and Toxic Substances has a number of standing "peer review" committees for carcinogenic risk and other issues, made up of officials from various offices at the agency. The Toxicology Branch Peer Review Group met on 25 August 1985 with six members in attendance and concluded, after a review of the Toth studies as well as documents related to the dispute with Uniroyal over the conflicting laboratory audits on those studies, that both daminozide and UDMH should be regarded as category $B_2$ carcinogens.[24] It is noteworthy that no mention was made of this judgment at the hearing conducted by the Scientific Advisory Panel just a month later.

The EPA's risk assessment followed the standard format of quantifying health risk as a function of both the nature of the hazard and of the exposure. The conclusions of its hazard profile were that both SADH and UDMH should be classified as "category $B_2$ carcinogens," that is, "probable human carcinogens"; the hazard profile ends with an overall estimate of life-shortening cancer potency ("$Q_1$*"), representing the application of a particular method of extrapolating probable human health effects from the dose-response curves in the animal test data. The decisive point for the future stages of controversy is the following statement (referring to daminozide): "The ... estimates of excess cancer risk presented here are based on the blood vessel tumors observed in the [1977] Toth study, taking into account their life shortening effect"; a similar comment on UDMH made reference to the 1973 Toth study.[25]

Note that at this time (mid-summer 1985) the same studies that had been reviewed exhaustively by the regulatory agencies in both the United States and Canada since 1978 – 1973 Toth, 1977 Toth,[26] and 1978 NCI – were still the chief buttress of the EPA's hazard profile. As indicated earlier, the regulatory scientists in Canada had raised questions (in confidential internal documents) about the Toth methodologies and evaluations from the beginning, without calling into question their basic scientific competence. But for a long time before 1985 a fierce fight over the Toth studies had been waged between EPA staff and Uniroyal's scientific personnel. The Toth studies had been "audited" repeatedly and exhaustively by both the EPA and Uniroyal (a scientific "audit" refers to another appraisal by a recognized scientist of all aspects of a laboratory study, including its methodology, procedures, record-keeping, pathology, and so forth); the two sides could not agree on the results. The EPA's "Draft Position Document" of September 1985 contained an extensive review of these prior audits and a defence of its contention that, despite all criticisms, those studies provided a reliable basis for a toxicological profile of daminozide and UDMH. But as we shall see, this matter was far from settled.

The "Draft Position Document" of September 1985 went on to give an elaborate, quantitative exposure estimate and detailed risk assessment. The exposure assessments were based on what appears to be abundant data on actual residues (in most cases) for both raw and processed food commodities of different types, measured in parts per million, as opposed to the theoretical calculations noted earlier; for each commodity, there is also an estimate of average daily consumption based on consumer survey data. Finally, the risk assessment was done, with this elaborate process of calculation proceeding through three discrete stages:[27]

1 Evaluating the tumour-generating effects in animals and choosing the method of extrapolation to human health effects, resulting in the measure of potency (i.e., the product of the two stages of hazard identification and dose response assessment: $Q_1$*);
2 Measuring the residues (and making estimates about the percentage of the total crop actually treated with the chemical at issue) and choosing figures for average daily consumption for each food commodity separately, resulting in the exposure measure (i.e., the product of two discrete components of exposure assessment);
3 Multiplying and summing the foregoing.

In summary: for each food type, [1] the average daily consumption (g/kg of body weight) is multiplied by [2] the residue level (ppm) to yield [3] an exposure measure (mg/kg/day), which is in turn multiplied by [4] the $Q_1$* to give the risk. For daminozide residues in raw apples: [1] 0.4567 × [2] 4.9 = [3] $2.2 \times 10^{-3}$ × [4] 2 $10^{-2}$ = 1 × $10^{-5}$ to $10^{-6}$. Looking at the total of nineteen different foods, for each of which this calculation was done, the overall excess risk from dietary exposure to daminozide was calculated as $10^{-4}$ (1 in 10,000). The same calculation for UDMH yielded an even higher risk, $10^{-3}$ (1 in 1,000).[28] The latter number – obviously a very high risk – is the one that Paul Lapsley, head of the EPA's Special Review branch, called attention to in public comments made after the press release on the "Position Document"; he also compared the level of risk to that associated with ethylene dibromide (EDB), about which there had been a huge controversy involving public concern over food safety a year or two previously.[29]

The risk-assessment section closed with a brief discussion of occupational exposure calculations and the general uncertainties known to be associated with all such assessments, and with an equally brief reference to the toxicity profiles of three other chemicals, registered for similar uses, that could be considered alternatives to daminozide. It did not, however, provide the comparative, overall risk assessment that would have been the only basis for a judgment that one or more of the alternatives was "better or worse" than daminozide. (We shall see in chapter 8 how a similar situation became a key element in another controversy.)

## EXPERT JUDGMENT (B):
## DISPUTES AMONG EXPERTS

We will restrict ourselves to indicating in general here that competing expert risk assessments were made by other interested parties; as would be expected, lower estimates were offered by the manufacturer, Uniroyal, and higher ones by its chief antagonist, the Natural Resources Defense Council (NRDC). So far as the manufacturer is concerned, Uniroyal seemed to spend most of its energy in seeking to undermine the scientific credibility of the Toth studies, apparently a wise move considering the EPA's almost complete dependence on them for its hazard profile of their product. Uniroyal's detailed response to the *Federal Register* notice, conducted by its own staff but also utilizing outside consultants, took up the three studies (Toth 1973 and 1977, NCI 1978) in turn, concentrating on the two by Toth. Its objections to their scientific procedure were listed under the headings of record-keeping, animal randomization, dose selection, control group, conduct of study and personnel, validation of test material, and quality assurance and pathology. The company concluded: "The oncogenicity studies which the Agency has relied upon to trigger the Special Review for daminozide are of questionable validity and inconclusive to support a significant finding of carcinogenicity."[30] It went on to state:

It is Uniroyal's position that the use of daminozide products does not pose any significant risk to humans. The Eppley [Toth] studies relied on by the Agency are seriously flawed. They are not indicative of adverse toxicological effects. Human exposure from daminozide use is so minute that even if a risk assessment were performed based on the flawed studies, the risk would be negligible – on the order of $10^{-6}$ [1 in 1,000,000] to $10^{-7}$ [1 in 10,000,000].[31]

Thus the range of estimates, from Uniroyal's lowest to the EPA's highest ($10^{-3}$), is four orders of magnitude – a huge gap, but not an unfamiliar one in these types of controversies. The company proposed to undertake new toxicological studies that would avoid the methodological errors of those done by Toth. Figuring the time required for both undertaking and reviewing the studies, this process would consume anywhere from twenty-four to thirty-six months.

On the other side, the NRDC continuously berated the EPA for underestimating daminozide's risk. In comments filed in response to the *Federal Register* notice, the NRDC claimed that problems with the

EPA's methods in calculating such things as dietary and non-dietary exposure suggest that the risk could be higher than $10^{-4}$, but they did not give an alternate quantitative estimate at that time (they did so only five years later).

### Benefits Assessment and the Risk/Benefit Analysis

Information on the economic benefits from daminozide use on food crops had been gathered over the years since it was first registered, and appears in the record in the form of studies submitted by Uniroyal, in huge numbers of letters from growers testifying to their need for this product (many of them initiated by Uniroyal through distribution of form letters to their customers and industry associations), and in the formal benefits assessment calculations by the EPA. We will refer in detail only to the calculations for apples, but this same process was carried out crop by crop for all food uses; we shall give only the summary figures for the remaining crops.

Uniroyal "opened the bidding" by estimating direct benefits to growers alone from daminozide use (or losses in its absence), for apple crops only, at $183 million, with the agency immediately countering that – especially since the chemical was then in use on only one-third of the nation's crop – this figure was wildly overstated, perhaps by a factor of five or six. The EPA then outlined a methodology for this purpose that begins by identifying ten separate benefits:

- increased colour on red varieties;
- firmer fruit at harvest and after a period of storage;
- delayed fruit maturity (extends harvest period);
- prevention of pre-harvest fruit drop;
- delayed development of watercore (internal rotting);
- reduced scalding (a disorder occurring during storage);
- reduced bruising;
- reduced vegetative growth (less pruning);
- promotion of flower-bud initiation;
- reduced fruit cracking.

For half of the above there was no alternative product on the market at the time. Where alternatives were non-existent, the qualitative impacts were assessed individually, focusing in, for example, on the unique benefits of daminozide for growers of McIntosh varieties. Another potential impact would be the shifting of some of the crop

from raw to processed end uses, due to the lower quality of the fresh
fruit. Of course, one of the market effects would be to encourage
substitution of varieties (such as Granny Smith) which did not
depend so heavily on this particular product, and therefore the qualitative impact would cause economic losses for certain producers and
regions (different varieties do better in different regions of North
America) and corresponding opportunities for others. These are the
nature of some of the impacts on users of the product; there is also
the impact on consumers of changing prices in response to supply-
and-demand fluctuations.

All these factors were calculated separately and then summed.[32]
Consumer prices were estimated to increase between 6 and 10 percent (translating into a little over $1 per bushel or 1 to 2¢ per apple
at retail). The net "social benefit" to both producers and consumers
from all of the above changes was estimated to decline, as a result
of the unavailability of daminozide, by anywhere from $60 to $108
million; this represents the conclusion of a theoretically constructed
argument that is said to reflect society's "willingness to pay" for the
benefits created by daminozide.

One of most pertinent aspects of all this money-counting is that
opposing groups such as the NRDC never chose to enter into the
debates about benefits, basing their opposition solely on the notion
of unacceptable health risk. It follows that they never participated in
the discussion of the reasonableness of particular sets of trade-offs
between risks and benefits. This is a common feature of environmental controversies and, indeed, one of the main sources of their
seemingly intractable nature. In many respects the "debates about
risk" among the group of interested parties represent a pseudo-
dialogue in which each party speaks but none listens, preferring not
to hear certain "facts" that others insist are important to their well-
being.

Following the specification of the net reduction in social benefit
for each crop, using the method described above, the EPA proceeded
to the risk/benefit analysis. This glimpse of the completed edifice is
something of a letdown after we have been treated to such a full
view of its elaborate foundations. Following a brief consideration –
and rejection – of the possibility that continued use might be acceptable if the way in which the product was applied to crops was modified, the summary risk and benefits assessments for each crop are
placed side by side; the formula given here for apples is repeated
verbatim for the rest: "After weighing the benefits from daminozide
use against the dietary risks from daminozide use, the Agency has
determined that continued use of daminozide on apples causes

unreasonable adverse effects to human health, and daminozide use on apples should be discontinued."[33] (The only concession to the registrant was that utilization of its product for ornamentals – the sole use originally approved in 1963 – could be continued subject to changes in application methods that would reduce occupational exposure.)

The other parties could be excused if the thought crossed their minds that, after being treated to the EPA's Herculean labours on the separate risk and benefits assessments, the ultimate product seemed rather insubstantial. No further reasoning was offered to assist the audience in moving from the premises (the two intensely quantitative assessments) to the hurried qualitative judgment. No explanation was offered as to how the two radically different measures (cancer risk versus economic benefit) could be compared at all; indeed, if the pun can be forgiven, this is a classic case of "apples and oranges." Thus there is no way to replicate the judgment; it appears arbitrary, a "black box" whose contents are forever hidden from the scrutiny of outsiders. It is hardly surprising that all those who thought that the estimated health risks were exaggerated, or that the economic fate of the users was inconsequential to other interested parties, or both, would be dissatisfied with the result.

Part IV of the EPA's "Draft Position Document" was reserved for the comments of a Scientific Advisory Panel, and only two weeks after the document was issued it became the subject of a formal hearing before such a panel (consisting of eight members); the verbatim transcript of its proceedings totals 167 pages. The EPA had no fewer than thirty-three officials present, the industry had almost as many, and there were as many again from other constitutencies, including the media, environmentalists, growers, and politicians (the NRDC did not attend, perhaps anticipating a set-up).

The benefits assessment played a minor role in the discussion, although Uniroyal's witnesses "upped the ante" again, estimating that 20 to 25 percent of the entire U.S. crop would be lost without daminozide, and referring to claims by Washington State growers that their losses alone would total $275 million annually. Virtually the entire discussion revolved around the carcinogenicity studies and the resultant risk assessments. The senior EPA official present told the panel: "The issue we have asked, needed [sic] the Panel's recommendation on is whether the currently available data support the weight of evidence conclusion that daminozide and UDMH are carcinogenic in animals, and has [sic] the potential to be carcinogenic in humans." But the panel chairman responded, referring implicitly to the Toth studies: "I would like to ask ... in view of this desire to get better science into risk assessment, whatever has induced the Agency to suddenly dash into this whole issue with data that frankly just don't seem to exist. This is not science."[34]

The EPA and Uniroyal experts argued again about their elaborate and conflicting audits of Toth's laboratory practices; one of Uniroyal's experts, who was previously Associate Director for Toxicological Sciences in the Bureau of Foods at the U.S. Food and Drug Administration, stated: "Now, let's go to UDMH, and, again, the Toth studies, to me, are just – they are not even within consideration. I don't even really want to call it science."[35] If we think back to our earlier discussion about the careful expert reviews on the Toth studies done by the Canadian officials, we will recall certain reservations about methods and findings, but nothing approaching the extreme views presented by Uniroyal's experts or the panel chairman at the SAP hearing.

At the resumption of hearings the following morning the panel's chairman gave his response on behalf of the panel to the request for its evaluation of the adequacy of the EPA's risk assessment (there were apparently no dissenting views):

The data available are inadequate to perform a qualitative risk assessment. The Toth Alar studies do give rise to concern over the potential oncogenicity of daminozide. The Panel feels that the other studies are equivocal. None of the present studies are considered suitable for quantitative risk assessment. Given the fact that the Toth data have been available for eight years, the Panel does not understand why EPA has neither requested, nor the registrant initiated in a more timely fashion, additional oncogenicity testing. Quantitative risk assessment cannot be appropriately carried out until data become available.[36]

The criticism of the EPA's inability to ensure that replacement studies were undertaken promptly by the registrant, once the registrant had raised fundamental objections to the published Toth work, is certainly well placed. But this rebuke was not what garnered public attention for the Scientific Advisory Panel. A few years later some congressmen levelled charges of pro-industry bias against certain SAP members, and the credibility of the EPA's entire scientific review process was called into question.[37]

Federal law requires the EPA to consult its Scientific Advisory Panels on interpretive matters in scientific risk assessment, but the panels' views are not binding on it.[38] Thus, following the SAP's rejection of its risk assessment, the EPA was certainly in a position to choose whether or not to back down on its proposed cancellation of Alar uses on food crops. The EPA backed down: on 22 January 1986 its press release stated that it was "following the panel's determination that the available animal studies are not adequate to characterize the potential risk of daminozide to human health." The press release also revealed that during the preceding fall the U.S. Department of Agriculture had intervened in the dispute with an argument (and 500 pages of supporting documentation!)[39] "that EPA had underestimated the benefits of continued use" and had "urged the agency to reevaluate the need for cancellation." The EPA's actions therefore were limited to the following: (1) requiring the registrant to produce new animal-feeding studies, a process that it was said would take four years to complete (although the EPA also said that interim data might be available in two years); (2) requiring the registrant to produce new residue studies; (3) reducing permitted application rates of the chemical on apples by 25 percent and reducing the MRL for raw apples downwards from 30 to 20ppm. These provisions were accompanied by an astonishing revision of its earlier, publicly announced data on exposure:

The agency has also made new exposure estimates using the actual percentage of crops treated with daminozide. Taking into consideration these new estimates and the actions to reduce exposure, the agency now calculates that exposure to daminozide will only be *10–15 percent* [our emphasis] of the levels the agency used in issuing its notice of intent to propose the cancellation of this product. Original estimates had been based on maximum exposure levels.[40]

It is hard not to suspect some bad faith here. The EPA sought to disguise the extent of its own earlier bias (towards the highest possible number for exposure) by wrapping together the effects of its backtracking on the data already accumulated, on the one hand, and on the other the *future* impact of the reductions in application rates it was mandating. Remember that the original, elaborate figuring of exposure estimates had been publicly advanced by these same officials only four months earlier! An informal calculation that removes the impact of the future measures still leaves us with the conclusion that in September 1985 the EPA had overstated (deliberately?) exposure to daminozide and UDMH residues by *up to a factor of seven*.

This ultimately unsatisfying risk-assessment debate would go on for another five years, but it is at this point that the forces driving the Alar issue shift from the "expert" to the "public" sphere. The NRDC, which had been engaged in legal and other manoeuvres against the EPA for its handling of pesticide regulatory matters (including daminozide) for some time already, objected immediately to the reversal of the EPA's position.[41] More to the point was the consumer boycott campaign launched by Ralph Nader and others, which before long began to have results, such as the announcements by the nationwide chain of Safeway stores that they would no longer sell apples treated with Alar, and similar announcements by the major baby-food manufacturers that they would not use Alar-treated products in their processed foods. The remaining notable steps in the evolution of the risk-assessment controversy itself are summarized in Appendix II at the end of this chapter.

### ALAR: "WHAT DID THE PUBLIC KNOW, AND WHEN?"

The first "public interest" entry in the EPA's Public Docket is a letter dated 6 March 1981 from the Environmental Resources Group, calling for a special review of daminozide. In the period before 1985 almost the only letters received from the public, judging by the contents of the Public Docket, were from growers testifying to the benefits of Alar and urging the EPA to maintain its availability.[42] Almost all of these were the result of a letter-writing campaign initiated by Uniroyal. The first calls in the correspondence file for cancellation of registration come in August 1984, after the announcement that the EPA's long-delayed "special review" would be undertaken, but for another full year and a half the supporting letters continue to outnumber the negative ones.

In other words, the preponderance of "public sentiment" as demonstrated by the volume of correspondence in the EPA files – which is pretty much the only indicator at this point – continued to weigh in Alar's favour. If the Public Docket's contents are a reliable guide, this continued for the five-month period between the announcement of proposed cancellation (August 1985) and the EPA's recantation (January 1986).[43] It is possible that Alar's opponents did not seek to generate a public letter-writing campaign against it during this time because they anticipated that the EPA would be carrying through with its announced intention to cancel.

This supposition is supported by a survey of coverage in *The New York Times*: there is not a single article on Alar before 30 August 1985, the day of the EPA's possibly unintended press release. Even after a flurry of interest during the first half of 1986, following the EPA's reversal of its position, the subject again disappeared from the newspaper; there is only one small item directly related to Alar in all of 1987, and only one in all of 1988.

In the August 1985 *New York Times* article, only apple growers and officials from the EPA and Uniroyal are quoted, indicating that no

Table 6-2
Overview of Quantitative Risk Assessments in the Public Domain

| "Number" | Source |
|---|---|
| $1.0 \times 10^{-3}$ | P. Lapsley, Senior EPA official, August 1985 [UDMH] |
| $9.1 \times 10^{-4}$ | NRDC, upper-bound estimate, February 1989* |
| $3.0 \times 10^{-4}$ | EPA Registration Standard, June 1984 [Daminozide] |
| $4.5 \times 10^{-5}$ | J. Moore, Senior EPA official, January 1989 |
| $9.0 \times 10^{-6}$ | J. Moore, Senior EPA official, January 1989** |
| $1.3 \times 10^{-7}$ | Uniroyal Chemical Co., 1985*** |
| $4.0 \times 10^{-12}$ | California Department of Food and Agriculture, 1989*** |

The first number is 1 case in 1,000; the second is just over 9 cases in 10,000; the sixth is slightly more than 1 case in 10,000,000; the seventh is 4 cases in one trillion.

* Note especially that the NRDC's number is not the highest the public would have heard at some point during the controversy.
** This is the risk to children *for an 18-month exposure only*; we place it here because it would have been easy for the public to become confused concerning the difference between lifetime exposure (represented by the previous number) and this special case.
*** We can safety assume that these numbers were known, especially to growers and other interested parties on the industry side.

environmental group was sufficiently "visible" on this issue at that time to attract the press's attention. EPA officials sought to play down possible public fears. Jack Moore, the senior administrator from this point right through the 1989 endgame, is quoted as saying: "I do not have an immediate concern about existing food products that may contain daminozide residues." Another agency official averred: "If we thought the risk was that great, we'd yank this stuff off the market."[44] On the other hand, the growers made alarming statements. One in New York, the nation's second-largest apple-producing state after Washington, said a ban on Alar would have "tremendous" effects; in Michigan, another major source, one large grower, referring to the time before Alar became available, exclaimed: "We know how we lived prior to this, and everyone says, 'Dear God, don't let us go back to that.'"[45]

It may be useful to recall at this point the range of the cancer-risk assessment "numbers" that various segments of the public may have heard from the principal interested parties in the period after the fall of 1985, when the controversy "went public." The list is assembled in Table 6-2 and is made up of a sample of statements made during the period 1985–89 (it overlooks the difference between daminozide and UDMH, on the grounds that this was not an essential difference from the standpoint of the public perception of risk).

There is no coverage again until January 1986. About a week before the EPA's press release announcing its about-face, an article revealed that Gerber Products, the largest manufacturer of baby-food products in the United States, had had its chemists looking for daminozide residues in samples of applesauce and apple juice. For the first time, the debate had been broadened. Spokespersons for two groups, Public Voice for Food and Health Policy (a consumers' organization) and the National Coalition Against the Misuse of Pesticides (an environmental group), are quoted in strongly negative terms, alongside the usual voices of Uniroyal, the growers, and the EPA. A grower from the State of Washington calls Alar "one of the greatest chemicals ever developed." The article discusses at length the controversy over the scientific studies and the SAP's rejection of the EPA's initial position in favour of cancellation; however, later in the story an EPA official appears unrepentant: "We are concerned because the evidence indicates daminozide and its breakdown product are potential carcinogens."[46]

The way in which the EPA presented to the citizenry the reversal of its position in January 1986 could only have increased the public's disquiet. Jack Moore said that it would take "more than four years" to acquire the new data that was needed to replace the studies that the SAP had ruled defective. Worse, he explained that once a product has been approved for use, the agency's enabling legislation puts the burden of proof on the government to demonstrate that its continued use is unacceptable. He remarked: "If this was a new product it would not be allowed on the market." In effect, he was saying that the agency still agreed with its original position, whatever the SAP thought! And for the first time the NRDC's voice is heard in the public controversy, with the public release of its letter to the EPA calling for a ban on daminozide.

By this time all of the major baby-food manufacturers, as well as Mott's, a well-known maker of processed fruit products for the general consumer market, had notified their suppliers that they would no longer accept Alar-treated apples beginning with the 1986 crop. The food processors stated that they had no position on the safety of Alar, but that they were faced with pressure from consumers and had to act to protect the integrity of their brands. Then *The New York Times* published a long article on Alar in May 1986, and once again the growers' dilemma was the lead-in to the story.[47] The growers whose problems were recounted in this story told once again of the wide range of benefits that this product had bestowed upon them. The new element was a statement from Nabisco, owner of the well-known "Planter's" label of peanut products, defending its refusal to order its suppliers to stop using Alar (the peanut crop always represented the second-largest use). There is no evidence that the same groups that were pressuring baby-food producers and supermarket chains to refuse Alar-treated apple supplies made a special target out of the peanut crop, or any of the numerous other fruit crops on which Alar continued to be sprayed. This may well have been a tactical move to concentrate the pressure at what was perceived to be the most vulnerable point: not only did apples represent the largest use pattern – at that time about 40 percent of the U.S. crop was treated – but apples have a special place in food lore, especially for children (in this respect they are similar to milk).[48]

By July 1986 all of the major U.S. supermarket chains, led by Safeway, had notified their suppliers that they would no longer buy apples treated with daminozide.[49] Another important element entered the public perception of events at this time, namely the characterization of Alar as a "fruit cosmetic";[50] in other words, the impression was conveyed that the reddening effect on McIntosh apples was the chief reason Alar was used (which was not the case, certainly from the growers' viewpoint, although it was one element among many others in the group of advantages it brought). To the extent to which this theme was emphasized, it would be detrimental to public acceptability of Alar. As Lester Lave of Carnegie Mellon University has remarked in another context: "Is having brightly colored maraschino cherries worth even a miniscule threat (the risk of red food color is estimated to be 0.02 cancers per million lifetimes)?"[51]

By this time the party under greatest pressure was clearly the apple growers. Although their chemical supplier stoutly maintained that there was no reason for the public to fear its product, the growers' largest institutional buyers saw no profit in resisting the consumer advocates, as well as the many individuals who had become concerned about their children's health and who were now writing to corporate executives, and many growers started to abandon Alar. The case of the British Columbia apple industry is instructive in this regard.[52]

British Columbia is second only to Ontario among Canada's five apple-growing provinces. Reactions from the B.C. Fruit Growers Association (BCFGA) were quoted in the Vancouver press as soon as the first widely reported story broke (the August 1985 EPA press release announcing proposed cancellation of Alar's registration). The BCFGA's president reiterated the industry's confidence in the chemical and said that the possible health effects were "no cause for alarm."[53] But the BCFGA reacted immediately to the July 1986 news of supermarket boycotts in the United States (where much of its market lies). On July 18, the same president told his 1,740 association members to stop using Alar;[54] it was the only provincial industry group to take this step, and in doing so it apparently broke a prior agreement with its counterparts in the rest of Canada. The decision was made jointly by the BCFGA, the board of directors of B.C. Tree Fruits Ltd. (BCTF), and the board of directors of the five packing houses contracted to BCTF. According to one person who participated in this decision, the growers had become aware of the controversy surrounding Alar over the preceding year through the media, but it only began to affect them when this information reached their buyers, who started questioning them regarding their use of Alar and requested proof from BCTF that its produce was Alar-free. As a result, the BCFGA, the BCTF, and the packing houses jointly "looked at what was happening" in the United States, considered "the risk in the market" and "the risk of being shut out of markets," and then "decided that it was in their best interest as marketers" to stop using Alar.[55] This move was estimated to reduce gross returns by $2 million on the $8-million crop in 1986. Compliance with this recommendation was voluntary, but in 1987 all member growers that sent their apples to any of the five packing houses contracted to B.C. Tree Fruits Ltd. had to sign affidavits certifying that they had not used Alar on their crop.

In considering the quick response of food producers and retailers to the pressure from consumer advocates, it is useful to recall that many of these same parties had gone through an unpleasant episode involving residues of a suspect chemical in food in the not-too-distant past. The well-publicized controversy over a fungicide called ethylene dibromide (EDB) surfaced in late 1983 and continued into 1984.[56] EDB, a pesticide widely used for many years around the world as a fumigant to prevent the growth of highly toxic moulds, primarily in grain, was found to be a potent carcinogen in new tests on laboratory animals after its EPA review. But there is general agreement that, following an announcement to this effect, the EPA mishandled the public perception of risk, leading to exaggerated fears of short-term health risks that saw health officials in a number of states scrambling to restaurants and hotel chains to test their menu items for EDB residues. Pancake and cake mixes and some seventy-seven grain-based commodities were recalled from wholesalers and retail shelves. The economic consequences were enormous: 7.7 billion bushels of grain and massive amounts of processed foods were destroyed.

Then, in the summer of 1985, about 1,400 people on the west coast of the United States fell ill after eating watermelons, suffering from diarrhoea, nausea, vomiting, and blurred vision. These watermelons were found to be tainted with residues of the pesticide aldicarb, an insecticide registered for use on cotton and ornamental trees and on numerous edible crops such as dry beans, bananas, potatoes, and peanuts – but not watermelons. The problem was traced to California farms that were illegally applying aldicarb products to their watermelon crops. Unfortunately, retailers typically first learned of all this from their local media rather than through official channels. In early June of 1985 about 125 people in the British Columbia Lower Mainland area and 25 on Vancouver Island had become ill after eating English cucumbers, and a contamination warning was issued by the federal health department against English cucumbers grown in British Columbia. Cucumbers distributed by the Western Greenhouse Growers Cooperative Association of Surrey were found to be contaminated by aldicarb and had to be recalled from the Lower Mainland and Washington State. These experiences go a long way to explaining why food retailers reacted quickly when the reports of possible problems with Alar-treated produce reached them.

As the Alar issue gradually faded away from public awareness again during 1987 and 1988, the large array of new scientific studies arranged by the registrant was underway, and, as it was later revealed, the NRDC was quietly preparing its own expert risk assessment. Then, as we have seen, on the last day of January 1989 the EPA made its second public announcement of its intent to ban food uses of daminozide, based on interim results from the new studies. In explaining why the agency would not take immediate action to suspend all food uses, Jack Moore said that, because Alar was registered before 1972, when new rules took effect, the burden of proof for unacceptability fell upon the government, and the agency did not yet have sufficient proof in hand to take that step.[57]

The "60 Minutes" program broadcast on February 26 opened with Ed Bradley introducing the NRDC report, titled *Intolerable Risk*, with these words: "The most potent cancer-causing agent in our food supply is a substance sprayed on apples to keep them on trees longer and make them look better." The most telling moment, however, came during the interview with a senior EPA administrator, the familiar Jack Moore, who patiently explained for a mass television audience the constraints imposed by existing law on his agency's ability to remove from the marketplace a substance that it considered to pose an unacceptable risk to health.

The next day, the NRDC report was unveiled for public distribution at media conferences held simultaneously in twelve U.S. cities. A week later additional publicity was generated when actress Meryl Streep announced the formation of a new group, "Mothers and Others for Pesticide Limits," and television footage showed her busily scrubbing raw fruits and vegetables with dish detergent (which, some experts would say, undoubtedly had never been assessed scientifically for the possibly toxic residues it might deposit on the food). School boards across the country removed apples from children's lunch menus. So alarmed were the U.S. federal authorities by the intensity of the public reaction that three agencies (the EPA, the Food and Drug Administration, and the Department of Agriculture), encouraged by the White House, issued a joint statement: "The Government believes it is safe for Americans to eat apples."[58] (The word "safe" is not one that the EPA would ordinarily use in these circumstances.) It did not help. A few months later, fourteen scientific bodies in the United States, with a total membership of over 100,000, made a stab at expert communication with the public, issuing a statement urging consumers to realize that, according to reliable risk assessments, the greatest threats to health from food contaminants had their source not in residues from industrial chemicals but from the actions of naturally occurring bacteria, fungi, and moulds. This too was insufficient to save Alar.

Consternation in various quarters increased when the *Wall Street Journal* revealed some time later that in October 1988 the NRDC had hired a professional firm, Fenton Communications, to plan a systematic campaign of media coverage for the release of its soon-to-be-completed report. Fenton made a deal with "60 Minutes" for exclusive coverage of the initial story and with several popular magazines for follow-up stories, and devised the two-stage strategy involving Meryl Streep. The results were indeed impressive, as Fenton Communications itself boasted in advertising the firm's abilities to other public interest groups:

Media coverage included two segments on CBS 60 Minutes, the covers of Time and Newsweek, the Phil Donahue show, multiple appearances on Today, Good Morning America, and CBS This Morning, several stories in each of the network evening newscasts, MacNeil/Lehrer, multiple stories in the N.Y. Times, Washington Post, L.A. Times, and newspapers around the country, three cover stories in USA Today, People, four women's magazines with a combined circulation of 17 million (Redbook, Family Circle, Women's Day and New Woman), and thousands of repeat stories in local media around the nation and the world ... . Consumer feedback devices were built into the campaign, including self-published book sales and the first use of a 900 phone number by a non-profit group ... .

And that was the score for round one. Round two, featuring Meryl Streep, followed a similar scenario.[59]

There has been a good deal of outrage vented and nonsense penned since that story appeared in the *Wall Street Journal*, dealing with the allegedly underhanded nature of the service provided to the NRDC by Fenton Communications. A report prepared by the British office of Uniroyal added spice to the criticism, which was especially intense in industry circles, by pointing out that the founder of Fenton Communications had supported "a variety of anti-establishment left-wing causes" in his youth and that his firm "has had clients ranging from the left to the far left."[60]

David Fenton's political views aside, the substantive basis for complaint about his firm's outstanding service to the NRDC is hard to fathom. Surely no one doubts that all major firms, as well as most governments these days, hire communications and public relations strategists at great expense to get out whatever message they wish to sell to their target audiences in the most effective possible manner. The contents of those communications occupy all the points along the spectrum of truthfulness and persuasiveness, as judged from the standpoint of individuals in the various audiences. Why would anyone think that an organization such as the NRDC, which had a message to sell and the means to do so, was not entitled to develop a professionally crafted strategy in order achieve the maximum possible dispersal for that message? One can read about similar campaigns both for products and for "concepts" or images (social marketing) every day. For example, presumably the critics of Fenton Communications would be equally alarmed at the strategy devised in 1991 by Ketcham Communications for Clorox Co., which was worried that Greenpeace would extend their campaign against chlorine from the pulp and paper industry to household bleaching agents (which do not in fact contain chlorine). Ketchum recommended to Clorox that it be prepared to dispatch teams of compliant scientists to counteract Greenpeace media events and to file slander lawsuits not only against Greenpeace members but against any journalist foolish enough to report on their activities. When Ketcham's strategy proposal to Clorox was leaked to Greenpeace, which promptly publicized it, Clorox spokespersons quickly distanced themselves from their adviser's over-eager methods.

Critics might be equally alarmed at the elaborate pre-emptive publicity strike against "60 Minutes" launched by the Glutamate Association, whose members make and use monosodium glutamate (MSG), which is widely employed throughout the entire food industry. The association had learned well in advance of the broadcast date that CBS was planning a "60 Minutes" segment on adverse health affects associated with MSG, and together with the International Food Information Council hired Nichols Dezenhall Communications Management Group to concoct a counter-offensive, with the objective of ensuring that MSG did not go the way of Alar.[61]

There are one or two other steps to recount in the public's knowledge base about this issue. After the "60 Minutes" broadcast, Canadian consumers and institutions such as school boards reacted much as their American counterparts did, by besieging their provincial and local government officials via national toll-free telephone lines and other means with requests for further explanations and, above all, reassurance about their children's health. As the national regulatory authority in such matters, Agriculture Canada got many of these calls, as they had over the years since 1986. The general tenor of Agriculture Canada's message is indicated by the following statement from mid-1987: "A large body of data exists to substantiate the position that use of daminozide does not represent a health hazard at this time. There is, however, some controversy on this issue and we will be closely monitoring new information as it emerges."[62] During the period of intense publicity beginning in late February 1989, however, the Food Directorate of Health and Welfare Canada bore the brunt of responsibility for answering to consumers on behalf of the Canadian regulatory system as a whole.

The Canadian government had decided that the new events did not warrant a change in its established position, namely, that while recent studies were being evaluated regularly and therefore the situation could change at any time, there was no cause for public alarm or different regulatory action based on what was known then, largely because the actual residues of both daminozide and UDMH on Canadian produce were so low and thus the safety factor margin was correspondingly very high. Under Canadian regulations, MRLs for daminozide were still set at 30 ppm for apples and sweet cherries; levels of UDMH could not exceed 0.1 ppm for any food.[63] Federal food inspection studies conducted in 1989 found the highest level of daminozide residues on raw domestic apples during 1986–1987 was 4.1 ppm (there were no detectable residues of UDMH); samples of domestic apple juice reached a maximum of 0.53 ppm for daminozide and 0.03 ppm for UDMH – the latter figure is 3 parts in 100 million. The corresponding figures for highest recorded levels of daminozide and UDMH on imported apples were 2.3 ppm and 0.02 ppm respectively, and for imported apple juice concentrate up to 0.47 ppm for daminozide and no detectable residues of UDMH.

In the days following the "60 Minutes" segment, the HWC Food Directorate's game spokesperson, Diane Kirkpatrick, fielded innumerable interview requests from the press, radio, and television, including an appearance on the CBC's popular interview program "The Journal," where Barbara Frum badgered her unmercifully, since Kirkpatrick would not budge from her position that no change in the government's existing position was warranted. This position was set down in a bulletin, parts of which follow:

Currently the [new rodent] studies are approximately half-way to their completion. Preliminary results from two of these studies show that UDMH is not carcinogenic ... . In the third study, which is a study of high dose application of UDMH in mice, preliminary data showed malignancy at the highest dose tested. A lower dose is being tested in this study and preliminary data so far show no malignancy at this dose. The findings of malignancy at the highest dose is inconclusive. Malignancy may have been due to certain "confounding" factors other than UDMH which make the findings of malignant tumors difficult to interpret.

Recent monitoring has shown Alar residues well below regulatory limits. Residues of the Alar breakdown product UDMH were not detected in most cases, and in the few where residues appeared, they were at very low levels (parts per billion).

Based on the information currently available, there is no evidence that Canadian consumers, including children, are exposed to hazardous levels of Alar or UDMH. Although the preliminary results of one high-dose mouse study showed problems at the highest dose tested, the Health Protection Branch estimates that a child would have to consume approximately 250,000 times more than their [sic] present daily intake of apples and apple products (such as juice, applesauce, etc.) in order to reach this high dose level.[64]

These themes were reiterated in the press and electronic-media interviews. The "bottom line" was clear: HWC was not going to jump on the EPA bandwagon and propose cancellation based on the preliminary results of the new studies.

In one interview, Kirkpatrick was quoted as saying that she felt "very sympathetic and sad" about consumers who had to sort out for themselves these conflicting expert views. The Consumers Association of Canada publicly supported HWC,[65] while Canadian environmental groups were furiously denouncing those same officials. Friends of the Earth had Alar "at the top of our 'really bad' list of pesticides," and environmental lawyer Toby Vigod said: "I think it's a risky product used largely for cosmetic purposes, and we should ban it." Most telling was the remark of a Canadian mother who said that her children drank huge quantities of apple juice and that she was especially bitter about having to deal with so much conflicting information.[66]

Our final entry is from a petition to the EPA from the U.S. Consumers Union in April 1989. Consumers Union had done independent testing of residues and research on use patterns and reported these with its own recommendations:

(1) finding: daminozide residues generally are lower than EPA assumptions but there are exceptions in the samples;

(2) finding: Alar is being used on a higher proportion of the total crop than EPA assumes, and use appears to be increasing again since the low point in 1986;

(3) conclusion: EPA has probably underestimated exposure during the period when cancellation proceedings are under way;

(4) EPA should replace the existing 20 ppm tolerance with an interim tolerance of 0.1 ppm for processed apple products.[67]

In the May 1989 issue of its magazine, *Consumer Reports*, the organization reiterated its call for a ban on daminozide. In that month also the International Apple Institute announced that its members would no longer use Alar, and shortly thereafter Uniroyal negotiated an agreement with the EPA whereby its product was voluntarily withdrawn for food crop uses from the marketplace.

## CODA

The answer to the question posed in our chapter title is that no one in society – neither individual producers, consumers, nor interested groups – benefits from the type of controversy that unfolded in the Alar case.

Some years later, with respect to a different but no less contentious issue involving health and environmental risks, a consensus-building exercise involving a wide range of interested parties would be brought into being by a government agency that decided to accept those other parties as partners in risk management decision-making; other agencies participated at the table, some actively co-operated with the exercise, and some provided funding for the expenses associated with this process. The unions emerged as decisive players, and occupational risk was at the forefront of discussions. Environmental groups continued to participate in the process despite their stated dislike for the risk/benefit trade-offs that all the other parties insisted on bringing to the table, in part because they saw that these matters were so vital to the situation of the unions. The industry participants demonstrated in a number of specific ways, including financial commitments for a research program aimed at delivering credible worker-exposure assessments, that they were serious about co-operating with all other parties on a long-term strategy to follow the ALARA rule, "as low as reasonably achievable," with respect to the health and environmental impacts of the products they sell.

It actually happened in British Columbia starting in 1989, and the story is recounted in chapter 8.

### APPENDIX 6.1

*A Methodology for the Study of Risk Controversies*

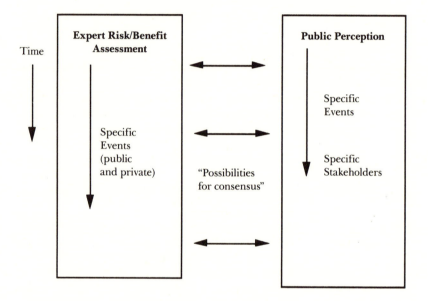

In this model, the "possibilities for consensus" depend upon such factors as:

- the relation between the two spheres as a *developing* phenomenon over time;
- the type of information base, in each sphere, as it evolves over time;
- the timing of specific events;
- how scientific knowledge is used at various times;
- priorities and choices of various stakeholders;
- whether a competent agency "assumes responsibility for" attempting to resolve the controversy at a particular juncture in the sequence of events; and
- other factors peculiar to each case.

Briefly described, the method is as follows. The material chosen for analysis is the record of a long-running controversy over a specific health or environmental risk – in the Alar case, the chemicals daminozide and UDMH. In Step One, the analysis seeks to follow the scientific understanding and description of the risk associated with its use, as documented in published and unpublished reports by industry sources, governments, and independent researchers. A special attempt is made to identify disagreements in the expert assessments of risk, for example between those working for industry and regulators working for governments, and to describe the processes whereby those disagreements are "negotiated," resolved, or exacerbated (public and private informal meetings, formal hearings, court cases, etc.). The impact of new scientific findings that appear at specific times is also watched for.

Accompanying the technical assessment of risk is often an equally technical description of the economic and other benefits associated with the use of a chemical such as daminozide, and also information on the evaluation processes used by government regulators in different jurisdictions to "balance" benefits against risks in order to arrive at a decision that will withstand a variety of challenges from different parties in different venues (the courts, the media, peer review, and so on). Tracking the interplay between the technical assessment of both risks and benefits becomes part of the study, because changes on either side can affect the risk manager's judgment that "benefits outweigh risks," or vice versa: for example, where a purely quantitative calculation is being used, a recalculation upwards of economic benefits (while the risk estimates remain unchanged) can itself reverse a risk-management decision. Finally, since industrial chemicals are used worldwide, both scientific assessments and public controversies may be occurring in different countries, within the same or different time-frames. The interplay among events in a number of countries may be a factor in the making of risk-management decisions.

In summary, Step One may be characterized by the attempt to answer the following question: "What did the experts know, and when did they know it?" Step Two traces the evolution of public controversy with an analogous question: "What did the public know, and when did they know it?" Here we are interested in how the public perception of risk and benefit was formed, what awareness there was of the evolving state of scientific understanding of the relevant issues, and precisely how a particular environmental or health hazard became controversial. The sources for this part of the study are newspaper accounts, the record of public hearings or inquiries, activities of public interest groups, and correspondence received by industry, government agencies, etc. Above all else, the exact chronology of events becomes very important: we seek to "match" the parallel tracks of the two dimensions (technical risk and perceived risk) to see when each is or is not influenced by the other, and why.

In Step Three, we examine closely all of the main points of divergence between technical and perceived risk and look especially for the risk communication exchanges, if any, that occurred at those points. We ask, for example: What effort, if any, did risk managers make to explain clearly to the public the risk and benefit assessments they had conducted? What effort, if any, did risk managers make to understand thoroughly the nature of public concerns? We also ask: What events fuelled public concern? What was the nature of media reporting of relevant events? Above all, the following overriding question is posed: As the public awareness of the issue was developing, did any agency seek to "take responsibility" for the issue and seek to forge a workable consensus among a broad range of interest groups? If so, what happened? If not, can we identify (in retrospect) any potential candidates for that role, and suggest – in the light of all relevant factors prevailing at a certain time – what that agency might have done?

## APPENDIX 6.2

### Expert Risk Assessments of Daminozide and UDMH, 1986–1989[68]

1. April 1986: EPA's reply to the NRDC letter states: "The Agency does not now believe it can demonstrate the oncogenicity of these substances [daminozide and UDMH] nor can it quantify the risk attributable to exposure to them."

2. January – June 1986: The Health departments in 3 eastern U.S. states join the risk-assessment debate with detailed reviews of the scientific issues and the data in the Toth and other studies. The New York DOH's Bureau of Toxic Substance Assessment supports the EPA's original Sept. 1985 position; in response to a critique from a scientist at Cornell, apparently solicited by an official at the New York Department of Agriculture, the DOH replies with an unyielding defence of its earlier paper. Maine's Bureau of Health also has its toxicologists join the fray; they agree with the classifications of both substances as probable human carcinogens. Scientists at Harvard's School of Public Health and the University of Massachusetts also write to the EPA with their toxicological assessments; in the former case, they also claim there is unacceptable worker exposure (which is not otherwise mentioned in the debate). The Department of Public Health in the State of Massachusetts joins the other two in urging far lower tolerance levels, and notes that Massachusetts has instituted lower levels under its own authority.

3. May & July 1986: NRDC brief and then formal (legal) petition – joined by the states of Maine and New York – that reviews the carcinogenicity and exposure data and demands the setting of a zero tolerance. State of Massachusetts also supports NRDC position.

4. January 1987: EPA's reply to the petition, reviewing the usual studies once again and maintaining the position it adopted in January 1986.

5. June 1987: HWC does risk assessment of UDMH (official calls it a "guess-timate" due to inadequate database and says that adequate data required to set an ADI will not be available until late 1990). Concludes: "(1) The data do not indicate that UDMH is a probable human carcinogen (primarily because it is positive only in the mouse). (2) The experimental data on which the estimates are based are poor." Recommends an ADI – using a 5000 fold safety factor – of 0.5 ug/kg bw/day; does not change MRLS (for apples, still 30ppm).

6. April 1988: EPA letter to the International Apple Institute (Virginia), noting that the preliminary data submissions from the new studies being done by the registrant "are suggestive of tumor formation in test animals caused by dietary exposure to daminozide and UDMH."

7. 1986–89: The EPA Special Review Public Docket on Daminozide lists annual bibliographies of studies on daminozide or related compounds submitted to EPA's Office of Pesticides Programs. There are a total of 339 scientific studies submitted between 1986 and March 1989 – which gives some idea of the "regulatory burden." (Koren [p. 242] notes that there are 40,000 scientific studies on the 600 registered pesticides' active ingredients in EPA files.)

8. 31 January 1989: Press Release: EPA "is accelerating the process which will propose cancellation of the food uses of daminozide." EPA administrator Jack Moore states: "There is an inescapable and direct correlation between exposure to UDMH and the development of life-threatening tumors in test mice ... [And] the receipt of additional data on daminozide continues to heighten the concern about possible cancer risks." So far as the quantitative risk assessment is concerned, "the agency has preliminarily estimated the lifetime risk of cancer for adults due to dietary exposure to daminozide to be 4.5 persons per 100,000 (or $4.5 \times 10^{-5}$)." In a letter of the same date to the International Apple Institute, the increased risk for a child for just the eighteen-month period (until July 1990) when legal tolerances for daminozide would expire was estimated at $9 \times 10^{-6}$.

9. January–March 1989: HWC completes review of the new studies from the registrant on product chemistry, metabolism, analytical methodology,

residues, and environmental fate (no new toxicology data analysed). MRLS unchanged. Regulatory position as of March 1989 is focussed on the fact that that actual residue levels are far below the MRLs: for daminozide, a mean level of 0.71 ppm for raw apples and 0.29 ppm for apple juice; for UDMH, 0.001 ppm for raw apples and 0.006 ppm for apple juice (in many samples there was no detectable residue at the limit of detection, which would be in parts per billion). Conclusion (at 03/03/89): "The level of UDMH purported to have caused cancer in mice is equivalent to 23 mg/kg body weight/day (i.e. the highest dose tested). Thus, the mean intake of 0.02 ug/kg body weight/day by a child 1–4 yrs old who consumes apples, apple juice, and apple sauce every day is approximately 1,150,000 times less than the dose causing a carcinogenic response in the mouse. The worst case intake of 0.08 ... is approximately 287,500 times less ..."

10. Late February 1989: Release of NRDC report (see Appendix 6–3)

11. April 1989: EPA's Health Effects Division's Peer Review Committee, consisting of sixteen in-house experts (only one of whom declined to sign the report), has reviewed the new toxicology data submitted by the registrant and states: "The Committee reiterated its position stated at the initial peer review meeting held August 25, 1985 ... that both Alar and UDMH be considered as $B_2$ category carcinogens using the EPA risk assessment guidelines." Of particular interest is the Peer Review Committee's revisiting of the Toth studies in the light of the new data. They say (the comment actually applies to a total of eight studies published between 1973 and 1984, including the three done by Toth, all of which had been dismissed by the SAP in 1985): "The Committee compared the data in Table 3 [the 1973–84 group] with that currently available for the more recent Alar/UDMH studies ... and noted that both chemicals appeared to be consistent in producing vascular and lung tumors in mice in both groups of studies. On the other hand, neither chemical appeared to produce treatment-related increases in the two types of tumors in rats in both groups of studies ... Although the SAP's opinion on these previous studies was that they were of limited value because of shortcomings in dosing, the Committee concluded that these studies now have gained renewed importance for the weight of the evidence determination of Alar/UDMH since the same tumor types were seen in the previous studies as in the more recent ones." This evaluation also has special relevance to the hazard profile that was generated by the initial toxicology studies and reviews done in 1967 (on the basis of which daminozide was registered for food crop uses), since the only rodent test populations at that time were rats.

12. May 1989: The California State Department of Food and Agriculture (CDFA) says that in *Intolerable Risk* the NRDC's use of upper-bound estimates yields figures that "are, in many cases, 10 to 100 times or more higher than would have resulted from using currently accepted techniques of risk assessment ... CDFA toxicologists were reluctant to perform a risk assessment for daminozide/UDMH because an important study has not yet been completed. However, because CDFA was concerned that the continued use of this chemical would be determined by public opinion rather than by scientific fact, our toxicologists developed an interim assessment. The findings of this assessment are that there is an estimated excess lifetime risk from damonizide/UDMH of $4 \times 10^{-12}$ [4 cases in one trillion], with an upper-bound of $3 \times 10^{-6}$ [3 in a million], levels one thousand to one billion times safer than NRDC's estimate."[69]

13. May 1989: EPA issues its "Special Review Technical Support Document – Preliminary Determination to Cancel the Food Uses of Daminozide" (this has the same format as the 1985 "Position Document"). It reaffirms the $B_2$ status of both compounds, but concentrates on UDMH and now puts the risk of dietary exposure to UDMH at $\frac{4}{5} \times 10^{-5}$ (four or five in 100,000), with an incremental risk over and above that for children. The benefits assessment now figured that there could be a 3 percent price increase for raw apples and a 2 percent price decrease for processed apple products (more apples would be diverted to processing); the net social cost is estimated to range from $18 to $81 million, probably towards the lower end of that range; these reductions are due to the fact that Alar use had been slipping steadily since 1986, and in 1989 was estimated to be used on about 10 percent only of the total crop. It concludes that the risk "outweighs" the benefits.

An interesting sidelight in the risk/benefit analysis section is the passing reference to the existence of alternative chemicals. In "Table IV-1: Summary of the Toxicity of the Alternatives to Daminozide," where six alternatives are listed, the most common evaluative entries are "no data available," "data awaiting review," and "additional data required"!

14. August 1989: Uniroyal disputes the EPA's classificiation of daminozide as a group $B_2$ carcinogen, claiming that the new 1988 data supplied by it does not support this action and that the agency is still basing its classification on the old Toth studies and maintaining that "the weight of the evidence supports the conclusion that daminozide is not oncogenic." It also objects to the agency's use of interim results from the new UDMH "high dose" study to calculate risk, since the extreme levels of toxicity in such doses (known as the Maximum Tolerated Dose or MTD) do not give reliable guidance when extrapolated.[70] Finally, it disputes the categorization of UDMH as mutagenic.[71]

15. November 1989: Great Britain's Ministry of Agriculture, Fisheries and Food reviews both the old and new toxicology studies; performs exposure calculations (using U.S. residue data for raw apples and "adult" apple juice) using maximum possible intakes of residues from consumption. It concludes: "When adult exposure to Daminozide and UDMH are compared with the no effect levels for these compounds, the resultant safety factors are very large indeed (greater than 6000). It can therefore be concluded that this exposure presents no risk to health ... [For infants and children] the safety factor for Daminozide is ... still reassuring, at 4000. For UDMH the safety factors are also reassuring [ranging under worse-case scenarios from 1000 to 150] ... A safety factor of 150 would generally be considered acceptable when setting an ADI on the basis of a carcinogenic effect resulting from a non-genotoxic agent." The group goes on to note that it is not in a position to actually establish an ADI (acceptable daily intake) for either compound.

16. July 1991: EPA Health Effects Division Peer Review Committee reports on its "Third Peer Review." It reviewed studies completed and submitted in the preceding two years and reaffirmed its April 1989 findings (see #11 above).

## APPENDIX 6.3

### *Natural Resources Defense Council,* Intolerable Risk

The report is written with abundant technical documentation and identifies the members of an expert peer-review group that supports the methodology and calculations. It says:

"NRDC estimates that the average excess lifetime carcinogenic risk to preschoolers from exposures to only eight pesticides or metabolites in 27 different types of fruits and vegetables from ages 0–5, may be as high as $2.5 \times 10^{-4}$ to $2.8 \times 10^{-4}$ (or one cancer case for approximately every 3,600 to 4,000 preschoolers exposed). This means that as many as 5,500 to 6,200 children from the current preschool population of 22 million children ages 0–5 may contract cancer some time during their lifetime solely as a result of exposure to these eight chemicals in food during their preschool years. UDMH, the carcinogenic metabolite of the pesticide daminozide, accounts for 86% to 96% of this risk.

"The average carcinogenic risk from consumption of UDMH-contaminated food from birth through age five is estimated to be $2.4 \times 10^{-4}$, or an additional cancer case for approximately every 4,200 children exposed. This risk is 240 times the level considered acceptable by EPA [i.e., one-in-a-million or $1 \times 10^{-6}$] following a full lifetime of exposure ... . For heavy consumers (those who are at or above the 95th percentile level of exposure), the carcinogenic risk from consumption of UDMH-contaminated food from birth through age five is estimated at $9.1 \times 10^{-4}$, or an additional cancer case for approximately every 1,100 children exposed. This is a risk level 910 times greater than that considered acceptable by EPA following a full lifetime of exposure."

*Intolerable Risk* includes a lengthy appendix, "Methodology for Estimating Cancer Risk from Preschooler Exposure to Carcinogenic Pesticides in Food," written by Professor William J. Nicholson of the Mount Sinai School of Medicine in New York. The appendix contains elaborate quantitative calculations of cancer risk and discussions of competing methodologies; thus NRDC chose to enter both the expert and the public debate on Alar.

# PART THREE

# *Towards Consensus*

# CHAPTER SEVEN

# Stakeholder Negotiation in Risk Controversies

## ALAR AGAIN: WAS CONSENSUS POSSIBLE?

As we've mentioned, almost every participant in the Alar controversy emerged with their credibility damaged, to varying degrees. Many of the most deeply involved parties sought to reassess their positions after the issue finally died down.

One particular episode in the months following the "60 Minutes" broadcast and the NRDC's publicity blitz is especially revealing and bears directly on the possibilities for consensus in controversies over health and environmental risks. Growers in various parts of the United States asked NRDC personnel to visit their operations, where they displayed warehouses full of stored apples that were unsaleable and would have to be dumped.[1] The NRDC's Janet Hathaway, who had played a prominent role in the launching of *Intolerable Risk*, was invited to participate on a panel at the International Apple Institute's annual meeting in June 1989, where she apologized for the economic damage that her group's report had caused to growers: "I apologize that environmentalists and growers have been divided. [If] the facts hurt growers, that represents a breakdown in a government program aimed to protect both growers and consumers." She went on to propose the forging of an alliance between growers and consumer groups to advance their mutual concerns.[2] The apple industry sought to draw its own lessons from the blows it took in those years, resolving to assume responsibility for taking the initiative to respond to public concerns about health risks, instead of deferring, as it had done in the past, to the chemical industry on the one hand and government regulatory agencies on the other.

Apparently the media have decided to be a bit warier with the communications strategies of environmental groups. Risk communication specialists berated the EPA for its mishandling of the Alar issue; in particular, Peter Sandman, a risk communication specialist, told the EPA that it should "share control with citizens" and "allow the public to be partners" in risk decisions, rather than trying to control the situation unilaterally.[3] Other commentators have pointed out that public outrage will arise when it takes so long (as it did with Alar) to clear up uncertainties and disagreements with the scientific databases, and urged chemical producers in particular to "initiate dialogues with consumers and discuss issues of concern honestly and openly before the concerns become media events."[4]

What if the various parties had followed their own good advice rather earlier: would the final outcome in the case at hand have been any different? Perhaps – if a process of seeking common ground had been started before all the parties had manoeuvred themselves into inflexible positions. Was it possible for these parties to have developed a consensus-building process that gradually would have yielded a higher level of mutual trust and respect, so that in the long term, as many of them met again over one or another controversial issues, their interactions could be conducted with less rancour? Without a doubt. In that event, are other types of outcomes conceivable, in controversies over health and environmental risks similar to the Alar case? Quite possibly, yes.

What might have transpired if the main contending parties had sat down around a table with each other and argued over what to do about Alar? Since there is such abundant information on the evolution of this dispute, it is possible to undertake an imaginary exercise, by constructing the hypothetical "opening" and "closing" positions of the various parties as well as the likely interactions among them over the years. At the outset we will suppose that all of the key players have been summoned to the table by an all-powerful agency.

## THE OPENING POSITIONS

The reader should be aware that a wide set of variations on the details of each position is imaginable. In particular, some fine-tuning of regulatory provisions – altering the use patterns and the permitted residue levels, for example – can significantly lower estimated risk. These adjustments go on all the time in administrative practice within regulatory agencies. As we shall see later, such adjustments can play a role also in the face-to-face bargaining between interested parties as they explore the paths towards a possible consensus position.

*The Scene:* At the consensus conference site in the United States the population density of lawyers among the participants approaches unity, while academic experts roam the halls handing out business cards with printed *per diem* rates and offering to testify in court on any side of the issue. Planeloads of media personnel and television camera equipment have descended, followed by even more numerous planeloads of campaigning politicians, attracted like insects by the bright lights, in search of useful sound bites. At the separate conference site in Canada, however, no lawyers are permitted within a radius of 500 metres, and the media are nowhere to be seen, having rushed to a lakeside retreat to cover the latest round of that country's perpetual constitutional negotiations.

*I. The Registrant: Uniroyal (or its national subsidiary):*
The status of Alar as a registered product will be defended forcefully; in particular, the company will not accept evidence from animal studies showing carcinogenic response unless and until faced with inescapable and overwhelming evidence of the same. The benefits are enormous and the product is solidly supported by users.

*II. The Federal Agencies:*[5]
*In the United States:*
Environmental Protection Agency (EPA): Risks outweigh benefits; registration should be cancelled.
U.S. Department of Agriculture (USDA): Benefits outweigh risks; registration should be continued.
Food and Drug Administration (FDA): Registration should probably be continued: no convincing proof of unacceptable risk.[6]
*In Canada:*
Agriculture Canada: In the absence of evidence of health risk convincing to Health and Welfare Canada, registration should be continued.
Health and Welfare Canada (HWC): No convincing evidence of unacceptable health risk.
Environment Canada: No unacceptable environmental risk

*III. State or Provincial Agencies:*
Both the state governments in the United States and the provincial governments in Canada would have representation from (1) Departments of Agriculture and (2) Departments of Public Health, from each of the main apple-producing or Alar-using jurisdictions. Based on public statements from a sample of the U.S. states noted earlier, the two agencies from each jurisdiction would take opposite positions on Alar.

*IV. User Groups:*

1. Growers and grower associations representing the main crop areas: Benefits, both qualitative and economic, are very substantial and continued availability is essential.

2. Unions representing farm workers: Worker exposure has been relatively neglected to date, in comparison with dietary risk, and better information on this point is demanded.

*V. Consumer Interests:*

1. Independent non-profit consumer organizations: There are sufficiently disquieting uncertainties in all dimensions of risk assessment (carcinogenicity, residues, exposure) to justify taking Alar off the market until they are cleared up.

2. Retailers (small grocer associations as well as large supermarket chains): In view of our recent experiences with EDB (a fungicide) and aldicarb, we agree with consumer organizations.

*VI. Public-Interest Advocacy Groups:*

"Environmental" organizations: An *immediate* ban is demanded for the following reasons:

1. It is unconscionable that there should be any further wait for the results of new rodent studies for a chemical that has been on the market for twenty years. Even the Scientific Advisory Panel, which has no credibility in our eyes, chastised the EPA in 1985 for not ensuring that replacement studies were under way long ago.

2. Benefits and trade-offs are irrelevant (we do not want even to discuss them) where proven carcinogenic risk is involved.

## THE CROSS-EXAMINATIONS

The following is a sample of the types of questions that the parties would put to each other as they sat around the table, ostensibly seeking a "consensus" position. Neither the voice tone nor the body language would be especially cordial, at least in many cases. The likely source of the question is indicated by the parenthetical reference to the category number (I, II, etc.) at the end. Note that the representatives of government agencies are not allowed the pleasure of participating in these nasty duels.

*A. Unfriendly Questions addressed to the Registrant by Other Parties:*

1. Why do you spend so much money, time, and effort trying to discredit the Toth studies, instead of taking the initiative long ago to provide voluntarily a complete database of unexceptionable scientific studies? (VI)

2. Why does your industry always appear to wish to evade truly independent peer review for scientific studies? (VI)

3. Why does your industry support the discrediting of existing toxicology reviews – for example, by claiming that we cannot perform valid human health extrapolations from high doses in the laboratory animal studies – when you know that there is no generally accepted substitute process? Do you want to market your poisons with no credible scientific review at all? (V)

B. *Unfriendly Questions addressed to the Federal Agencies by Other Parties:*

1. Why did we have to go to court (in the United States) to force you to reveal relevant documentation for all interested parties, such as the minutes of meetings you hold with the industry representatives? And – for the Canadian scene – why is so little comparable information readily available? (VI)

2. To the EPA: How can we believe your quantitative risk estimates when the numbers appear to change all the time? For example: the evidence on the table demonstrates beyond the shadow of a doubt that in September 1985 you deliberately overstated residues by a factor of seven, obviously in order to make sure that the "bottom line" risk number that fell out of the calculations was the one you had decided upon before even starting the process. (V)

3. What were you doing between 1973, when the first Toth results were published in the open literature, and January 1986, when you ordered replacement studies – especially since you knew for most of this period that the registrant disputed the entire scientific basis of the only available studies of this kind? (VI)

C. *Unfriendly Questions addressed to States/Provinces by Other Parties:*

1. Why do the state/provincial agriculture departments always seem to be merely public relations spokespersons for the chemical user interests? (V, VI)

2. Why have you taken so little interest over the years in farm-worker exposure to toxic chemicals? (IV.2)

3. What real capacity do you have for initiating proper toxicology reviews for anything except an arbitrary, small sample of those substances that become matters of public concern? (I, V)

D. *Unfriendly Questions addressed to the Growers by Other Parties:*

1. Why do you appear to take so little interest in dietary risk issues and instead just repeat the chemical industry publicity releases and ads you read in your farm journals? (V)

2. Why have you been so trusting of everything the chemical industry tells you, when you are (or should be) aware that it has so

little interest in assessing risks honestly – including occupational exposure risks to owner/growers such as yourselves? (VI)

3. Why have you been so indifferent all these years to worker exposure issues relating to the chemicals you use? (IV.2)

*E. Unfriendly Questions addressed to Consumer Interests by Other Parties:*

1. Why are food retailers so afraid of addressing public concerns honestly, instead of quickly folding under pressure from a few crackpot letter-writers? (I)

2. In particular, since food retailers know how important the modern chemical industry has been generally in improving the safety of the food supply for consumers, why are you so reluctant to help inform consumers of these benefits? (I)

3. Why have the non-profit organizations traditionally been so quiet (and ineffective) in their advocacy of consumer interests? (VI)

*F. Unfriendly Questions addressed to Advocacy Groups by Other Parties:*

1. Few of you have any science competence at all: what makes you think you know anything about cancer risk, or even who is entitled to be considered an expert in such matters? (I)

2. Why are you so completely indifferent to the interests of growers, many of whom are small farmers who, with their families, have committed the labours of a lifetime and the entirety of their financial resources to the viability of their enterprise? Are you prepared to see them ruined to satisfy your own egos? (IV)

3. Why are you so arbitrary in the selection of risks that you seek to scare the public about? Don't you know – perhaps you don't – that health risks from food contamination pale beside many others in our society? And that even with respect to the food supply itself most serious dietary risks – except for rare accidents – are not those associated with pesticide residues? (I)

### ASSUMING (OR EVADING) RESPONSIBILITY FOR TRADE-OFFS

Since this is an imaginary exercise, we have the luxury of postulating the existence of an all-powerful convening entity who can compel the various parties to respond to the following types of questions. In practice, the questions are rarely tolerated and the unspoken answers become the tacit presuppositions of the positions taken.

*I. The Registrant: Uniroyal (or its national subsidiary):*

1. If the much-delayed carcinogenicity studies show dietary health risks well in excess of your stated risk estimate ($10^{-7}$), how will you compensate the public for this mistake?

2. If the much-delayed carcinogenicity studies show occupational exposure health risks well in excess of the estimated risk to date, how will you compensate farmworkers and growers for this mistake?

3. What level of health risk, for both occupational and consumer exposure, do you consider acceptable, and why?

*II. The Federal Agencies:*

1. What level of health risk, for both occupational and consumer exposure, do you consider acceptable, and why?

2. How do you make trade-offs between risks and benefits, when you say that one "outweighs" the other?

3. If you accept the argument – as you seem to do – that, generally speaking, health and environmental risks are adequately assessed, that risks from pesticide use are acceptable, and especially that risk/benefit trade-offs as made are appropriate, why do you not make a more determined effort to communicate these truths to the public?

*III. The State/Provincial Agencies:*

1. Is excess risk – especially occupational exposure, and most especially for farmworkers – adequately assessed and compensated? By what standard? If not, who should be responsible for redress?

2. If you accept the argument – as you seem to do – that, generally speaking, health and environmental risks are adequately assessed, that risks from pesticide use are acceptable, and especially that risk/benefit trade-offs as made are appropriate, why do you not make a more determined effort to communicate these truths to the public?

3. What efforts do you make to involve the public as partners in risk-management decision-making, so that citizens may gain experience in what it means to assume responsibility for risks? Specify.

*IV. User Groups:*

1. Do the owners among you accept full responsibility for the levels of risk you impose upon your employees? How do you satisfy yourselves that these risks have been assessed adequately?

2. What actions do you take to reduce risks to levels as low as reasonably achievable for the technologies you employ? Specify.

3. Do you actively seek to find the lowest-risk technology among alternatives that are roughly equal in cost-effectiveness? If so, what is the evidence?

*V/VI. Public Interest Advocacy Groups:*

1. Do you agree with the collective statement made by many American scientific associations to the effect that the greatest threats to health from food contaminants have their source not in residues from industrial chemicals but from the actions of naturally occurring bacteria, fungi, and moulds? If so, why do you not say so to the public? If not, what is the basis for your disagreement with this statement?

2. You must acknowledge that many individuals voluntarily incur risks at levels far in excess of the ones described in *Intolerable Risk.* Does the mere fact of their voluntary nature make them "tolerable," despite their high social cost – no matter how risky or costly they may be? And is it not irrational, self-defeating, and economically punishing for society to tolerate a whole set of double standards for risk (one for "natural," one for "artificial"; one for voluntary, one for involuntary; and so forth)?

3. Do you accept the need for trade-offs between risks and benefits? If not, are you prepared to welcome the end of industrial society?

## THE (PROBABLE) CLOSING POSITIONS

*I. The Registrant: Uniroyal (or its national subsidiary).*

*Possibility #1:* The company will voluntarily and permanently withdraw its product from the marketplace, in the face of convincing evidence that users have been persuaded to abandon it permanently, and despite its unshakeable conviction that no unacceptable risk has been demonstrated. It will do so in part to maintain the goodwill of its customers, to whom it expects to sell many other chemical products in the future.

*Possibility #2:* The company will voluntarily and temporarily withdraw its product from the marketplace until all of its new studies, currently under way, have been completed and reviewed by regulatory agencies. (The relevant parties have agreed upon a series of special measures to proceed as quickly as possible to this point.) If the company disagrees with the review results, the company will pay the expenses of a special panel of experts, internationally recognized and indeed drawn from around the world, the names of whom are agreed to by all parties. These experts will be convened on an expedited basis to judge the dispute, and the company agrees in advance to be bound by the contents of that judgment.

*Possibility #3:* The company announces its intention to sue a group of the other parties present, who have been acting in collusion to unfairly undermine its business interests by destroying the market demand for Alar, for $1 billion in damages. (But only in the United States; after careful evaluation, the company decides that such a move would be fruitless in Canada.)

## II. The Federal Agencies:

*In the United States,* after many, near-violent internal bureaucratic struggles, as well as desperate secret lobbying and counter-lobbying of everyone above the position of janitor in both Congress and the Executive Branch by all interested parties (who had all pledged not to do this), the three agencies announce a unified position:

- *Alar will stay on the market* with reduced tolerances, expanded residue testing with more sophisticated technologies, new worker-exposure monitoring, more detailed market basket surveys, and an accelerated program of review – including a fast-tracked reference to a new expert advisory panel whose members are acceptable to a broad range of interest groups – as the pending animal and product chemistry study results are submitted by the registrant.

*In Canada* internal bureaucratic negotiations are quiet and cordial, and the external lobbying is restrained. The agencies agree to leave Alar on the market, but with a much-reduced set of ancillary commitments by comparison with the United States; this is said to be the result of lack of funds due to government fiscal restraint programs.

## III. The State and Provincial Agencies:

After protracted but less bloody internecine bureaucratic warfare, including dire private threats by the public health authorities to publicly crucify the agricultural interests if they do not agree to go along with their wishes, in most U.S. and Canadian jurisdictions the consensus position supports the ban on Alar; those that disagree are bought off with concessions in other unrelated areas, and a unified position is announced.

## IV. User Groups:

1. After intensive negotiation with consumer interests and environmental groups, growers state that they will phase out use of Alar, on a schedule that will minimize economic losses, with compliance to be monitored by a voluntary multi-party group, in return for

pledges from environmental groups to work co-operatively with them in the future on food safety issues.

2. Farmworkers' concerns about inadequate attention to exposure assessment over the whole range of pesticides that they are obliged to use are forgotten after the side deal is struck between the growers, the food retailers, consumer organizations, and environmental groups to support voluntary withdrawal from all uses of Alar.

*V/VI. Consumer Interests and Environmental Groups:*
Join forces to make the growers an offer they can't refuse for complete cessation of Alar use on food crops.

Environmental groups still refuse to discuss the matters of risk/benefit trade-offs, risk comparisons, voluntary/involuntary risk dilemmas, the spurious difference between natural and artificial risks, or any other topics remotely resembling the foregoing, citing lack of resources for research. Since the government agencies present have very little leverage, given their dilatoriness in providing a publicly credible risk assessment in this case, they are unable to shame these parties into entering such discussions.

## STAKEHOLDERS

Although no such episode as described above actually occurred in the struggle over Alar, events much like it have actually transpired in North America during the last five years or so. These events, attempts to negotiate settlements to risk controversies, have involved a wide range of interested parties often referred to as "stakeholders."[7] They have evolved in response to the steadily increasing incidence of environmental and natural resource conflicts over the last two decades. Conventional decision-making and dispute-resolution processes (legislative, administrative, and judicial) were being taxed to the limit; more and more decisions were being protested, appealed, or ignored. As a result, there has been a growing interest on the part of industry, government officials, and others in negotiated approaches to consensus-building.

What are "stakeholders"? The term is now in wide use and undoubtedly covers a multitude of sins. Nonetheless, in practice it is usually not difficult to identify relevant stakeholders. Stakeholders are those organizations that are "entitled" to be consulted as a result of legal standing or public regard and that have a prior record of involvement in the issues or localities involved. Where there has existed longstanding controversy (as in the case of the antisapstain chemicals discussed in chapter 8), combined with established labour-management industrial relations, the naming of the principal stakeholders is relatively straightforward. At the other extreme, where incipient controversies involve broad but unfocused community concern, there are great difficulties for anyone charged with the responsibility of deciding who should be "at the table." In such cases, another guideline is helpful: Stakeholders are those organizations and individuals without whose participation any resulting agreement will be ineffectual or inoperative.

Who is entitled to pick the set of stakeholders? This question seems to be vitally important in principle for reasons of natural justice, but in practice, deciding who will choose the stakeholders turns out to be one of the least contentious aspects of these processes. A number of options are available:

- the agency(ies) with statutory authority
- the stakeholder that has the "problem"
- by consensus among self-selecting stakeholders

The reason why it is largely immaterial who does the initial selection of stakeholders and their representatives is that any stakeholder group will formally constitute itself at its initial meeting, and the group itself is never bound by the initial selection process. The group can and must review the issue of appropriate representation at that time, making additions (and even deletions) under its own authority; if those actions are unacceptable to either the sponsoring agencies or the major interested parties, then the entire process will be nullified at the outset.

In stakeholder negotiation the outcome usually sought is called "consensus." As with other aspects of this process there is actually no hard-and-fast set of rules to serve as a guideline in answering the question: What is consensus? Of course each stakeholder group, in setting out on its mission, ought to try to come to an agreement on this point, for each case is situation-specific, and what will be "acceptable" in one instance will not be in another. In the end, the answer will be found in the larger context of the group's activities itself; in other words, whether or not there is thought to be a "consensus of interested parties" on a particular issue depends on the perceptions of the larger public decision-making structure within which the stakeholder group's deliberations take place. Governments, for example, may take the position that there is a sufficient consensus among interested parties to justify adopting a course of action even if some of the stakeholders disagree, and depending always on the particular circumstances at hand such a move indeed may be recognized widely as "legitimate."

In principle, each stakeholder group can seek unanimous agreement, but unanimity should be neither a necessary criterion for "success" in such matters nor always an *a priori* condition for participation. These is one obvious reason for this: a unanimity requirement gives every participant a veto power over the proceedings and makes bargaining and trade-offs harder to consummate.[8] So, in practice, a reliable guideline is that agreement among approximately 75 percent of participating stakeholders represents a consensus, with the following important proviso: among the 75 percent must be all stakeholders without whose consent any agreement is ineffectual or inoperative. Again, this is a purely practical matter, not a statement of principle, reflecting the simple fact that in almost all such circumstances some stakeholders will be more equal than others. (The constitutional proposals that surfaced in 1992 in Canada about "weighted" voting power in a new Senate, although they were not included in the final agreement, provide an interesting illustration.)

Consensus-building requires informal, face-to-face interaction among specially chosen representatives of all interested parties; a voluntary effort to seek "all-gain" rather than "win-lose" solutions or watered-down political compromise; and, often, the assistance of a neutral facilitator or mediator. Such approaches are treated as supplements to conventional decision-making, not alternatives to it: officials with statutory power retain their authority as guarantors of due process as well as political and legal accountability.

Consensus-building negotiation is an approach to resolving disputes that is:

- ad hoc – participants design the process;
- informal – parties deal with each other in a non-bureaucratized fashion;
- consensual – achieved when parties agree to live with a particular problem formulation and solution because the settlement is the best available under the circumstances, and because it addresses each party's most important concerns;
- face-to-face – specially selected representatives of all stakeholders sit around a table and work together until they produce an agreement or decide to give up;
- supplementary to conventional dispute-resolution processes – if agreement is not reached, the parties will fall back upon existing structures.

The goal of consensus-building negotiation is to encourage joint problem solving. Its success "depends on establishing linkages among issues, packaging elements valued differently by the various participants, arranging compensatory actions or payments, and guaranteeing future behavior."[9]

Consensus-building negotiation can be unassisted (managed by the parties to the dispute) or assisted (managed by an neutral third party). The neutral manager is independent of the other parties and the immediate issues and mutually acceptable to all of the parties.

Facilitation is the simplest form of assisted negotiation; the facilitator focuses almost entirely on process and sometimes acts as a moderator. Mediation intensifies the substantive involvement of the neutral manager. A mediator can act as a convener of meetings to assist the parties in defining the terms and conditions of the process; "a broker representing interests, concerns and ideas of one party to another outside joint sessions and in caucus; a facilitator in joint sessions; and an instructor or coach on how to negotiate effectively."[10]

Negotiated approaches to consensus-building employ the basic methods of "principled negotiation" rather than the more pervasive form of positional bargaining implicit in conventional dispute-resolution and decision-making processes.[11] Fisher and Ury identify four propositions of principled negotiation: separate people and their personalities from the problem; focus on basic interests, not stated positions; invent a range of options for mutual gain; and insist on using objective criteria where possible. Negotiations hinge on the concept of BATNA, or "best alternative to a negotiated agreement."[12] If a party is not confident of victory away from the bargaining table or wants to satisfy more than its minimum objectives (i.e., the party sees an opportunity to get more than its BATNA through negotiating), it has an incentive to negotiate.

In our concluding chapter we shall have more to say about the implications of the stakeholder negotiation process for the conduct of democratic societies. But in order to set the stage for the case study that follows in Chapter 8 we will give brief consideration to the question: Why is it necessary to engage in stakeholder negotiation to seek a resolution for environmental- and health-risk controversies?

There are two replies that are relevant to the type of cases presented in this volume. First, because democratic governments are increasingly facing types of issues that cannot be resolved definitively by law, regulation, or policy pronouncements; issues about managing health and environmental risks, which are pervasive in contemporary industrial societies and about which there is a wide range of strongly held opinion in society, are prime illustrations of this type. Second,

because increasingly the informed consent of a wide range of potentially affected parties is required for public policy to be translated
into effective action, as more and more groups are capable of
obstructing through the courts or by other means the implementation
of policies and practices that appear to them to violate principles of
natural justice.

There are also some distinct benefits for society flowing from the
involvement of individuals and organizations in multi-stakeholder
negotiation processes. For example:

• the full set of trade-offs between benefits and disadvantages,
  reflecting the perceived interests of all relevant parties, can be
  made apparent to everyone;
• each party must defend openly in front of all others its own interpretation of benefits and disadvantages;
• the issue of equity in the distribution of benefits and disadvantages
  among all of the parties may be confronted openly.

Often the alternative is for each group to plead its case separately
for the success of its own position, either publicly through the media
or (more frequently) privately in lobbying politicians. In neither of
these settings is any group forced to confront the views of others or
to consider the impact that the adoption of its position would have
on the legitimate interests of other groups. Around the table this will
not wash, however: with other stakeholders physically present no
group can afford to dismiss the concerns of others out of hand, or
to resist for long making compromises, with the interests of others
in mind, through the brokering of trade-offs and incremental solutions.

## THE TURN TO A MULTI-STAKEHOLDER PROCESS IN NORTH AMERICA

Multi-stakeholder negotiation, as a formal or quasi-legal process of
decision-making based on a consensus among interested parties, was
pioneered in the United States over the past twenty years or so and
is now encountered frequently, especially in attempts to resolve environmental disputes.[13] What is still unique about the process in the
United States (at least so far) is the willingness of government agencies to formally convene multi-stakeholder bodies, organize their proceedings, and commit themselves (within certain limitations) to
turning a consensus of interested parties into a set of legally binding
rules under administrative law. This process has been given the

names "regulatory negotiation" (or "reg-neg") and "negotiated rule-making."[14] Consensus-building negotiation has typically been used in local, site-specific disputes. It has also been applied more generally in the policy arena in the form of "policy dialogues" on environmental policy issues at the regional or federal level, where representatives of interest groups are brought together "to identify areas of agreement and disagreement and develop mutually agreeable proposals for policy makers."[15] An early example is the U.S. National Coal Policy Project of 1976.

Negotiated rulemaking or regulatory negotiation involves bringing together representatives of the regulating agency and interest groups affected to draft a proposed rule. The concept of reg-neg was orig-inated and developed in the United States by Philip Harter in the early 1980s in response to an initiative of the Administrative Con-ference of the United States, a federal agency created to study ways to improve administrative procedures.[16] Reg-neg has since been used by a number of U.S. federal and state agencies under the Adminis-trative Procedure Act; the first three cases involved negotiation of regulations on crew flight and duty time at the Federal Aviation Administration, on non-conformance penalties for vehicle emissions at the Environmental Protection Agency, and on benzene exposure at the Occupational Safety and Health Administration.[17] Others have dealt with air pollution in the Grand Canyon area resulting from a coal-burning generating station and an environmental protection plan for a gold mining operation near the Nevada–California border.[18]

Similar processes have been evolving in Canada, generally of a more informal nature but slowly evolving into more structured forms and enjoying more explicit support from government agencies. Informal rounds of stakeholder consultation were pioneered by an independent body called the Niagara Institute in Ontario, which directed a major exercise in the preparations leading up to the passage of the Canadian Environmental Protection Act. More struc-tured processes have been implemented in a number of important disputes or environmental controversies during the last few years: mercury pollution on Native reserves in northern Ontario; land man-agement in the "Height-of-the-Rockies" wilderness area (in south-eastern British Columbia near the Alberta border); a major over-hauling of the entire national regulatory scheme for pest manage-ment; and the administration of the Fraser River Basin in British Columbia's Lower Mainland.[19]

More recently, interest has been focused on institutionalizing dis-pute-resolution systems, that is, incorporating such techniques into the framework of established institutions and rules. For example, the

B.C. provincial government recently created the Commission on Resources and Environment with a mandate to develop a land use strategy for the province, including a dispute-resolution system; preparatory work for regional negotiation processes is under way.[20] At the federal level, Bill C-13, an act to establish a federal environmental assessment process, grants the Environment minister authority to refer a project assessment to a process of mediated negotiation. In the U.S., the EPA has institutionalized reg-neg: its Negotiation Project evaluates rules under development for possible reg-neg and provides assistance to rule-making offices in establishing procedures. Several states have established institutions or agencies to mediate environmental issues and are available to assist in convening or facilitating reg-neg efforts.[21]

### KEY COMPONENTS OF A CONSENSUS-BUILDING PROCESS

Environmental and natural resource disputes are complex and differ from one dispute to the next in terms of the scope, substance, participants, and procedures involved. Yet a sufficient body of experience with consensus-building negotiation of these and other complex public policy disputes is available to provide reasonably clear guidance on the conduct of the consensus-building process. The B.C. Roundtable on Economy and the Environment recommends that nine conditions "be met in designing and implementing an effective consensus process":[22]

- *A conflict*: There must be an unresolved conflict or potential for conflict. Those affected must be dissatisfied with existing decision-making processes.
- *Incentive*: The parties must perceive that they are better off seeking solutions collaboratively rather than pursuing individual courses of action (e.g., lobbying, protesting) or leaving matters to a higher authority.
- *Stakeholder involvement*: The full range of stakeholders must be represented, including those who will be affected by the decision and those who can block or undermine the agreement if they are not included. The parties should be recognized principals in their respective constituencies so that they are responsible to those interests and can deliver assent on behalf of those constituents.
- *Government involvement*: "Government authorities must participate to represent the broad provincial [federal] perspective, to bring public policies and legal requirements to the process, and to keep decision-makers informed of the process."

- *Accepted process rules*: All participants must agree to the objectives of the process, its format, and the rules and procedures of operation.
- *Time limits*: Time limits for reaching a conclusion and reporting on outcomes must be clear and reasonable. (Otherwise some parties may use the process as a stalling tactic.) The process must also be flexible to allow for delays if the process is leading to consensus.
- *Full mandate*: "The parties must be provided the opportunity to participate in defining the problems, identifying options, and seeking solutions."
- *Government commitment*: Parties must be reasonably satisfied that the agreement has a reasonable prospect of being implemented, as quickly as possible, especially in the form of government action. If government cannot act on the agreement, it must provide clear reasons for this inability to the parties involved.
- *Fallback*: "There must be a clear understanding that there are alternatives for making necessary decisions if agreement is not reached." However, these alternative are generally perceived to be less desirable and therefore provide an incentive for parties to participate in good faith.

Susskind and Cruikshank add "three preconditions for the success of unassisted negotiation": (1) the issues in dispute, as well as the array of stakeholder parties, should be relatively few in number and readily identifiable; (2) the stakeholders must be able to establish sufficient channels of communication to permit joint problem-solving; and (3) the uncertainty surrounding the outcome of unilateral action must be moderately high for all stakeholders.[23]

These preconditions for applying negotiated rule-making may be summarized more briefly as follows:

1 There is a limited number of interests that are significantly affected, and a limited number of individuals to represent them.
2 The issues are known.
3 No party will have to compromise a fundamental value.
4 The proposed rule involves diverse issues.
5 The outcome is genuinely in doubt.
6 The parties view it as being in their best interests to use the process.
7 The regulatory agency is willing to use the process and participate in it.
8 No one interest is able to dominate the proceedings or eventual consensus.
9 There is a reasonable deadline for achieving consensus.

10  It is clear that in the absence of a consensus, the rule will still be developed and established by the regulatory agency.[24]

DESIGNING AND
IMPLEMENTING A CONSENSUS
PROCESS

The consensus-building process generally evolves through three stages:

• pre-negotiation, to lay the framework for the conduct of the process;
• substantive negotiation, to try and reach agreement; and
• post-negotiation, to implement and enforce the agreement.

For each of these stages, a number of guiding principles indicative of "common practice" have been identified. However, there is no one correct way to settle a complex public policy dispute; a process must be tailored to fit the issues, interests, and institutions involved.[25] The cardinal rule is for the parties themselves to design the process, from the point of deciding whether a consensus-building approach is appropriate right through to an implementation strategy.

*Pre-negotiation.* Determine whether the process is appropriate. If so, identify and convene the stakeholders (may be done by government or any of the other stakeholders). Establish ground rules. Topics can include:

• purpose and scope of the process;
• working definition of "consensus";
• structure of the process (e.g., committees, caucuses, meeting formats, presence and role of a neutral manager);
• participants' responsibilities (e.g., informing constituents, providing information);
• protocol (confidentiality, provision of data);
• deadlines for reports and milestones;
• steps to be taken should there be a failure to reach agreement;
• provisions for revision.

Draft an agenda of issues to be discussed and their order of discussion. (A neutral manager is usually selected at this point.) Engage in a process of joint fact-finding. Identify the issues, contexts, and experiences relevant to the dispute, and describe information necessary for stakeholders to consider moving away from their initial positions. Specify ways of gathering data jointly, perhaps with the assistance of independent experts.

*Negotiation.* Identify options for mutual gain: after stakeholders identify their concerns, they generate for consideration (not commitment) a list of ideas that address the agenda items. Evaluate and select options to achieve an acceptable outcome (known as "packaging" or "trading"). Produce a written agreement (include a description of mechanisms for binding the parties to their commitments). Review and ratify the agreement.

*Implementation.* Link the agreement to government decision-making processes (for example, appropriate laws or regulations can be passed or an agency can be mandated to implement the agreement as a matter of policy). Design a process to monitor implementation, including checking compliance, measuring success, and designating a body to inform newcomers of the terms of the agreement. Create a context for renegotiation, identifying the terms of and procedure for reconvening.[26]

If consensus is not reached, the process can still enhance understanding of the concerns and viewpoints of all parties, explicate causes of conflict, narrow the issues in dispute, identify information necessary to resolve issues, stipulate areas of disagreement remaining, and specify alternate means of resolving the remaining issues (e.g., adjudication, legislative action, polling of the affected electorate).[27]

## GOOD OUTCOMES OF NEGOTIATED SETTLEMENTS

Definitions of success inevitably will differ. Assuming that a good process produces a good outcome and a better process a better outcome, Susskind and Cruikshank identify four characteristics of a good negotiated settlement: fairness, efficiency, wisdom, and stability. A satisfactory agreement is one that is perceived as fair, is reached efficiently, seems technically wise, and endures.[28]

*Fairness.* Because it is unlikely that parties to a dispute would accept any single indicator of substantive fairness, the best way to determine the fairness of a negotiated solution is to evaluate the attitudes and perceptions of the parties most affected: Among other things, if they think a given process has been fair, they are more likely to abide by its outcome. There are four tests for perceived fairness:

1  Was the offer to participate genuine, and were all the stakeholders given a chance to be involved? Did the offer to participate come at a timely juncture? Were all parties given access to the information and technical resources they needed to express their views effectively?
2  Were opportunities provided for systematic review and improvement of the decision process in response to stakeholder concerns?
3  Was the process perceived as legitimate after it ended, as well as when it began? Did anyone feel "taken advantage of" as a result of the negotiation?
4  In the eyes of the community, was a good precedent set?[29]

*Efficiency.* A stakeholder negotiation process is unacceptable if it takes too much time away from the main business of the various parties; is too costly in monetary terms; or if it results in missed opportunities for trade-offs that would have benefited everyone without imposing costs on anyone. Obviously there can be a tension between fairness and efficiency: ensuring fairness means that all stakeholders must listen patiently to each other's concerns, many of which have accumulated over a long period of time and may not be directly relevant to the matter at hand. At the same time, consensus must usually be reached within a specific time frame to be useful.

*Wisdom.* Dispute-resolution processes usually involve forecasts, and the wisdom of such forecasts often cannot be ascertained until months or even years later. Sometimes there is no relevant experience and "prospective hindsight" is difficult to muster. At other times, as we have seen in our case studies so far (and as will be evident in the one still to be discussed), there is intense disagreement about the interpretation of shared experiences, or about the fund of received knowledge, both informal and scientific. In the worst cases, the parties bring in their own "experts" to seek to discredit others' positions, which inevitably leads to a situation where legitimate scientific and technical differences are exaggerated instead of being examined and resolved.

The search for wise resolution of differences requires a collaborative inquiry that breaks down a complex problem into a series of mutually agreed-upon pieces. The pieces can be defined by a series of questions:

• "What small-scale experiment could we perform to test a critical assumption upon which we disagree?"

- "What information should we try to get that would settle a key disagreement?"
- "Can we identify which evidence, obtained by agreed-upon means, would cause us to abandon our own argument and accept someone else's?"
- "Can we be educated together in the complexities of this issue?"[30]

*Stability*. Participants should emphasize feasibility – they should be able to implement the agreement (so, for example, parties representing coalitions must take responsibility for cultivating support from all coalition members), and timetables should be realistic. Conversely, the commitments that parties make to each other must be realistic in technical, legal, economic, and financial terms. Agreements should include provisions for renegotiation; thus negotiators should include a summary paragraph in the written agreement stating that if they based their agreement on a mistaken assumption then they will reconvene and correct that mistake. Parties should agree to meet regularly to monitor implementation and to review new information.

A useful caution has been emphasized by a number of commentators to the effect that evaluating mediation on the basis of the "signed agreement test" has pressured mediators into advocating an outcome, not a process, even in cases in which all parties might well be acting rationally. The first and foremost objective of such exercises, therefore, should be to facilitate a fair and reasoned dialogue among the parties, most of whom are engaged in the issues under dispute on a long-term basis.[31]

Indeed, several concerns have already been raised regarding consensus-building negotiations.[32] They include: time and expense; ability to participate (financial resources, time, and negotiating skills); the role of government (danger of compromising government authority); the role of the mediator (conflict of interest); adequate representation and the varying expertise of stakeholders; inequitable distribution of power and influence; and anomalies in using a process designed to deal with issues of fairness in an effort to arrive at agreements on issues of science.[33] And practical solutions have been suggested to address some of them, for example, coalition-building, schemes for organizational or financial assistance, and the use of "stand-ins" for unorganized interests to keep the process manageable while also ensuring that all legitimate interests or social values are fully represented.[34]

Although most observers concur that the use of consensus-building negotiation processes is still in the experimental stage, there is also general agreement that these processes have one overriding advantage, so far as controversies over health and environmental risks are concerned – namely, that they can "open up backroom lobbying to a broader array of stakeholders" and subject their dealings "to greater public visibility and scrutiny."[35]

# CHAPTER EIGHT

# Antisapstain Chemicals

## Introduction

Antisapstain chemicals are fungicides designed to control the growth of a mould caused by sapstain fungi on freshly sawn or stored lumber; they have been used in the wood products industry for over fifty years. Such a mould does not affect the structural integrity of lumber, but the extensive and highly noticeable bluish-black stains it produces affect the marketability of wood products. In a global industry where competition is strong and where antisapstain treatment is the norm (at least in certain markets), stained lumber will be refused by buyers or will give rise to claims for monetary compensation brought against the manufacturer.

In the late 1980s Canada was producing about 150 million cubic metres of primary wood products annually – about half of this total in British Columbia alone – with a value in export markets of about $16 billion (amounting to 40 percent of the world softwood lumber market). As of 1990 the British Columbia wood products industry was treating annually with antisapstain chemicals about 3.5 billion board feet of softwood lumber (hemlock and fir), with a value in excess of $2 billion annually, mostly in overseas export markets.[2]

Not all softwood lumber needs to be treated with chemicals. The tree species, the amount of moisture in the wood, the prevailing ambient temperature, the distance to markets and type of transportation used, and the availability of alternative technologies all affect the decisions as to what type and extent of action against sapstain fungi is required. Kiln drying, which kills the fungus through extended heat treatment, is a preferred option for certain tree species and also for growing areas where the wood is relatively dry to begin with and where markets are served by rail over relatively short distances. In addition, even where the use of antisapstain chemicals is necessary under present circumstances, technological innovations currently in use can reduce the amounts of chemicals required for efficacious treatment of lumber and also reduce worker exposure to those chemicals. Finally, researchers are actively seeking effective biological control agents (microfungi and bacteria) that can act as biopesticides for sapstain fungi.

B.C. softwood lumber comes from two quite different regions, coastal and interior. Interior lumber is drier by nature and is shipped by rail, with costs based on weight; in this area, kiln drying is the preferred mode of sapstain control. Conversely, approximately 90 percent of lumber produced from coastal species in British Columbia is treated with antisapstain chemicals. This is due in part to the type of species prevalent there; in part to the high moisture content and relatively warm ambient temperatures; and in part to the distance to the overseas markets and the type of transportation required (ship transport, with the warm, moist holds, offering an ideal environment for fungal growth). In addition, buyers in overseas markets demand green (undried) lumber, and 90 percent of B.C. coastal production is shipped overseas. The large volume of lumber produced annually by a substantial workforce has meant widespread occupational exposure to the chemicals; thus the longstanding controversy over those chemicals has been especially severe in British Columbia.

Antisapstain chemicals are pesticides, and as such they come under the federal regulatory authority of Agriculture Canada, though they may also be subject to additional provincial regulations (for example, controls on effluent levels for stormwater runoff from sawmill sites).

The group of organochlorine compounds known as chlorophenates, first registered in Canada in 1941, was soon shown to give excellent results for wood treatment in terms of both efficacy and cost, and from the 1940s right through until the mid-1980s these were the chemicals of choice for the wood products industry.[3] The chlorophenate mixtures used in sawmills – composed almost entirely of sodium tetrachlorophenate, not pentachlorophenol as is commonly supposed – were rated as 100 percent effective for sapstain control. In 1989 the cost of treatment per thousand board feet of lumber using these mixtures ranged from $0.25 to $0.70, whereas the only other product then available with a comparable efficacy cost on average seven times as much (see Table 8-1).[4]

Beginning about 1975 a storm of controversy began to swirl around the chlorophenate compounds, especially pentachlorophenol (PCP), both in Canada and elsewhere.[5] There were serious concerns about occupational exposure for a variety of both short-term and long-term worker health effects, and about environmental impacts due to the long persistence of PCP itself, as well as the dioxins that were produced as contaminants during its manufacture. A chronology of major events in the PCP controversy is given at the end of the chapter in Table 8-7.[6]

Controversies over chlorophenate use came to wide public attention in the late 1970s with the issue of potential food contamination as a result of leaching from treated wood in mushroom houses, seed flats, and other greenhouse materials. Also a matter of concern were wood materials used in farm structures (silos, stalls, feed troughs) and animal bedding (wood shavings). Permission for all of these uses was revoked by 1981. Today the major remaining registered use for pentachlorophenol is for pressure-treatment of utility poles and railway ties: in 1987 annual use in Canada for this purpose amounted to 1,200 metric tonnes.[7]

*The Developing Controversy*

One of the most significant aspects of this developing controversy was the emergence of new scientific research results on the chlorophenate compounds, including the analytical methods necessary for the detection and measuring of their dioxin contaminants. As late as the mid-1970s, for example, the dioxin analyses were still proving to be difficult, leading to major efforts to improve analytical methods. The scientific basis of health studies on the organochlorine compounds, especially the herbicide 2,4-D, became the subject of intense and bitter international controversy.[8] In Canada a whole range of federal government expert committees eventually got involved during the early 1980s: the Associate Committee on Scientific Criteria for Environmental Quality of the National Research Council; the Interdepartmental Committee on Toxic Chemicals; and the Expert Advisory Committee on Dioxins.

But what became quite clear over time to the interested parties was that the established Canadian regulatory structure and the way science was utilized therein could not provide a definitive resolution to those problems. The resolution to the controversy over PCP that

Table 8-1
List of Antisapstain Chemicals In Use After 1980

| Chemical Active Ingredient* | Common Name |
| --- | --- |
| A. Older Products | |
| 1. Pentachlorophenol | PCP, Penta |
| 2. Sodium tetrachlorophenate | Tetra |
| | |
| B. Products in increasing use during the 1980s | |
| 3. 2 (thiocyanomethylthio) benzothiazole | TCMTB |
| 4. Copper 8 quinolinolate | Copper-8 |
| 5. Borax (+ Sodium Carbonate) | Ecobrite® |
| | |
| C. New Products in Canada in 1990 | |
| 6. Didecyldimethyl ammonium chloride | DDAC** |
| 7. Iodo propynyl butyl carbamate | IPBC** |
| 8. Azaconazole | Rodewod® |

* A wide variety of products for actual use may be made from a single active ingredient or from combinations of active ingredients.
** A product in widespread use is NP-1®, which uses a combination of DDAC and IPBC.

the major stakeholders (industry, unions, and environmental groups) demanded from the government could be stated as follows: make available through the pesticide registration process *any product* that can deliver both the requisite efficacy (control of sapstain), on the one hand, and a scientifically verified level of acceptable risk (in terms of both worker health and environmental impact), on the other.

As a result of the escalating controversy over PCP, during the latter part of the 1980s the wood products industry began to switch voluntarily to other antisapstain products that had been registered earlier but were not in wide use (for one thing, they cost considerably more than the chlorophenates did). The immediate difficulty was twofold. First, in most cases less was known about the potential adverse health and environmental effects of the alternative active ingredients than was known at that point about PCP! And second, the two most widely used alternatives themselves soon became the cause of both complaint and concern on health and environmental grounds.

Accepting the industry's need to treat its products with chemicals in this context meant making choices among equally undesirable courses of action, in the view of the unions and environmental groups; however, the regulatory system could not offer a way out of this Hobson's choice. In other words, it could not deliver to industry, unions, and environmental groups any product that was satisfactory both in terms of adequate efficacy and of a scientifically verified statement of acceptable risk. This was so despite the fact that by 1989 the federal regulatory system for toxic chemicals required companies who wished to apply for registration of new products to complete a seemingly exhaustive list of detailed scientific studies (Table 8-2), on the basis of which reasonably reliable estimates of health and environmental risk ought to be able to be made.

Fewer tests were required in the past, and the further back one goes in time the poorer the scientific database tends to be. From time to time, companies can be required to bring their databases on older registered products into line with newer reporting requirements, but in many such cases, in view of the considerable costs of doing the newly required scientific studies, the company chooses to withdraw the product from the market. This can have economic impacts on industries that use such a product if no substitute is available or can be had only at a higher price.

The list of studies in Table 8-2 could be misleading if the reader were not also informed at once that a chemical with a complete database submitted to regulatory authorities is the exception rather than the rule. Of course this is due in part to the fact that data requirements by regulatory authorities are always changing, usually in the direction of requiring additional studies based on more advanced analytical methods. Chemicals already in use normally do not have to comply with these enlarged requirements unless and until they are subject to a later data call-in, in the context of a re-evaluation – except in special circumstances, where there is other evidence of greater risk, for example, as a result of publications in the journal literature. Those who have been exposed to many such chemicals in the workplace have complained for years about incomplete databases for adequate health and environmental risk assessment.

To explain adequately why no authoritative statement on acceptable risk could be given by the regulatory officials to the industry, and most importantly to the unions, would require the construction of the entire history of toxic chemical assessment in Canada. Unfortunately, such a history cannot be given here.[9] At its root the problem is this: the government's regulatory system for the toxic chemicals used in industry is not charged by law with the mandate to find the means whereby the most acceptable solution to the technological problem – i.e., the solution that "does the job" at an acceptable level of risk – is made available, one way or another. Instead, the regulatory system is set up to respond to technological solutions initiated by industry, and is limited to approving, rejecting, or modifying (through the imposition of conditions of use) those solutions.

Table 8-2
List of Scientific Studies Making Up a "Complete and Comprehensive Database"
(1989) for Regulatory Purposes*

---

*A. List of Studies required by Health and Welfare Canada*
Acute toxicity: oral (2 species), dermal, inhalation; irritation (eye, dermal),
sensitization; delayed neurotoxicity (when indicated)
Short-term toxicity: 90 day oral (2 species), 12 month oral; short term dermal or
inhalation (when indicated); delayed neurotoxicity (if acute test positive)
Chronic toxicity (one species)
Oncogenicity (two species)
Reproductive toxicity
Teratogenicity (2 species)
Mutagenicity
Phamacokinetics
Occupational exposure

*B. Studies required by, or of interest to, Environment Canada*
Volatilization, water solubility**
Hydrolysis**
Phototransformation
Adsorption/desorption, leaching in soil**; leaching from wood**
Biotransformation; bioconcentration
Environmental toxicology
Disposal from treated wood
Stormwater concentration
Analytical methodology**
** also of interest to Fisheries & Oceans

*C. Studies required by, or of interest to, Fisheries & Oceans*
Acute toxicity to fish
Chronic exposure (sub-lethal toxicity to fish)
Kow value
Bioconcentration in fish
Acute toxicity to invertebrates
Chronic exposure (sub-lethal toxicity to invertebrates)
Effects upon phytoplankton and aquatic macrophytes
Vapour pressure
Persistence in soil
Photolysis in water
Persistence in water

---

* Exactly which of these studies are relevant to a regulatory decision depends on a number of
factors, including the nature of the chemical involved.

Persistent complaints from the unions about the antisapstain chemicals used in sawmills and the lack of adequate health and environmental risk data was one of the factors that led to a series of meetings,
among officials from various bodies, designed to search for solutions.
The first consultative group in this area, the B.C. Federal-Provincial

Table 8-3
List of Organizations Represented on the Steering Committee of the Lumber
Antisapstain Advisory Subcommittee (1985–88)

*Industry:*
Council of Forest Industries (COFI) Head Office Staff
COFI Northern Interior Lumber Sector
COFI Sawmill Operations Committee

*Unions:*
International Woodworkers of America-Canada
Canadian Paperworkers Union
Pulp, Paper and Woodworkers of Canada

*Federal Government:*
Agriculture Canada, Pesticides Directorate, Ottawa
Health and Welfare Canada, Health Protection Branch, Ottawa
Environment Canada, Pacific and Yukon Region

*Provincial Government:*
B.C. Ministry of Environment, Waste Management Branch

*Research Organizations:*
B.C. Research, Vancouver (for Forest Industry Industrial Health Research
Program)
Forintek, Vancouver

Wood Protection Task Force, formed in 1980 at the initiative of
Environment Canada, had by 1982 produced a "Code of Good Practice" for the use of chlorophenate wood preservatives in the lumber
industry. But although PCPs were subject to increasingly intense scrutiny and regulatory restrictiveness during the 1980s, the controversy
intensified steadily, exacerbated by fundamental disagreements
between the industry and the unions over the conduct of Forest
Industry Industrial Health Research Program (FIIHRP) health studies
(see Table 8-7). In 1985 the first consultative group had metamor-
phosed into a second, the Lumber Anti-Sapstain Advisory Subcommittee (Table 8-3), but by 1989 the parties were completely at odds
with each other and frequently registered bitter complaints, both
privately and publicly (for example, at a public meeting held in
Vancouver in 1988 to discuss worker health complaints about an
alternative to PCP known as TCMTB).

The sharp divisions between the key interested parties were made
abundantly clear in August 1989 when, following an accidental spill
of TCMTB into the Fraser River that closed the salmon fishery for a
time, a broad coalition of labour and environmental groups called

publicly for the immediate banning of all antisapstain chemicals from use in the wood products industry[10] – a position that was, of course, completely unacceptable to the industry, which did not have a viable, non-chemical alternative technology available to it. At this point (late 1989), the established public decision-making process for this health and environmental risk controversy was paralysed: neither the political nor the regulatory process appeared to be capable of providing a resolution to the practical problem faced by the interested parties in British Columbia.

In September 1989, barely one month after the Fraser River spill and only a few days after the public call for banning all "toxic" wood preservatives, Agriculture Canada released its "Discussion Document on Anti-Sapstain Chemicals." Eighteen months in preparation, this document had been eagerly awaited by many of the chief interested parties, especially the wood products industry, the labour unions, and the B.C. provincial government. Co-ordinated by Agriculture Canada on behalf of the five interested federal departments, this document dealt with all three groups of antisapstain chemicals used during the 1980s (see Table 8-1). There was an update by Health and Welfare Canada (HWC) on PCP as well as a three-part risk evaluation on health and safety (by HWC), on environmental impacts generally (by Environment Canada), and on aquatic impacts (by Fisheries and Oceans) on the three active ingredients then in use (TCMTB, Cu-8, and borax) and three new "candidate" chemicals (DDAC, IPBC, and Azaconazole). Thus seven different chemicals in all were separately put through a scientific review by technical specialists in three different federal departments, for a total of twenty-one distinct risk assessments.

Agriculture Canada's document also included a report entitled "An Economic Benefit Assessment of Anti-Sapstain Chemicals used in B.C. Sawmills," prepared by a consultant under contract to Forestry Canada. To no one's surprise the report confirmed the economic value of antisapstain treatment, estimating its annual dollar value at $388 million as of 1989.[11] At the time of the document's release Agriculture Canada also called a one-day meeting scheduled for 8 November 1989 in the Vancouver area, at which time federal officials would be present to discuss the report and its recommendations. Agriculture Canada also issued strictly limited invitations to the meeting: two representatives from each of the interested parties in British Columbia (labour, industry, provincial government, and environmental groups) – later amended to allow three for labour –, plus two representatives from each of the numerous manufacturers, formulators, and suppliers of antisapstain products.

At the time when this document was issued, virtually all stakeholders representing B.C. industry, unions, and environmental organizations had already publicly gone on record as favouring a complete ban on the use of chlorophenate compounds in B.C. sawmills. Thus, although the technical risk assessment for PCP was of some historical interest, no one (including industry) was prepared to advocate publicly its continued use, no matter what the outcome of the review was. However, there was the strong impression among stakeholders outside the federal agencies that the "Discussion Document" would contain a hierarchy of non-PCP alternatives, ranked in order of relative merit with respect to the two dimensions of interest: health risk for exposed workers and general environmental impacts. They were to be sorely disappointed.

For the remaining six chemicals (aside from PCP), all of the health risk assessments by HWC noted the absence of one or more key studies (mostly in toxicology) that are required for regulatory assessment; thus the hazard profile was incomplete to varying degrees in the case of all alternative compounds. Much worse, however, were the implications of HWC's statement that for *all* alternatives, including those already registered, "a lack of exposure data precludes an overall assessment of risk at this time." Recall that a risk assessment is the combined product of hazard identification and exposure assessment: no scientific risk assessment could be done, for *any* candidate antisapstain compound, because no scientific protocol for measuring exposure of workers in the sawmill industry had ever been put into place, despite the fact that antisapstains had been used in that industry for well over fifty years!

So far as the matter of environmental impacts was concerned, in Agriculture Canada's "Discussion Document" Environment Canada gave a "status report" noting which required studies had been filed and evaluated and which were still outstanding; for none of the chemicals was the file complete, and the Environment Canada advisers used this fact to justify making no summary assessment at all. Likewise, the six evaluations by the Department of Fisheries and Oceans all noted a variety of data gaps, and all concluded with a statement such as "the risk [from use of this product] to fish, fish habitat and fishery resources is considered to be unassessable." In summary, for the eighteen possible non-chlorophenate risk assessments – six chemicals reviewed separately by three federal agencies –, covering the two dimensions of interest (health and environmental risk), *none was available*. This includes the risk assessments for the three actives in general use in B.C. sawmills during the time when the document was being prepared.

At the end of the foreword to its "Discussion Document," Agriculture Canada indicated that it had considered four regulatory actions:[12]

1 Continue the use of PCP-based products as an anti-sapstain treatment on lumber, limiting the registration of the alternatives to those with a complete and comprehensive database.
2 Suspend/cancel immediately the use of PCP-based products as an anti-sapstain treatment on lumber, limiting the registration of the alternatives to those with a complete and comprehensive database.
3 Elimination of anti-sapstain use for PCP by June 1991, with the registration of alternative compounds only as they became fully supported by a complete and comprehensive database, to permit an evaluation of the potential effects on health and the environment.
4 Phase out the use of PCP-based products as an anti-sapstain treatment on lumber, providing immediate temporary registration to alternative products which at present lack sufficient test data to assess their potential impact on health and the environment.
The Government has concluded that the most practical solution is adoption of option number three.

The irony of the situation – namely, that a relatively "complete and comprehensive database" (Table 8-2) existed only for PCP, the one chemical that all interest groups wished to see banned! – was not lost on the attendees at the November 8 meeting. Option number three represented the *status quo*: its practical effect, although that is only implicit in its wording, was to leave available to the industry only the existing group of active ingredients already in general use (TCMTB, Cu-8, borax). Option number one was meaningless, for the use of PCP had been discontinued permanently by the industry; option number two was equally meaningless, save for the formality of deregistering PCP; and option number four was unacceptable to Agriculture Canada because it had been criticized severely during the past few years, especially by environmental groups, for "abusing" the process of granting temporary registrations, a process that allows the database requirements to be bypassed for a certain period of time while a product is being used.

In the period between late September and early November 1989 some chemical manufacturers, COFI, and the B.C. Ministry of Environment all wrote to Agriculture Canada proposing additional alternatives for regulatory action. These proposals included a variety of actions – most of them mutually exclusive, of course – with respect to the three groups of chemicals (Table 8-1). As a result of these representations, as well as the long history of controversy over antis-apstains, no one was better aware than the Agriculture Canada officials that this document was unlikely to answer the questions that had been in the minds of many participants, especially the labour representatives, when the project to produce it had been launched two years earlier. Thus, acting in anticipation of the general unhappiness that was bound to result from the meeting it had called to review the "Discussion Document," Agriculture Canada's Pesticides Directorate made the following proposal to interested parties in British Columbia: It would recognize the *British Columbia parties only* which it had invited to that meeting as a multi-stakeholder consultative group, consisting of representatives from nine organizations including unions, the industry, provincial government departments, and environmental groups (see Table 8-4). Agriculture Canada did not "officially" endorse this group nor did it pay for the conduct of its activities but it pledged to do two things: first, to delay any further initiative of its own for a reasonable time, to see whether those parties could reach a "consensus" position in support of specific regulatory actions on antisapstain chemicals; and second, if a consensus position were indeed reached it pledged informally to consider the substance of that position in taking further regulatory action.

It is very important to note that all of the stakeholder representatives from labour and environmental groups regarded this offer as a "second best" option. For them the preferred option was the resolution noted earlier: namely, an assurance from the responsible government agencies that some technological solution to the wood product industry's problem with sapstain would be made available at an acceptable level of health and environmental risk (as defined by those agencies). The agencies were in no position to give such an assurance, then or now. On the other hand, the majority of British Columbia stakeholders in the Forum were persuaded that some new resolution to the situation prevailing in late 1989 was essential, in terms of their perceived interests. In effect, they were led to define for themselves a level of acceptable risk.

Although a majority of union stakeholders (but not the two environmental ones) accepted the consensus position that was eventually reached, they did so reluctantly, after it became clear that only the "second best" option was available to them. All of the labour and environmental stakeholders continue to be firmly in agreement on one point, namely, that it remains the responsibility of Canadian government agencies generally to ensure that a long-term solution, guaranteeing the combination of acceptable efficacy and an accept-

Table 8-4
List of Stakeholders & Other Interested Parties in the B.C. Stakeholder Forum on
Sapstain Control

A. British Columbia Stakeholders (11)

*Provincial Government Ministries:*
British Columbia Ministry of the Environment
British Columbia Ministry of Forests and Lands

*Unions:*
Canadian Paperworkers Union (CPU)
International Longshoremen's and Warehousemen's Union (ILWU)
International Woodworkers of America-Canada (IWA-Canada)
Pulp, Paper & Woodworkers of Canada (PPWC)

*Industry:*
Council of Forest Industries of British Columbia (COFI)
Sawmill Industry of British Columbia (COFI Members)
Wharf Operators of British Columbia

*Environmental Organizations:*
Earthcare (Kelowna, B.C.)
Westcoast Environmental Law Association (WCELA)

*Note:* Agriculture Canada originally named nine of the above; when the group was convened for
the first time, its members agreed to add two others deemed essential to making the process
work.

B. Other Interested Parties (5):

*Federal Government Departments*
Agriculture Canada (Pesticides Directorate)
Health and Welfare Canada (Health Protection Branch)
Environment Canada (Commercial Chemicals Branch)
Department of Fisheries and Oceans
Forestry Canada

---

able level of health and environmental risk, will be made available to
them. Whether or not this will ever happen still remains to be seen.

PART II: CONSTRUCTING
A NEW PATH

*The Stakeholder Meetings*

At the opening of the first meeting of the B.C. Stakeholder Forum
(BCSF), a question was raised as to the meaning of "consensus." There

was a general wish not to attempt to give an exact (numerical) meaning to the term but rather to locate it somewhere between a bare majority and full agreement of all representatives. It was also suggested that one or more stakeholders or representatives might indicate disagreement with the majority, and register that disagreement in a number of ways, without directly challenging the view that a consensus had been achieved, and this proviso was agreeable to everyone. To facilitate the process of arriving at decisions the group agreed that each stakeholder should be represented at every meeting.

At the first meeting, the group also took up the issue of whether the appropriate stakeholders were represented around the table. As indicated in Table 8-4 there was immediate agreement to the effect that the initial Agriculture Canada list had omitted two key stakeholders (one labour union and one industry), and these were admitted at once. They also quickly agreed to accept a person not attached to any of the stakeholder groups as a "neutral" Chair for their proceedings. The main issue, however, was whether or not the chemical industry manufacturers and suppliers (all of whom had been on Agriculture Canada's invitation list for the November 8 meeting) ought to be recognized as stakeholders. The decision to exclude them was implicit in article 3 of a "Statement of Principles" adopted by the eleven B.C. stakeholders: "All uses of toxic sapstain control products in British Columbia are to be discontinued as soon as it is practicable to do so ... "[13] Although it might be thought that the wood products industry would object to this provision, a moment's consideration will reveal why it did not do so. Antisapstain products are a cost of production for the sawmill and shipping industry – and a cost that increases as each new generation of products comes onto the market. This industry has no interest in such products *per se*, and would gladly dispense with them entirely if it could do so and still market its own products.

The decision on the part of the B.C. stakeholders to exclude chemical manufacturers was an indispensable ingredient in the very possibility of their reaching a consensus position on anything at all. There is no question that reaching a consensus would have been impossible with the product manufacturers (including the suppliers of chlorophenate products) sitting at the table. For anyone who harboured doubts on this point the November 8 meeting, which ended in bitterness and disarray, offered sufficient proof. Had the representatives of those chemical suppliers been sitting around the table, the anger built up over twenty years of fighting between industry and unions over PCP, TCMTB, and other products would alone have been enough to completely scupper the possibility of any agreement.

On the other hand, all the B.C. stakeholders knew full well that what had occasioned their presence "around the table" was specific antisapstain products and their use in the sawmill industry. Thus the eleven stakeholders immediately made provision for "receiving" invited deputations from the product suppliers while retaining the right to issue the invitations and to state exactly what information they were interested in being provided with on those occasions. (All such invitations were quickly accepted.)

Another initial matter for the B.C. stakeholders to assess was the implication of the refusal of the federal agencies to sit "directly" at the table during the first six meetings of the Forum. The main reason for not doing so was once again the long history of the dispute over antisapstains. As Table 8-3 shows, the group that preceded this one, the Lumber Anti-Sapstain Advisory Subcommitee, did include such direct representation – and it had failed over a number of years to resolve any outstanding issues. One argument supporting the decision not to appear in this round was the fact that when the federal agencies were directly at the table, their own problems in managing pesticides – under the terms of legislation and regulations that were full of defects, from the perspective of most non-government stakeholders[14] –, as well as the dissatisfaction of all non-government stakeholders with their management (which was voiced repeatedly and loudly at every opportunity) tended to dominate the discussions. The decision to remain "at a distance" during the BCSF meetings was (as things turned out) an insightful one, showing a clear understanding of group dynamics. In their absence, the B.C. stakeholders were able to focus clearly on their own interpretation of their problems and the possible solutions for them; like the decision to exclude the product suppliers, this element was a key ingredient in the ultimate success of the negotiations.[15]

There was also a strong desire to open this series of meetings with one or more consensus positions, symbolizing the desire of the group to reach general agreement. This was initiated by a formal ratification of the "Statement of Principles" that had been put forward provisionally by the COFI representative on behalf of B.C. stakeholders at the November 8 meeting. At its first meeting the group went on to formulate another position:

**Agreed**, there is a stakeholder consensus that Agriculture Canada should cancel registration of pentachlorophenol for sapstain control uses, and that this position should be communicated to the Pesticides Directorate, Ottawa.

**Agreed**, there is a stakeholder consensus on the status of all currently registered active ingredients for sapstain control uses, as follows:

(1) that Agriculture Canada should confirm that a complete data package on each has been formally requested from the manufacturers;

(2) that the submission of the complete data requirements should be done as soon as reasonably possible;

(3) that Agriculture Canada should inform this group what the deadlines for the submission of complete data packages in each case are, that is, when completion of the data packages can be expected. Further, that this position should be communicated to the Pesticides Directorate, Ottawa.

Then an "action plan" for arriving at a consensus position that would support the provisional registration of new active ingredients for sapstain control was discussed at length. The active ingredients DDAC and IPBC and the products NP-1®, F2®, and Timbercote® were designated the most obvious candidates, especially since there was the presumption that efficacy with these products was likely to be at acceptable levels. In accordance with the "Statement of Principles," a consensus position on this matter was required to be oriented towards identifying products and practices that demonstrated promise of lesser toxicity (or lower adverse impact) in either or both of environmental and human health dimensions, and no greater toxicity in either dimension, when judged in comparison with existing uses. To realize this objective, the group understood its need to secure an acceptable expert comparative-risk assessment, in environmental and health dimensions, for active ingredients, considered independently and in proposed combinations.

At its first meeting the group also stated its intention to seek a consensus position on the following matters:

(1) Establishment, by the Workers Compensation Board or other organizations, of suitable worker health monitoring and study programs for all registered products, based on acceptable procedures for evaluations of exposure levels, including both production and maintenance workers, and those workers who may be exposed to contaminated by-products;

(2) Modified application technologies, or substitute sapstain control technologies, which would reduce environmental or health risks;

(3) Possible provisional registration of other alternative active ingredients and products not reviewed in the Agriculture Canada discussion document.

Finally, discussion turned to the arrangements for funding to support the continued activities of the Forum. From the outset, when the Pesticides Directorate of Agriculture Canada had "invited" COFI to assume responsibility for the initial exploration of a stakeholder consensus, the Directorate took the position that it would not take direct responsibility for either the process or its funding require- ments; the rationale seemed to be that, since it was the agency that must respond to an initiative from a group of provincial stakeholders, to sponsor the group directly would constitute a potential conflict of interest. (By contrast, agencies in the United States do not appear to believe that this is a barrier to their direct participation in effective multi-stakeholder negotiation.) However, once the stakeholder rep- resentatives began to meet as a group, it was unacceptable to other stakeholders for one of their number (COFI), as a directly interested party, to continue to support the process financially. The solution was found in an offer from the B.C. Ministry of Forests, indicating that there was an agreement in principle between Forestry Canada and the ministry for a cost-sharing arrangement to support the Forum. This was acceptable since the stakeholders viewed the ministry, although a participant, as a party that did not have a direct interest in any specific outcome. This offer was limited to an initial expen- diture of $40,000 and provided support for the following types of expenditure: (1) fees and expenses of expert consultants; (2) fees paid to the Chair; (3) travel expenses for the stakeholder represen- tative who lives outside the Lower Mainland. Subsequently, this funding arrangement was continued indefinitely.

The second meeting was preoccupied with the attempt to reach agreement on an overall strategy for a series of meetings, limited in number, that might lead to a consensus position. The single most important desideratum, especially for the unions and environmental groups, was obtaining an independent comparative-risk assessment of sapstain-control products by one or more recognized experts. This flowed directly from the profound sense of disappointment they felt with both the Agriculture Canada "Discussion Document" and the November 8 meeting, which in their opinion left them with no guid- ance whatsoever on those issues that mattered most to them – in particular, a judgment by a competent scientific authority that one or more products, actually or potentially in use, represented an acceptable level of risk. A decision was made at once to seek a comparative-risk assessment from one or more independent academic experts, to be retained by the Forum itself, even if it meant that their experts would go over once again the same ground that had been covered in the "Discussion Document."

The group also recognized that time pressures likely would come into play during its deliberations. In particular, a 1 September 1990 deadline was looming: at that point, the industry would need to be in compliance with new provincial leachate regulations (concerning allowable concentrations of active ingredients in stormwater runoff from sawmill and wharf treating sites) pertaining to the antisapstain products then in use (TCMTB, Cu-8). The industry believed that existing technologies were incapable of enabling them to be in compliance with the new regulations. In other words, there was the possibility that within nine months the existing products could not be used and no alternatives would be available. However, some stakeholder representatives indicated that, unless a satisfactory resolution of the key issues in the comparative-risk assessment had already been achieved, the existence of such a deadline itself was not likely to provide sufficient impetus for reaching a consensus agreement.

The foundations for an agreement to be based on an integrated set of multiple objectives was also laid at this meeting. Various stakeholders indicated that among the essential ingredients for a viable agreement were provisions to deal with the following issues:

(1) an effective monitoring and reporting system for on-site experiences with both new and older products;

(2) an agreement with the supplier(s) of products granted temporary registration to report promptly to the Forum on new information – from worldwide sources – about on-site experience and expert assessments of such products;

(3) provision for regular reporting by the industry on new application technologies and on market opportunities for kiln-dried lumber.

Others noted that the concerns identified in this list were also a matter of record in the long series of earlier meetings of the Lumber Anti-Sapstain Advisory Committee, and agreed that it was most appropriate to put them "on the table" again now.

The union members, however, felt these provisions were inadequate. They noted that, despite a lot of discussion over the years, little had been resolved, and there remained much unhappiness among them with the ways in which sapstain-control products now being used were introduced into the mills; in the future, they insisted, there must be consultation, better information exchange, and serious attempts to monitor health impacts. More specifically, locals at two mills in particular were reported to be very unhappy with the use of one particular product under existing conditions due to skin sensitization problems, and members at these locals wanted that product withdrawn from use at the earliest possible opportunity. This demand also put pressure on the group to find a comprehensive solution for themselves, since the "default" option for Agriculture Canada was to leave things as they were for an indefinite period, and this meant that the antisapstain product then most widely employed in coastal treating sites would continue in use.

In early March 1990 the Forum met in an all-day session with the two expert toxicologists it had engaged for the comparative-risk assessment, Dr. H.B. Schiefer, Director of the Toxicology Research Centre at the University of Saskatchewan, and Dr. K.R. Solomon of the Canadian Centre for Toxicology at Guelph, Ontario. Both were asked to prepare an analysis, attend a Forum meeting, and submit a written report. The following is the charge they received:

With reference to two active ingredients in antisapstain products which are currently registered for use in Canada, and which are described in the Agriculture Canada "Discussion Document on Anti-Sapstain Chemicals," namely Copper-8-Quinolinolate or Cu8 (sect. 4, pp. 46–60) and TCMTB (sect. 8, pp. 97–118); and,

With reference to two active ingredients in antisapstain products which have been proposed for registration in Canada, but are not now registered, and which are also described in the "Discussion Document," namely DDAC (sect. 5, pp. 61–72) and IPBC (sect. 6, pp. 73–85); and,

With special reference to the information contained in additional materials supplied to you, and furnished by the manufacturers of certain products, namely
  (1) NP-1®, from Kop-Coat, Inc., which uses a combination of DDAC and IPBC, in proportions as described;
  (2) Timbercote®, from Napier Pacific, which uses only the active ingredient DDAC; and
  (3) F2®, developed by Forintek Canada, which uses only the active ingredient DDAC,

**Please prepare an expert assessment in the following terms:** Based on the documentation furnished to you, and any other relevant data that is available to you in the published scientific literature,
  1. Compare the presently registered ingredients (Cu8 and TCMTB) with both the product which combines DDAC and IPBC, and the products that use DDAC alone, in terms of
    (a) effects on human health, especially workers in industrial plants using antisapstain products, and
    (b) effects on the environment, especially leaching into water and effects on fish and other wildlife species.
  2. Specifically, give an expert opinion on the matter of whether either the DDAC/IPBC product, and/or the DDAC-only products, may be regarded as being "safer" than either or both of the products based on Cu8

and TCMTB, in terms of both human health and effects on the environment.

3. Prepare your assessment both in terms of accepted scientific terminology and also in terminology that can be understood by the layperson.

Please be advised that we have invited representatives from Kop-Coat, Napier, and Forintek to be available for direct consultations during the March 9 meeting. Of course, you will have the right to address the Stakeholder Forum representatives privately, in sessions that do not include the manufacturers' representatives, if you so wish.

Discussion during the March 9 session on Dr. Schiefer's report, which was entitled "Summary Evaluation of Anti-Sapstain Chemicals," focused on two summary charts, "Mammalian Toxicity" and "Environmental Toxicity" (see Tables 8-5 and 8-6). These charts were compiled from the following sources of information: published literature; Agriculture Canada, "Discussion Document on Anti-Sapstain Chemicals" (September 1989); and materials furnished to the Forum by Kop-Coat Inc., Napier Pacific Industries, and Forintek Canada. Dr. Schiefer emphasized the lack of independently verified scientific data for many of the critical areas of evaluation – as noted earlier, a source of great frustration for all stakeholders – especially for the long-term tests listed under "Other" and for "Human Health Data" on the "Mammalian Toxicity" chart, and in many categories of the "Environmental Toxicity" data. In the absence of such verified data, no sound judgment could be made, from a toxicological standpoint, comparing the degree of hazard among the specific set of materials considered in his report. There was considerable discussion between Dr. Schiefer and various stakeholder representatives about the implications of this lack. These discussions also focused on the implications of the differences between the tests on the active ingredients themselves versus the formulated products considered as a whole.

Dr. Keith Solomon presented a report that focused on the environmental toxicity aspects of the materials in question (these materials are the same as those considered by Dr. Schiefer, except that Dr. Solomon added Azaconazole to his list, since there were quite a few references to it in the published literature). Dr. Solomon explained that environmental toxicity is a function of both the inherent toxicity of a compound and its bioavailability, which is itself a function of such factors as movement, persistence, and biomagnification. His report gave a comparative evaluation of the materials in question in

Table 8-5
Mammalian Toxicity

| | | | | | Compound | | | |
|---|---|---|---|---|---|---|---|---|
| Descriptor | TCMTB | Cu-8 | Borax | F-2 DDAC (11.4%) + Borax (16.8%) | NP-1 DDAC (64.8%) + IPBC (7.6%) (DMSO = 5%) | IPBC IPBC (40%) Naphta (25%) DMSO (17.5%) dipropylene glycol (17.5%) | DDAC | DDAC 20% "Timbercote" |
| **Acute Toxicity** | | | | | | | | |
| $LD_{50}$ oral | + to ++ (?) | + | + | ND | ++ | + | ++ | ++* |
| $LD_{50}$ inhalation | + | + | not required | ND | ++ | + | + | –* |
| $LC_{50}$ inhalation | ? | +++ | not required | ND | +++ | ? | ND | ND |
| **Irritation** | | | | | | | | |
| eye | assumed | + | ++ | ND | +++ | +++ | +++ | +++* |
| dermal | + | ND | – | ND | +++ | + | +++ | +++* |
| sensitization | +++ | ND | ND | ND | – | – | ND | ND |
| **Short-term Toxicity** | | | | | | | | |
| oral rat | + | ? | + (++) | ND | ND | + | ND | ND |
| oral dog or | – | ND | + | ND | ND | ND | ND | ND |
| **Other** | | | | | | | | |
| Chronic toxicity | ND | + | ND | ND | ND | ND | ND | ND |
| Carcinogenicity | ND | ?** | – | ND | ND | ND | ND | ND |
| Reproductive Toxicity | ND | ? | ? | ND | ND | + | ND | ND |
| Teratogenicity | – (?) | ND | – | ND | ND | – | ND | ? |
| Mutagenicity | – | – | – | ND | – | – | – | –* |
| Pharmacokinetics | – | – | ND | ND | ND | – | ND | ND |
| **Human Health Data** | | | | | | | | |
| (from manufacturing/pilot testing/use) | ND | ND | + (?) | ND | –* | ND | ND | ND |

\* Data supplied by compagny.

\*\* "Animal, Suspected Carcinogen" according to Gosselin *et al*, 1984, but: "Inadequate evidence" according to IARC, 1987.

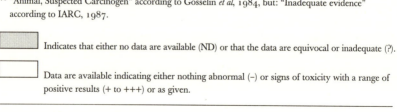

Indicates that either no data are available (ND) or that the data are equivocal or inadequate (?).

Data are available indicating either nothing abnormal (–) or signs of toxicity with a range of positive results (+ to +++) or as given.

Table 8-6
Environmental Toxicity

| Descriptor | TCMTB | Cu-8 | Borax | F-2 DDAC (11.4%) + Borax (16.8%) | NP-1 DDAC (64.8%) + IPBC (7.6%) (DMSO = 5%) | IPBC IPBC (40%) Naphta (25%) DMSO (17.5%) dipropylene glycol (17.5%) | DDAC | DDAC 20% "Timbercote" |
|---|---|---|---|---|---|---|---|---|
| **General** | | | | | | | | |
| Volatilization | – | – | – | ND | ND | – | – | ND |
| Vapour Pressure | ND | low | – | ND | ND | low | – | ND |
| Water Solubility | 40 mg/L | < 220 µg/L | soluble | ND | ND | moderate | soluble | ND |
| Persistence in Water | t½=15 days | ND | ND | ND | ND | < 7 days | ND | ND |
| Hydrolysis | assumed | – | ? | ND | ND | – | ND | ND |
| Phototransform-ation/Photolysis | rapid | stable | ND | ND | ND | ND | ND | ND |
| Adsorption/ Desorption/ Leaching in Soil | + to ++ | ND | ND | ND | ND | ND | ++ | ND |
| Biotransformation | occurs | ND | ? | ND | ND | little | ? | ND |
| Bioconcentration | – (?) | 0 to 2,000 | ? | ND | ND | low | – | ND |
| **Fish** | | | | | | | | |
| Acute: 48h LC$_{50}$ | ND | ++ | ND | ND | ND | +++ | ++ | ND |
| Acute: 96h LC$_{50}$ | +++ | +++ | + | ND | +++ | +++ | +++ | ++* |
| Chronic | ND | ND | ND | ND | ND | ND | ND | ND |
| **Invertebrate Toxicity** | | | | | | | | |
| Acute (e.g. Daphnia) | +++ | + | ND | ND | ND | ND | ND | ND |
| Chronic | ND | ND | ND | ND | ND | ND | ND | ND |
| *Avian Toxicity* | – | ND | ND | ND | ND | + | ND | ND |
| **Other** | | | | | | | | |
| Effects on Phytoplankton | ND | ND | ND | ND | ND | ND | ? | ND |
| Kow Value | 25 | ND | ND | ND | ND | ND | "0" | ND |
| Leaching from Wood | ND | ND | ND | below tox. to fich=– (?) | 800 ppb* | ND | ND | ? |
| Disposal of Treated Wood | yields SO$_2$ | ND | ND | ND | ND | ND | incin.safe | ND |
| Storm Water Concentration | 300 ppb (?) | 300 ppb (?) | ND | ND | ND | ND | ND | ND |
| Analytical Methodology | ? | ND | yes ? | ND | ND | ND | ND | ND |
| Environmental Residues | ND | ND | yes ? | ND | ND | ND | ND | ND |

*Data supplied by compagny.

Indicates that either no data are available (ND) or that the data are equivocal or inadequate (?).

Data are available indicating either nothing abnormal (–) or signs of toxicity with a range of positive results (+ to +++) or as given.

terms of charts on chronic and acute toxicity, leaching, biomagnification, persistence, movement in various media, completeness of the database, and acute toxicity of the most sensitive organism. The discussions with stakeholder representatives focused again on the adequacy of the verified data, which was virtually complete for acute effects but non-existent for chronic effects. In response to questions, a number of points were made: (1) a 1986 scientific paper appeared to show that there is a good correlation between acute and chronic toxicity in aquatic organisms, and therefore one may be able to use the former as a guide to the latter, at least in these cases; (2) there were a quite limited number of species tested for acute effects; (3) there was a clear pattern in the acute toxicity results, with Azaconazole towards the lower end of the distribution, IPBC and DDAC around the middle, and TCMTB and Cu-8 towards the higher end.

In the general discussion with Drs. Schiefer and Solomon, a variety of topics were raised for discussion by stakeholder representatives, notably:

- cancer rates in the population: Dr. Schiefer gave a brief exposition on this matter, pointing out that, if lung cancer due to smoking is excluded, cancer rates have been decreasing in industrial societies over a long period.
- mutagenicity tests: these have limited significance. In general, human health continues to improve (as indicated by increasing life expectancy), but there is a potential problem in the greater sensitivity to various substances on the part of a portion of the population, and this problem is not sufficiently understood yet.
- human health data, based on scientifically valid measures of exposure, for sapstain-control products is poor in general.

In later discussion Dr. Hans Ward of Kop-Coat noted that in the United States (where NP-1 had been registered for sapstain-control use by the EPA since 1985) there were in 1989 about 700 mills using sapstain-control products, distributed approximately as follows: NP-1, 600 mills; Cu-8, 50 mills; TCMTB, 30 mills; other (including chlorophenates), 20 mills. It was noted that about thirty-five other products had been experimented with at various mills during the past five years and had not been adopted.

Towards the end of this session, Mr. Calvin Sandborn, stakeholder representative from the West Coast Environmental Law Association, stated that the data inadequacies described that day led to an inescapable conclusion, namely, that it would be unwise to short-circuit the full registration process. He argued further that there was no

apparent basis for saying that the materials discussed at the stakeholder meeting which were not then registered were "safer" than
those then being used, with respect either to worker health or to the
environment. Products that are unacceptable by today's standards
indeed may have avoided proper scrutiny by being "grandfathered,"
but if so, these eventually would be removed from use; it is no
solution to allow others to be used which also have inadequate databases.

Dr. Schiefer noted in conclusion that the family of "quats" (qua-
ternary ammonium compounds, such as DDAC) is very widely used
in society generally, for example as hospital disinfectants, and perhaps it would be possible to examine data held by Agriculture
Canada with respect to the registration of DDAC-based products for
uses other than that of sapstain control. Second, judging from the
published literature in Germany, where DDAC-based products had
been widely used for over fifty years and where there were as yet no
reports of carcinogenetic effects, it was unlikely that DDAC would be
shown to be a carcinogen when further tests were done. Dr. Solomon
concluded: (1) on the basis of the fish toxicity data in hand, the
DDAC-based products should represent a significant reduction in
environmental hazard by comparison with products then in use;
(2) completion of adequate human-exposure and short-term aquatic
toxicity studies could be made a condition of any temporary registration decision.

At the next meeting Mr. Phil Gilbert, stakeholder representative
from the Council of Forest Industries, tabled a draft of a proposed
health-monitoring agreement, resulting from discussions between
IWA-Canada and COFI representatives; extensive modifications to the
draft were made in the Forum meetings, and the complete text of
this agreement, in its final form, appeared as "Sub-Agreement C" of
the Framework Consensus Agreement (see Appendix 2). This sub-
agreement is in fact the centrepiece of the Framework Consensus
Agreement, and its centrality reflects the longstanding (but to that
point unanswered) demand of the unions for a direct and ongoing
role in the monitoring of health effects and in the making of decisions
about remedial measures for identified problems. Its complexity was
such that the initial drafting had to be done outside the scope of the
main Forum meetings, but subsequently (after minor changes) it
received the unanimous and enthusiastic support of all stakeholders.

Also at this meeting Professor Clyde Hertzman from the Department of Epidemiology and Health Care at the University of British
Columbia gave a preliminary report on the data generated by his
ongoing questionnaire study of the reporting of symptoms of acute

adverse health effects by workers at sawmills. There were a total of 1229 symptoms reported in his sample, of which approximately 25 percent could be associated with the use of sapstain-control products; however, fewer than 10 percent of these symptoms were said to have been reported to the first-aid stations, and not all of these could actually be found in the first-aid reports maintained at the mills. His preliminary conclusion was that the method of reporting symptoms then in force was not even good enough to correlate the symptom reporting with first-aid reports; some progress was being made in developing a suitable methodology for symptom reporting, however.

### Towards Agreement

Then the Chair asked permission of stakeholders to table a draft of a comprehensive Framework Consensus Agreement which had been prepared by the Chair, who also noted that meetings about the possibility of a consensus had been going on regularly since September 1989, and that at least some stakeholders wished to assess at this point whether it was likely that a consensus agreement might be reached in the near future. The stakeholder representatives agreed to review this document and began making a number of additions to the draft.

Discussion on acceptance of the consensus agreement was interrupted by other business, however. Mr. Sandborn inquired as to the existence of a report on NP-1 which had been completed and submitted to MacMillan Bloedel some time ago by Professor Hertzman. Mr. Hu Martin, an alternate representative from the B.C. sawmill industry and an employee of the company, acknowledged that such a report existed and had been prepared in 1989 as part of an ongoing contractual arrangement between MacMillan Bloedel and Professor Hertzman (in fact, he had this report in his possession at the meeting but had no authority to distribute it). Mr. Sandborn vigorously noted his dismay and disappointment that the existence of this report had not been indicated earlier to the Stakeholder Forum, and Mr. Martin agreed to seek immediate approval from his superiors by telephone to release this report to the stakeholders; once he had received approval, copies were prepared and distributed to all stakeholders at once. The Chair was instructed to send copies to Drs. Schiefer and Solomon and to request that they review its contents and discuss them by telephone with Professor Hertzman, and to request further that they include the results of their evaluation and discussions in their final written reports to the Stakeholder Forum.

Mr. Martin agreed to ascertain whether there were any other pertinent documents held by MacMillan Bloedel on this matter, with respect to MacMillan Bloedel's "internal review" of NP-1. Mr. Martin subsequently provided eleven pages of such documentation to the Chair and this material was then distributed to all stakeholders. The Chair also was instructed to invite Professor Hertzman to the next meeting to discuss his report.

This episode illustrates one of the potential pitfalls of multi-stakeholder negotiation: a single case of perceived bad faith, especially on the part of a major stakeholder, can undermine temporarily or permanently an otherwise good record of co-operation and progress towards consensus. In this case the company's reasons for not volunteering the existence of this most relevant study were never clarified, but the fact of its unexpected disclosure almost caused the union and environmental stakeholders to walk out of the meeting and did result in reversing the generally improving relations among stakeholders that had been in evidence until that moment. Directly as a result of this episode a new point on information disclosure was added immediately to the "Framework Consensus Agreement," binding each stakeholder to disclose promptly any information in its possession that was likely to be regarded by other stakeholders as of material significance to their deliberations.

The Hertzman report on NP-1 was written in the accepted scientific style of a professional epidemiologist. Nevertheless, although few stakeholder representatives present at the meeting had scientific training of any sort, they were all able to scan its contents and understand its general thrust, mainly because they had spent an entire day of intensive discussion with Drs. Schiefer and Solomon only two weeks earlier, and they had had detailed presentations from and exchanges with these experts (whom they had hired and trusted), in language appropriate to the "educated layperson," about the technical issues in risk assessment. Most stakeholders were thus able to scan the Hertzman report in the meeting room and come to the conclusion that there were "no surprises" in it – in other words, there was nothing that contradicted the general thrust of what they had learned from their experts. Had this not been the case, and had the stakeholders been required to wait a few weeks until their experts had confirmed their own intuitive reading of this document (as they did subsequently), the forced disclosure of this document would have disrupted the course of subsequent discussions much more severely than it did, and might even – in view of the deadline mentioned earlier, which at this point was only five months away – have ensured the collapse of the entire process. The receipt of the additional documentation from MacMillan Bloedel seemed to repair some of the damage to stakeholder relations, and the series of meetings was resumed three weeks later.

The representatives requested that, before consenting to resume discussion on the "Framework Consensus Agreement," the industry give an overview of the current state of development in sapstain-control technologies. Mr. Gilbert gave such a presentation in early May, which covered the topics of sapstain-control systems and products presently in use, current market acceptance issues, Code of Good Practice compliance, leachate regulations compliance, and alternative application technologies in development around the world (such as charged drop technology, waxing, kiln drying, and biotechnology). A provision was incorporated into the Agreement requiring the industry to provide an annual update on this subject to the Forum.

When the Agreement was re-tabled, its key feature was apparent: it was a package of six separate but interrelated features, and it had to be accepted or rejected as a whole (subject to modifications in the actual text that were agreed to, of course). This is a necessary feature of any such agreement, for obvious reasons. (The entire document is reproduced in Appendix 2, Document #1.)

For the union and environmental representatives, Sub-Agreement "E" of the proposed Agreement was "the bottom line." The provisions of this sub-agreement announced the support of its signatories for the granting of temporary registration by Agriculture Canada to products using the active ingredients DDAC and IPBC, which were not then registered for sapstain control in Canada. In the regulatory scheme in place, "full" registration (covering an initial period of five years and renewable) is given only to those products for which complete data packages have been submitted and evaluated. In all other cases registration is "conditional" or "temporary," pending receipt and evaluation of required data, and is normally limited to one year (although such registration is also renewable on a year-to-year basis). As noted earlier, the union and environmental stakeholders had been very reluctant all along to state publicly their support for a pesticide registration decision on one or more specific chemical compounds. In the end, half of this combined group of six stakeholders did so because they got an acceptable "package" in the Agreement as a whole. In simple terms, the key trade-off was the industry's support for the health-monitoring process and the unions' support for the temporary registration of NP-1. What the unions did appreciate very much about the temporary registration status was that it enabled both the Forum and the federal agencies to monitor closely developments at the treatment sites upon introduction of NP-1 (which was being used widely at coastal sites within months of its registration), and to take appropriate action, if problems appeared, with a minimum of regulatory fuss as the registration expired each year.

The final version of the Agreement was accepted and signed by eight stakeholders:

British Columbia Ministry of Environment
British Columbia Ministry of Forests
Canadian Paperworkers Union
Council of Forest Industries of British Columbia
International Longshoremen's and Warehousemen's Union
IWA-Canada
Sawmill Industry of British Columbia (COFI Members)
Wharf Operators of British Columbia

Three stakeholders declined to sign the Agreement:

Earthcare
Pulp, Paper and Woodworkers of Canada
West Coast Environmental Law Association

The Agreement was forwarded to the federal agencies involved in pesticide registration, while the three stakeholders who declined to affirm the Agreement communicated directly to those agencies the reasons for their decision. The dissenting stakeholders did not make any public statements that called into question the wisdom of the Agreement, however, and when Forum meetings resumed the following fall they continued to participate.

Even before learning of Ottawa's response, the British Columbia stakeholders moved immediately to implement the provisions of the Agreement, especially the sub-agreement on health monitoring, as a sign of good faith among themselves. The IWA-Canada representative was named Interim Chair of the Health Protection and Monitoring Subcommittee and convened its first meeting two months later. The representative of one of the dissenting stakeholders (the Pulp, Paper and Woodworkers of Canada) stated that his union would participate in the activities of the Health Protection and Monitoring Subcommittee established under the Framework Consensus Agreement. This decision was accepted by the other stakeholders, including all of the other unions and the industry groups whose representatives formed this subcommittee.

Naturally, arriving at a consensus position of any kind was by no means a foregone conclusion, nor was there any predetermined content for a consensus position. To the extent to which the final outcome was acceptable to a majority of participants, there was more than a bit of luck involved. However, the fact that the Agreement has held up in a satisfactory way since May 1990 is some indication of the underlying soundness of the package that was negotiated.

On August 1, 1990, the Pesticides Directorate of Agriculture Canada issued CAPCO (Canadian Association of Pesticide Control Officers) Note No. 90–10, "Wood Treatment Materials."[16] (The part of this document dealing with antisapstains is reproduced in its entirety as Document #2 in Appendix 2.) Thus the federal agency took regulatory actions having the force of law that were consistent with the Forum's consensus position (Sub-Agreement "E") with respect to all three groups of antisapstain products (see Table 8-1). In giving an explanation for these decisions, Agriculture Canada made explicit reference to the actions of the B.C. Stakeholder Forum on Sapstain Control, including the consensus position contained in the Framework Consensus Agreement as well as the nature of the dissenting views. In effect, the federal agency accepted the 8–3 split in the Stakeholder Forum as a "consensus," taking into account the line-up of stakeholders on the majority side, but also both the thoughtful and extensive deliberations of the Forum on the issues at stake and the nature of the dilemmas facing B.C. stakeholders as a whole, in view of the long history of these disputes and the changed situation represented by the new provincial leachate regulations.

*Developments following the consensus agreement*

The Health Monitoring Subcommittee of the Stakeholder Forum, consisting of representatives from the union and industry stakeholders only, has met on average once every quarter since June 1990. The regular responsibilities it has assumed are as follows:

1 Preparation of an "Anti-Sapstain Log Sheet," containing a record of the type of active ingredient, and the concentration level of the active in the resultant spray mix, at every site;
2 Preparation of a permanent registry for the log sheets to be maintained at the offices of the B.C. Workers Compensation Board;
3 Preparation of a permanent first-aid record book, and a questionnaire form for reporting acute health symptoms during the two-week monitoring periods specified in the Agreement;

4 Meetings with suppliers of newly introduced products, to review
  and discuss the training programs and protective-gear requirements for workers at treatment sites;
5 Meetings with prospective suppliers of new products, who wish to
  make the case that their products would pose lower risk to health
  and environment than existing products do;
6 Discussions of information filed on questionnaire forms; problems
  arising at treatment sites; levels of compliance with safety precautions; new types of protective gear; and related matters.

Despite this record of impressive progress in labour-management
relations, the single most important longstanding issue concerning
health-effects monitoring remained unresolved: the lack of a scientific exposure assessment, an essential ingredient in a proper risk
assessment of products in actual use. It was the responsibility of
Health and Welfare Canada, as an advisory department to Agriculture Canada, to evaluate the data, but it was industry's responsibility
to gather the data, and there existed no generally accepted protocol
for doing so. Thus, in August 1990, the Pesticides Directorate wrote
to the IWA-Canada representative, who chaired the Health Monitoring Subcommittee, suggesting that the Stakeholder Forum become
involved in a process leading to the formulation of an acceptable
protocol for the scientific assessment of worker exposure to antisapstains at treatment sites; the Forum was encouraged to take the
lead role in devising this process, with the assurance of co-operation
from the federal agencies involved.

When the work on the actual protocol was set to begin, after a full
year of preparatory work, the roles and responsibilities had been
arrayed as follows:

1 The Stakeholder Forum was the agency responsible for managing
  the process, in particular, for selecting a team of independent
  experts to produce the protocol.
2 A three-member expert panel, epidemiologists from the University
  of British Columbia and the University of Washington, was responsible for developing a protocol acceptable to Health and Welfare
  Canada.
3 Agriculture Canada had formal authority as the regulatory agency,
  and assumed responsibility for enlisting the support of all suppliers
  or potential suppliers of antisapstain products, based anywhere in
  the world, to the Canadian market.
4 Seventeen manufacturers of antisapstain products, with head
  offices in Canada, the United States, and Europe, agreed to share

equally the costs for the expert team, even though they would not have exclusive rights to the use of the scientific protocol which was developed by the panel.

5 The Chair of the Forum, who is a university faculty member, was responsible for collecting the industry contributions, paying the costs of the expert team, and ensuring good communications among all of the above parties as the project progressed.

In February 1992, some time before the protocol was finished, Agriculture Canada announced that all future regulatory review of antisapstain products would incorporate a requirement for a worker-exposure assessment.

The completed protocol was accepted by Health and Welfare Canada during the fall of 1992, and the first actual exposure assessment studies conducted according to its terms (which are very expensive to undertake) are expected to be carried out in early 1994.

Finally, at its May 1992 meeting, the Stakeholder Forum agreed to expand its participation in the evaluation of new products and technologies for sapstain control that promise lower risk both for worker health and environmental impact by establishing a subcommittee to receive representations from manufacturers along these lines. Both the main stakeholder group and its health-monitoring committee appear by now to be permanent participants in this area of pest management in Canada. Their relationship with the federal agencies, who of course retain legal authority over these matters, is working well. The stakeholders have learned that their efforts to devise consensus positions that both reflect their own sense of acceptable solutions and also respect the boundaries of formal bureaucratic authority will be informally integrated into the decision-making structure; similarly, the federal agencies have found that their own strong encouragement of a regional stakeholder consensus group has assisted them in carrying out their responsibilities in a domain that had been fraught with bitter controversy for a long time.

Two results in particular stand out, so far as Canadian public policy is concerned, in the record of events that began in the fall of 1989: first, the explicit referencing of a stakeholder consensus agreement (along with the dissenting views) in an actual regulatory decision; and second, the unusual matrix of responsibility, involving industry, governments, academic experts, and stakeholders, that brought into being the scientific protocol for worker exposure assessment. So far as we know, neither had occurred previously in Canadian regulatory practice.

PART III: ISSUES IN
STAKEHOLDER NEGOTIATION
AND ACCEPTABLE RISK

*Inadequate Databases for Risk Assessments*

Where potentially toxic chemicals are in use in industries with important economic significance (including those that provide significant employment), all stakeholders (except the chemical manufacturers) are put at a considerable disadvantage as a result of insufficient data. Considerable frustration is expressed at the regulatory system for allowing this to happen: stakeholders are puzzled and annoyed that, many years after a certain chemical is registered, important studies are either still outstanding or not even under way.

The controversy over antisapstain products may or may not represent an extreme case, but consider the factors involved:

- an industry of great importance to both a provincial economy and, in terms of export markets, the nation's balance of payments;
- a technological solution for sapstain control utilizing toxic chemicals that has been in place for over fifty years;
- an elaborate government regulatory apparatus, also in place for a long time, charged with expert assessments of risks and benefits.

Now consider the facts. Despite the above, as of 1989 no scientific procedure was in place to do any worker-exposure assessments (rendering a full health-risk assessment impossible); there had been almost a decade of consistent complaints by various stakeholders about the inadequacy of the existing state of affairs; and, to cap it all, at the end of 1989 a situation existed in which there were serious data gaps for all candidate chemicals except the one that stakeholders unanimously agreed should be discontinued![17]

This can only be described as a "system failure" of massive proportions. As indicated in Section I, the established Canadian regulatory structure and the way science is utilized therein cannot provide the resolution to these types of problems. To repeat, the resolution to the controversy over antisapstains that the major stakeholders – industry, unions, and environmental groups – demanded from governments can be stated as follows: Make available through the pesticide registration process any product that delivers the requisite efficacy (control of sapstain), on the one hand, and a scientifically verified level of acceptable risk (in terms of both worker health and environmental impact), on the other. We contend that this system failure stems from the absence of an explicit, legal mandate that would enable regulators to take a "proactive" approach in areas where deficiencies are identified. As of this time no such remedies exist.[18]

### Regulatory Decisions based on Risk/Benefit Trade-offs

What would have been the situation if more complete hazard assessments, at least, had been available for both currently used and proposed antisapstains? Judging on the basis of established practice, the regulatory authority (Agriculture Canada) almost certainly would have registered a wider variety of active ingredients, perhaps with differential restrictions on use based on acute effects such as skin sensitization, for example. One can surmise this with confidence because of the unsurprising conclusion of the economic benefits assessment for sapstain control in the B.C. wood products industry, which showed significantly positive results. The risk/benefit trade-off approach to decision-making that is evident in many current Agriculture Canada "decision documents" on pesticide registration, if it had been applied in this case, almost certainly would have shown that "benefits outweigh risks" for a large assortment of currently available antisapstain products.[19]

The problem here is that risk/benefit trade-offs represent a "black box" approach to decision-making; you can see the result, but not the reasoning behind it. Risks are quantified in terms of adverse health impacts, which are traditionally assessed in Canadian regulatory practice in qualitative, not quantitative, terms (risk of sickness or premature death, sometimes expressed as "quality of life-years lost or impaired"); whereas benefits are quantified in terms of actual dollars. And there are simply no rules that allow the two to be "weighed" against each other in a way that has been publicly defended and is generally acceptable. In our view, even a much more complete hazard assessment of antisapstains would not have helped the situation in 1989, since it would not have led necessarily to a removal of products from the market by an action of the competent regulatory authority, even though these products were the subject of loud and persistent complaints from the unions.[20] This is simply because there was definitive and unshakeable evidence showing the economic benefits of using them, whereas the radically incomplete health-risk assessment simply persisted and the cumbersome regulatory process did not have the capability of responding to demands for procuring an adequate risk assessment within any kind

251 Antisapstain Chemicals

of reasonable time frame. In this case, given the history of controversy over PCP in the industry, the tradition of active unionism, and the large number of workers routinely exposed to antisapstain chemicals, it is our belief that regulatory decisions based on conventional risk/benefit trade-offs would not have been acceptable to either union or environmental stakeholders.

Furthermore, the way in which Health and Welfare Canada's (HWC) PCP update is presented in the 1989 "Discussion Document" shows the inherent limitations of expert risk assessment as a basis for a judgment on acceptable risk. In the first place, despite the comparatively large published (and thus peer-reviewed) literature on these chemicals and their extensive industrial use over a long period in Canada, what can only be described as the scandalous lack of scientifically reliable exposure data defeated the very possibility of an adequate health-risk assessment. The HWC update notes: Neither daily absorbed doses nor amounts excreted in urine can be "directly" calculated from any available Canadian data (only "rough estimates" may be made); although "the degree of dermal penetration is a determining factor in the estimation of human occupational exposure and assessment of risk," HWC notes that the published literature on this point is too limited to permit a reliable assessment. And it concludes: "The results of published human monitoring studies, after a single oral dose *or after chronic occupational exposure*, do not present a consistent profile on which to assess human risk" (emphasis added).

The "bottom line" in this situation can be stated simply:

- In light of the above, and recognizing that Agriculture Canada is completely dependent upon Health and Welfare Canada for its risk assessment expertise, if Agriculture Canada had been required to make a regulatory judgment on chlorophenate compounds on the basis of its established risk/benefit trade-off framework, those compounds would not have been withdrawn from use as antisapstains.
- Only consistent pressure from unions and environmental groups was responsible for ending chlorophenate use in the wood products industry.

Thus, so long as the toxicological data and hazard profile of a chemical does not show unacceptable cancer risk, the uncertainties that arise from the lack of a scientific basis for exposure assessment means that, to this day, definitive health-risk assessments cannot be done in Canada for antisapstain products. Fortunately this situation is expected to change soon.

*Acceptable Risk*

The limitations on expert risk assessment in the antisapstain case are symptomatic: similar key gaps turn up in almost every area of health and environmental assessment. (This is not a generic problem for risk assessment as such, however: where good data exist for both hazard estimation and exposure, such as for formaldehyde in homes, tobacco use, or prescription drugs generally, a reliable health-risk assessment can be made.)[21] In the type of cases exemplified by antisapstains, almost always, even when some very good and relevant quantitative data exists, there are some key pieces missing that forestall a complete risk assessment. And almost always the incomplete (and therefore questionable) risk assessment is juxtaposed against a confident statement of economic benefits: "Five hundred jobs will be created [or lost]," etc.

What should one conclude from this seemingly inescapable lack of essential data and analysis? Certainly it does no harm to dream of a time when all essential data for the risk assessment of all potentially harmful technologies currently in use will be at hand in a thoroughly reliable form – so long as we remain cognizant of the difference between our dream and waking states. For, given the relentless advance of industrial technologies, where qualitatively new phases of product development (think of biotechnologies) force themselves upon us and somehow win general acquiescence well before we have the means in hand to assess their impacts at all adequately (and indeed well before we have finished with the arduous task of coming to terms with their predecessors), we have reason to suspect that our society will always be lacking somewhat in its conduct of risk assessment. Thus we conclude that in the absence of the "complete and comprehensive database" fondly referred to by regulatory agencies but infrequently available in practice, all relevant stakeholders ought to become involved in judgments about acceptable risk, for the following reasons:

- First, although most stakeholders cannot independently evaluate expert risk assessments, they ought to be given a chance to hear for themselves the review of evidence and (especially) an account of the key data gaps and how they may be remedied – and also, where it exists, the "clash of experts" on the issues that concern them;
- Second, the main rationale is that for health risks the willing co-operation of potentially affected parties can assist the process of

filling key data gaps (personal record-keeping or suitable blood/ urine samples for exposure assessment, for example);

• Third, and most generally, respecting environmental- as well as health-risk assessment, active stakeholder involvement holds the promise of correcting, if only in part, some of the "system failures" in Canada.[22] When they are empowered to do so, stakeholders can insist on appropriate accountability and can assist governments towards institutionalizing a better system.

This involvement by stakeholders in *de facto* judgments on acceptable risk also means being an invited party to the making of risk/ benefit trade-offs: it is intuitively obvious that a health or environmental risk, especially of an involuntary nature, is acceptable *only* in the light of offsetting benefits. Given the inherently arbitrary nature of decision-making on risk/benefit trade-offs (the "black box"), such decisions are acceptable only where relevant stakeholders have been involved in making such trade-offs explicitly in a public forum. Acceptance by stakeholders of risk/benefit trade-offs can be gained only through negotiation, specifically by a process of bargaining among themselves.

1 Experts in risk assessment must accept the fact that the bargaining will be carried out in terms of risks and benefits as perceived by the stakeholders themselves and as expressed in layperson's terms. When it comes to *acceptable* risk, in a democratic society all parties are equally expert.

2 There must be clear and quite concrete short-term benefits for key stakeholders in terms of their perceived interests, in return for which they assume part of the burden of the scientific uncertainties associated with incomplete risk assessments.

3 The notion of concrete gains means that implementing decisions by competent authorities should follow quickly from any specific round of stakeholder negotiation that those authorities have called into being (directly or indirectly).

4 The process is at least as important as the result, especially in the "first round," because most environmental controversies are ongoing matters that will not be resolved completely in the near future. Thus the main objective early on is to build a relationship of trust among the participants.

5 A consensus position should involve as many key stakeholder interests as possible, but unanimity is almost always impossible to achieve; however, something less than unanimous acceptance of a

Table 8-7
Chronology of Key Events in the Antisapstain Controversy (1941–91)

| | |
|---|---|
| 1941 | Chlorophenates registered in Canada as wood preservatives |
| 1959–1970 | Additional registrations of Penta for other materials (e.g., animal hides) and uses (e.g., soil sterilant) |
| 1971 | First recommendation against use (in preserving animal hides); controversy in U.S. and Canada over chick edema |
| 1975 | First indication of possible occupational health problems in B.C. lumber industry |
| 1975–1990 | Public controversy about PCP involving unions, environmental groups, industry, and governments in many different countries |
| 1976–1989 | PCP under ongoing regulatory scrutiny in Canada by three federal departments, expert committees, etc. |
| 1977 | Publicity over contamination of feed grain from railway car previously used to transport PCP, which is thereafter listed as a dangerous commodity under the Railway Act |
| 1978 | Ban on PCP for sapstain control in Sweden |
| 1978–1979 | U.S. EPA "RPAR" Notice (1978); Agriculture Canada official notice of re-evaluation (1979) |
| 1980 | Two alternatives to PCP [TCMTB, Cu8] "grandfathered" under new Agriculture Canada rules (i.e., registered with inadequate data) |
| 1980 | B.C. Federal/Provincial Wood Protection Task Force convened by Environment Canada, along with Agriculture Canada; B.C. provincial ministries (Health, Forests, Environment); B.C. Workers' Compensation Board; Council of Forest Industries (COFI); and B.C. labour unions. |
| 1981 | IWA-Canada sponsored report on occupational health effects of chlorophenates |
| 1979–1983 | Forest Industry Industrial Health Research Program [FIIHRP] in B.C. (controversies over health studies) |
| 1985–1988 | Meetings of COFI's Lumber Anti-Sapstain Advisory Sub-Committee (see Table 8-3) |
| 1987–1990 | Wood products industry phases out use of PCP and begins using registered alternatives (TCMTB, Cu8, Borax) |
| June 1987 | Agriculture Canada "Discussion Document on Penta-chlorophenol" |
| Sept. 1989 | Agriculture Canada "Discussion Document on Anti-Sapstain Chemicals" |
| Nov. 1989 | Meeting in Vancouver, convened by Agriculture Canada; invitees included B.C. stakeholders (Table 8-4) and the manufacturers and formulators of antisapstain products |
| Nov. 1989 | Initial consensus position of British Columbia stakeholders |
| Dec. 1989 | Initial meeting of the B.C. Stakeholder Forum on Sapstain Control (BCSF); a total of six meetings were held between December 1989 and May 1990 |
| May 1990 | Framework Consensus Agreement (FCA) and public announcement |
| June 1990 | First meeting of the Health Monitoring Subcommittee (HMS) of the BCSF, as established under the terms of the FCA |
| July 1990 | Agriculture Canada document, "Wood Preservative Chemicals," including regulatory decision on new antisapstain products |
| Sept. 1990 | B.C. Ministry of Environment, "Anti-sapstain Chemical Waste Control Regulation" |
| Fall 1990 | B.C. registry of antisapstain product uses, health-monitoring protocol, exposure study protocol, and other activities under the auspices of Health Monitoring Subcommittee of the BCSF |
| Fall 1991 | Generic Worker Exposure Protocol project started under the auspices of the BCSF |
| Fall 1992 | Canadian regulatory agencies begin to implement provisions for worker exposure assessments in product registration process |

position should be reasonable enough to ensure that all stake-holders "stay at the table."

6  This also means that for any particular "round" the scope of the consensus that is sought should be restricted: from a purely prag-matic standpoint, stakeholders should distinguish between what they can tackle in one round and what they can agree to postpone for future rounds.

It is too early to say whether the multi-stakeholder consultation approach, as a way of dealing with seemingly intractable health and environmental risk controversies, will take root and flourish in Canada. We shall return to the task of estimating its prospects in our final chapter.

# CHAPTER NINE

# Useful Lessons

So, what do most of the policy makers' constituencies care about? I suggest TLC: trust, liability, consent.
   a. Are the institutions that make the decisions that manage and regulate the technology worthy of fiduciary trust?
   b. Is the principle that will be used to apportion liabilities for an undesirable consequence acceptable to those affected?
   c. Is the procedure by which collective consent is obtained for a course of action acceptable to those who must bear its consequences?

Steve Rayner[1]

## PRELUDE

Risks are trade-offs: to take a risk is to incur a certain loss in expectation of a larger but uncertain offsetting gain. Where health and environmental risks are concerned, the loss is not necessarily an actual adverse effect, because the undesirable outcome may not ever occur for anyone. Rather, the loss is characterized by an element of uncertainty. Those individuals who actually do suffer a diminution of health or well-being may never become aware of the cause-and-effect relation, or if they do, their knowledge might arrive too late to benefit them; moreover, the effect can be distributed among the exposed population (such as workers in a particular industry) with apparent randomness, with no explanation as to why some persons are afflicted and others similarly exposed are not.

   To take responsibility for a risk is to accept explicitly the role one has played in generating a set of trade-offs. A firm that requires its workers to use an industrial chemical, an individual who drives an automobile, a government that subsidizes a coal mine venture with loan guarantees and tax breaks all willingly play a role in risk-taking activity and necessarily a role in generating trade-offs. Where some of these parties do so in effect on behalf of others who may not be aware of the exact nature of the trade-offs that have been made – for example, if the plant workers have not been fully apprised of the assessed risks associated with the chemical they must use, or if the miners are not fully cognizant of the site-specific risk of an underground explosion – such parties bear a far heavier share of responsibility than they would have if they were acting solely on their own account.

The great hope of modern society is to substitute, through the conquest of nature, self-initiated risks for naturally imposed ones. In continuous technological innovation modern society has sought to reduce the naturally occurring hazards to which the human race traditionally has been exposed (pestilence, disease, famine – but not alas the other "Horseman", war) to an irreducible minimum and to replace them with better bargains, namely, risks deliberately undertaken because the potential benefits are calculated to outweigh the potential losses by a wide margin. But there is a hefty price to pay, for the machines that make up the technological shield we have erected against nature now bid us to service them faithfully. The pesticides that suppress insect populations, the food production that sustains ever-increasing numbers, the drugs that hold infectious diseases at bay, the energy that underpins the whole enterprise – none can rest in its labours on our behalf. All these and other technologies must be renewed incessantly (for the insects and bacteria mutate and soils and energy sources become depleted), and all the while our needs and our dependency grow. Even the promise of "sustainable development" is unthinkable without continuous technological innovation, and such innovation is inherently risk-taking activity. Therefore our first proposition is this: As a society we are hooked on risk.

When we look back across the trajectory of the modern era, few would deny that on the whole the benefits of industrialism have outweighed the actual and potential new losses. And when we examine our own personal proclivities, relatively few individuals are found who fail to indulge themselves in at least some risky activities that are voluntarily assumed and not imposed. In fact there appears to be a curious paradox in the idea of individual freedom, namely, that we seek to liberate ourselves from domination by involuntarily imposed risks, originating either in nature or in society, in order to be able to indulge ourselves more and more in risky voluntary activities. Therefore our second proposition is this: Most of us seek out at least some risks to enjoy.

Both our subtle technological manipulations of nature and our own lifestyle choices yield a complex web of interacting forces in terms of the impacts they can have on our well-being, making the isolation of particular cause-and-effect relations difficult and often impossible. In addition, the essence of market-driven economic transactions (as a virtually infinite series of discrete private contracts motivated with an eye to proximate advantage) discourages the attribution of specific liability for impacts that occur at a distance in time and space. In the process of continuous technological innovation within a market-driven context, the two foregoing factors pretty much assure for the risk-proponent – with respect to health and environmental (as opposed to financial) risks – what we may call the nearness of benefits and the remoteness of losses. Thus, while both institutions and individuals have an interest in developing opportunities for risk-taking behaviour on utility-maximizing grounds, many also realize that there is a good chance they may retain a nice portion of the resultant benefits for themselves whilst off-loading much of the potential loss on someone else. Therefore our third proposition is this: In our society, everyone has an interest in evading responsibility for risks.

As long as both institutions and individuals are motivated to offload potential losses for the risks they propagate – that is, to try to avoid accepting responsibility for their risk-taking behaviour – we will continue to experience intense disagreements about managing risks. Some level of disagreement is inevitable in any case, given the inherent uncertainties that are built into the very nature of risky activity itself. But much of the disagreement is pointless and unhelpful, some of it paralyses our social transactions, and some is very costly in terms of health and economic loss (both for inadequately assessed risks and for unnecessary risk reduction).[2]

There is simply no doubt that many of our major institutions and equally many of our fellow citizens do indeed underestimate risk, more or less consciously, in order to maximize the benefits to themselves of risky activities. As explained earlier, institutions do so largely by failing to assess scientifically the relevant hazards and failing to avoid or reduce potential losses by implementing adequate safety measures, even though they have the means to do so; they trust that, when and if such losses actually emerge, they will be able to avoid accepting responsibility for them since there will be insufficient evidence (especially as argued in courtrooms by their platoons of expensive legal talent) to establish convincing cause-and-effect relations.[3] On the other hand, individuals indulge themselves in experiences fraught with excess risk, even though abundant information is circulating about some important hazards and their consequences, trusting that, when and if the odds run against them, the losses can be mitigated and the bills paid by a social agency. On both sides, many of the propagators of risky activities pretend not to know what the risks are.

The proposition that both institutions and individuals have a strong interest in under-assessing and underestimating risk may seem unduly harsh, but in fact it is not; it is past time to introduce a larger dose of honesty into society's debates about risk. If this were not the case, why would there be no occupational risk assessment at all over such a long period of time for such industrial chemicals as formaldehyde and antisapstains, which help to produce enormous economic benefits (a fund of benefits that is surely large enough to pay for those assessments, plus decent mitigation and compensation measures for those unlucky enough to bear the excess risk on behalf of society)? If it were not the case, why would both the private owners of Nova Scotia's Westray coal mine and their government backers ignore abundant warnings of high methane and coal dust readings in 1992, after more than two centuries of having miners and their families bear unacceptable levels of excess risk so that the rest of society could benefit? And if it were not the case, why would so many individuals continue to pump carcinogenic smoke into their lungs, despite being surrounded by abundant and graphic warnings about the dire consequences of tobacco use? Or continue to kill and maim themselves on streets and highways with such apparent abandon?

In our view, this methodical avoidance of responsibility by both individuals and institutions for the risks being incurred at their insistence – this dishonesty, to speak bluntly – is one of the chief sources of mistrust among the parties to risk debates, and also one of the chief obstacles to our arriving at a consensus on how to manage health and environmental risks.

### RISK CONSTITUENCIES

If the stakeholders for environmental and health risk issues were to meet regularly around a table,[4] who would be present? In our experience there are, roughly speaking, three types of stakeholder constituencies, each of which has a distinctive outlook on risk: the corporate/government, the labour/local community, and the public interest constituencies.

*1. The corporate/government constituency.* Historically, this has been the chief innovator and promoter of involuntary risks in its joint advocacy of industrial development. In a market economy, the private sector is usually the risk-initiator, but everywhere – even in the United States – public authority has been an integral part of industrialism through the legal and regulatory framework it establishes for the conduct of business. Moreover, in most other capitalist nations, including Canada, the state has always been an active partner in economic development as such. For reasons that should be obvious by now, this constituency has a direct interest in exaggerating benefits and under-assessing risks, that is, in manipulating or "massaging" both the available information and (even more importantly) the inevitable uncertainties associated with risk estimates so that the "bottom line" judgment will confirm that "benefits outweigh risks."

Another fundamental aspect of this constituency is that those responsible for promoting risk activities (the managerial strata in business and government who are ultimately responsible for decision-making) are, for the most part, insulated from personal exposure to the most hazardous materials used in industry. This observation is not meant to be an ethical objection as such, simply a statement of fact that has great relevance to the highly charged atmosphere in which face-to-face meetings on health risks occur among labour and management representatives.

Obviously, governments, especially national governments, also have a role in health and environmental protection, one that began long ago in such areas as food safety and gradually has been expanded during the course of the twentieth century. This role is fulfilled best where there exist strong legislative mandates based on continuing public demand; for Canada, the clearest cases are the Food and Drug Act and the Hazardous Products Act, both having their origins in abundant scandals involving contaminated or bogus consumer products. Occupational safety legislation also has a long history, but the results are far less satisfactory in this domain, with workers all too often being the guinea pigs for the unintended adverse impacts of industrial innovation.[5] The achievements of environmental protection legislation have also been, on the whole, far less satisfactory, although with some exceptions its origins are more recent and so the battles over its basic scope are still being fought; reliable environmental impact assessment practices, which, like health-risk assessment, seek to incorporate scientific research findings to provide an "objective" basis for uncertain choices are in a still more primitive state of development.

We could further distinguish among the component parts of this constituency, as we might expect to see them arrayed around a table where negotiations on health and environmental risks are taking place. More recently, the main risk-promoting segment has been formed by an alliance between business and regional government

(U.S. states, Canadian provinces), while the national authorities, if and when they are present, may either represent a multiplicity of interests (as reflected in the positions of different agencies or departments) or seek to stand apart from particular interests and assume a "brokering" or facilitating mission at the negotiating table.[6] The same is true on the business side. Whereas in the past we would expect to see for the most part a unified front, the situation is more complex now, especially where environmental risk-issues are at stake. Thus, in forest-management or ecosystem-preservation controversies, tourism and recreation businesses will be taking a position different from that of the more traditional industrial interests.

2. *Labour/local communities.* These are lumped together here for a specific reason, even though they often do not recognize their own commonality of interest with respect to health and environmental risks. They are the constituencies that usually bear a disproportionate share of the identifiable losses from particular risk-taking projects (remember that we are dealing with exposure to involuntary risks only for the moment). So far as labour is concerned, occupational-risk exposure levels almost always exceed general population exposures for the same or similar substances; so far as local communities are concerned, the most serious hazards are almost always place-specific rather than dispersed uniformly throughout the natural and social environment, leading to the "not in my back yard" (NIMBY) syndrome. And yet, at the same time, this is the constituency – especially in its labour component – that is best able to recognize and acknowledge that the risk/benefit trade-offs inherent in industrial economic development are vitally important to its well-being.[7]

Thus, out of all the constituencies and their component parts listed above, this one (and especially its labour component) has the most direct interest in arriving at a well-founded conception of acceptable risk, both as an intrinsic measure of human dignity and also as a foundation for the acceptability of the resulting calculations of risk/benefit trade-offs. Such a conception requires that there be a reasonable effort made by the risk-promoters to produce a truly disinterested risk assessment, that the nature of the uncertainties be described as fully as possible, and that the nature of the risk be communicated in a language comprehensible to the members of that constituency. What is extraordinary about this, considering the sheer number and relative severity of occupational hazards, is how rarely those conditions have been met over the course of the history of industrial society.

*3. The public interest constituency.* This is composed largely of environmental and consumer groups with very broad organizational mandates and membership bases. The diffuse character of their membership normally gives the groups themselves no direct stake in most outcomes, with respect to environmental- and health-risk controversies. This is a source of strength and uniqueness in the positions they take, notably in such areas as protection of endangered wildlife species; in their absence, no one else will speak on behalf of such affected parties and the short-term interests of most other stakeholders will prevail. However, the nature of most of these groups also results in their taking risk-averse positions as a matter of course, that is, exaggerating involuntary risks, endorsing worst-case scenarios, and ignoring trade-offs.

As just described, the first and third constituencies occupy two opposite ends of a spectrum of views on acceptable risk, with the second taking an intermediate position. How would the interplay of risk and responsibility unfold were the representatives of these and other relevant constituencies to meet regularly face to face, with the objective of seeking to arrive at a consensus on acceptable risk and risk/benefit trade-offs? The only truthful answer to that question is, slowly and rancorously, at least for some considerable amount of time. Yet this is only what ought to be expected, for there are very high stakes on the table for all parties. The practice we have described as one of off-loading risk onto others has not been indulged in for so long for entirely whimsical reasons; on the contrary, both institutions and individuals derive substantial long-term benefits from engaging in it. What might happen if all were induced to stop?

## MANAGING RISKS THROUGH NEGOTIATED CONSENSUS

There is enough experience to date in North America with negotiated rule-making and consensus-building processes to suggest that the parties concerned will indeed come to the table. Usually this is because government agencies with statutory authority have indicated that it would be a good idea for them to do so, although non-governmental parties can also initiate the process.[8] Those with a direct stake in the outcome (usually industry and labour or industry and environmentalists) have little choice but to appear; those with an indirect stake have more flexible options, but they could not avoid all such events and still retain credibility as a stakeholder in risk debates. As to what would happen when all arrived at the negotiating table, we shall try to answer this by first continuing to sketch a likely general position for each of the constituences, then lending each position more substance by referring to the case-study materials.[9]

All the risk controversy cases analysed in the literature with which we are familiar have a common feature: at the point when the controversy erupted, some risk-assessment data that was regarded as indispensable from the standpoint of at least one key stakeholder was unavailable. (This data is "expected" to be generated by the risk-promoter, and the absence of essential parts of it is what we have referred to all along as the main type of the under-assessment of risk by the principal risk-promoters.) Since this is not the kind of data that normally can be generated on the spot, this deficiency always goes unremedied for a considerable length of time and, depending upon how long the initial controversy lasts, may still be missing when it dies down again. Nevertheless, the inherent circumstances of face-to-face meetings, as well as the need for all parties to take reasonable positions in order to demonstrate that each is serious about seeking to reach consensus, means that the outstanding deficiencies in the risk-assessment database will be regarded as regrettable and, if completing the database is considered to be essential to an agreement, a commitment by the risk-promoter to do so expeditiously will almost certainly be forthcoming.

Second, the representatives of those stakeholders who bear the most immediate level of excess risk will normally insist upon choosing independent expert consultants to: evaluate the pre-existing risk assessment (or, if none is available, to prepare one); to present their findings in terms comprehensible to the non-expert; and to engage in a dialogue with them about what ought to be considered an acceptable level of risk under the particular circumstances at hand. Even if the initial findings were to show unacceptable levels of excess risk to a key stakeholder, this need not be more than a temporary obstacle to a settlement, because almost always some risk-reduction technologies or strategies are available to bring the numbers within acceptable limits. This is a matter of money – of capital investment or worker training and safety equipment programs – and thus becomes part of a straightforward risk/benefit trade-off to be made "at the table" by the risk-promoter.

There are enormous advantages inherent in the immediacy of feedback that is available when the parties are all sitting around the table. This is bargaining in the classic sense, involving bluff, bluster, threats, portents of doom, denunciations, mock outrage, recriminations, and the like. Those who are concerned that the level of excess risk is too high and who propose that the risk-promoter commit funds so as to reduce it take a chance that the expenditures demanded will tip the risk-promoter's benefit-cost ratios against undertaking or continuing the project, with the concomitant threat – to labour, the local community, and the regional government – of unemployment and monetary losses. The others have to evaluate their "bottom line" acceptable-risk numbers, including the uncertainty ranges around those numbers, taking into account the fact that *all risk estimates represent possible outcomes only and that the actual adverse health effect may be zero.* If any will object that this appears to be "bargaining with people's lives," the rejoinder is: correct, so it is; and furthermore, every one of us, every day of our lives, willingly – albeit more or less wittingly – engages in the same sort of activity, both for ourselves and for those dependent upon us (such as our children or pets) as we make a running series of judgments in choosing what foods to eat, how to operate on city streets, what medical and exercise regimens to follow, what discretionary pleasures to indulge in, and so forth.

To summarize, these are the types of specific risk debates that will characterize the dialogue between the risk-promoters and those constituencies most directly affected by the possible elevated level of risk. Examples of the two sides are: industry and labour unions, for new or newly assessed occupational hazards; industry and a local community, for siting a chemical manufacturing plant; government and one or more local communities, for siting a waste-treatment facility; government and industry, for regulations setting limits on discharges of potentially hazardous materials into air and water or for scientific standards on how to measure those discharges. Among other topics, the debates will centre on the availability or quality of the existing risk assessment, the credibility of that assessment for all stakeholders, the extraction of commitments for an improved (independent) risk assessment (if necessary), the determination by all affected stakeholders of the limits of acceptable risk, and the negotiation of risk-reduction strategies in light of their impact on benefit-cost ratios.

A different type of dialogue is likely to take place in general between all of the parties to the above-mentioned debates and any remaining stakeholders (usually the public interest groups) who are risk-averse as a matter of principle and consequently will not countenance negotiations over acceptable risk and the resultant trade-offs. Some will insist on "zero risk," period. Others will take the position that only a very large margin of safety is appropriate, given the uncertainties involved, even if the consequence is to eliminate any positive benefit-cost outcome for the promoter and so doom the project. Still others will maintain that all stakeholder negotiation on such matters is inappropriate and that only the government agencies have a right to say what acceptable risk is – even if those agencies steadfastly refuse to do so, or are willing to do so only by hinting darkly at what the number might be.[10]

Such pronouncements serve as a warning – from the risk-averse stakeholders to those more inclined to bargain over acceptable risk – to be cautious while traversing this treacherous ground. Such a warning may well be timely if the risk assessments are unreliable or incomplete, as they often are. These pronouncements will also be a valuable counterweight to the smooth reassurances from the risk-promoters. However, to the extent to which they can sway the outcome for all stakeholders, the presuppositions they carry should be unveiled for all to examine and judge. The weightiest of these presuppositions may be phrased as follows: For all cases of involuntary risk we must safeguard the interests of citizens by imposing an extremely risk-averse standard, even if large numbers of those same citizens then voluntarily expose themselves to risks carrying much higher probabilities of harm.

We fully expect to be chastised by the adherents of risk-averse standards for involuntary risks by phrasing the point thus. Undoubtedly many will say that the one standard has nothing to do with the other, that no one has the right to challenge the risk choices that individuals make for themselves in their private lives. Obviously, we disagree. We believe that those who enter risk debates not only have a right but a duty to join these two dimensions. We suggest that it is unreasonable, illogical, economically ruinous, and ultimately self-defeating to seek to protect citizens from involuntary exposure to certain risk levels if, simultaneously, many of those selfsame citizens voluntarily expose themselves to levels of other risks that are often higher by several orders of magnitude. We do not disagree that in a democracy those citizens have the right to seek protection against imposed or involuntary risks at whatever level of acceptable risk – down to zero risk – they choose in any particular case. But we have a duty to advise them that if this strategy is chosen across the board, they will pay dearly for it in the end.

## APPORTIONING RESPONSIBILITY

Those who promote a risk-averse philosophy for involuntary exposure usually invoke a worst-case scenario as the limit of acceptable risk, which in quantitative terms is expressed as the upper-bound 95 percent confidence limit. This means that there is a 95 percent chance that the risk is no higher than assessed, but it may be lower, indeed much lower: in fact, *it may be zero*. The Natural Resources Defense Council (NRDC) told us what it considers to be "intolerable risk" with respect to pesticide residues in foods, especially for children, but not what it considers to be tolerable risk. It urged Congress to "establish health-based standards for pesticide residues in foods" and consumers to demand "food without pesticide residues."[11] Does the NRDC really think that the U.S. Congress, largely a labyrinth of smoke-filled rooms where covert deals are struck among special-interest groups, is capable (even if so inclined) of making sensible decisions in such matters? We would like to see a probability estimate for this scenario. Does the NRDC wish to eliminate all pesticide residues in foods at the limit of detection (now in the parts per quadrillion range, but new technology will drive it lower) so that, in effect, none can be used, even those that protect us against the potent toxins produced by some moulds, bacteria, and fungi?[12] If so, will they warn consumers that, on balance, their safety almost certainly will decline under those conditions?

The possibility that in the food-safety area an extreme risk-averse philosophy will bring more grief than succour is one of the ways in which the citizenry could pay dearly for adopting such a stance.[13] But why limit our concern to food safety? What about the domain where risk is almost always higher, namely occupational exposure?[14] Why is this domain so often simply ignored by public interest groups, especially for much-abused sectors such as farmworkers? In all the public commentary sent to the EPA we reviewed on the Alar case, there was but a single reference to the likelihood that risks were seriously underestimated here;[15] there is no mention of occupational risk at all in the NRDC's *Intolerable Risk*.

From an ethical standpoint it is intolerable that we should permit higher direct exposures to chemicals for those who labour to produce useful things for us in our factories and on our farms than the rest of us wish to find residually in our diets or homes for those same substances, but this appears to be the logical outcome of risk controversies to date. Formaldehyde was and is widely used in industry, and yet there was no great public concern about it, and no quantitative risk assessment done by regulatory authorities, before residential owners became worried about their exposure as a result of installing UFFI in their homes. UDMH was (and probably still is) used as a rocket fuel, but although we know a great deal about the dietary risks of UDMH as a result of the Alar controversy, who has ever heard of an occupational risk assessement for that chemical?[16] Were we to adopt an equitable standard, however, effectively setting occupational as well as dietary exposure to carcinogens at zero level, there would be trouble for the risk-averse philosophy, because we would have to shut down immediately all our industrial production facilities (including agriculture) and return to a hunting-and-gathering mode for sustenance – whereupon, alas, we would be exposed to some rather hefty naturally-occurring hazards, including carcinogens. The zero-risk standard would not long survive this experiment.

Since undoubtedly we have already offended the adherents of a risk-averse philosophy, we have nothing to lose in pushing further along this line of argument. We suggest that those persons might also assume responsibility for helping to educate citizens about genuinely unreasonable fears that originate in an extreme risk-averse stance. We can offer a case in point. In late 1991 public hysteria about allegations of toxic substances (pesticides) contaminating water supplies spread through some Fraser Valley communities in British Columbia. According to media reports, the public fears appear to have had their origins in a diagnosis by a local physician to the effect that pesticide residues had "caused toxins to lodge in people's bodies, affecting the central nervous system"; the doctor even coined a name for a unique syndrome ("cybernetic paresis") based on the set of symptoms he had observed, and since in his opinion these had appeared in a number of patients residing in contiguous areas, he referred to the phenomenon called "cluster disease."

Although B.C. Ministry of Health and Ministry of Environment officials were very active in responding to the concerns of local communities, and even sent a team of University of British Columbia epidemiologists to investigate, a local residents' group decided to raise funds to bring in their own "expert" from Florida. Shortly after arriving, taking water samples, and having an "analysis" done in an astonishingly short time period, this "expert" made alarming statements about cancer risk, associating it with residues from EDB, a substance banned five years earlier, although no independent proof was ever offered that such residues existed. So far as can be determined, both the original diagnosis and the allegations of the Florida "expert" were entirely unfounded.[17] The hysteria gradually dissipated. Our question is: Why do public interest groups not get involved in these types of controversies and use their reputations for concern about health and environmental risks to assist government agencies to defuse obviously unfounded fears? Why should their mission be restricted to raising alarms only, rather than also aiding the public in learning how to evaluate health risks in general?

In effect we are proposing that the advocates of a risk-averse philosophy take full responsibility for the consequences flowing from this position.[18] So long as society's risk debates are not conducted face to face by stakeholders, however, but only indirectly, where every-one speaks but no one listens, they are not compelled to do so. We must emphasize the point here that any individual or group in our society has a perfect right to adopt this philosophy and to seek to persuade others to do likewise. Moreover we reaffirm here our own belief that groups promoting this philosophy have made and continue to make indispensable contributions to our risk debates; in their absence our society's earlier, secret dialogues on risk, conducted in the past entirely within the dominant institutional bureaucracies, were all too often indifferent to unacceptable levels of risk imposed, for example, upon workers and upon non-human species in our environment. But we do want to urge all participants to move society's risk debates onto another, higher plateau.

We have asked those who hold a risk-averse stance to accept responsibility for the consequences of generalizing that position across all sectors of risk activity in society. What would we ask in turn of the chief institutional risk-promoters?

For openers we would ask them to stop fooling around with their scientific risk assessments. In our view this is precisely what was truly intolerable in the Alar case. For over ten years Uniroyal and the government of the United States played a game of bluff over the toxicology studies, a game that had its origins in an earlier era and was conducted on the assumption that the only players allowed to sit at the table would be the company and the regulators.[19] All the  dealings in that older game, including assessment of the data and reviews for the product's hazard profile, were confidential, protected by law from disclosure to any other parties; the protracted industry–government negotiations over the results of those reviews were also conducted in secret.

Only an assumption that the conduct of both parties was predi-cated on the continued credibility of this older set of rules can explain the elaborate choreography of increasingly absurd moves on the "audits" of the Toth studies, for example, where Uniroyal's and the EPA's scientists, as well as consultants hired by both sides, went back and forth to Kansas to labour over the most minute details of Toth's laboratory practices (even though his studies were undertaken before there was a regulatory standard for good laboratory practices). As Toth finally was compelled to state for the public record, these were not perfect studies, but there was no basis for anyone to claim that they were not done according to the generally accepted scientific standards of their day. All were published in highly reputable jour-nals and, as we have seen, the EPA's Second Peer Review Committee commented in 1989 that Uniroyal's new studies confirmed the sub-

stance of Toth's original analysis. Part of the reason why the Scientific
Advisory Panel discredited itself in the Alar case was that it was still
giving far too much weight to Uniroyal's massive campaign to undermine the credibility of those studies, the oldest of which had been
published fully twelve years earlier, even though there were in the
EPA's files perfectly good counter-arguments to Uniroyal's allegations
made by both EPA staff and well-regarded independent experts.

If Uniroyal really thought that Toth's research was so scientifically
disreputable, why did the company not simply go ahead and produce
better studies on its own initiative – well before 1986, when for the
first time they were legally compelled by the EPA to initiate them?
We can only guess that the answer may reside in the key presupposition that subsists tacitly in the thinking of many institutional risk-
promoters: If one suspects that there is even a low probability that
additional information will give rise to concerns, and if one is not
being compelled to produce such information, it is preferable not to
know.

EPA staff first raised concerns about the Toth findings in 1977; in
the highly politicized environment at the EPA during the early 1980s
Uniroyal managed to delay the official announcement of the data
call-in – the point at which the company was legally required to *begin*
the process of undertaking new studies – until January 1986,
knowing full well that their completion and the EPA's review of the
new data would consume fully another three or four years. The net
result was that their product would be sold and used for at least
thirteen years after the first concerns about excess risk were raised,
and indeed probably much longer, because the agency's cancellation
proceedings, when and if they were begun, could be tied up in court
for years. All this time some element of genuine uncertainty would
exist about the risk assessment, but under the old rules of the game
the public was not supposed to find out about it. Those rules began
to change beginning in the 1980s, both in the United States and in
Canada, but many parties to the Alar dispute failed to understand
in time the significance of those changes. Uniroyal may have been
congratulating itself following the EPA's retreat in January 1986, but
if so, such self-praise was short-sighted in the extreme: the consumer
boycott of Alar-treated apples launched shortly thereafter was the
beginning of the end for its product.[20]

From the standpoint of the public interest, playing elaborate games
with uncertainties in the science of risk assessment, with or without
the additional layers of obstructionism that lawyers can supply, is
intolerable.[21] Such tactics, however tempting for the risk manager,
fuel the fears of the unknown felt by many non-expert stakeholders

and cause them to harden their view that, in the face of a substantial range of unknown factors, many of which appear to stem only from the risk-promoter's evident wish not to find out whether there might be any bad news in the missing data, the only prudent course of action is to be extremely risk-averse. In other words, if the risk-promoters fail to accept responsibility for making the most determined effort to secure complete and unbiased risk-assessment data, they have only themselves to blame if other stakeholders find their confident risk/benefit trade-off projections to be little better than pie-in-the-sky fabrications and take a hard line against them in the ensuing negotiations.

On the other hand, where the risk-promoters are forthcoming and co-operative in doing everything they can to secure an unbiased risk assessment, we believe that most other stakeholders will reciprocate by moving away from extremely risk-averse positions. Simply put, it is usually in their interest to do so, given the relatively low probabilities of adverse effects they are likely to be dealing with, not to mention the real possibility that in many cases the actual adverse effects may be zero. In the antisapstain case, the willingness of the risk-promoters to spend the time and money to work through the outstanding risk assessment deficiences at the table was a vital part of the eventual solution, even though substantial uncertainties remained. (We must also remember that under present conditions the worst of the potential involuntary risks have already been screened out and, with possible rare exceptions, would never be brought to the negotiating table as the subject of trade-offs.)[22] Remember also that when a good risk assessment is available, which by definition includes a reliable exposure estimate, it is almost always feasible to narrow the outstanding differences on acceptable risk among the parties by investing additional resources in risk-reduction strategies, or to make other types of concessions on health-risk issues, such as we saw in the antisapstain case study with the formation of a standing committee on health monitoring, that facilitate the making of trade-offs.

In addition to being more forthcoming with disinterested risk assessments, institutional risk-promoters ought to take every opportunity, when meeting other stakeholders face to face around negotiating tables, to clarify the judgmental rules they utilize in weighing benefits and risks against each other. We are not thinking here of a short course in formal techniques such as are employed in the field known as "decision analysis," but rather a frank account of the quite informal rules that government agencies actually have called upon over the years in arriving at their regulatory decisions. Those who have some acquaintance with these rules know that there is little magic and even less mystery concealed in the "black box" of risk/ benefit trade-offs; instead, for the most part purely pragmatic considerations dominate these proceedings. Explaining what usually happens there will not necessarily satisfy all stakeholder concerns, but doing so can only help to clarify the strategies all employ – institutions and individuals alike – in steering through these tricky waters.

Finally, as noted earlier in the context of negotiated agreements, the parties can agree on interim solutions pending the completion and review of missing data, and if, on balance, the trade-offs in that deal are advantageous to the risk-promoter, there is a strong incentive to remedy those deficiencies. It is only when no guidance is even on the horizon from the standpoint of scientifically assessed risk – especially if the other parties suspect that the risk-promoters are not dealing fairly with their obligations on this score – that negotiation on acceptable risk and risk/benefit trade-offs is next to impossible.

## A RETROSPECTIVE LOOK AT THE CASE STUDIES

Our case studies looked at power frequency electric and magnetic fields (PF E/MF), Alar, and antisapstains. We shall summarize the useful lessons they offer in the light of our discussion on the responsibilities of various parties under conditions of multi-stakeholder negotiation concerning acceptable risks and risk/benefit trade-offs.

### Power Frequency Electric and Magnetic Fields

The Courtenay public inquiry was not an appropriate forum in which to resolve expert disagreement over PF E/MF health effects.[23] Could any of the mechanisms discussed in chapter 5 – the science court, scientific panel, or scientific consensus-finding conference – have helped clarify or even resolve some of the disagreement? As Ozawa and Susskind (and others) point out, each mechanism presumes that scientists can best contribute to the resolution of policy disputes by operating independently of the affected interests and the decision-makers. But such a separation may be "unjustified, unwise and undesirable." Differences in scientific judgments often arise from differences in hypotheses and in simplifying assumptions – factors that are not strictly "scientific" in character. Isolating the scientists from the dialogue will not serve to inform decision-makers and affected interests about the underlying factors that may be responsible for the differences among the experts.[24] We agree with Ozawa and Susskind and others that mediated negotiation of science-intensive disputes can help alleviate this problem.[25] However, given the complex nature of the scientific debate about possible PF E/MF human health effects, we also believe that a "separation" in the form of an international scientific consensus-finding conference must occur prior to any negotiation or mediation process. The experts must first come to terms with the reasons for their own differences of opinion.

This scientific consensus-finding conference would be comprised of scientists from a variety of relevant disciplines and representing a broad range of opinion. They would be asked to come to consensus on where they agree and disagree, on the basis for that agreement or disagreement, and on the quality of the scientific database. This conference would encourage scientists to revisit their respective disciplines and fields in terms of rules of evidence, rules of reasoning with evidence, and general theoretical understandings. Lay observers (including social scientists, humanists) would help tease out the value assumptions that are inevitably made. Conferences would be held periodically as new evidence emerged.

The findings of the conference would then be brought to a multistakeholder consensus-based negotiation process. The findings should not minimize the existence of uncertainty; data gaps and areas of significant disagreement among experts should be disclosed; and some indication of the level of confidence of the estimates and the significance of scientific uncertainty should be conveyed.[26]

The stakeholder forum would then address questions such as: How much proof is enough? On whom does the burden of proof lie (public, industry)? And what is the burden of proof (harm or safety)? Is it up to the public to prove harm or to industry to prove safety? Who should make these decisions? And what interim action should be taken while these decisions are being made? These are questions that science cannot answer for society. The stakeholder forum would be an ongoing process – subject to a broader societal decision about how much of our limited resources (time, money, people) we want to devote to this potential risk versus other known risks.

A recent experiment in consensus-based negotiation was undertaken in California. In October 1991 the Public Utilities Commission (PUC) approved an administrative law judge ruling creating the "California EMF Consensus Group." The group, consisting of seventeen stakeholders representing various organizations involved with the PF E/MF health effects issue, was asked to develop consensus recommendations on interim policies for dealing with the issue. In March 1992, these representatives from utilities, unions, state agencies, and citizen, consumer, and environmental groups signed off on the recommendations. Although the group was not able to reach consensus on all issues, it did agree on the need for more research, unbiased public information and education, and for appropriate no-cost and low-cost field management. Of particular note, the group recommended that the PUC establish a research management structure with independent arm's-length supervision and stakeholder involvement, and that research activities be funded in specific categories as prioritized by the group with the assistance of their scientific advisers. It also recommended that a "stakeholder advisory committee" (including no more than ten representatives from labour, electric utilities, ratepayers, citizens, and local government, appointed by the PUC) be established to guide the PUC on the implementation of the PF E/MF program, that interim policy options be reviewed at least once every three years, and that "public participation hearings" be held by the PUC prior to adoption of the group's consensus positions. In the report, areas of disagreement are outlined but without attribution or numbers of dissenting members.[27]

On a broader scale, the State of Washington, as part of its Environment 2010 initiative (a joint project with the EPA), used consensus-based negotiation to establish environmental priorities for the state. First, a team of twenty-five technical experts identified and analysed the relative human health, ecological, and economic risks posed by twenty-three different threats to those resources, ranging from air pollution to wetlands destruction to oil spills. A citizen's committee representing local government, the legislature, and the tribal, business, academic, agricultural, and environmental communities then digested the assessments and prioritized threats according to: the risk to human health and to ecological systems; the potential to cause economic damage; the trend and manageability of the threat; and personal judgment. The result was a ranking of the twenty-three threats into five levels of priority action. "Non-ionizing Radiation" (including radio frequency and power frequency, excluding occupational exposure) was assigned to the lowest priority level.[28] The ranking will be reconsidered in about seven years.[29]

Although these experiments are examples of policy dialogues and not regulatory negotiation *per se*, they do illustrate the potential for multi-stakeholder negotiation processes to move forward the debate over a seemingly intractable public policy dispute. However, evaluations of the two processes should be undertaken based on Susskind and Cruikshank's criteria for "good outcomes": fairness, efficiency, wisdom, and stability.[30]

In our opinion, a fundamental requirement for a "good outcome" from an initial consensus-finding conference and subsequent stakeholder forum would be for the experts to take responsibility for their role in public policy-making. Changes will be required both within and outside of the scientific community to encourage the necessary self-reflection[31] and public candour about the PF E/MF and human health issue, and about mandated science and science more generally. As discussed in chapter 5, the risk managers have the major responsibility to ensure that the inherent limitations of the risk-assessment process are acknowledged and compensated for. However, the experts must take the first step. Taking responsibility for their role in public policy-making will not resolve the PF E/MF health effects issue – there will always be some differences of opinion – but such an act is crucial if we are to hope to begin making risk-management decisions that are more fair, efficient, wise, and stable.

*Alar*

After late 1985, the Alar controversy began to take on a life of its own. Once the roles and relations of the parties who would be most influential on the eventual outcome had become fixed, a final result different from the one which actually transpired became hard to imagine.

By that time, Uniroyal was locked into its strategy of simply harassing the EPA about the Toth studies while showing no interest of its own in the generation of a more complete and adequate toxicological database for daminozide and UDMH. Its other concern was to ensure that its complacent clients among the food commodity producers and state agricultural agencies would generate reams of happy testimonials, for the EPA's edification, about their product's benefits. Meanwhile, the EPA had just emerged from the first wave of Reagan's extremist deregulatory ideology with a strong need to rebuild its shattered credibility. The NRDC had had to fight the U.S. government in court in order to gain a better window on how the pesticides regulatory system worked in practice; but in no sense had the NRDC or similar groups been accepted at that time as legitimate stakeholders in such matters by the traditional players (industry and governments), and moreover there were no alliances among consumer, environmental, grower, and labour interests. Among apple and other food commodity producers, many had become quite dependent on Uniroyal's Alar, which had many uniquely useful properties and had contributed substantial financial benefits to their operations. Finally, at that point the large food retailers had gone through some nasty public scares over food safety (EDB and aldicarb) within the preceding year or two, and were approaching the controversy with understandable caution.

Under the foregoing circumstances, the only way that a publicly visible struggle could have been avoided was if the pesticide regulatory system had remained the exclusive property of the traditional stakeholders.[32] Once the U.S. public interest groups decided to force their way into the game the stakes changed, but only in retrospect was it possible to gauge how great the change was: at the time (late 1985), not all of the cards they had to play were showing and the traditional stakeholders had no way of knowing how strong their hands really were. The 1986 consumer boycott led by Ralph Nader and others was a significant intervention, but there is some evidence that by 1988 the growers' use of Alar was gradually increasing again from its 1986 low point. The decisive stroke was the NRDC's decision first to prepare quietly its own expert risk assessment and second to retain a professional communications firm to construct a media strategy around its release.[33] The tactic worked brilliantly – although it will be very hard, if not impossible, for any group to repeat it with the same effect, especially since the media are now a bit warier of being used as an instrument in some other player's game plan.[34]

Had the sequence of events begun to unfold a decade later, is it possible to imagine that the outcome might have been different? The answer depends entirely, in the first instance, on whether the registrant company might have pursued a different strategy and early on taken the initiative voluntarily to complete and submit for review a proper set of scientific studies. Let us also suppose that a multi-stakeholder negotiation had been set in motion at that point, with all interested parties around the table, *before* the consumer boycott and the NRDC's other plan had been set in motion. Let us further suppose that the food retailers were not then still smarting from the EDB episode. Now it is possible to think that some other outcome indeed was possible, based on a complex series of negotiated trade-offs. For example, even if most of the parties (not including Health and Welfare Canada) stuck to the contention that UDMH represented a serious hazard, a risk-reduction scenario in which growers consented to refrain from using daminozide on apples intended for processing, as opposed to raw apples (where UDMH residues were likely to be very low and therefore to represent a trivial risk), may have been acceptable to almost all stakeholders. Other measures might have been agreed upon to reduce worker exposure. In addition, Uniroyal may have volunteered to undertake still more studies in order to clarify some points that were still outstanding, and the stakeholders could have established an ongoing forum to which they would return when those results were available. Or, if the competing risk assessments of the various parties still yielded conclusions that were too varied for comfort, Uniroyal might have pledged to under-write the costs of a scientific consensus conference, made up of truly independent experts, to see whether the degree of difference could be reduced or eliminated. These are only a small sample of the types of bids that could have been made by the various parties in order to ascertain whether a consensus position would emerge from their negotiations.

Under these conditions it is not unreasonable to think that Alar might have continued to be applied to food crops, certainly with some changes in the use pattern. This would clearly have been the case in Canada even in 1989 (had Uniroyal not withdrawn it from world markets as a result of the controversy in the United States), since Health and Welfare Canada never moved from its stated posi-tion that there was no unacceptable risk to consumers from its con-tinued use, based upon its own scientific risk assessment.

### Antisapstains

Our final review of the antisapstain case study can be briefer. Here the opposite considerations apply, for although a multi-stakeholder consensus in fact was reached, it might not have been. For example, had the proposed new chemical not already been widely employed in the same industry in the United States, so that the unions had some anecdotal evidence about its apparent acceptability (at least so far as acute human health effects were concerned), the labour stake-holders might have been far less comfortable with acceding to its use in Canada. Still, the uncertainties over the incomplete database for a risk assessment proved vexatious. In this regard, the availability of funds for the group to retain its own expert consultants proved decisive, even though what they had to say did not differ significantly from what was available earlier. The opportunity to work through these types of issues "around the table," using terminology that all the parties could understand, went a long way towards creating *in the minds of the stakeholders themselves* a greater confidence in their own abilities to make judgments about acceptable risk.

The detailed agreement on health monitoring was the centrepiece of the consensus document so far as the unions were concerned, and without the willingness of the industry to accept it there would have been no resolution. The existence of the "temporary registration" status for the new product was also a key item, for it allowed the stakeholders the security of not committing themselves to the deal for more than one year at a time, and of having an opportunity annually to alter the nature of the agreement if circumstances should warrant. Finally, if the crisis over the study that MacMillan Bloedel failed to divulge voluntarily had not been overcome, a number of the parties whose co-operation was essential would have walked away from the table, and we have no way of knowing what ultimately would have happened thereafter.

There is a sense in which this case provides a perfect illustration of our central theme, in that the stakeholder agreement named a group that was willing to assume responsibility for a difficult decision in a situation where others could not or would not do so. As we have seen, decisions in the context of health and environmental risk controversies have two overriding dimensions: first, the need to make risk/benefit trade-offs, and second, the existence of irreducible uncertainties and incompleteness in the relevant knowledge base. In the antisapstain case, the sheer magnitude of the uncertainties was the decisive factor; among other things it prevented all the parties from knowing what the actual trade-offs were likely to be and was the reason why the regulatory agencies refused to make a ruling on the basis of guesses about those trade-offs.

The stakeholder agreement has an explicit reference to this point. The recommendation that the agencies should grant temporary registration status to two then-unregistered chemicals was accompanied by the following statement: "In making this recommendation, the Forum recognizes the inadequacy of available data to evaluate many critical end-points relating to health, safety and environmental impact..."[35] This statement appeared in the document at the insistence of a senior federal official in one of the regulatory agencies, who dictated its exact wording and who stated that he would not co-operate in implementing the agreement if it were not included (those who signed the document were aware of these circumstances). In other words, *someone had to assume responsibility for the risk-related uncertainties that had inhibited the regular decision-making processes*, and the British Columbia Stakeholder Forum, a group with no legal standing, was named as the party that would have to do so. That they accepted this burden and went on to craft an agreement which has stood the test of time is a great tribute to the courage and clear-sightedness of the signatories, as well as of the Agriculture Canada personnel who bestowed official sanction on their work.

TOWARDS CONSENSUS

Returning briefly to the typology of risk management issues presented in chapter 2, we have been concerned in this book almost entirely with some of the latter categories on our list, namely issues in the areas of industrial hazards, where there are strong concerns about distributional equity and about the incommensurable character of the risks and benefits that are proposed to be traded off against each other. It is in these areas that industrial societies have experienced bitter disagreements over acceptable risk and risk/benefit trade-offs. Controversies are not unknown in the first three areas – natural hazards, prescription drugs and medical procedures, and infectious disease – but they tend to have a very different character. We will not tax the reader's patience at this point with an extended commentary on these types of cases, but only observe that here the public will normally be content if there is an honest attempt by recognized experts both to arrive at a consensus among themselves, first on the scientific risk assessment and then on a risk-management strategy, and to make thereafter a reasonable effort to communicate the nature of that consensus to the general public in understandable language.

For the rest, it is in everyone's interest – in a society hooked on risk – to move from disagreement towards consensus. We have suggested that the most promising route to this end is for the major participants in risk debates to accept a fuller share of responsibility for the consequences of the positions each advocates on risk-taking: for industry and governments, to look ahead in the zones where health and environmental risk controversies are likely to arise (not a particularly difficult exercise now) and to pay more attention to the basic needs of other stakeholders, namely, to have available a disinterested risk assessment that uses the best available scientific methods; for goverments, to continue to explore "around the table" with other stakeholders the ways in which responsible choices can be made in trade-offs between risks and benefits; for public-interest groups, to help citizens to move away from unreasonably risk-averse standpoints, where such appear to exist, and to try to find a way of balancing their attitudes towards involuntarily imposed and voluntarily assumed risks. There is not meant to be any trace of condescension is this last remark, for risk is a devilishly convoluted business in itself which gets even more so when we seek to sum everything up in a handy prescription to guide the individual who wishes to make sensible choices in everyday life.[36] The entire set of health and environmental risks we experience today, both involuntary and voluntary in nature, is, in the last analysis, a seamless web: all the consequences of our choices of both kinds tend towards a unified outcome so far as our individual and social well-being is concerned.

However, we have not framed this notion that major stakeholders in risk debates might embrace an enlarged sense of responsibility merely as an abstract ethical ideal, so as to be able to preach to the risk stakeholders about repentance and good works. Rather, we have suggested that there is an already existing practical framework in which the interested parties have an opportunity to assume an appropriate portion of these enlarged responsibilities, in a setting that, of necessity, is dominated not by competing claims of moral purity but by the nitty-gritty details of toxicology, law and regulation, statistics, sustainable ecosystems, civic duty, actual conditions of work in the farmer's field and on the factory floor, and above all the shadowy outlines of irreducible uncertainties. That framework has been tried here and there with a variety of outcomes, but it has not yet been tested on more than a small fraction of the controversies we have witnessed to date over health and environmental risks. We all have little to lose in essaying those wider trials.

# Appendices

# Power Frequency Electric and Magnetic Fields (PF E/MF) and Human Health: Basic Concepts

## PF E/MF

Electric and magnetic fields and electromagnetic forces arise from many natural sources and are found throughout nature and in all living things. They hold matter together (in both living and non-living things) and are necessary for the operation of the nervous system. Atmospheric processes generate large static electric fields at the earth's surface, culminating in lightning, and the earth's core produces a static magnetic field that makes navigation by compass possible.[1] Electric and magnetic fields and electro-magnetic radiation are also produced artificially, for example, by power lines, radio and television broadcast, and microwave ovens.[2]

In North America, electricity alternates at a frequency of 60 cycles per second (Hz); i.e., the voltage and current change strength and direction 120 times per second.[3] The alternating voltage and current (AC) produce electric and magnetic fields (E/MF) that oscillate at the same frequency as the voltage and current. These power frequency (PF) E/MF are invisible fields of force that surround any conductor carrying electricity. They are present wherever electricity is in use.[4] The "electric field" relates to the electric force a charged object is capable of exerting on other charges in its vicinity. The electric field intensity is directly proportional to the strength of its force. Electric fields are produced by electric charges that are "pumped" onto wires by electric generators. The "magnetic field" relates to the magnetic force. The magnetic field intensity around a current-carrying conductor is directly proportional to the amount of current flowing.[5]

The electromagnetic spectrum (represented in Figure A-1) measures energy using a scale based on frequency and wavelength. All forms of electromagnetic energy are fields of force. The various spectral regions differ in terms of the physical and biological effects that are produced.[6] Non-

Figure A-1
The Electromagnetic Spectrum

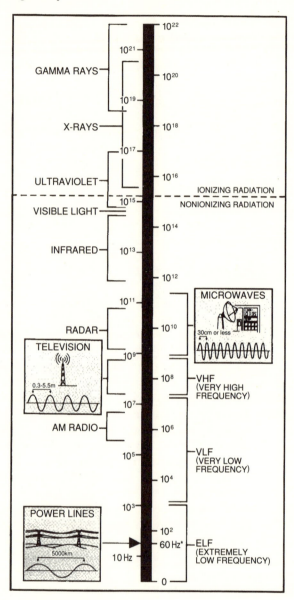

*Note:* The limits of human hearing are from 20 Hz–20 kHz.

Reproduced with permission from Ontario Hydro, *Electric and Magnetic Fields and Human Health Research.*

ionizing radiation (NIR), unlike ionizing radiation, is not powerful enough to break molecular or chemical bonds or to create charged particles called ions. The high energy associated with ionizing radiation (IR) strips electrons from molecules. PF E/MF are a type of NIR. PF E/MF and other "extremely low frequency" (ELF) fields (ranging from 30 to 300 Hz)[7] do not heat tissue significantly compared to radiation from intense microwaves. Energy from higher frequency fields (of shorter wavelength) is absorbed more readily by biological material and can produce heating (e.g., microwave ovens). The extra long wavelength at 60 Hz allows the transfer of only a minute amount of energy to objects the size of a person.[8]

When the distance from a source of electromagnetic energy is large with respect to the wavelength, the electric and magentic fields are linked and considered together as a radiating electromagnetic field (EMF). The area in which the linked fields can be observed is called the "far" or "radiation" zone. When the distance from the source is small with respect to the wavelength, the electric and magnetic fields are not linked. The fields are independent and can be considered (from an engineering point of view) as separate entities. One is always in the so-scalled "near" or "static" zone of PF fields due to their long wavelength. This is why we use the term "electric and magnetic fields" to refer to power frequencies, rather than "electromagnetic radiation."[9]

Although PF E/MF are considered to be 50 or 60 Hz sinusoidal waveforms of a given strength and direction, the currents and fields associated with power lines, wiring, and appliances at the same location can interact, and resultant field strengths and directions will depend upon, among other factors, the location of the object, the location of nearby objects, and the electrical conditions of use.[10] Furthermore, other strengths and frequencies may be introduced by switching transients, power surges, or harmonic distortions, and unique energy patterns are induced in transmission lines by solar flare activity.[11]

Radio frequencies modulated by ELF are used in radio transmission, television transmission, and radar. Electric currents and fields of varying field strengths and frequencies, from DC to microwave, are also used for medical diagnostic purposes and treatment. Several such applications are now in routine use. Electricity has been used for many years by some physicians in efforts to repair fractures by stimulating bone formation.[12]

## Electric Fields

Electric field strength is measured in volt/meter (V/m). Table A-1 shows the typical and maximum electric field strengths from power lines. The field strength is greatest in the area immediately surrounding the line and decreases rapidly with distance.

The electric fields created by the voltage on wiring and appliances are generally much weaker than those close to power lines (see Table A-2). The

Table A-1
Typical and Maximum Power Line Electric and Magnetic Field Strengths
(kV, kilovolt; μT, microtesla)

| | | Beneath power line | Edge of ROW | 100 ft from power line | 200 ft from power line | 300 ft from power line |
|---|---|---|---|---|---|---|
| 12 kV | kV | .01–0.1 | | | | |
| | μT | .0001–0.001 | | | | |
| 115 kV | kV | 1.0  (2) | 0.5 | 0.07 | 0.01 | 0.003 |
| | μT | 2.0  (4.0) | 0.5  (1.0) | 0.1  (0.2) | 0.03  (0.06) | 0.01  (0.03) |
| 230 kV | kV | 2.0  (3) | 1.5  (1) | 0.3 | 0.05 | 0.01 |
| | μT | 3.5  (7.0) | 1.5  (3.0) | 0.5  (1.0) | 0.1  (0.2) | 0.05  (0.1) |
| 500 kV | kV | 7.0  (9) | 3.0 | 1.0 | 0.3 | 0.1 |
| | μT | 7.0  (14.0) | 2.5  (5.0) | 1.2  (2.5) | 0.3  (0.7) | 0.1  (0.3) |
| 750 kV | kV | (12) | (2) | | | |
| | μT | (30) | (7) | | | |

*Notes:* Parentheses indicate maximum strengths.
   Measured 3.3 ft (1 metre) above ground.
   Actual field strength and right-of-way (ROW) width depend on line design and voltage and
   current levels.
   The right-of-way (ROW) is a strip of land for which a utility acquires a permanent
   easement from the owner. This easement allows the utility to build, operate, and maintain
   its transmission lines and to keep the ROW clear. In some cases the land is purchased
   outright. The ROW is usually a specified amount of feet wider than the towers and lines,
   e.g., 56 ft (17 metres) either side of the centre line for a 230 kV line.

*Sources:* U.S., BPA, DOE, *Electrical and Biological Effects*, June 1989, 14, 19; Dan Bracken,
"Properties and Effects of A.C. and D.C. Line Fields," paper in Ontario Hydro, *Health Effects of
Electric and Magnetic Fields*

fields are present whenever the electric appliances are plugged in, unless the
appliance has a three-prong plug, in which case the electric field will not be
present when the appliance is off, due to grounding.[13] The field strength is
greatest in the immediately surrounding area and decreases rapidly with
distance. The electric field levels inside most homes and workplaces are not
greatly affected by power lines. This is because building materials, fences,
vegetation, and other conducting objects can greatly reduce the strength of
the external electric field. The amount of shielding depends on the conduc-
tivity of the material.

## Magnetic Fields

Magnetic field strength is measured in ampere/meter (A/m). In air, magnetic
field strength is proportional to magnetic flux density. The magnetic flux

Table A-2
Typical Values of 60 Hz Electric Field Levels
in the Home
(V/m, volts/meter)

| Appliance | Electric field strength 30 cm from 115-V home appliance |
|---|---|
| Broiler | 130 |
| Coffee pot | 30 |
| Color TV | 30 |
| Electric blanket | 250 |
| Hair dryer | 40 |
| Hand mixer | 50 |
| Incandescent bulb | 2 |
| Electric iron | 60 |
| Refrigerator | 60 |
| Stereo | 90 |
| Toaster | 40 |
| Vacuum cleaner | 16 |

| Location | Electric field strength at centre of room |
|---|---|
| Bathroom | 1.2–1.5 |
| Bedroom | 2.4–7.8 |
| Dining room | 0.9 |
| Hallway | 13.0 |
| Kitchen | 2.6 |
| Laundry room | 0.8 |
| Living room | 3.3 |

Source: *Environmental Health Criteria 35: Extremely Low Frequency
(ELF) Fields* (Geneva: World Health Organization, 1984)

density, measured in tesla (T) or gauss (G), is sometimes called the magnetic field. The simpler nomenclature is adopted here (1 microTesla, μT = 10 milliGauss, mG.)

The amount of current flowing in a power line varies as the demand for electric power changes throughout the day. Therefore the magnetic field strength varies over a wide range; it can easily change by a factor of two under normal conditions. Table A-1 shows typical and maximum power line magnetic field strengths. The field strength is greatest in the area immediately surrounding the line and decreases rapidly with distance. Field patterns can be calculated given the geometry of the line and the line current.

Building wiring and appliances also create magnetic fields (see Table A-3). Magnetic fields in wall wiring can be quite small because parallel wires (hot and neutral) can cancel if they are close and the fields are equal and

Table A-3
60 Hz Magnetic Field Levels Near Various Applicances

| Appliance | Magnetic Field Strength ($\mu T$, microTesla) | | |
|---|---|---|---|
| | 3 cm | 30 cm | 1 m |
| Blenders | 25–130 | 0.6–2 | 0.03–0.12 |
| Can openers | 1000–2000 | 3.5–30 | 0.07–1 |
| Coffee makers | 1.8–25 | 0.08–0.15 | <0.01 |
| Drills | 400–800 | 2–3.5 | 0.08–0.2 |
| Electric shavers | 15–1500 | 0.08–9 | <0.01–0.3 |
| Hair dryers | 6–2000 | 0.01–7 | <0.01–0.3 |
| Irons | 8–30 | 0.12–0.3 | 0.01–0.025 |
| Mixers | 60–700 | 0.6–10 | 0.02–0.25 |
| Portable heaters | 10–180 | 0.15–5 | 0.01–0.25 |
| Refrigerators | 0.5–1.7 | 0.01–0.25 | <0.01 |
| Television | 2.5–50 | 0.04–2 | 0.01–0.15 |

Source: Environmental Health Criteria 69: Magnetic Fields (Geneva: World Health Organization, 1987)

opposite. Otherwise, they can be significant sources. A major source of the fields is the electric motor in appliances, with the number of coils essentially determining the magnetic field strength. The fields exist only when current is flowing (i.e., the appliance is plugged in and turned on). The magnetic field is greatest in the immediately surrounding area and decreases rapidly with distance.

Outside sources of magnetic fields can contribute significantly to fields found inside the home and workplace. Buildings, vegetation, and most other objects do not provide appreciable shielding. Magnetic fields are shielded only by structures containing large amounts of ferrous or other special metals.[14] The contribution from outside sources such as power lines is complex because of the different field directions/orientations and phases from various other sources[15] and, until recently, was not well understood. Calculation is difficult. Except for houses close to transmission lines, the major sources of magnetic fields in homes are external distribution lines. A few homes have significant ground return currents from distribution lines and building wiring.[16]

## PF E/MF INTERACTIONS WITH BIOLOGICAL SYSTEMS

When a conducting object is introduced into PF E/MF, the electric field is perturbed but the effect on the magnetic field is negligible. All biological systems are good conductors in comparison with air.[17]

*Perception*

Strong electric fields can stimulate the skin of animals, by vibrating hairs or by triggering various skin sensors; (human perception occurs at about 12–15 kV/m, related to the unperturbed electric field).[18] A person standing in an electric field of 20 kV/m or greater will likely feel a slight tingling sensation. A variety of studies have shown that animals can also feel strong electric fields.[19] Generally, people cannot detect the presence of magnetic fields. However, extraordinarily strong magnetic fields (found only in special situations such as the laboratory) cause flashes of light in the eye. Some animals have developed special sense organs that can sense the presence of very weak electric or magnetic fields. The organs are used in navigation and in searching for prey.[20]

*Electric and Magnetic Induction*[21]

The human body contains free or nearly free electron charges that move in response to forces exerted by charges and currents on appliances and nearby power lines. These movements, or body currents, are produced by electric and magnetic induction.

*Electric Induction*

In electric induction, charges on a power line, for example, attract or repel the body's charges. The electric force causes the charges to move to the body surface because body fluids are good conductors of electricity. As the charges on the power line alternate from positive to negative 60 times per second (and negative to positive 60 times per second), the charges induced on the body surface also alternate. Thus PF electric fields induce currents in the body as well as charges on the surface (see Figure A-2).

*Magnetic Induction*

Magnetic fields and electric fields are interrelated. As previously discussed, alternating current produces magnetic fields that oscillate with the current. In turn, the alternating magnetic fields produce electric fields that exert forces on the electric charges contained in the body. This process, called magnetic induction, induces currents that flow in loops. In a simple model, these "eddy currents" are greatest near the periphery of the body and smallest at the centre (see Figure A-2). Detailed data on the distribution of magnetically induced currents in humans and animals is sparse.

The magnitude of surface charges and internal body currents induced by PF E/MF depends on many factors, including the magnitude of the charges

Figure A-2
Currents Induced by Electric and Magnetic Fields in a
Human Standing Directly Under a Power Line

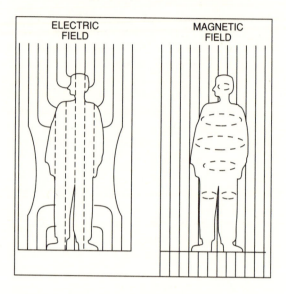

*Notes:* Solid lines represent invisible field lines. Dotted lines
indicate direction of induced current flow.

Reproduced with permission from U.S., BPA, DOE, *Electrical
and Biological Effects*, 16

and currents in the source, the distance of the body from the source and
ground, the presence of other objects that might shield or concentrate the
field, body posture, shape and orientation relative to the field, and whether
and how the body is grounded. (Therefore, induced surface charges and
currents are very different for different animals.)

Compared to contact currents when touching, for example, a refrigerator,
induced currents are typically small except in very strong fields.[22] For
example, an electric field of 1 kV/m or a magnetic field of about 40 μT
induces about 0.016 mA. A 10 kV/m electric field induces about 0.16 mA.[23]

### Contact Currents

When physical contact is made between a body and a conducting object
carrying an induced voltage (e.g., a vehicle parked under a transmission line
or a refrigerator door handle), contact currents flow into the body. If a
person touches a vehicle parked under a power line, for example, the body

provides a path to ground through which the charge induced on the vehicle by the power line's electric field can flow. High current densities are often produced in the tissue near the point of contact, resulting in some of the most intense exposures. However, they usually last for only a brief period of time (e.g., as long as it takes to open the car door or refrigerator).

The magnitude of a contact current depends on several factors, including the local field intensity, the size and shape of the contacted object, and how well grounded the contacted object and person are. The largest contact current is drawn by a well-grounded person touching a large metal object well insulated from the ground. Most common contact currents are imperceptible (less than 0.2 mA); however, if large enough, they can result in an annoying spark discharge or painful shock. For comparison, adult humans can typically detect a PF current of about 0.4 to 1 mA, "let-go" current is of the order of 5–15 mA, and ventricular fibrillation occurs at currents of 60–120 mA.[24]

Power line and appliance contact currents (and therefore exposure) are limited to a certain extent by existing safety standards. For example, the U.S. National Electric Safety Code (NESC) recommends that power lines be designed to limit contact currents from large vehicles to 5 mA.[25] The NESC also limits the "short-circuit" current (the contact current that flows into a well-grounded person with wet hands) of new appliances to 0.5 mA (for portable units) and 0.75 mA (for stationary units). Typical appliance short-circuit currents are 1–100 μA.[26] In British Columbia, similar standards are established by the Canadian Standards Association and Provincial Workers' Compensation Board, as well as by B.C. Hydro.

### EXPOSURE

#### Exposure Assessment

Exposure assessment involves the determination of the amount of exposure that may be encountered in homes, offices, and factories. Direct measurement or, if direct measurement is unavailable or impractical, exposure modelling (i.e., theoretical estimates) are used to assess exposure.

#### Direct Measurement

Instruments to measure exposure from both electric fields and, more recently, magnetic fields have been developed. Electric field instruments measure either the unperturbed electric field or the time integral of the electric-charge density on some area of body surface. Magnetic field instruments measure either the magnetic field or the time integral of the magnetic field produced on some area of the body surface (see Figure A-3).

Figure A-3
A Personal 60 Hz Magnetic Field Exposure Record

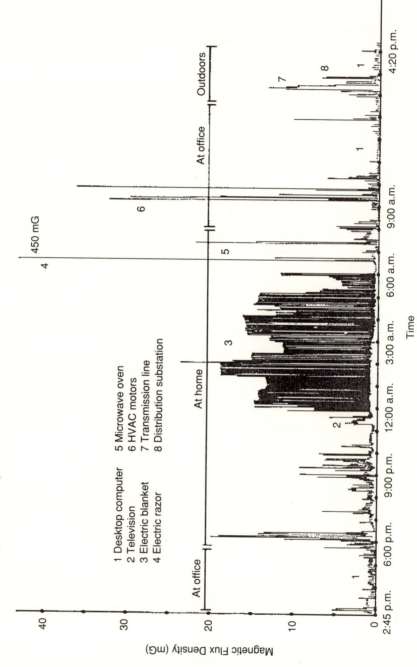

Reproduced with permission from Taylor Moore, "Pursuing the Science of EMF," 9

Electric utilities will now measure PF E/MF in homes. A number of engineering consulting firms take measurements as a commercial service. Some instruments are moderately expensive and involve downloading to a computer for data analysis. Because there are multiple sources, the procedure can be complicated.[27] Relatively inexpensive single-axis dosimeters are also available. Recently, dosimeters that are small enough to be carried in a pocket or worn like a watch have been developed.

### Exposure Modelling

In simple situations, e.g., a transmission line crossing an open field, PF E/MF can be calculated very accurately using formulas from physics and electrical engineering. Electric field calculations are often used in designing or approving transmission lines. In recent years, magnetic field calculations have been increasingly common. Direct measurement may be more practical in complex settings due to the complex shapes or complex current and voltage patterns involved. The fields may add or subtract, depending on phase. Other frequencies, including those due to harmonics, also have to be taken into account.

Exposure models consist of two elements: estimates of instantaneous exposure intensity as a function of time, and estimates of the length of time that people spend in such positions. The unperturbed field is often used as a measure of instantaneous exposure because it is easy to compute and measure profiles of the field, and, for some common exposures, the field is well correlated with other measures of instantaneous exposure, such as internal current or surface-charge densities. (Of course, precise relationships between external unperturbed fields and other quantities depend on factors such as the impedance between the body and other conductors, body shape and position, and field duration.)

The interpretation of results from direct measurement or exposure modelling is difficult, not only because there are multiple sources but, more importantly, the exposure measure may not be appropriate because dose has not been defined. Even so, most studies have characterized exposure in terms of the unperturbed electric field or the magnetic field strength.[28]

### Exposure Parameters[29]

The PF E/MF and induced currents that people are exposed to can be measured or computed. However, scientists do not know which, if any, quantity or combination is related to human health. The mechanism(s) for field/biological effects have not yet been established and consequently the relevant exposure parameters have not been identified. Possible variables include (average or peak) field strength, change in field strength over time, (average

or peak) currents induced in the body, and exposure duration (time spent
in field or number of times subject passes in or out of field).[30]

For most known environmental hazards, such as chemical agents (arsenic)
or physical agents (ionizing radiation), it can safely be assumed that if some
of an agent is bad, more of it is worse. However, in the case of PF E/MF, much
of the biological experimental evidence suggests that this assumption cannot
always be justified. The problem involves defining "dose," i.e., identifying
which, if any, aspect (or combination of aspects) of the field can affect human
health.[31] Some studies have suggested a dose measure proportional to the
long-term average of magnetic field exposure. Other studies have suggested
very different measures of dose such as:

- frequency and intensity "windows" – biological effects are seen in specific
  narrow ranges of field intensity and frequency;[32]
- time thresholds – biological effects are observed only after several weeks
  of exposure;
- time "windows" – biological effects are seen after long- and short-duration
  exposure periods;
- field strength threshold – biological effects are observed only when field
  strength exceeds some threshold value.

Although each study involved different protocols and biological systems,
together they suggest that dose is not necessarily proportional to field
strength or to time spent in the field.

### Comparing Exposures from Different Sources

A great variety of sources can contribute to total exposure.[33] However,
because scientists do not know what measure is relevant in determining
biological effect, comparisons cannot be made on the basis of relative contributions to effective dose. Only physical quantities that are amenable to
measurement or theoretical estimates, including electric quantities such as
induced surface charge and internal currents, exposure duration, frequency
of exposure, and number of people exposed, can provide the basis for
comparisons among sources. Although such electric quantities may not be
related to possible health effects, they can be used to indicate how similar
or different people's exposures to various sources are.

As indicated in Figures A-4 and A-5, the rank of different exposure situations along one dimension can look quite different from the rank along
another dimension. (The range of values indicated represents both uncertainty
in the various factors needed to estimate dose and variability across exposed
populations.) Assuming that field strength is the relevant variable, appliances
can generate fields that are higher than transmission lines. On one hand,

Figure A-4
Three Different Exposure Measures Applied to Eight Exposure Situations

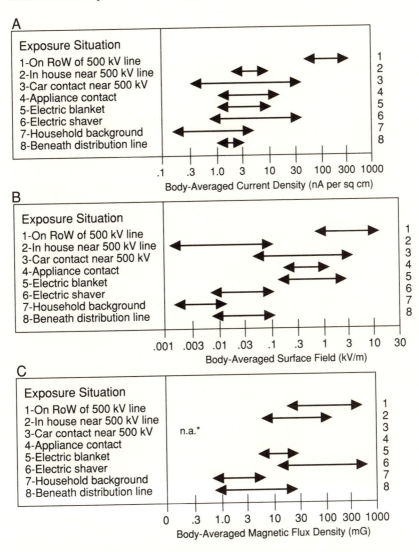

* Contact currents themselves produce negligible magnetic field. Of course the magnetic fields from the nearby 500 kV line would be comparable to those of exposure situations C1 and C2.

*Notes:* Exposure measures are: A) the density of electrically and magnetically induced currents averaged over the body; B) the induced electric field averaged over the body surface; and C) the average magnetic field within the body. Ranges represent the span of typical values.

Figure A-5
Three More Exposure Measures Applied to Eight Exposure Situations

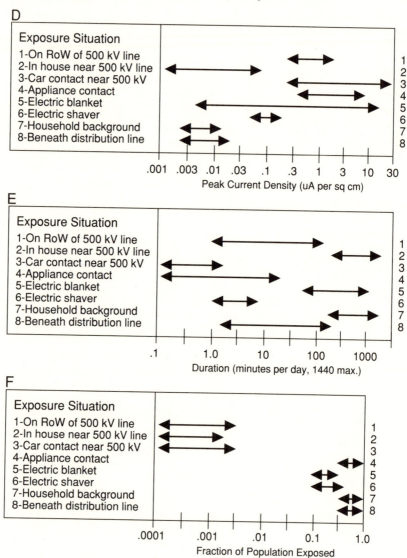

Notes: Exposure measures are D) peak electrically or magnetically induced current density anywhere in the body; E) the duration of the field encounter; and F) the fraction of the population that regularly encounters the exposure situation. Ranges represent the span of typical values.

Reproduced with permission from U.S., Congress, OTA, *Biological Effects*, 23 these fields in most cases decrease rapidly with distance and produce only intermittent exposure. On the other hand, electric blankets expose users for long periods of time and, like hair-driers and electric shavers, are operated close to the body. Assuming that induced current is the relevant variable, contact currents from appliances and video display terminals (VDTS) are greater than power lines even when integrated over time.[34]

## RESEARCH METHODS

Studies concerning the effects of PF E/MF exposure on human health fall into two general categories: laboratory studies and epidemiological studies. They differ qualitatively in approach, sensitivity, analytical power, and potential relevance to the question at hand.

### Laboratory Studies

Laboratory studies allow scientists to generate and examine specific hypotheses[35] and are capable of developing hard cause-and-effect relationships from experimental evidence.[36] Properly designed, performed, and controlled laboratory studies can define mechanisms of action, provide indicators for studies in humans, and permit extrapolation to the human response.[37]

Under controlled conditions, biological subjects are exposed to carefully defined fields for known periods of time and compared to subjects treated in a similar manner (to the best of the investigator's ability) except for field exposure. Exposures can be graded and confounding effects such as diet, genetics, and environment are minimized.[38] If large numbers of subjects are used and appropriate statistical analyses applied, it is possible in principle to detect differences between exposed and "control" or "sham exposed" populations that are even smaller than the normal variations that occur spontaneously in all biological systems. Thus (with skilful experimental design), laboratory studies are able to reveal subtle effects that would be missed in epidemiological studies or casual observation.

Yet the most sophisticated statistical techniques can tell only what the odds are that the two groups are different. Whether the difference resulted from field exposure or other factors depends on the skill and ingenuity given to the experimental design. There are few general principles to guide scientists; each experiment is its own challenge. Success depends not only on the concepts of the experimental design but also on meticulous attention to detail during execution.[39]

### Cell and Tissue Studies

Both *in vitro* and *in vivo* techniques are used in laboratory studies. *In vitro* studies use isolated and artificially maintained preparations of cells or tissues; *in vivo* studies use living organisms.

*In vitro* studies are used to determine the biological effects of PF E/MF exposure on the functions of cells and tissues, with an emphasis on establishing mechanisms of interaction. However, the studies are limited by the scientific inability to predict physiological responses of biological systems on the basis of fundamental mechanisms. Cells are simple and their relationship with higher organisms is too tenuous. With some exceptions, notably relating to bone growth, *in vitro* functional changes are not closely linked *in vivo*. Even when effects are demonstrated consistently at the cellular level in laboratory experiments, it is difficult to predict whether and how they will affect the whole organism. Cell processes are integrated through complex mechanisms and feedback loops in the animal. Other processes may compensate for cellular process perturbation by an external agent so that there is no overall disturbance to the organism.[40] It is also difficult to extrapolate *in vitro* to *in vivo* exposure conditions, nor may it be appropriate to do so. Ultimately, *in vivo* testing is required.[41]

### *Whole Animal Studies*

Laboratory animal studies can be used to assess the existence and general nature of a health risk, and to give general guidance for safety levels. In studying the biological effects of PF E/MF, the emphasis is often on providing information for eventual use in assessing the potential for biological effects on humans.[42] (In some situations, the animal may be the end-point, e.g., cattle on a transmission line ROW.)

It is normally not practical to conduct an animal study to determine if an agent causes chronic disease such as cancer or heart disease. However, the existence of physiological effects such as neuroendocrine response, altered brain waves, and depressed serum enzyme levels can be revealed.[43]

Animal studies are valuable in testing for possible deleterious effects. If chromosome damage cannot be demonstrated in the laboratory, it is unlikely to occur in exposed humans. However, if an effect is demonstrated in the laboratory, it does not necessarily follow that exposed humans will also show effects.[44] For example, experimental effects on chick embryos have not been found to be predictive of any human fetal effects from the same agents.[45] Developmental control is very different in the two species.

Determining the relationship of animal data to human disease is usually a matter of judgment, not demonstrable fact. Extrapolation to humans is very tenuous for a number of reasons: the relationship of the controlled laboratory to the real world; the relevance of effects on laboratory animals to humans; dosimetric considerations, including scaling of the species; and evaluation of the biological consequences of observed effects.[46] To accurately extrapolate the results of laboratory animal studies to humans requires detailed knowledge of the physical and biological mechanisms involved.[47]

It is difficult to compare exposures in laboratory studies with human exposures because of uncertainties about dose. For example, if the magnetic field is the measure of interest, the exposure of a rat at a given magnetic field intensity would be equivalent to human exposures at the same intensity. If magnetically induced currents are of interest, exposure of a rat at given magnetic field strength is much less intense than human exposures at the same field strength, because magnetically induced currents are proportional to body size.[48]

Indeed, it is not even possible to duplicate human electric field exposure using laboratory animals. To some extent, animal exposure can be scaled to approximate that of humans, taking into account how body size, shape, and orientation influence field interactions; for example, exposing swine to unperturbed electric fields of 30 kV/m or rodents to 100 kV/m reflects, to some degree, the same situation as a human standing beneath a 765 kV transmission line.[49] However, strong electric fields can result in relatively high current density through the animal's legs, thus increasing the possibility of skin or hair stimulation. In addition, field perception for mice, swine, and birds occurs from 25 to 35 kV/m while for rats it occurs from 4 to 10 kV/m.[50]

### Human Studies

Ideally, the best data for determining the biological effects of PF E/MF would come from laboratory studies of humans. General physiological and psychological responses of human volunteers can be observed. However, the scope of these studies is severely limited due to ethical considerations, the difficulty of controlling genetic and environmental variables and exposures, and the length of the human lifespan.[51] (For example, the quasi-invasive measurement techniques routinely employed with animals are unthinkable in humans.)

### Epidemiological Studies

Research with human populations in real-world situations is termed epidemiology. It is the study of the frequency and distribution of disease, or a physiological condition in human populations, and of the factors that influence its frequency and distribution. Epidemiological research is generally limited to establishing statistical associations or correlations rather than cause-and-effect relationships.[52] (An "association" means statistically that the things occur together but not necessarily that one causes the other.)[53]

Epidemiology takes advantage of the fact that certain subjects are exposed to some agent over the normal course of their daily activities at work (occupational) or at home (residential). Their health is compared with the health of unexposed subjects. Because the subjects voluntarily chose the exposure conditions, it is possible to study what would otherwise be ruled out in laboratory or controlled testing situations due to ethical considerations.

However, because there is no direct control by the investigator over the length of time or magnitude of exposure, or over other environmental influences that the subjects experience, epidemiological studies are expected to reveal only large-scale or unusual effects.[54] Exposed and unexposed groups of subjects can differ in terms of many factors, including age, residence, occupation, and sex ratio. Some of these factors (e.g., age and sex) are known to influence the incidence rate of many diseases and can be accounted for in study design or analysis.[55] Other factors associated with disease (and with exposure potential) may be unknown (even impossible to control for); such "confounders" may lead to an incorrect interpretation of a study.

Bias can also be introduced due to uncertainties in determining the actual exposure status of an individual, variations in disease definition and diagnosis in different geographic areas or in different hospitals, loss of study subjects who leave the area, unwillingness of subjects to participate, and inaccuracies in data sources such as death certificates and clinical records.[56] Furthermore, data on exposure is often drawn from incomplete medical records, personal recall, or personal descriptions of symptoms.[57] Practical solutions to many of these problems have been developed, but they are frequently not adequately addressed.[58] Although bias can give rise to a spurious effect – that is, make the study show an apparent effect that does not exist in reality – bias can also mask a true effect.[59]

The quality of the study depends to a very large degree upon the skill and originality of the investigator in selecting groups of subjects and controls for comparison and, after determining that there are statistically significant differences between groups, in devising methods to ascertain which of the many possible environmental influences may be responsible.[60] Epidemiology has provided valuable clues in the search for causes of disease,[61] often providing the only available direct evidence linking human exposure to a disease.

A commonly used epidemiological study design is the correlational or cross-sectional study in which factors of interest in a defined population are examined at a particular point in time. It is a broad screening type of study correlating the occurrence of disease or death in some group (selected by occupation or geographic area) with the assumed presence or absence of exposure to some agent. The proportional mortality rate (PMR), or ratio of exposed subjects who died of a specific cause to the unexposed subjects who died of the same cause, is often used to measure risk.[62]

Another common design is the retrospective case-control study, often simply referred to as a "case-control" study. Individuals who have already developed the disease are identified. An attempt is then made to compare the previous exposure experience of these "cases" with that of "controls" who have not developed the disease. Both groups are selected to be as similar as possible in all other characteristics.[63] The exposures have already occurred so they must somehow be estimated. The odds ratio (OR), or exposure odds among cases to exposure odds among controls, is often used to measure risk.[64]

A third common design is the cohort study. The exposure status of non-diseased individuals is first identified. Then the subsequent rate of disease development in the cohort is determined. The two types of cohort studies, concurrent (or prospective) and non-concurrent (or retrospective), differ in terms of when the study variables (exposure and disease) occur in relation to the onset of the study. Prospective cohort studies are most similar to the classic laboratory experiment and result in a "true" measure of relative risk (RR), the ratio of incidence among exposed to the ratio among unexposed (or less exposed).[65]

Epidemiological studies are very persuasive because they deal with people.[66] But this is a difficult science and one that is subject to many pitfalls, particularly when the differences in incidence of disease between groups is small[67] or the agent is weak with non-specific effects.[68] Very large populations are then required to attain statistical significance. In addition, because of the inherent biases in epidemiology, a great number of studies are usually required to establish pervasive scientific evidence about causal links.[69] However, a series of carefully designed epidemiological studies, all indicating a positive association supported by cellular and animal data, can provide persuasive evidence for cause.[70]

### Cause and Effect

Criteria commonly invoked to distinguish between causal and non-causal associations include:

- strength of association – ratio of incidence rate in exposed to non-exposed populations, e.g., RR;
- consistency – same association observed in different populations under different circumstances;
- specificity – single rather than multiple effects;
- temporality – cause precedes effect in time;
- biological gradient – dose-response relationship;
- biological plausibility and coherence – association consistent or supported by known facts or observations;
- experimental evidence; and
- analogy – analogous agent.

These criteria, developed by Sir Austin Bradford Hill, are not "hard and fast" rules of evidence. For example, specificity, biological plausibility, experimental evidence, and analogy are not necessarily required to demonstrate cause and effect. The criteria can help experts decide if there is another way of explaining the set of facts that is equally, or more, likely than cause and effect. As Hill points out, formal tests of significance cannot answer this question. They only indicate the effects of chance and the likely magnitude of those effects.[71]

Experts agree that a considerable degree of scientific judgment is involved in evaluating any epidemiological association. However, different experts stress different criteria; not all agree that certain factors are useful.[72] For example, one epidemiologist has suggested that cause-and-effect associations are only clearly established when relative risks are large (i.e., 5 or more) and results of epidemiological studies are consistent.[73] (In the past, epidemiology has been successful in identifying hazards when relative risks were greater than 10, e.g., cigarettes and asbestos.) Temporality may be the only factor universally accepted as an essential criterion. However, it can be difficult to demonstrate with many chronic diseases (e.g., cancer), which generally have long latency periods.[74]

# Framework
# Consensus Agreement
# and CAPCO Note
# B.C. Stakeholder Forum
# on Sapstain Control

## DOCUMENT #1: FRAMEWORK
## CONSENSUS AGREEMENT

There is a consensus among the undersigned stakeholders on the following matters, including the six Sub-Agreements, all of which shall be treated as a single overall agreement, and not as separate or separable parts.

1. The B.C. Stakeholder Forum on Sapstain Control is affirmed by these stakeholders as a continuing organization, and each of them makes a commitment to participate in its future meetings, according to the provisions of Sub-Agreement "A." The "Statement of Principles," agreed to as of November 8, 1989, has been incorporated into these terms of reference.

2. Expenses incurred by the Forum shall be managed according to the terms of Sub-Agreement "B."

3. A health monitoring program for those engaged in the use of sapstain control technologies shall be established, according to the terms of Sub-Agreement "C."

4. An annual report to the Forum on technologies and markets for wood products shall be submitted by the Council of Forest Industries, as per Sub-Agreement "D."

5. Recommendations on the registration status of sapstain control products shall be forwarded to Agriculture Canada, according to the terms of Sub-Agreement "E."

6. The B.C. Ministry of Environment agrees to work in harmony with Agriculture Canada, in determining effluent regulations for registered sapstain control products, and with the Forum on training and education matters, as per Sub-Agreement "F."

*Sub-agreement "A": Terms of Reference*

1. The Stakeholders supporting this Agreement are as follows:
British Columbia Ministry of Environment
British Columbia Ministry of Forests
Canadian Paperworkers Union
Council of Forest Industries of British Columbia
International Longshoremen's and Warehousemen's Union
IWA – Canada
Sawmill Industry of British Columbia (COFI Members)
Wharf Operators of British Columbia

2. Other Stakeholders who wish to affirm this Agreement at a later date shall be invited to do so by consensus among the above-mentioned Stakeholders.

3. The Forum is charged with the mission of seeking to arrive at a stakeholder consensus on all matters pertaining to the uses of sapstain control products in British Columbia. In particular, the Forum shall monitor the activities called for in the Framework Consensus Agreement and its subagreements, and shall consider changes to that Agreement as required.

4. Each of the named Stakeholders undertakes to disclose promptly, to all of the others, all information known to itself that is relevant to the purposes of the Agreement.

5. The B.C. Stakeholder Forum on Sapstain Control shall meet at least once annually, in the month of September; other meetings may be called by a majority of Stakeholders (in case of a tie, the voices in favour of holding a meeting shall prevail).

6. The Stakeholders shall designate a Chair/Secretariat for a term of office, who shall conduct meetings, prepare minutes, and undertake activities between meetings at the direction of the Stakeholders.

7. The B.C. Stakeholder Forum on Sapstain Control shall establish subcommittees as required.

8. It is understood by all Stakeholders that adherence to these Terms of Reference and participation in any activities, mentioned in the Framework Agreement and its Sub-Agreements, is on a voluntary basis only. It is further understood that any Stakeholder may discontinue such adherence and participation by giving notice to this effect to the other Stakeholders.

9. It is understood that a consensus position of the Stakeholder Forum may not represent the viewpoint of every individual stakeholder on every point.

Stakeholders who wish to record reservations to consensus positions may do so in the official minutes of meetings.

## Appendix: Statement of Principles

1. Acceptable wood sapstain control must meet the objectives of adequate
   • environmental protection;
   • health protection, especially of workers;
   • efficacy; and
   • economic feasibility.

2. Taken together, these four objectives as a whole are likely to be achieved, for the foreseeable future, by some combination of a variety of wood treatment technologies.

3. All uses of toxic sapstain control products in British Columbia are to be discontinued as soon as it is practicable to do so, taking into account the four objectives listed above.

4. Where sapstain control products are used, the adverse health and environmental impacts of such products must be as low as is reasonably achievable.

5. All future substitutions of new sapstain control products, for those presently in use, must produce, on a province-wide basis, a lower net adverse environmental and health impact.

6. Criteria and benchmarks, acceptable to all stakeholders, for determining what new products and practices will result in such lower adverse impacts, should be established and monitored.

## Sub-agreement "B": Finances

1. The B.C. Ministry of Forests will endeavour to ensure that sufficient funds are available to enable the B.C. Stakeholder Forum on Sapstain Control to carry out its activities.

2. The funds provided in the Forum budget shall be used for the following purposes:
   • payment of fees and expenses of the Chair/Secretariat;
   • payment of fees and expenses for expert advisors retained by the Forum;
   • payment of travel expenses to Stakeholders for attendance at meetings;
   • other expenses associated with the Forum's activities, as authorized in advance by the Stakeholders.

*Sub-agreement "C": Health Protection and*
*Monitoring Procedures*

1. A new Industry/Union Health Monitoring SubCommittee of the B.C. Stakeholder Forum on Sapstain Control will be established to monitor the development and implementation of suitable programs, designed to ensure the minimization of all health risks associated with the use of any sapstain control products in B.C. sawmills and terminals.

2. Where considered necessary, the SubCommittee will seek appropriate sources of funding for relevant research or education programs.

3. The SubCommittee will focus on the following activity areas:

   a. Establishment of a central registry of the usage of sapstain control products, maintained on a current basis by product and by mill or terminal, and available on request to all Stakeholder Forum members. (This might best be done through the WCB [Workers Compensation Board].)

   b. Establishment of effective training and education programs at each operation for each sapstain control product in use, or about to be put into use, involving managerial and supervisory personnel, workers (including casual and weekend workers), first-aid attendants, safety committee members and local unions. (This might best be done through individual operations management and safety committees, in conjunction with suppliers and other external resources as required.)

   c. The development and ongoing use of appropriate instruments, such as periodic questionnaires and/or a separate "sapstain control" record book in the first-aid room at each mill using any sapstain control products, in addition to the current general first-aid record book, in which to record all details pertinent to possible worker exposure and reported health symptoms.

   d. Development and use of suitable protective equipment, hygiene practices and engineering controls for each sapstain control product. (B.C. Research may be asked to play a role in this, subject to funding availability, in addition to the WCB.)

   e. Receipt and evaluation of all pertinent new information, related to possible health implications of existing or new sapstain control products, which triggers appropriate new or modified actions. Such actions might include more intensive monitoring of certain workplaces, including biological monitoring or changes in protective equipment and/or application technologies to reduce exposure.

   f. Seek to have operations safety committees notify the SubCommittee when new items of concern have been identified, and report on them to the SubCommittee for its consideration and possible assistance.

4. At the time when, at each treatment unit, a dilution level is established for each sapstain control product used, a two-week monitoring study of acute health symptoms will be commenced at once, to be administered by an appropriate body, for example the local health and safety committee, and a report thereon will be filed with the SubCommittee and with other appropriate bodies. If the dilution level is changed subsequently at that unit, a new study of the same type will be undertaken. A standard questionnaire format for these studies will be approved in advance by the Sub-Committee.

5. The SubCommittee will meet as required, and will report on its activities to the full Stakeholder Forum at least once per year. A representative of the WCB should be invited and encouraged to attend all meetings of the Sub-Committee, to provide advice and to share information. The first meeting should be held no later than September 1990.

6. Members of the SubCommittee will be appointed by those industry and union organizations that are members of the Stakeholder Forum, and these appointees in turn will then elect or appoint their own chairperson or co-chairs. (Total SubCommittee membership should probably comprise six to eight individuals.)

### Sub-agreement "D": COFI Report

The Council of Forest Industries undertakes to provide an annual written report to the Forum dealing with the following matters:

(a) current markets for kiln-dried lumber and forecasts of future market prospects;

(b) current developments in new application technologies for the use of sapstain control products; and

(c) current developments in other strategies as alternatives to the uses of sapstain control products.

### Sub-agreement "E": Product Registrations

The B. C. Stakeholder Forum on Sapstain Control recommends to the Pesticides Directorate, Agriculture Canada, the following steps:

A. That the re-evaluation process be initiated immediately for all products which are currently registered for sapstain control and which contain the active ingredients TCMTB, Copper-8, or Borax; and

B. That products based on the active ingredients DDAC and IPBC be granted conditional registrations, to be reviewed annually, for sapstain control uses.

In making this recommendation, the Forum recognizes the inadequacy of available data to evaluate many critical end-points relating to health, safety, and environmental impact (as noted in the "Summary of Toxicity Data on Antisapstain Products" in the "Discussion Document on Anti-Sapstain Chemicals").

With respect to these two recommendations, the Forum requests the Pesticides Directorate to take note of the following points:

1. It is the intention of the Stakeholders to establish the B.C. Stakeholder Forum on Sapstain Control as an ongoing organization.

2. Should the Stakeholders become aware, during the period when a registration is held by any sapstain control product, of information that indicates adverse conditions with respect to either health or environmental impacts, which appear to arise out of the uses of this product, this information will be communicated to Agriculture Canada at once for its advice and consideration.

3. The Forum will request the manufacturers and formulators of the products holding registration for sapstain control in Canada for an undertaking to supply the Stakeholders, in a timely fashion, with all information about the product, known to those firms, and arising from uses anywhere in the world, that is relevant to the matters of occupational health and environmental impacts.

*Sub-agreement "F": B.C. Effluent Regulations and Pesticides Applicator Licensing*

1. The Environmental Protection Division, B.C. Ministry of Environment, will work in harmony with the Pesticides Directorate, Agriculture Canada, to determine, in a timely manner, in accordance with Section 4 of the "Antisapstain Chemical Waste Control Regulation," the minimum effluent quality in effluent for those chemicals that are registered for use by Agriculture Canada.

2. With reference to the special education and training programs (Sub-Agreement "C," art. 3-b and any related provisions) provided for under this Agreement: The Pesticide Control Branch, B.C. Ministry of Environment, will collaborate with the B.C. Stakeholder Forum on Sapstain Control, at future meetings, to explore the feasibility of utilizing the framework of the B.C. pesticide control regulations to achieve these objectives, either through voluntary compliance mechanisms or by some other means.

DOCUMENT #2: AGRICULTURE
CANADA, CAPCO NOTE 90—10

SAPSTAIN

*Introduction*

Fresh sawn softwood lumber is generally treated with a pesticide (antisapstain chemical) to protect it from surface mould and fungal deterioration during transportation and prolonged storage. Over 3.6 billion board feet of coastal softwood lumber from British Columbia were treated in 1986 with antisapstain chemicals. This treatment is essential to meet lumber quality requirements for export markets.

The use of chlorophenate chemicals, the traditional protectants, has become controversial, both in Canada and elsewhere, particularly in relation to three concerns:

• potential carcinogenicity;
• dioxin contamination; and
• toxicity to aquatic organisms.

Many alternative chemicals to the chlorophenates do exist. Three are currently registered in Canada, under the Pest Control Products Act, namely, TCMTB, Copper-8, and borax. However, these alternatives do not effectively control the full spectrum of organisms. Furthermore, their health and environmental databases do not meet current Canadian registration standards. Several additional replacement chemicals are required to control the broad range of sapstain organisms occurring on the various wood species encountered in Canada.

Although registered and used in a number of other countries, none of the alternative antisapstain chemicals have the comprehensive database normally required for registration in Canada under the Pest Control Products Act.

There are two types of regulatory approaches commonly used in Canada and internationally:

• A complete package of scientific studies supporting a generally acceptable course of action.
• A less than ideal science database frequently associated with controversial decisions that nevertheless must be made.

To deal with the dilemma posed by the latter type of situation, agencies world-wide often make use of regulatory management techniques.

Federal departments have been working for some time to introduce regulatory management principles to strengthen the pesticide decision making process. Progress in this initiative has been gradual, but steady, over time. The current sapstain example represents the most ambitious application of this regulatory management approach to date, in terms of federal involvement and stakeholder participation.

## *Background*

In 1989 Agriculture Canada – in co-operation with Health and Welfare Canada, Environment Canada, Forestry Canada, and the Department of Fisheries and Oceans – prepared a Draft Discussion Document on Antisapstain Chemicals.

The Draft Discussion Document:
- summarizes the scientific studies on a series of compounds identified, in consultation with the Council of Forest Industries for British Columbia (COFI), as chlorophenate replacement products;
- provides an update on new or additional health and safety information that had emerged over the previous 18 months on pentachlorophenol (PCP);
- includes a value assessment prepared, under contract for Forestry Canada, by Deloitte Haskins and Sells International, with the assistance of the forest industry; and,
- identifies some possible regulatory options.

In November 1989, Agriculture Canada (in concert with Health and Welfare Canada, Environment Canada, Fisheries & Oceans, and Forestry Canada) sponsored a consultation meeting in Vancouver on sapstain control. Other participants in this consultation included COFI, the B.C. government, labour unions, and public interest groups, as well as representatives of primary suppliers of the control products described in the Draft Discussion Document on Antisapstain Chemicals.

## *Decision-Making Process*

Although the participants did not reach a consensus on specific chemicals, the November 1989 consultation meeting was worthwhile. Participants were unable to endorse additional alternative chemicals in the absence of full data packages, but were willing to consider this possibility after further review by an independent multi-stakeholder forum (MSF), with representation from:

The British Columbia Ministry of the Environment
The British Columbia Ministry of Forests
The Canadian Paperworkers Union
The Council of Forest Industries of British Columbia (COFI)
Earthcare
The International Longshoremen's and Warehousemen's Union

The Industrial Woodworkers of America (IWA)–Canada
The Pulp, Paper and Woodworkers of Canada (PPWC)
The Sawmill Industry of British Columbia (COFI Members)
The West Coast Environmental Law Association (WCELA)
The Wharf Operators of British Columbia

Federal government efforts in preparing background documentation (the Draft Discussion Document) and hosting the November 8, 1989 consultation, were a prerequisite to formation of the MSF.

Federal departments involved were pleased to see this independent initiative and committed to carefully consider any advice, counsel, or suggestions that would emerge from this process.

The MSF, established late in 1989, has already met several times and has also engaged its own private consultants to assess the supporting scientific studies. These assessments, available from the MSF Chairman, were consistent with those developed by federal government scientists and summarized in the Draft Discussion Document on Antisapstain Chemicals.

Arising from these discussions has been a position developed independently by the MSF, with no direct involvement of the federal officials. This position reflects careful consideration of the existing knowledge base by a majority of the interest groups represented on the MSF and by their contract consultants. Against this background, there is little reason for the federal response to run counter to the majority view and expressed wishes of the MSF whose members are likely to be the first affected and most directly impacted by whatever direction is adopted.

Agriculture Canada will continue to pursue the fullest possible scientific evidence to demonstrate the safety, merit, and value of pesticides. However, at the same time, the Department recognizes that it is not possible to provide infallible assurances of infinite safety, even with today's intensive testing procedures and the Canadian government's high standards.

Situations are frequently encountered where products are widely used and accepted internationally as pesticides or, in nonpesticidal applications, accepted as having no recognized hazards or known risks. Nevertheless, these same products may have information gaps when measured against the high standards set for the registration of pesticides in Canada. The incremental risk involved in extending coverage to include pesticidal uses is likely to be perceived as acceptable, particularly if the material is intended to replace registered pesticides that have become linked to clearly defined and recognized risks.

Circumstances such as these may well support, in the public interest, a decision to register certain pesticide products using regulatory management decision-making principles, supported by full public disclosure of information, along with consultation and communication with affected parties of interest.

Agriculture Canada has led initiatives to develop and introduce this type of decision-making process. The Department will continue efforts to develop and apply these principles.

While this process requires extensive time and energy, it is seen as a useful alternative for major, critically important user situations that are not fully supported by complete data packages. This approach to decision-making is widely used in other countries and has been applied in this case, dealing with new antisapstain materials, as well as in other areas.

## *Results*

The outcome emerging from this particular effort on antisapstain chemicals has been a majority expression of support by the MSF focusing on:

- registration of products containing DDAC and IPBC, as additional antisapstain alternatives, recognizing existing limitations in the current science base;
- re-evaluation of products containing the active ingredients TCMTB, copper-8, and borax;
- establishment of a B.C. provincial health protection and monitoring committee (union and industry members) to oversee the collection and analysis of information on worker health effects. This information will enable industry to adjust technological practices to enhance worker safety;
- cooperation of the B.C. Ministry of Environment in establishing appropriate effluent standards for registered antisapstain chemicals;
- on-site training and education program for mill managers and workers.

The MSF Report reflects the interests and informed input of the majority of the participants. The position developed by the MSF forum did not carry the support of Earthcare, The Pulp, Paper and Woodworkers of Canada (PPWC), or The West Coast Environmental Law Association (WCELA).

The PPWC provided a dissenting view focusing on the inability, based on currently available data, to scientifically support definitive conclusions regarding the safety of the new chemicals. Their comments also touched on the relationship between exposure, end-use product concentration, and occupational hazard.

The WCELA also provided a dissenting view based on recognized data gaps and the resultant inability to "declare or establish scientifically, that the new chemicals are probably safer to the environment and to workers than the present chemicals."

While these represent minority positions, the PPWC and the WCELA viewpoints are appreciated, particularly in light of the number of end-points that must be compared and the range of chemicals involved.

The risk associated with any treatment is by definition a function of the hazard inherent in the product and the degree of exposure to that hazard.

Worker exposure is reduced and, conversely, protection of health and safety enhanced, by new closed system application technology which is now common in many mills.

The diversity of practical situations encountered (e.g., wood species, weather conditions, application techniques ranging from dip tanks to spray boxes) necessitates availability of a range of end use product concentration options. Engineering design of the application system (e.g., vented spray boxes) responds to this reality by minimizing exposure to concentrated solutions while producing a finished product (i.e., treated lumber that is virtually "dry") thereby reducing the potential worker exposure during subsequent handling. Regardless of the product concentration and application technique, actual dosages are targeted for a standard application of active ingredient per unit surface area (i.e., micrograms (ug) of active ingredient/cm of wood).

It has been recognized from the outset that the database currently available could not provide complete scientific support for any final decision on the relative overall safety, to the environment and to workers, of the various antisapstain chemicals. This situation is evident in reviewing the fact base described in the Draft Discussion Document and was highlighted during the November 1989 consultation meeting. Independent experts engaged by the MSF reached a similar conclusion.

Awareness of the current database and ongoing studies were KEY factors in the undertaking, by federal pesticide regulatory authorities, to resolve the antisapstain question on the basis of regulatory management principles (i.e., a combination of science and public policy considerations based on an accepted fact base, plus informed consultations and input). Recognition of the scientific fact base, together with the MSF majority report, has influenced the regulatory position summarized in this Note to CAPCO (e.g., annual review of the temporary registrations and annual monitoring of schedules for additional data).

Advice and input from key stakeholders is an essential component of this approach to decision-making. Having benefited from broad consultation, advice, and council, it is Agriculture Canada's responsibility, under the authority of the Pest Control Products Act, to make regulatory decisions and to implement actions arising from them. At the same time, to be acceptable, the selected course of action must also recognize and respect the legitimate interests of all five federal departments involved in, and directly impacted by, the decision.

Against this background, and in the light of input and advice received via the process described above:

1. Registration of all sapstain control uses of tetrachlorophenol and pentachlorophenol in Canada will be terminated, as requested by manufacturers, effective December 31, 1990.

2. Agriculture Canada is:

i) granting temporary registration, subject to annual review, for the following new DDAC and IPBC antisapstain products which are considered
essential for effective control of the full range of organisms that cause
sapstain in various wood species:

| Product Name | Guarantee (%) | |
| --- | --- | --- |
| NP-1 (Kop-Coat) | DDAC 64.8 | IPBC 7.6 |
| Ecobrite III (Canfor) | SCB 10 | DDAC 2 |
| | BOA 2 | BNS 2 |
| F2 (Walker Brothers) | DDAC 11.4 | BNS 16.8 |
| Timbercote II | DDAC 20 | |
| (Napier Pacific) | | |

Additional terms and conditions will also be associated with the registration of the technical active ingredients, DDAC and IPBC, relevant to
compliance with schedules for ongoing studies and additional data, as
outlined in the Draft Discussion Document on Antisapstain Chemicals.
Compliance with these schedules will be monitored annually, as a condition for continuing regulatory status.

As part of the agreement developed by the MSF, the B.C. Ministry of
Environment has committed to work cooperatively to establish appropriate effluent standards for registered antisapstain chemicals, in
accordance with Section 4 of the B.C. provincial "Antisapstain Chemical Waste Control Regulation".

The B.C. Ministry of Environment will work, in concert with federal
colleagues in Environment Canada and in Fisheries & Oceans, to
develop technical details regarding appropriate standards, analytical
technique, and compliance monitoring.

Progress in this area will also be reviewed annually as part of the
commitment to a regular re-examination of this important area. Since
the MSF intends to continue to function on an ongoing basis, it will be
asked to commit to this undertaking, as well as to the education and
training programs also discussed under sub-agreement "F" of the MSF
Report.

ii) formally initiating re-evaluation of antisapstain products containing
TCMTB, copper-8, and borax. A great deal of work has already been
done in this area, such as the preparation of the Draft Discussion
Document on Antisapstain Chemicals.

This best balanced decision will accomplish several major objectives:
• Early phase-out of antisapstain use of the chlorophenates.
• Access to the range of products necessary to protect lumber export
markets valued at over four billion dollars per year.
• Establishment of sufficient information and options to allow for an
informed choice by users to:

– select products best suited to their specific operations, wood species, etc.
– switch away from materials that they may have been forced to use (because of the limited range of alternatives available) even though they were not the product of choice in their particular operation or circumstance.

# *Notes*

ABBREVIATIONS

BPA     United States, Department of Energy, Bonneville
Power Administration

DHS     Deloitte Haskins & Sells

EPA     U.S. Environmental Protection Agency

EPRI     Electric Power Research Institute

*Free Press*     *Comox Free Press.*

HWC     Health and Welfare Canada

MWN     *Microwave News.*

NRC     National Research Council

NRDC     Natural Resources Defense Council

NYPA     New York Power Authority

NYSPLP SAP     New York State, Department of Health, *Biolog-
ical Effects of Power Line Fields: New York State
Power Lines Project Scientific Advisory Panel's Final
Report*, Albany, July 1, 1987.

OTA     United States, Congress, Office of Technology
Assessment.

OTA Oversight     United States, Congress, Office of Technology
Assessment, "Health Effects of Power Frequency
Fields," in United States, House, Committee of
Interior and Insular Affairs, Subcommittee on
General Oversight and Investigations, *Electric
Power Lines: Health and Public Policy Implications:
Oversight Hearing*, 101st Congress, 2nd session,
8 March 1990.

PSC     Public Service Commission

R&R    British Columbia Utilities Commission, B.C.
       Hydro and Power Authority Proposed 230 kV
       Transmission Line Dunsmuir/Gold River:
       *Report and Recommendations*, Vancouver, 26 July
       1989.

Record    *Courtenay Comox Valley Record*

TDHSR    *Transmission/Distribution Health & Safety Report.*

TR    British Columbia Utilities Commission, B.C.
       Hydro and Power Authority Proposed 230 kV
       Transmission Line Dunsmuir/Gold River: *Pro-
       ceedings at Inquiry*, Courtenay, B.C., 11–14 July
       1989, Vol. 1–6 (Vancouver: Allwest Reporting
       Ltd., 1989).

CHAPTER ONE

1 "The Social Amplification of Risk: Progress in Developing an Integrative Framework," 155.
2 The importance of compensation has been emphasized recently by Inhaber, 2–3.
3 "New York Court Backs Wide Claims on the Drug DES," *New York Times*, April 5, 1989.
4 Peto *et al.*, "Mortality from Tobacco in Developed Countries," 1270, reporting on the results of a cross-country study carried out jointly by the World Health Organization, the American Cancer Society, and the Imperial Cancer Research Fund (U.K.). For a comparable risk one looks to something like estimated occupational risk of premature death from lifetime exposure to arsenic originating in ore smelting operations (36 cases in 100: Lave, "Health and Safety Risk Analyses," note 14). The calculation of what is termed "smoking-attributable mortality" is a matter of some controversy among epidemiologists and statisticians. Nevertheless, whatever may be the range of opinion at the moment on this issue, there is general agreement that smoking represents a very high risk in relation to all others.
5 Nothing that has been said here should be taken as implying that technical risk estimates are *always*, or in principle, reliable, well-founded, and preferable to qualitative judgments. The remainder of this book gives abundant illustrations of profound disagreements over the accuracy and adequacy of technical risk estimates.
6 There have been many such controversies in the past twenty years or so. A decent sample of them will be found in the volumes by the following authors whose works are referred to in our bibliography (as well

as the cases discussed herein): Bosso; Ellis; Graham, Green, and Roberts; Harrison and Hoberg; Jasanoff; Krimsky and Plough; and Salter. A sample of what the controversies are about would include: alachlor, alar, arsenic, asbestos, benzene, biotechnology (engineered organisms), bovine somatotropin, cadmium, captan, chlorophenates (2,4-D; 2,4,5-T; pentachlorophenol), DDT, dioxins and furans, electrical and magnetic fields, ethylene dibromide, forest resource management, formaldehyde, hazardous waste treatment, lead, medical devices (breast implants, Dalkon Shield), mercury, nuclear power generation, pesticides generally, PCBS, prescription drugs (female contraceptives, diethylstilbesterol, thalidomide), radioactive wastes, radon, and tobacco; the full list would be much longer.

7 Covello and Mumpower, "Risk Analysis and Risk Management: A Historical Perspective," 6–7 (this article gives a most interesting overview of the historical development of risk assessment since antiquity).

8 Krewski emphasizes the element of uncertainty as a key factor in explaining why risk decisions are controversial ("Risk and Risk Management," 34). Robin Gregory reminds us that it is useful to distinguish between resolvable uncertainty (will this pump work when I turn it on?) and unresolvable uncertainty (what will the weather be like three days hence?). As mentioned later, the unresolvable uncertainties associated with environmental and health risks have to do with the fact that, because we are exposed to so many different potential impacts, it is difficult or impossible to sort out particular cause-and-effect relations (say, in epidemiological studies) even after a long history of exposure to a known toxic agent.

9 "Perception of Risk: Reflections on the Psychometric Paradigm," 150.

10 See "The Asbestos Removal Fiasco"; Mossman et al., "Asbestos"; D'Agostino and Wilson, "Asbestos: The Hazard, the Risk, and Public Policy."

11 This paragraph is a contribution to our continuing dialogue with our friend Robin Gregory.

12 MacCrimmon and Wehrung, Taking Risks, 14–15.

13 Ibid., 19.

14 As mentioned in the Preface, the presentation in chapter 2 is intended for those who are unfamiliar with these materials; those who are already acquainted with the field may wish to skip to chapter 3.

15 Litigation in Minnesota about the so-called "Reserve Mining" controversy, dealing with taconite tailings in Lake Superior, went on intermittently between 1967 and 1978 (Bartlett, "Appendix: Chronology of Events"); the Uniroyal Chemical Co. paid its lawyers to fight the EPA over the risk assessment of Alar for about a decade (see chapter 6). In the United States, but not in Canada, the risk assessment for formalde-

hyde ended up in the courts; for a brief account see Merrill, pp. S424–5, and for a fuller story Graham, Green, and Roberts, ch. 1 and Harrison and Hoberg, *Risk, Science, and Politics*, ch. 6.

16 Among chlorine's many industrial uses is as a component in the pulp and paper bleaching process; Greenpeace and other environmental groups have "targeted" chlorine as an issue and propose its complete elimination from paper-making. At the time of writing, the dynamics of the chlorine issue stood about where the Alar issue was in 1985–86 at the mid-point of that controversy; the outcome is up in the air.

17 For an American example (waste disposal in New York City) see Ozawa, especially pp. 51–60 on expert disagreement. The "clash of experts" over risk assessments occurs frequently in U.S. courts; for a rare Canadian example see the record of the Nova Scotia herbicide trial, *Palmer v. Nova Scotia Forest Industries (1983)*, 26 C.C.L.T. 26, 2 D.L.R. (4th) 397 (N.F.T.D.).

18 In her book *Mandated Science* Liora Salter defines the title phrase as scientific assessment that occurs in the context of public policy decision-making.

19 The tribunal, whose members included distinguished Canadian toxicologists and U.S. risk experts, presented its decision in *Report of the Alachlor Review Board*; the hearings took place in 1986–87.

20 $10^{-4}$ is a risk of one in ten thousand cases; $10^{-5}$, one in a hundred thousand; $10^{-6}$, one in a million.

21 *Federal Register* 52 (1987) 49480. A selection of items from the Special Review Public Docket on Alachlor are: D-1347 (Position Document 1), D-5730 (Technical Support Document), D-6597 (SAP transcript), D-6829 (NRDC comments). Although the final result was dramatically different in the two countries – a ban on continued use in Canada, continuation in widespread use in the United States – the marginal difference between the two regulatory risk assessments is not particularly great. A reading of the Alachlor Review Board transcripts gives the impression that the HWC risk assessment could have had a different conclusion, especially if there had been a willingness to make different assumptions about exposure, but also (we suspect) with respect to the evaluation of cancer potency and extrapolation to human health effects. (Obviously we are not saying that the conclusion ought to have been different, just that it is not unthinkable that it might have been, at other times and under other circumstances.) On the other hand, had the EPA stuck to its original (1984) quantitative risk assessment, by refraining from manipulating its residue data, the agency might have found that the risk/benefit trade-off was tipped against Alachlor. It is impossible to resist the impression that the disagreement between the EPA and its Scientific Advisory Panel (SAP) in the Alachlor case was less

"damaging" to both sides than it was with Alar largely because the EPA was not recommending cancellation of registration in this case. See chapter 6 for further discussion on the SAP.

22  Brunk, Haworth, and Lee do not deal with the simultaneous U.S. proceedings.

23  In presentations to the EPA and the SAP in the United States, and to the government agencies and the Alachlor Review Board in Canada, Monsanto insisted on repeatedly raising the issue that studies on monkeys were preferable to studies on rats, because (Monsanto submitted) the monkey's metabolism (for this type of chemical at least) is closer to that of humans than is the rat's. Monsanto's scientists continued to do so even after they had conceded to the SAP in September 1986 that Monsanto did not have a clue as to the significance of any monkey data with respect to extrapolations to human health effects (EPA, Alachlor D-6597, pp. 36–7); for further discussion on this point see pp. 372–3.

24  Brunk *et al.*, 11–20.

25  Ibid., ch. V, esp. p. 112.

26  The clash of experts over power line EMF is really just beginning: there is plenty of time yet for public despair and frustration to materialize here.

27  The numbers come from Schiefer *et al.*, p. 2. An example where there is such agreement is the relation between vinyl chloride and a rare form of liver cancer; in general, the more restricted is the exposed population, the quicker and more reliable is the possible risk assessment. On the vinyl chloride case see Badaracco.

28  This is to be taken as a general observation about the gap between expertly assessed and publicly perceived risk, and not as a judgment that in particular cases either side is "right" or "wrong."

29  See especially the writings of Liora Salter, Sheila Jasanoff, and K.S. Shrader-Frechette.

30  Brunk *et al.*, 151 (italics in original).

CHAPTER TWO

1  "Perception of Risk: Reflections on the Psychometric Paradigm," 119.

2  Canada. Health and Welfare Canada, Environmental Health Directorate, "Risk Assessment/Risk Management: A Handbook on Risk Management for use within the Bureau of Chemical Hazards"; for an excellent overview see Lave, "The State-of-the-Art of Risk Assessment Approaches."

3  United States. National Science Foundation, "Risk Assessment and Risk Assessment Methods," 16.

4 For a much fuller discussion see Harrison and Hoberg, *Risk, Science, and Politics,* chapter 2.

5 The best introduction to this subject is still Slovic, "Perception of Risk" (1987), but see also: Gough, *A Review of the Literature Pertaining to 'Perceived' Risk and 'Acceptable' Risk*; United States National Research Council, *Improving Risk Communication,* ch. 2.

6 Kahneman, Slovic, and Tversky, eds, *Judgment Under Uncertainty.*

7 United States National Research Council, *Toxicity Testing* (based on a random sample of 675 substances). For the active ingredients in pesticides compounds, which are registered under the Federal Insecticide, Fungicide and Rodenticide Act (FIFRA) in the United States: "Only six of some six hundred active ingredients mandated for reregistration under the 1972 amendments [to FIFRA] had been fully tested [by 1985], and most of the more than 40,000 products on the market were unknown quantities in terms of their health and safety implications" (Bosso, *Pesticides and Politics,* 226). For a detailed discussion of a particular case, see chapter 8.

8 For example, Fischoff, Slovic and Lichtenstein, "Lay Foibles and Expert Fables in Judgements About Risk"; for more recent summaries see generally United States, National Research Council, *Improving Risk Communication,* ch. 2; Otway, "Public Wisdom, Expert Fallibility"; and especially the section entitled "The Pitfalls of Expert Judgment" in Otway and von Winterfeldt, "Expert Judgement in Risk Analysis and Management," 88–92.

9 Graham, Green, and Roberts, *In Search of Safety,* 218.

10 Kraus *et al.* "Intuitive Toxicology," 230.

11 The best recent overview is Gough, *A Review of the Literature Pertaining to 'Perceived' Risk and 'Acceptable' Risk,* sections 6 and 7.

12 It is demonstrably unwise, in the example cited, on two presumptions only: (1) In the case of public (governmental) expenditures for environmental protection, that it is actually possible to divert resources for reducing risks from one domain to another, rather than frittering away the funds otherwise expended on unnecessary risk reduction on frivolous gratifications of the vanities of politicians. (2) In the case of private-sector expenditures, that funds saved from avoiding expenditures on unnecessary risk reduction will be reinvested towards gaining genuine economic efficiencies rather than in enhancing the private gratifications of executives and shareholders.

13 One of the consistent themes in risk management is the "labelling effect." Something (usually a chemical) attains special prominence, largely for accidental reasons, and often because the adjective "cancer-causing" gets stuck to it in media reporting; thereafter the possibilities for dealing with it as "just another substance" vanish. But the public

remains unaware that as it is withdrawn from use, in many cases other substances with similar or even elevated risk profiles are quickly substituted for the one that has been damned.

14 Risk comparisons are notoriously a difficult matter to deal with: see Roth *et al.*, "What do we know about making risk comparisons," and the references cited therein.

15 The otherwise tacit dimension of presumed benefit was a key element in the Alar controversy (see chapter 6).

16 We acknowledge the force of an ethical argument that seeks to apply this same principle to the "higher animals" (monkeys, dogs, and the like) that are sacrificed for the sake of human well-being in medical research.

17 A broad overview of the field may be found in Kasperson and Stallen, eds, *Communicating Risks to the Public*.

18 Covello, von Winterfeldt, and Slovic, "Risk Communication," 171.

19 Leiss and Krewski, "Risk Communication," 100 (Figure 4).

20 The identification of the issue of trust as the key to risk conflicts has been a consistent theme in the influential writings of Brian Wynne; for a summary comment see his "Risk and Social Learning," 277–8. For another brief but important comment see Rayner, "Cultural Theory and Risk Analysis," 95, and for an extended treatment Renn and Levine, "Credibility and Trust in Risk Communication."

21 For a selection of the abundant recent research see G.W. Fischer *et al.*, "What risks are people concerned about?" and D. Golding *et al.*, "Evaluating Risk Communication," and the references cited therein.

22 This distinction was made widely known by United States, National Research Council, *Risk Assessment in the Federal Government*.

23 For examples of how contentious these matters can be, see the "Excursus on Cadmium" in chapter 3 and the more extensive discussions of the "clash of experts" in our accounts of the Alachlor, EMF, and Alar controversies (chapters 1, 4, and 6). For other accounts see "Risk Assessment of Pesticides"; Shrader-Frechette, *Risk and Rationality*; Graham, Green, and Roberts, *In Search of Safety*.

24 Kraus *et al.*, "Intuitive Toxicology," 230.

25 See further the "Excursus on Cadmium" in chapter 3.

26 It is well known that industrialized nations can "export" excess risk to less developed nations, when industries relocate production processes from areas of more stringent risk standards to those with less stringent ones. We have not elaborated on this important topic here because it has been dealt with recently and authoritatively in chapter 10 of Shrader-Frechette's *Risk and Rationality*.

27 This discussion is based on Peter Victor, "Techniques for Assessment and Analysis in the Management of Toxic Chemicals"; see also the

more recent and extensive discussion in Lind, Nathwani, and Siddall, *Managing Risks in the Public Interest.*

28 For a recent commentary on benefits assessment see United States, National Research Council, *Improving Risk Communication*, 262–8; the most complete treatment is Bentkover, Covello and Mumpower, eds, *Benefits Assessment.*

29 Canadian Standards Association, "Risk Analysis Requirements and Guidelines," Q-634.

30 Canadian Public Health Association, *Benefit, Risk and Cost Management of Drugs* (1993), as modified slightly by the authors.

31 Krewski, "Risk and Risk Management," pp. 32–4; see also Krewski and Birkwood, "Risk Assessment and Risk Management."

32 Canada. Health and Welfare Canada. Drugs Directorate, "Guidelines for Preparing and Filing New Drug Submissions." See generally Torrance *et al.*, "Risk-benefit and Quality-of-Life Analyses of Prescription Drugs."

33 *The Globe and Mail*, 28 March 1989, p. A12; Health and Welfare Canada, Health Protection Branch, "Dear Doctor Letter," September 1988.

34 For examples of how this explanation can be done, see the series of publications entitled "Discussion Document" and "Decision Document," issued by Agriculture Canada, Pesticides Directorate, Ottawa. As noted elsewhere in this volume, with respect to this key aspect of risk management – the judgment that "benefits outweigh risks" or vice versa – much more remains to be done in conveying to the public how such judgments are made and rationalized. For example, officials at the U.S. Environmental Protection Agency have acknowledged often that there are no "written guidelines describing how the agency balances risks against benefits" (Correia, "'A' is for Alar," 872 note 56).

35 See especially the writings of Sheila Jasanoff on this general point; and for the specific case of how science and policy interact in the regulation of carcinogens in the United States, see McGarity, "Substantive and Procedural Discretion in Administrative Resolution of Science Policy Questions."

36 See further chapter 3, pp. 70–1.

37 Krewski and Birkwood, "Risk Assessment and Risk Management," 59.

38 We agree very strongly with Shrader-Frechette (*Risk and Rationality*, ch. 11) on this important point.

39 Slovic, Kraus, and Covello, "What *Should* We Know About Making Risk Comparisons?" 391.

40 As our own discussion in this volume proceeds, we shall end up at the position staked out by Harry Otway ("Public Wisdom, Expert Falli-

bility," 222): "Acceptability is finally decided by political negotiations among stakeholders, informed by expert advice."

41 The following discussion is based on McColl and Leiss, "Formalde-hyde." See also the articles by Robert L. Sielken, Jr., and Ian C. Munro and Keith R. Solomon in the collection *Environmental Health Risks: Assessment and Management* (McColl, ed.), and Chapter Three in Graham, Green, and Roberts, *In Search of Safety*. For a full account of the UFFI episode see Harrison and Hoberg, *Risk, Science, and Politics*, ch. 6.

42 Formaldehyde has been in commercial production since 1901, and according to one U.S. estimate it is used in products accounting for 8 percent of all GNP; yet as of 1978, "very little was known about its chronic health effects": Graham, Green, and Roberts, *In Search of Safety*, 9, 39.

CHAPTER THREE

1 "Risk and Social Learning," 281.

2 See Leiss, *C.B. Macpherson*, ch. 4; Ulrich Beck's *The Risk Society* presents very forcefully the case against institutions, but his argument is not balanced by a recognition of the interests of individuals in avoiding responsibility for the risks they seek to enjoy.

3 Cf. Shrader-Frechette, *Risk and Rationality*, 132–4.

4 (1) *Tobacco:* The tobacco industry devised a massive "disinformation" campaign during the 1950s to undermine the force of the first wave of publicity about scientific studies linking cigarette smoking and lung cancer (Pollay, "Propaganda, Puffing, and the Public Interest"). At first the idea that conclusive proof of the link was lacking was the standard gambit in law against damage claims from smokers and their families; more recently the defence is that smokers understand the risks, which have been well publicized (thus the manufacturers' liability is nil).

(2) *Asbestos:* Paul Brodeur, "The Asbestos Industry on Trial," recounts at length the story of Johns-Manville; more recent cases are mentioned in *The Globe and Mail*, 31 July 1992, p. B3.

(3) *DDT:* Bosso, *Pesticides and Politics*, 115–25.

(4) *IBT:* Castrilli and Vigod, *Pesticides in Canada*, 13–14; Koren, *Handbook of Environmental Health and Safety* (p. 269) states: "EPA has invalid or fraudulent data on 36 pesticides including 35 used on food."

(5) M. Mintz, *At any cost*.

(6) *Westray:* see the coverage in *The Globe and Mail* during 1992, especially the articles by Stevie Cameron: 11, 12, 18, 25 May and 8, 29 June 1992; Jennifer Wells, "The Fault Line."

5  In June 1993, the tobacco companies launched the latest (but not the last) of their forays, challenging the EPA's risk assessment of environmental tobacco smoke (the EPA has classified it as a proven human carcinogen) in U.S. courts.

6  Bob Davis, "Risk Analysis: When science enters the political arena," *The Globe and Mail*, 10 August 1992, p. B1 (reprinted from *The Wall Street Journal*).

7  Keith Schneider, article in *The New York Times*, 28 July 1992, p. A6.

8  See Hajo Versteeg, "The Conflict between Law and Science," for an excellent account of the consequences flowing from this complexity.

9  "We tolerate voluntarily assumed risks more than those such as environmental hazards over which we have no control" (Viscusi, *Fatal Trade-offs*, 152).

10 William Freudenberg writes ("Heuristics, Biases, and the Not-so-general Publics" 239): "[T]he underestimation of risks does appear to be widespread in 'risky' occupations ... "; he mentions fishing, coal mining, offshore oil drilling, police work, high-steel iron work, and parachute jumping. We do not regard occupational risks as falling into the category of voluntary risk, and so they are excluded from our own list in the text. Nor do we believe that excess occupational risks are adequately compensated in market-based wage differentials, because we believe it is far-fetched in the extreme to think that the necessary precondition (perfect information) prevails in such transactions.

11 (1) Canada. Statistics Canada, *Accidents in Canada* (1991), cat. 11–612E, p. 72, 1987 data: accident occurring in the home defined as an event that resulted in activity limitation for at least half a day or resulted in property damage of $200 or more.

(2) Statistics Canada, *Accidents in Canada* (1992), p. 68: "incidence of sports accidents" measures accidents that occurred while playing games or participating in sports. This restrictive definition will result in lower estimates of accidents.

(3) Statistics Canada, *Accidents in Canada* (1991), p. 61.

(4) Personal communication, Dr. M. Kaiserman, Tobacco Products Control Unit, Health Canada, Ottawa, October 1993 (cf. chap. 1, note 4); we tried to find a number to represent "smoking-attributable morbidity" but were unable to do so.

(5) Statistics Canada, *Occupational Injures and their Costs 1988–1990* (1992), Table 8, Number of Accepted Time-Loss Injuries, by Industry and Province, pp. 13 and 14; Meng, "How Dangerous is Work in Canada?"; Leigh, "Estimates of the Probability of Job-related Death"; Covello, Brandt-Rauf, and Bendixen, "The Occupational Risk of Death from HIV Transmission in Health Care Workers," Table 1.

12 In an important article in this area Keeney and von Winterfeldt noted that the risk measures most commonly used by experts to date do not provide very useful guidance for people in deciding how to approach risky activities. They set themselves the following question (523): "How can a measure of risk be defined that is a useful guide for an individual's decision-making and that is consistent with the individual's beliefs and values?"

13 Even where such universal, tax-funded entitlement systems do not exist, especially in the United States, group insurance plans provide an opportunity for individuals to transfer the costs of high-risk lifestyle choices to others. In both cases these "external costs" are large. See Manning *et al.*, *The Costs of Poor Health Habits*, for detailed estimates of the external costs imposed by smoking, heavy drinking, and sedentary lifestyles.

14 In North America, farmworkers are a notorious case of a group of individuals who have been left largely unprotected by other social interests. See Sandborn, "The Democratization of Risk Decisions."

15 These features are in evidence in our case studies on Alar and anti-sapstains (chapters 6 and 8).

16 These abbreviations will be used later in the summary matrix for our risk management typology (Table 3–1).

17 Castrilli and Vigod, *Pesticides in Canada*, 537.

18 See, for example, Paul Riegert's account of the terrible effects of insect populations on humans and domestic animals in the Canadian West during earlier times, *From Arsenic to DDT*.

19 As indicated, they are not relevant to Type A.

20 Slovic *et al.*, "Risk Perception of Prescription Drugs," 101–2 (Figures 11.8 and 11.9).

21 Ibid., 105 (Figures 11.11 and 11.12).

22 Gregory and Mendelsohn ("Perceived Risk, Dread, and Benefits," 262) state that "average risk ratings are found to be significatly affected by perceived individual benefits, which suggests that perceptions of risk are net rather than gross indicators of harm."

23 Bettman *et al.*, "Cognitive Considerations in Designing Effective Labels for Presenting Risk Information," 6.

24 Sandman, "Hazard versus Outrage in the Public Perception of Risk."

25 For an introduction to the large literature on the effectiveness of health hazard warnings against tobacco use, see Australia, Centre for Behavioural Research in Cancer, Anti-Cancer Council of Victoria, "Health Warnings and Contents Labelling on Tobacco Products."

26 The phrase "amplification of risk" comes from Kasperson *et al.*, "The Social Amplification of Risk," but they do not apply their concept to the area of perceived benefits.

27  Slovic, "Perception of Risk," Table I.

28  The nuclear power industry is currently using this message in media advertising, as part of its ongoing (but so far futile) attempt to sway public opinion in its favour.

29  Canadian Nuclear Association, "Communications Plan within the Canadian Nuclear Association," 8 April 1987 (unpublished).

30  Christie McLaren, *The Globe and Mail*, 23 July 1988, p. A6.

31  Mary Gooderham, *The Globe and Mail*, 3 June 1989, p. A8. (There is a description of the CNA marketing campaign in *Marketing*, 28 August 1989, p. 1.) As a result of the low level of general support and the active campaign by local citizens against specific plants, at least three fully completed nuclear generating plants in the United States, each costing about $5 billion to construct in the mid-1980s, were not allowed to operate: Martin Mittelstaedt, *The Globe and Mail*, 5 July 1988, page B1. Paul Slovic has commented on the obtuseness of experts in their inability to understand the public attitude towards nuclear power in "Perception of Risk," 284–5.

32  McGee and Levy, "Herbicide Use in Forestry."

33  For example, one will not find in the media campaign any reference to the protracted "expert disagreement" over nuclear reactor safety design between the Canadian regulatory agency (Atomic Energy Control Board) and Atomic Energy of Canada Ltd., the Crown corporation that designs and builds reactors: Christie McLaren, *The Globe and Mail*, 20 August 1987, p. 1.

34  The bibliography on health risks from tobacco use is almost limitless. Our description is based on two summary reports: Kenneth E. Warner, "Smoking and Health: A 25-Year Perspective," and an unpublished review paper by Donald T. Wigle (Laboratory Centre for Disease Control, Health Protection Branch, Health and Welfare Canada), "Illness and Death in Canada by Smoking."

35  Royal Society of Canada, *Tobacco, Nicotine, and Addiction*.

36  There are other effects from different forms of tobacco use, especially chewing, that are not covered here.

37  In other words, smokers have a risk of contracting coronary heart disease which is twice to four-times as great as that for never-smokers.

38  Warner, "Smoking and Health," 142 (italics in original).

39  Pierce, "International Comparisons of Trends in Cigarette Smoking Prevalence," Tables 1–4 (selections).

40  Ibid., Table 5; see also Pierce *et al.*, "Trends in Cigarette Smoking in the United States" and "Projections to the Year 2000."

41  Many observers have pointed out the monumental hypocrisy involved in the massive effort by the U.S. government to open up markets for its cigarette manufacturers in Third World countries and Asia.

42 For example, Fischer *et al.*, "Recall and Eye Tracking Study of Adolescents viewing Tobacco Advertisements"; compare the massive new research report, Australia, Centre for Behavioural Research in Cancer, "Health Warnings and Contents Labelling on Tobacco Products," sponsored by the Anti-Cancer Council of Victoria. In his *Smoking: Making the Risky Decision*, Viscusi states that, based on survey responses, the perceptions of lung cancer risk from smoking are greatly exaggerated both by adults and young children, and he suggests that this finding should prompt changes in health policy, such as encouraging more risk information on "safer" types of cigarettes as opposed to efforts to ban smoking entirely. We think that this is a rather incomplete premise on which to base a policy change in such an important area of public health. A number of the further questions and considerations that should be addressed first are: (1) Viscusi acknowledges that he does not deal with the issues of passive smoking from environmental tobacco smoke (ETS) or compensation claims arising from ETS; most observers would regard these as rather pertinent ones. (2) The lung cancer risk may be reasonably well known, but other cancer risks arguably are not: Why not get more complete survey information before recommending policy changes? (Note that in the survey instrument, which is reprinted in the Appendix and lists possible responses from the interviewees, a whole list of relatively unknown types of smoking-related cancers – of the esophagus, pancreas, renal pelvis, and bladder – are absent.) (3) It is not clear from Viscusi's data whether, comparing the most recent expert knowledge with the public perception of smoking risk, there are any significant differences in the *overall* health risk perception between the two: Is this not the most important consideration, however? (4) Gender breakdowns are very important to policy strategies (e.g., proportion of young women deciding to smoke); very few such breakdowns appear in Viscusi's data, although they are readily available. (5) Chewing tobacco is not mentioned, although it is a vital health policy consideration, especially with respect to young persons. (6) Children aged seven and over may well report an awareness of the lung cancer risk associated with smoking, but are we really going to say that this is all we need to know? Should we not also try to ascertain what that knowledge *means* to them – as well as to others up to the age of young adulthood – in relation to behavioural motivation? In our view, what is known about attitude- and behaviour-formation supports the comment by Manning *et al.*, *The Costs of Poor Health Habits* (p. 21, referring to the fact that four out of five smokers start before the age of twenty): "At that age, people are usually not well informed and have not matured to the point where future ill health or mortality have much compelling reality for them." (7) Viscusi's acknowledged omission

of the addiction issue gives his entire book somewhat surreal overtones. The common thread in his book is that the "rational smoker" can evaluate risk information properly and make an informed decision; he contrasts the image of the rational smoker with that of the "stylized smoker," propagated by health authorities, as one incapable of making informed decisions. This argument is plausible, at least for adults, *only so long as one agrees to omit entirely the addiction issue from the discussion.* But we know that nicotine is a powerful psychoactive drug, and that (according to an expert panel of the Royal Society of Canada) the nicotine addiction resulting from cigarette smoking shares characteristics of drug addiction with other drugs such as heroin or cocaine; so why on earth would one choose to leave the addiction issue out of the discussion?

43  Fischer *et al.*, "Brand Logo Recognition by Children aged 3 to 6 Years."
44  DiFranza *et al.*, "RJR Nabisco's Cartoon Camel promotes Camel Cigarettes to Children"; Pierce *et al.*, "Does Tobacco Advertising target Young People to start Smoking?"; Mazis *et al.*, "Perceived Age and Attractiveness of Models in Cigarette Advertisements"; Pollay and Lavack, "The Targeting of Youths by Cigarette manufacturers."
45  "Effects of the Antismoking Campaign: An Update."
46  A nice connection between them is provided by two cases of occupational hazards among tobacco workers, noted a century apart. The first, nicotine poisoning among tobacco factory workers, was reported in the *Journal of the American Medical Association* in 1891; the second, asbestos-type diseases among workers in cigarette-filter plants, in 1989. ("The Toxic Effect of Tobacco Vapors"; Talcott *et al.*, "Asbestos-associated Diseases in a Cohort of Cigarette-filter Workers.")

CHAPTER FOUR

1  Those readers without an understanding of the nature of PF E/MF or of the methodologies used in health effects research are strongly encouraged to refer to Appendix 1 at this time. Such an understanding is crucial to understanding the PF E/MF health effects debate.
2  Hauf, "Electric and magnetic fields at power frequencies," 176.
3  Janes, "Background Information on High Voltage Fields," 141.
4  Energy Information Administration, Washington, DC, cited in Randy Ross, "Do Power Line-Generated Electromagnetic Fields Have Any Association with Certain Disorders?" *Journal of the American Medical Association* 259, 8 (26 February 1988): 1131–3.
5  The purpose of this section is to give the reader a general idea of the research that had been conducted to December 1988. Unless otherwise noted, the discussion is based on OTA, *Electric Power Wheeling and*

*Dealing.* The OTA report is, in turn, based on *Biological Effects of Power Frequency Electric and Magnetic Fields: Background Paper,* an OTA contractor report by Indira Nair, M. Granger Morgan, and H. Keith Florig, Department of Engineering and Public Policy, Carnegie Mellon University (CMU). The OTA report is cited for two reasons: the OTA is a U.S. federal agency, and the OTA report further reviews the CMU report. Although the OTA report itself was not widely available until early- to mid-1989, the literature reviewed was available in one form or another to December 1988. Not all experts would necessarily agree on the effects reported by the studies, let alone the interpretations. (See, e.g., BPA, *Electrical and Biological Effects,* June 1989.) There are even some subtle differences between the OTA and CMU reports. If nothing else, the OTA report indicates the range of scientific opinion when compared to the various reports presented during the Courtenay controversy. (We deal with expert disagreement in the Courtenay controversy, see chapter 5.)

6  Morgan, *Electric and Magnetic Fields,* 10.

7  See Appendix 1 for definitions of this and related terminology.

8  W.R. Adey, "Electromagnetic Fields, Cell Membrane Amplification, and Cancer Promotion," paper from the National Council on Radiation Protection and Measurements Annual Meeting, NAS, Washington, DC, 1986, cited in OTA, *Electric Power Wheeling and Dealing,* 232.

9  Calcium flows regulate physiological processes such as muscle contraction, egg fertilization, cell division, and activate certain enzymes important during cell development and growth.

10  The cell's primary biomolecules are DNA and RNA. DNA carries the genetic code; RNA transcribes the DNA command codes into proteins for cell physiological functioning.

11  Adey, cited in OTA, *Electric Power Wheeling and Dealing,* 233.

12  The circadian timing system synchronizes the daily cycle of various physiological and biochemical processes. Although many aspects of the biology of timing systems are not well understood, considerable understanding of some system elements has occurred in the last two decades.

13  Banks, cited in TDHSR 6, 8:2.

14  BPA, *Electrical and Biological Effects,* June 1989, 41. Although most workers in 230 kV and 500 kV transmission line environments were exposed to electric fields greater than 4 kV/m for "only minutes per day," accumulated exposure is roughly three orders of magnitude greater than exposures for office workers (T.D. Bracken and V. Chartier, "Occupational Exposure of High Voltage Workers to 60-Hz Electric Fields. Part 2 – Analysis and Results," paper from the Twenty-Third Hanford Life Sciences Symposium, 2–4 October, 1984, Richland, WA, cited in BPA, *Electrical and Biological Effects,* June 1989, 49);

V.L. Chartier, T.D. Bracken, and A.S. Capon, "BPA Study of Occupational Exposure to 60-Hz Electric Fields," *IEEE Transactions on Power Apparatus and Systems* PAS-104, 3 [1985]: 733–44, cited in BPA, *Electrical and Biological Effects,* June 1989, 49).

Another study reported that total cumulative electric field exposure for farmers working near 500 kV and 765 kV transmission lines was comparable to cumulative domestic exposure. About half of domestic exposure was related to electric blanket use. Exposures from recreational activities, including jogging, bicycling, horseback riding and skiing, were, in general, lower than estimated for both agricultural and domestic exposures (M. Silva, Enertech Consultants, *AC Field Exposure Study: Human Exposure to 60 Hz Electric Fields,* RP79–16 [Palo Alto, CA: EPRI, 1985], cited in BPA, *Electrical and Biological Effects,* June 1989, 49–50).

A third study found that 230 kV substation operators were exposed to an average daily magnetic field of 410 nT. In contrast, office workers were exposed to 74 nT (T.D. Bracken, *Measurement of Occupational Exposure of Substation Workers to 60-Hz Magnetic Fields,* Vancouver, WA: BPA, 1988, cited in BPA, *Electrical and Biological Effects,* June 1989, 50).

15 Adult brain cancer is rare (1 percent of all cancer incidence, a 5 in 100,000 risk), peaking at about sixty years of age. Brain cancer is the second-highest-risk cancer for children from birth to eight years of age.

16 Metastasis refers to secondary growth of cancer that spreads from a primary site.

17 Even the exposure of electricians may not be significantly higher than those not in the electrical field because they often work with circuits turned off. Various types of occupations involve the construction, operation, or repair of electrical equipment and devices (TDHSR 3, 1:2).

18 As of December 1988, no comprehensive history about the PF E/MF health effects issue had been written. A considerable amount of information was available on very specific events and activities but there was little information on their interrelationships. For a detailed chronology of events to Fall 1988 see Chociolko, "The Controversy Regarding Power Frequency Electric and Magnetic Fields and Human Health," 37–100.

19 OTA, *Biological Effects,* 1.

20 Kavet, "Biological Effects of Electric Fields," 2115.

21 OTA, *Biological Effects of Power Frequency Electric and Magnetic Fields – Background Paper,* 24; Morgan et al., "Controlling Exposure to Transmission Line Electromagnetic Fields," 82; Slesin, "Power Lines and Cancer," 55, 58.

22 Marino and Becker, "High Voltage Lines: Hazard at a Distance," 6–7.
23 Ibid., 7; M. Granger Morgan, "Public Perceptions of Risk from Electric and Magnetic Fields," paper from Ontario Hydro, *Health Effects of Electric and Magnetic Fields*. Popular literature was critical of the ways in which transmission lines were sited, constructed, and operated (BPA, *Electrical and Biological Effects*, June 1989, 22). See, e.g., Louise B. Young, *Power over People* (New York: Oxford University Press, 1973).
24 Morgan *et al.*, "Power line fields and human health," 62.
25 Furby *et al.*, "Public Perceptions of Electric Power Transmission Lines," 22.
26 Janes, "Background Information on High Voltage Fields," 141. The U.S. electric utility industry began research as early as 1962. The American Electric Power (AEP) Co. funded two small-scale studies at Johns Hopkins University investigating the general health of extra-high-voltage transmission line workers and the effects on mice of strong 60 Hz electric fields exposure. AEP was the first U.S. utility to build an extra-high-voltage transmission line several years earlier (OTA, *Biological Effects*, 69).
27 Corona is a sometimes visible electric discharge resulting from a partial electric breakdown in a gas, as in the air surrounding a high-voltage power line.
28 William Feero, "The Evolution of Electromagnetic Effects Issues," paper from Ontario Hydro, *Health Effects of Electric and Magnetic Fields*, 2.
29 Reported effects included nausea, fatigue, headaches, irritability, insomnia, and decreased sexual drive. As a result, regulations were established for Soviet substation workers limiting exposure to fields greater than 5 kV/m (BPA, *Electrical and Biological Effects*, June 1989, 22; OTA, *Electric Power Wheeling and Dealing*, 227).
30 Like the Soviet studies, Spanish studies reported changes in CNS and physiological function in workers exposed to 500 kV and 750 kV transmission line electric fields.
31 Janes, "Background Information on High Voltage Fields," 144; BPA, *Electrical and Biological Effects*, June 1989, 22.
32 OTA, *Electric Power Wheeling and Dealing*, 228; BPA, *Electrical and Biological Effects*, June 1989, 22.
33 Bulawka *et al.*, "The U.S. Department of Energy 60-Hz Electric Fields Bioeffects Research," 4432.
34 Kavet, "Biological Effects of Electric Fields," 2115.
35 Project Sanguine was later renamed Project Seafarer, and, more recently, Project ELF (BPA, *Electrical and Biological Effects*, June 1989, 30). Original plans were to locate 6,200 miles of cable and 100 transmitters in Northern Wisconsin (MWN 10, 1: 5–6).

36 Marino and Becker, "High Voltage Lines," 7. A group of civilian experts, including Becker, reviewed the studies for the U.S. Navy in 1973 and recommended further research.

37 BPA, *Electrical and Biological Effects*, June 1989, 30. Project ELF remained controversial, with the Navy commissioning another literature review on ELF bioeffects. The conclusions reported by the American Institute of Biological Sciences (AIBS) in 1985 were consistent with the earlier NRC report. Project ELF was eventually completed with a 28-mile-long transmitter in Wisconsin and a 56-mile-long transmitter in Michigan (MWN 10, 1:5–6).

38 The NYPA is the largest U.S. non-federal public power organization, providing nearly one-third of the electricity in New York State (James M. Cunningham, testimony from Subcommittee on General Oversight and Investigations, *Electric Power Lines*, 202).

39 By the mid-1970s, health effects had become a central issue in transmission-siting hearings in several states (OTA, *Biological Effects*, 1).

40 Carstensen, *Biological Effects of Transmission Line Fields*, 5; Feero, "The Evolution of Electromagnetic Effects Issues," paper from Ontario Hydro, *Health Effects of Electric and Magnetic Fields*, 2. For example, Marino and Becker reported decreased growth, increased mortality, and changes in blood composition in rodents exposed to 15 kV/m electric fields. However, they also reported that some effects may have been due to shocks received while drinking and eating (BPA, *Electrical and Biological Effects*, June 1989, 22).

   In 1980, an out-of-court settlement with the PSC approved licensing conditional on NYPA funding a one-time program of research on PF E/ MF health effects. The $5-million program (later known as the New York State Power Line Project, or NYSPLP) was under way in 1982 (Feero, "The Evolution of Electromagnetic Effects Issues," 2; Cunningham, testimony from Subcommittee on General Oversight and Investigations, *Electric Power Lines*, 205–6).

41 Carstensen, *Biological Effects of Transmission Line Fields*, 46, 50–51. The investigator could be looking for the wrong end-point under the wrong exposure conditions, or using methods that are not sensitive enough to detect subtle effects.

42 EPRI is a non-profit research organization. Its 600 member companies together account for two-thirds of U.S. electric power sales (Sagan, testimony from Subcommittee on Water and Power Resources, *Health Effects of Transmission Lines*, 111). Some Canadian utilities are also members.

43 OTA, *Biological Effects*, 35; OTA, *Electric Power Wheeling and Dealing*, 234. Artifactual interference would thereby be minimized (Feero, "The Evolution of Electromagnetic Effects Issues," 2).

44 Feero, "The Evolution of Electromagnetic Effects Issues."

45 Ibid.; Bulawka *et al.*, "The U.S. Department of Energy 60-Hz Electric Fields Bioeffects Research," 4433; OTA, *Biological Effects*, 35; OTA, *Electric Power Wheeling and Dealing*, 234.

46 Morgan *et al.*, "Controlling Exposure to Transmission Line Electromagnetic Fields," 89. BPA is the U.S. federal power marketing agency. As required by the NEP Act, BPA has prepared literature reviews on transmission line health effects. The first, published in 1975, found that few biological studies were directly related to transmission line E/MF and only a handful of literature reviews had been published (BPA, *Electrical and Biological Effects*, June 1989, 1, 22). From 1977 until 1984, BPA would operate a prototype 1200 kV transmission line. BPA now operates nearly 15,000 miles of high voltage lines to the U.S., Canada, and elsewhere (Jack M. Lee, Jr., testimony from Subcommittee on General Oversight and Investigations, *Electric Power Lines*, 179).

47 OTA, *Biological Effects*, 69.

48 Tim Aldrich, "E/MF – Epidemiologic evidence for occupational and non-occupational health impacts and cancer mortality," paper from B.C. Hydro, in co-operation with B.C. Ministry of Health, "Symposium on the Biological Effects of Electric and Magnetic Fields," Richmond, B.C., 20 October 1988.

49 OTA, *Electric Power Wheeling and Dealing*, 232.

50 Since the EPA's inception, NIR has been an important element. RF was the initial focus, with some modest efforts on ELF. The EPA is responsible for providing advice to the U.S. President (Richard Guimond, testimony from Subcommittee on General Oversight and Investigations, *Electric Power Lines*, 134).

51 NYSPLP, 86. From 1979 to 1984, some studies also examined fertility problems, suicides, and other health effects (TDHSR 2, 6). The suicide study received considerable criticism from the scientific community on methodological and statistical grounds (TDHSR 2, 4:4).

52 Wertheimer and Leeper found that children with high exposure levels were twice to three-times as likely to develop cancer, particularly leukemia, lymphomas, and nervous system tumours. Several potential confounders, including social class and neighbourhood, could not account for the results. However, their findings were considered questionable because it was not clear if wire code configuration corresponded to magnetic field exposure, and because wire codings were not conducted blind (i.e., the surveyor knew the case and control homes) (TDHSR 2, 9:2).

53 They found an association between cancers of the nervous systems, uterus, and breast, with systematically increasing risk for higher current configurations, i.e., a dose-response relationship. The results did

not appear to be due to age, urbanicity, or socio-economic level (OTA, *Electric Power Wheeling and Dealing*, 236; TDHSR 2, 9:8).

54  OTA, *Electric Power Wheeling and Dealing*, 235. Earlier studies of electrical workers examined general employee health and were generally not designed to detect possible increases in rare diseases such as leukemia (Ontario Hydro, *Electric and Magnetic Fields and Human Health Research*).

55  OTA Oversight, 182.

56  NYSPLP, 86. In the residential studies, exposure was classified on the basis of the characteristics of and proximity to nearby distribution and transmission lines or other electrical facilities at the birth, death, and/or diagnosis address (TDHSR 2, 9:2). In addition, leukemia was the only end-point examined, sample populations were small, and there were confounders (Carpenter and Ahlbom, "Powerlines and Cancer," 97–8).
   The occupational studies appeared as letters to the editor. Letters typically do not undergo as rigorous a peer-review process as published articles, nor do they provide many specific details of study method and analysis. They were PMR studies; one was also case-control. No personal risk factors other than age and sex differences were considered. Personal exposure was not measured; it was assumed that "electrical workers" had excess exposure (TDHSR 2, 10:2).

57  TDHSR 3, 1:12. There had been an apparent increase in a few types cancer over the past several decades but it did not appear that the rates of most types of cancer had increased.

58  Ibid., 2, 12.

59  Rish and Morgan, "Regulating Possible Health Effects," 1416.

60  In 1988, the line was approved to operate at 16 percent of capacity, i.e., 1.56 kV/m and 160 mG at maximum load and 37 mG at the edge of a 100 foot ROW (MWN 9, 2:1; MWN 8, 4:3). Rule-making for the state continued, with limits for transmission lines and substations proposed in 1988.

61  Michael Freeman, "The courts and electromagnetic fields," 21. In 1987, the Texas Court of Appeals denied the award of punitive damages but upheld the lower court's finding that there were potential health effects. Houston Lighting and Power was prevented from using the line pending appeal of the decision. Meanwhile, the utility rerouted the line around the school property at a cost of $8.6 million (MWN 7, 6:1). In 1988, the Texas Supreme Court refused the school district's request for review of the Court of Appeals decision to overturn the punitive damages judgment against the utility (MWN 8, 4:10). Some scientists testified that exposure was an inadvertent prospective experiment.

62  Morgan, *Electric and Magnetic Fields*, 37–8.

63  The basic problem with risk analysis was the inability to define dose. Bounding analysis attempted to set upper and lower bounds on the

magnitude of effects that might exist if there were adverse health consequences (Morgan, *Electric and Magnetic Fields*, 76). CMU would also design a new study of public risk perception and conduct background work on decision-analytic problems such as "stopping rules." (TDHSR 4, 7:1). Both the Florida Department of Environmental Regulation (DER) and U.S. OTA would later contract CMU to help deal with assessment and regulatory problems related to 60 Hz fields (Morgan, *Electric and Magnetic Fields*, 37–8).

64 OTA Oversight, 127–8. The DOE research program included: exposure, instrumentation, and dosimetry; scaling and modelling; non-human screening studies; human studies; mechanistic studies; ecology and agriculture (BPA took the lead); and risk analysis methodologies (Robert L. San Martin, testimony from Subcommittee on General Oversight and Investigations, *Electric Power Lines*, 127–8).

65 MWN 7, 6:16.

66 OTA Oversight, 191.

67 BPA, *Electrical and Biological Effects*, October 1985, 18.

68 Bulawka *et al.*, "The US Department of Energy 60-Hz Electric Fields Bioeffects Research," 4432.

69 OTA Oversight, 191.

70 Morgan *et al.*, "Controlling Exposure to Transmission Line Electromagnetic Fields."

71 "Strategies to Reduce Population Exposure to 60 Hz Electric and Magnetic Fields," Final Report of the EPP/SUPA/SDS Project Course, Fall 1984, Dept. of Engineering and Public Policy, CMU, cited in Florig, "Management options for power-frequency fields," 87.

72 M. Granger Morgan et al., "A Framework for Thinking About, and Making Regulatory Decisions About, Power-Frequency Electromagnetic Fields," Tech. Report, Briefing Paper 2, prepared for the Florida DER under DER Contract SP117 (March 1987), cited in Florig, "Management Options for power-frequency fields," 88.

73 MWN 6, 5:2.

74 OTA Biological Effects, 70. BPA's level of funding continued at about $200,000 per year. The U.S. Navy continued to sponsor ecological field studies in the vicinity of Project ELF; funding remained at about $2 million per year (OTA, *Biological Effects*, 70).

75 Carpenter and Ahlbom, "Powerlines and Cancer," 96.

76 The five-year research program, funded largely by New York State electric utilities, was administered by the New York State Department of Health (DOH) and overseen by a Scientific Advisory Panel of scientists and engineers.

77 Both wire coding and actual field measurements in homes with the lights and appliances on and off were used to characterize the residential field environment. A relation was found between wire coding and

all cancers (OR = 1.7) and between wire coding and leukemia (OR = 2.1).
A positive but lesser relation was found between wire coding and brain
tumours. There was some indication of a dose-response relationship.
No relation was found between lights turned on/off and all cancers. A
relation was found between appliances turned on/off and all cancers,
slightly lower than between wire coding and all cancers (Carpenter and
Ahlbom, "Powerlines and Cancer," 97–8).

78 Carpenter and Ahlbom, "Powerlines and Cancer," 97–8. An attempt to
control for several major potential confounders (e.g., socio-economic
class, family cancer history, exposure to x-rays, local traffic density, use
of appliances) was made. Coding was done blind. Other measures of
potential field exposures were assessed – electric heat and hot water
use, use of heating pads and electric blankets by children and pregnant women, and the total number of electric appliances in home.
Savitz later investigated and rejected traffic density as a possible con-
founder (MWN 10, 1:5).

79 Slesin, "Power Lines and Cancer," 52.

80 Providing that the RRs reported by Savitz were correct and representative of the rest of the United States, and the number of homes with
elevated magnetic fields due to distribution systems in Denver was similar to other parts of the country (Carpenter and Ahlbom, "Powerlines
and Cancer," 99). An analysis of total childhood cancers occurring in
the Denver area was also done later; they were found to share the same
overall risk as elsewhere (OTA, *Electric Power Wheeling and Dealing*, 236).
David Carpenter, director of the NYSPLP, research physician for the
New York State DOH, and Dean, School of Public Health, State University of New York, estimated that exposure from LF EMF such as power
lines could account for 30 percent of all childhood cancers. Carpenter
was one of the many SAP members who changed their position on PF E/
MF health/magnetic field effects because of Savitz's results (Carpenter
and Ahlbom, "Powerlines and Cancer," 100; Slesin, "The danger of
ignoring non-ionizing radiation," 22).

81 Morgan, *Electric and Magnetic Fields*, 57. The NYSPLP had looked for
genetic/chromosomal changes in animals and isolated humans cells.
The results were uniformly negative, suggesting that PF E/MF was
unlikely to cause cancer through genetic change (Carpenter and
Ahlbom, "Powerlines and Cancer," 98).

82 OTA, *Electric Power Wheeling and Dealing*, 236. Although the study (by
Stevens) had fewer design flaws, it was criticized for having few subjects and possible misclassifications of exposure. In 1988, Wertheimer
and Leeper re-evaluated Stevens's data and found evidence for cancer
risk from residential exposure (TDHSR 6, 6:3).

83 OTA, *Biological Effects*, 36, 69–70.

84  Slesin, "Power Lines and Cancer," 56.

85  The working group was set up in response to a request from Canadian labour. Members included labour, electric utilities, academia, and federal and (some) provincial governments. The purpose was to assess the existence and scope of PF E/MF health effects to identify gaps in knowledge, to foster research to fill the gaps, and to educate the Canadian public on the state of scientific understanding. The working group recommended in 1989 that its final report be published by HWC, and that HWC intensify its ongoing PF E/MF research and set up a multi-stakeholder advisory committee (comprised of representatives from industry, labour, academia, and government) to advise on its research. (HWC, HPB, EHD, *Electric and Magnetic Fields and Your Health*, 2, 12; MWN, 10, 4:2).

86  Ontario Hydro began a six-year, $7-million program of research including occupational health, public health, and laboratory studies (Ontario Hydro, "Information: Electric and Magnetic Fields"). Both Ontario Hydro and Hydro Québec had previously conducted some research on PF E/MF health effects. In 1984 the Quebec government required Hydro Québec to undertake an epidemiological study, in conjunction with the Quebec Departments of Environment and Health and Social Services, on power line/human health effects as a condition of certification for a disputed transmission line. By 1985, Electricité de France had expressed interest, followed by Ontario Hydro. The Ontario Ministry of Health had conducted a literature review.

87  Carpenter and Ahlbom, "Powerlines and Cancer," 98. The NYSPLP had not addressed occupational exposure.

88  Ibid., 99.

89  Scientists whose research was sponsored by DOE or EPRI presented their research at the joint Contractors' Review. The Review was open to the public.

90  OTA, *Electric Power Wheeling and Dealing*, 228; OTA, *Biological Effects*, 3. If there was a risk of human cancer, most scientists believed the risk was likely small.

91  OTA, *Electric Power Wheeling and Dealing*, 233; OTA, *Biological Effects*, 1, 2.

92  Carpenter and Ahlbom, "Powerlines and Cancer," 98–9; MWN 9, 4:7. Ontario Hydro would co-sponsor a laboratory study on cancer promotion in rodents with HWC (Ontario Hydro, "Information: Electric and Magnetic Fields").

93  OTA, *Electric Power Wheeling and Dealing*, 239–40; BPA, *Electrical and Biological Effects*, June 1989. Countries included the United States, Sweden, West Germany, Britain, Canada, Japan, Italy, France, Finland, and Norway.

94 TDHSR 6, 6:10.

95 MWN 9, 1:1, 14.

96 TDHSR 7, 1:2. The program would include a study on exposure assessment, a case-control study of childhood cancer in New York State, replication of an earlier study reporting retarded learning performance in exposed rats, replication of a study on adult cancer and residential exposure, and a study on brain cancer and residential exposure. This research program has not yet been undertaken.

97 Savitz et al., "Methodological issues in the epidemiology of electromagnetic fields and cancer," 74–5. Residential exposure assessment generally relied on coding wiring configurations, while occupational exposure assessment was limited to the generally uncorroborated assumption that various groups of electrical workers had elevated field exposures. A persistent criticism of Savitz's study was that the association with wire codes was greater than with measured fields. A few scientists, including Savitz, speculated that if wire codes were a surrogate measure, then the surrogate would be linked even more strongly (MWN 8, 6:6). In addition, if PF E/MF caused cancer, improved exposure estimation should provide evidence of a stronger association.

98 TDHSR 6, 7:1; Savitz et al., "Methodological Issues in the Epidemiology of Electromagnetic Fields and Cancer," 59.

99 BPA, *Electrical and Biological Effects*, June 1989, 4.

100 OTA, *Electric Power Wheeling and Dealing*, 227.

101 For example, in early 1987 a group of 58 (later 135) New York State landowners filed a $66.5-million (later, over $100-million) class-action lawsuit against the NYPA, claiming that the fear of health effects had had a negative impact on the value of property along a new 345 kV transmission line. (The 345 kV Marcy South transmission line connected to the 765 kV transmission line that spurred the NYSPLP.) Crowell and Moring, counsel for the NYPA, claimed that landowners were not entitled to compensation because it could not be established that there was reason for fear because there were no significant effects, that fear actually existed, or that fear affected property values.

Crowell and Moring had worked with regulatory and utility counsel in PF E/MF health effects litigation throughout the United States over the past ten years. Before the NYPA case, they began a world-wide search for experts in disciplines thought key to resolving the scientific and legal issues. From over 1,000 experts, over 125 were interviewed, and 7 were selected, 3 of whom were NCI employees. In their own special database, they have over 4,000 PF E/MF health-effects-related studies and an index of litigation.

By late 1988, the NYPA had spent $1.2 million on attorney and witness fees while landowners had spent $300,000 (including $65,000 on expert testimony and $100,000 on land appraisal). The decision would be made in late 1989 (MWN 8, 2:6; Cunningham, testimony from Subcommittee on General Oversight and Investigations, 208–9; MWN 8, 5:1; TDHSR 6, 6:2).

102    OTA, *Biological Effects*, 73.

103    Fitzgerald *et al.*, "Special report – electromagnetic fields," 28.

104    Weiss, "The power line controversy," 378–9. For example, a new California law allocated $2 million for a three-year project to study medical risks that may be related to exposure produced by electrical utility facilities. The State PUC, with the assistance of the Department of Health Services, would review and summarize E/MF research and related biological theories. State utilities would fund the project through a one-time tax, to be added to the $100,000 government budget (MWN 8, 6:7; MWN 8, 5:7).

105    Florig, "Management Options for power-frequency fields," 87.

106    TDHSR, 7, 1.

107    TDHSR 5, 10:10, 11–2.

108    EPRI was currently sponsoring ELF research on statistical studies of human disease patterns, measurements of actual human exposure, and laboratory studies on animals and cells (OTA, *Electric Power Wheeling and Dealing*, 239).

109    A separate cancer assessment group within the EPA would still conduct studies on NIR (Slesin, "The danger of ignoring non-ionizing radiation," 22). EPA scientists in the Office of Health and Environmental Assessment were preparing an assessment of the human cancer threat posed by "LF" (including PF E/MF) and "HF" NIR. A draft report was expected by the end of 1988 (MWN 8, 5:13).

110    Slesin, "The danger of ignoring non-ionizing radiation," 23. Furthermore, concern had been raised about the planned NIH/NCI study because several key NCI officials had been paid witnesses in legal proceedings (including the "cancerophobia" case) on behalf of electric utilities.

111    Morgan, *Electric and Magnetic Fields*, 79.

112    See Florig, "Management options for power-frequency fields."

113    Ontario Hydro, cited in MWN 8, 4:9.

114    Fitzgerald *et al.*, "Special report – electromagnetic fields," 28.

115    Savitz *et al.*, "Methodological Issus in the Epidemiology of Electromagnetic Fields and Cancer," 29; Florig, "Management options for power-frequency fields," 86; Carpenter and Ahlbom, "Powerlines and Cancer," 99.

116    Morgan *et al.*, "Power-Frequency Fields," 81–91.

117    Florig, "Management options for power-frequency fields," 89. See Morgan, *Electric and Magnetic Fields*.

118    TDHSR 6, 6:12.

CHAPTER FIVE

1 Much of the information in this chapter was taken from local newspapers and inquiry transcripts. It was often unclear what frequencies were being referred to when information sources used the terms electromagnetic radiation (EMR) and electromagnetic fields (EMF). We did not attempt to clarify terminology.

2 TR, 546–7, 553–4. The partnership included a number of international newspaper publishers.

3 The ROW was acquired between 1947 and 1961.

4 Exhibit 14, Response to "Information Request of BCUC Re: Proposed 230 kV Transmission Line – Dunsmuir/Gold River by B.C. Hydro, July 4, 1989, tab 2, cited in R&R, 1; Exhibit 22, CPFP – Prepared Testimony, 2, cited in R&R, 2; TR, 446–7, 547.

5 R&R, 3.

6 R&R, 2; TR, 461, 546–551, 553.

7 TR, 551, 564, 625; Exhibit 22, 2, cited in R&R, 2. A "fast track" approach implies that construction commences immediately after or before design completion.

8 TR, 677; Robert Pellatt, cited in "Hydro ordered to halt transmission line job," *Vancouver Sun*, 15 June 1989.

9 TR, 449–451, 794; Exhibit 14, tab 2, cited in R&R, 2–3.

10 "Canadian Utility Offers to Buy Homes Next to Power Line ROW," MWN 9, 3:1; "British Columbia Utilities Commission Gives Go-Ahead to 230-kV Line," TDHSR 7, 6; TR, 489.

11 The full width of the ROW crossed Marton's property. The house in which he, his wife, and three children resided was 55 metres from the edge of the ROW. Marton was aware of the scientific debate over PF E/MF health effects.

12 March was also chairman of B.C. Hydro's Biological Effects of Electromagnetic Fields Task Force. B.C. Hydro had been following scientific developments, evaluating public and employee exposure, and participating in utility and technical forums on the PF E/MF and human health issue for several years.

13 See Ontario, Disease Control and Epidemiology Service, Public Health Branch, MOH, *Health Effects of Extremely Low Frequency Electromagnetic Fields*, and United States, BPA, DOE, *Electrical and Biological Effects*, October 1985.

14 John Marton, letter to L.I. Bell, Chairman, B.C. Hydro, 16 March 1988; TR, 617–8, 653–5.

15 The letter was requested by the New York State PSC and put on file for future public queries after Savitz's findings were released in 1987 as part of the NYSPLP SAP Final Report.

16  Marton, letter to L.I. Bell; TR, 657–8; Linda S. Erdreich and Antonio
Sastre, "Prepared Evidence and Report of Linda S. Erdreich and
Antonio Sastre," 5; David A. Savitz, School of Public Health, Department of Epidemiology, University of North Carolina at Chapel Hill,
letter to "Persons concerned about reports of electromagnetic fields and
childhood cancer," n.d. Savitz also stated in the letter a safe distance
from power lines could not be determined with any certainty. Ultimately,
a person's response to a "possible, but unproven hazard" required an
"individual judgement about risk, much as a decision regarding suspected dietary hazards, flying in airplanes, or drinking alcohol or coffee
reflects differing individual judgements." If it were learned that PF E/MF
did increase risk, it would be of "great concern" as a public health issue;
fortunately, childhood cancer was a very rare event, with "about *1 in
10,000* children developing cancer [per year]. If the risk really were 1.5
to 2-fold greater among persons with elevated magnetic field levels, the
risk would be 2.5 or *2 cancers in 10,000* children" (emphasis added).
Again, this would be "very important but minor relative to childhood
injuries or risks from known cancer hazards to adults such as cigarette
smoking or asbestos exposure." Savitz also stated, "The only readily
changed personal exposure to magnetic fields would be through avoidance of electric blankets or heated waterbeds."
17  Marton, letter to L. Bell; TR, 660.
18  The BCUC is the regulatory body responsible for energy projects in
British Columbia.
19  R&R, 3; Richard Gathercole, personal interview, 14 November 1989.
The BC PIAC, funded largely by the Law Foundation of B.C., "provides
[free] counsel to assist unrepresented or under-represented public
interest groups in areas of practice generally not served by the private
bar, the Legal Services Society or other organizations" (BC PIAC, *Annual
Report*, Vancouver, 1988, 4).
20  Robert Freeman, "Hydro gets fight over new line," *Free Press*, 1 February 1989. Although Jack Clifford, a Courtenay resident, had already
signed an agreement, he wanted control of the land under the new
line. His position was that if B.C. Hydro wanted control of the land
then B.C. Hydro should buy the land rather than just the trees. The
ombudsman was reviewing his demand.
21  Freeman, "Hydro gets fight over new line;" TR, 856–7, 866. The home
where Kavka, his wife Darlene, and their two children resided was 100
metres from the ROW.
22  B.C. Hydro originally offered $1,296 for the trees after inspection by
an independent timber cruiser.
23  Freeman, "Hydro gets fight over new line"; Jeff Barker, Manager,
Transmission Projects, B.C. Hydro, personal communication, 21

November 1989; Derek Cowan, "Owner calls it theft," *Record*, 5 August 1989, A3.

24  R&R, 4.

25  TR, 866; Lee MacKenzie, "Hydro roasted at last session on power line," *Free Press*, 19 July 1989, 1.

26  The health effects included learning disabilities, irritability, headaches, dizziness, depression, "general malaise," death of cells, and cancer.

27  Russ Paradice, "Hydro-line concerns RD: Radiation, cancer link questioned," *Free Press*, 31 March 1989; "Region joins call for move of Hydro line," *Record*, 31 March 1989.

28  The motion was made by the mayor of Gold River.

29  Sharon Carmichael, "Cancer threat not imagined says resident," *Record*, 14 April 1989, A1, A2. The schoolyard was 300 metres away from the ROW.

30  TR, 657–67, 880; Gathercole; "B.C. Hydro to Purchase Property of landowners concerned about EMF," TDHSR 7, 5:1–2.

31  Sharon Carmichael, "Hydro reviews powerline impact," *Record*, 5 May 1989, A1-A2.

32  Linda Erdreich, Research Scientist, ERI, telephone interview, 28 November 1989; Erdreich and Sastre, tab 1, 1; TR, 48; Antonio Sastre, Research Scientist, ERI, telephone interview, 20 December 1989. ERI, organized about five years ago, has offices in Watertown, MA and Palo Alto, CA, and employs about thirty scientists and other staff. Clients can purchase legal counsel, scientific counsel, and guidance on risk communication. ERI produces written reports for both informal and formal settings, makes presentations to utilities and state health officials, educates the public and regulators, and provides expert witnesses. The states of Minnesota, Vermont, Massachusetts, and Maryland have retained ERI.

B.C. Hydro first approached ERI for their assistance in dealing with the PF E/MF health effects issue in November 1988 at the annual DOE-EPRI Contractors' Review. Because of B.C. Hydro's plans for 500 kV transmission lines and their awareness of the emerging PF E/MF health effects issue, Boatman had asked March to hire an "independent expert" to assist them. (ERI has been funded three times by EPRI but was not at the DOE-EPRI meeting as a result of doing work for EPRI.) Informal contact between B.C. Hydro and ERI continued sporadically until early April 1989, when contracts were formalized to retain ERI on an ad hoc basis to provide information, in terms of state-of-the-art literature and analysis, and, informally, the results of ERI's own research. B.C. Hydro also anticipated the possible need for expert testimony at future hearings (TR, 37–42, 49–51, 619–20, 822–3; Erdreich and Sastre, tab 1, 1).

33 The average would be taken if the two appraisals were within 10 percent. If the difference was greater than 10 percent, a third appraiser,
agreed to by both parties, would be selected. Property owners who
changed their minds after the appraisals would be required to reim-
burse B.C. Hydro for appraisal costs.

34 "B.C. Hydro to Purchase Property of Landowners Concerned about
EMF"; TR, 665, 876, 657ff, 787–92, 513; Karin Wilson, "Resident skep-
tical about Hydro plans: Darlene Kavka: residents should be con-
cerned," *Free Press*, 12 May 1989, A1; R&R, 5; C.W.J. Boatman, Vice
President, Corporate and Environmental Affairs, B.C. Hydro, letter, 9
May 1989; "Hydro will offer powerline buyout," *Record*, 12 May 1989;
Karin Wilson, "Hydro offer 'unique': Residents delighted by property
purchase offer to escape high volt lines," *Free Press*, 12 May 1989.

35 Arden Elementary School was not included in the private property
buy-out offer.

36 TR, 835–835, 883; Karin Wilson, "Trustee frustrated by Hydro," *Free
Press*, 12 May 1989, A3.

37 Boatman wrote the letter after discussing the situation with Bell (TR,
633, 838, 507).

38 B.C. Hydro did not expect many property owners to accept the buy-
out offer and intended to put any properties acquired back on the
market (TR, 665, 876, 657ff, 787–92, 513).

39 TR, 633, 838, 507; "B.C. Hydro to Purchase Property of Landowners
Concerned about EMF."

40 TR, 42–3, 240, 192; Kabot *et al.*, *Background report on health issues associated with exposure to power frequency electric and magnetic fields.*

41 Karin Wilson, "Hydro offer 'unique'"; "Canadian Utility Offers to Buy
Homes Next to Power Line ROW," 14; "New spots for Hydro," *Record*,
17 May 1989.

42 The community of Bridlewood, Ontario, has been battling with
Ontario Hydro since 1986 over the siting of a transmission line. Darlene Kavka had corresponded and exchanged information with the residents.

43 Zig Hathorn, Senior Environmental Coordinator, B.C. Hydro, presentation at Edison Electric Institute Seminar on Transmission Lines in
Residential Neighborhoods: Issues in Siting and Environment Planning, Portland, 12–13 October 1989; "Hydro will offer powerline
buyout"; "Canadian Utility Offers to Buy Homes Next to Power Line
ROW," 14; Karin Walsh, Treasurer, CVRC, telephone interview, 11
December 1989; "B.C. Hydro to Purchase Property of Landowners
concerned about EMF."

44 "B.C. Hydro to Purchase Property of Landowners concerned about
EMF"; Wilson, "Hydro offer 'unique.'"

45 Darlene Kavka thought that eligibility would be based on any change in peak PF E/MF values. The *Free Press* reported that the buy-out letter actually stated this and that property owners along the ROW, whether on an easement or not, could request that B.C. Hydro purchase their property (TR, 890ff; Wilson, "Hydro offer 'unique.'"). Later, the *Free Press* reported that all properties within 300 metres of the ROW were eligible ("Hydro deadline looms," *Free Press,* 24 May 1989; Pamela Allen, letter, "Buy-out deadline," *Free Press,* 31 May 1989).

46 TR, 943, 436, 943, 541, 762–5, 957, 866ff, 817.

47 *The Upper Islander,* 24 May 1989; TR, 844–5. The purpose of the notice was to detect any eligible property owners not sent the buy-out letter.

48 TR, 866ff. The CVRC created a form letter for concerned property owners to forward to B.C. Hydro and to Stan Hagen, MP. The letter, available at the ABC Print Shop in Courtenay's Washington Mall, stated, "I am concerned with the dangers associated with electromagnetic radiation. If these lines cannot be rerouted safely away from populated areas, I wish to be placed on your list of potential properties to be purchased" ("Hydro deadline looms"; Allen).

49 The school expansion was scheduled for completion by September 1991 and already had provincial funding approval. A delay of more than a month or two would put the project into jeopardy. A longer delay could result in the money being reallocated. In the meantime, students would continue to use portable classrooms.

50 According to Randy Ross, Radiation Protection Service, B.C. MOH, the readings from two different meters, after calibration, can differ by as much as 50 percent. Or, if a reading is obtained that "you don't like," a reading that "you do like" can be obtained simply by shifting the position of the meter. He also said, referring to the measurements taken at Arden Elementary School, that "people don't realize that the levels are high everywhere" (Ross, personal interview, 10 November 1989).

51 Karin Wilson, "Hydro fears stall work: Arden school kids' health worries board," *Free Press,* 19 May 1989, A1; "Cancer fears stall plans for school," *Record,* 19 May 1989, A1, A2.

52 Kavka had originally asked Becker if he would meet with residents but he declined, wishing to avoid any "cross-examination," and suggested that she contact Marino (Darlene Kavka, Chair, Comox Valley Rerouting Committee, telephone interview, 22 November 1989).

53 "Hydro facts disputed," *Record,* 2 June 1989, A3; Karin Wilson, "Many Hydro concerns raised by letters," *Free Press,* 31 May 1989, A3.

54 Wilson, "Many Hydro concerns raised by letters"; Kavka; Marton, Psychologist, telephone interview, 17 November 1989.

55 Biolectricity is a recently developed area of biophysics. Biophysics involves using physical methods to understand how living things work.

Bioelectricity focuses on understanding the interactions of biological systems with electromagnetic energy.

56 TR, 307–15, 328–9, 366–70, 321–2.

57 "Canadian Utility Offers to Buy Homes Next to Power Line ROW"; R&R, 5.

58 "Hydro ordered to halt transmission line job"; Erdreich and Sastre, tab 2: 2; Karin Wilson, "Power line put on hold," *Free Press,* 14 June 1989, A1; Carl Gustafson, Lawyer, Michener, Lawrence and Shawl, telephone interview, 15 December 1989.

59 "Buy-out on hold," *Free Press,* 14 June 1989, 3; R&R, 5.

60 Usually, inquiries were chaired by senior BCUC staff, not by the Chairman of the BCUC. In addition, it was the first time that a fellow commissioner had been appointed to act as an adviser (John McIntyre, Chairman and CEO, BCUC, personal interview, 21 November 1989).

61 R&R, 5–6; McIntyre; TR, 969–70. In contrast, at a hearing, panels consisted of a minimum of three commissioners; their report was final.

62 Bev Hollingsworth, "Hydro lines could mean excess ozone," *Free Press,* 28 June 1989; "Group imports line expert," *Record,* 24 June 1989; Kavka; "Residents are already sick," *Record,* 5 July 1989, A1, A8; "Lesson in public advocacy," *Free Press,* 7 July 1989; Russ Paradice, "B.C. Hydro will have to explain itself," *Free Press,* 30 June 1989; Walsh, telephone interview.

63 This requirement was modified after Boatman informed the Chairman that one of B.C. Hydro's contacts – the law firm of Crowell and Moring – had been following the issue for fifteen years and had spent over $300,000 gathering 5,000 volumes of information (C.W.J. Boatman, telephone interview, 19 December 1989).

64 W.J. Grant, Director, Engineering and Accounting, BCUC, letter to C.W.J. Boatman, Vice-President, Corporate and Environmental Affairs, B.C. Hydro, Re: Proposed 230 kV Transmission Line-Dunsmuir/Gold River. Mimeo, 21 June 1989.

65 In a three-part series of articles in *The New Yorker,* author-journalist Paul Brodeur cited research indicating that exposure to low-intensity RF, microwave, and ELF fields could endanger health. He also suggested that utilities and the U.S. government tried to cover up or discredit such research.

66 Walsh, telephone interview; Kavka; TR, 662.

67 "Residents are already sick"; Lee MacKenzie, "Re-route advocates cite illness cases," *Free Press,* 5 July 1989, 1, 3; TR, 858ff.

68 MacKenzie, "Re-route advocates cite illness cases."

69 Gallagher is the principle investigator in a Canada-wide study on childhood leukemia, under way at the time of his BCUC appointment and scheduled for completion in 1994. PF E/MF is one of the factors being

studied. Sponsors include Health and Welfare Canada, EPRI, and the Canadian Electrical Association. The BC CCA (now the B.C. Cancer Agency) is a registered society whose mandate is to treat cancer patients and conduct research. They have representatives at the Children's Hospital and within the B.C. Hospitals Program. Savitz, the BCUC's original choice of expert, was unavailable, but he had suggested Gallagher as someone who had the expertise and was objective.

70  R&R, 6; Richard Gallagher, Epidemiologist, B.C. Cancer Control Agency, telephone interviews, 13 October 1989 and 16 November 1989; "EMF-Cancer Epidemiological Studies," MWN 9, 6:4; Neptune Smith, Manager, Engineering and Project Review–Electrical, BCUC, telephone communication, 23 November 1989. According to Gallagher, he was hired to be an "independent referee." He had not previously acted as an expert adviser before and avoided participating in assessments because they were "enormously time-consuming."

71  According to McIntyre, it was "normal to appoint staff and experts" to assist in an inquiry. According to Gustafson, although it was not uncommon, neither was it usual for the BCUC to bring in "technical expertise." In most instances, the BCUC had in-house expertise; for example, BCUC staff had attended seminars on PF E/MF health effects. Smith was knowledgeable and had "read the literature." However, he had not dealt with the issue in depth. One staff member had attended several conferences and the BCUC was preparing a paper on the subject.

72  McIntyre; Gustafson; Smith, telephone communication, 23 November 1989; Richard Gathercole, BC PIAC, personal interview.

73  Erdreich, an epidemiologist with a B.A. in biological sciences, M.Ed. in science education, M.Sc. in biostatistics and epidemiology, and Ph.D. in epidemiology, has been a senior research scientist with ERI since April 1989. Her work is in the review and evaluation of studies; she has conducted no research on PF E/MF health effects. Erdreich is a member of several societies, including the American College of Epidemiology, the Society for Risk Analysis, and the Sigma XI Scientific Research Society. Previously, Erdreich was senior epidemiologist at Clement Associates and performed public health evaluations for hazardous-waste sites and for incinerators. She was a group leader for the U.S. EPA, Office of Research and Development, Methods Evaluations and Development staff, managing a group that developed risk assessment methods and guidelines. Erdreich has served as a reviewer and scientific adviser concerning health risk assessment issues for industry and government agencies, and lectured to professional groups or organizations numerous times. She has published a number of articles in a variety of scientific journals, written chapters in books, and served as an editor

for proceedings published from scientific conferences. (TR, 44–8, 25–6; Erdreich and Sastre, tab 1, 1–5.)

Antonio Sastre, a laboratory scientist, has a B.A., M.S., and Ph.D. in applied mathematics and neurobiology. He was a post-doctoral fellow in neurobiology and pharmacology at Cornell University. Sastre has been a senior research scientist at ERI since 1988 and is an adjunct associate professor, Department of Pharmacology, Cornell University Medical College. He was an associate professor, Department of Neuroscience, Johns Hopkins University School of Medicine. Sastre's general area of expertise is in the electrical properties of cells from the nervous system, heart, and blood vessels (at the whole animal, cell, and molecular level). He has analysed and evaluated responses of biological organisms to AC E/MF. Sastre has studied the interaction of one of the key stress hormones, cortisol, on the nervous system. He has published about twenty research articles (in peer-reviewed journals) on the physiology and pharmacology of electrical excitability. He has written two chapters in research monographs and co-authored a chapter in a widely used textbook on medical physiology. He is on the editorial boards of two journals, the *American Journal of Physiology: Cell Physiology*, and *Blood Vessels*. Sastre has served as a reviewer of research grant proposals submitted to the U.S. National Institutes of Health (NIH), the National Science Foundation, and the American Heart Association. (TR, 137, 29–31; Erdreich and Sastre, table 1, 6–9.)

74  Lee MacKenzie, "Illness link supported," *Free Press*, 14 July 1989; Charlotte Ostrowski, "Expert says dangers suppressed," *Record*, 15 July 1989, A8; Zig Hathorn, telephone interview, 17 November 1989; Kelly Gibney, Manager, EMF Issues, B.C. Hydro, personal interview, 12 September 1989.

75  TR, 688; R&R, 6.

76  Erdreich and Sastre, 35.

77  Marino, "Submission to the British Columbia Utilities Commission in the Matter of the Routing of the 230-kV B.C. Hydro Dunsmuir to Gold River Transmission Line," 8–9.

78  R&R, i-ii.

79  Apart from Radiation Protection Services conducting measurements of PF E/MF levels at Arden Elementary School and a few residences, the B.C. MOH maintained a low profile during the controversy. Once the inquiry was called, people who contacted the MOH with concerns about PF E/MF health effects were generally referred to the BCUC (TR, 777–8; Smith, telephone communication, 23 November 1989; Brian Phillips, Director, Radiation Protection Services, B.C. MOH, letter to School District 71, 6 June 1989; "Hydro will test school").

80 TR, 20–1.

81 TR, 180–3, 186.

82 TR, 177–9.

83 TR, 207–10. Graham's unpublished data was available from his sponsor.

84 TR, 186.

85 See Morgan *et al.*, "Controlling Exposure to Transmission Line Electromagnetic Fields."

86 TR, 282–6, 288–9.

87 TR, 155–6, 158, 161, 245.

88 TR, 256–9.

89 TR, 286–8.

90 TR, 262–9, 214–5.

91 TR, 251–6.

92 TR, 269–70.

93 TR, 272–3.

94 TR, 91.

95 TR, 93, 102–3.

96 TR, 175–6.

97 TR, 105–6, 196.

98 TR, 130–1, 190–3, 239–42.

99 TR, 62.

100 TR, 81.

101 TR, 82–4.

102 TR, 86, 88.

103 TR, 116–7.

104 TR, 132–4.

105 TR, 135–6.

106 According to Erdreich, a "regulator's nightmare" occurs when the science is uncertain and there are large economic costs involved (Erdreich, telephone interview).

107 TR, 233–4, 304–6.

108 TR, 276–7.

109 TR, 299–304.

110 TR, 313–4. Marino's style of oral testimony was decidedly passionate compared to that of Erdreich and Sastre.

111 TR, 316–20, 350, 372–8, 469–80; Kavka.

112 TR, 320–2, 357.

113 TR, 232–4.

114 TR, 324–5.

115 TR, 329–31. Graves was also the Chairman of the AIBS 1985 study of Project ELF.

116 TR, 331–2.

117 TR, 351–2.

118 TR, 352–4.
119 TR, 355–6.
120 TR, 356–8.
121 TR, 358–61.
122 TR, 361–5.
123 TR, 401–5.
124 TR, 408–9.
125 TR, 409–12. Gustafson knew of Marino and his "conspiracy theory." He was concerned, along with the other scientists and BCUC staff, that the Chairman would be unable to go beyond Marino's "rhetoric." He had tried to "shock but not aggravate" Marino and thus provide Marino with an opportunity to restore his credibility (Gustafson). According to McIntyre, the conduct of both Marino and Gustafson was questionable (McIntyre).
126 TR, 412–5.
127 TR, 415–7.
128 TR, 418–22.
129 TR, 422–4.
130 TR, 424–6. Sastre and Erdreich were impressed with McIntyre's ability to "channel" Marino (Sastre; Erdreich).
131 TR, 533–43.
132 TR, 853–4.
133 TR, 851.
134 TR, 613–4.
135 TR, 621–2.
136 BCUC, "B.C. Hydro and Power Authority Proposed 230 kV Transmission Line Dunsmuir/Gold River," Order Number G-44–89. According to McIntyre, the other two BCUC commissioners had many questions regarding his findings because they did not understand the issue (Mcintyre). The terms EMF, E/MF and EMR were not defined in the Report.
137 R&R, 7–8.
138 McIntyre was referring to *Biological Effects of Power Frequency Electric and Magnetic Fields,* a background paper prepared by Nair, Morgan and Florig, Dept. of Engineering and Public Policy, CMU, as part of OTA's assessment of *Electric Power Wheeling and Dealing: Technical Considerations for Increasing Competition.* The background paper (not reviewed or approved by OTA) discusses the present state of knowledge on PF E/MF, describes current U.S. funding levels and research programs, and provides information on regulatory activity, including existing and proposed field exposure standards. The OTA report focuses on the technical and public policy aspects of proposals to expand access to U.S. transmission systems and to increasing competition in power

generation. CMU was contracted by OTA to review the health effects of high-voltage transmission lines at the request of the subcommittee on water and power resources of the Committee on Interior and Insular Affairs (OTA, *Biological Effects*, iii).

139 R&R, 31–2.

140 Ibid., 32–3.

141 According to McIntyre, the buy-out offer was the same as setting a standard that was so high, it was meaningless. He cited the recently passed Florida E/MF rule as an example (McIntyre).

142 R&R, 33–7.

143 According to Boatman, it is not possible to follow this recommendation. B.C. Hydro could not charge buy-out costs back into its rate structure because it was not investor-owned.

144 R&R, 36, 38.

145 Ibid., 38–9.

146 Ibid., 39; Jeff Barker, personal communication. According to Barker, B.C. Hydro upper management was expecting the CPCN order for 138 kV lines for other reasons.

147 R&R, 40. The BCUC absorbed the cost of the inquiry (McIntyre).

148 Editorial, "Protests passe," *North Island News*, 20 August 1989.

149 "Line now hot," *Record*, 1 September 1989; Jeff Barker, telephone communication, 17 November 1989.

150 "B.C. Hydro buy-out begins," MWN 9, 5:3; Gibney, personal interview, 12 September 1989; Barker, personal communication; "Power Line Talk," MWN 9, 6:3; Hathorn, telephone interview.

151 Barker, 21 November 1989; "Power Line Talk," MWN 9, 6:3; Hathorn, telephone interview.

152 Garland E. Allen, "The Role of Experts in Scientific Controversy," in Engelhardt and Caplan, eds., *Scientific Controversies*, 169–70.

153 Nelkin, "Controversies and the Authority of Science," 289.

154 Salter, *Mandated Science*, 5–6.

155 Ibid., 194–5.

156 Mazur, "Scientific Disputes over Policy," 273.

157 In June 1989, a Florida judge, in response to a court action initiated by concerned parents, ordered a school board to prevent the children from playing in a portion of the playground because of the presence of power lines. The judge discounted some evidence presented by school board witnesses due to their ties to the power industry (MWN 9, 4:6, 7; TDHSR 7, 5). Also in 1989, the California State Department of Education adopted a school siting policy setting limits for how close a new school could be to power lines (Weiss, "The power line controversy," 378–9).

158 Of particular note is the emerging view among some scientists that the assumption "more is worse" may not be appropriate in the case of PF

E/MF exposure. See, for example, OTA, *Biological Effects*, and OTA, *Electric Power Wheeling and Dealing*.

159 Salter, *Mandated Science*, 5.

160 Ibid., 198.

161 Once the inquiry was called, B.C. Hydro would not discuss the new line with Courtenay residents. Queries were directed to the BCUC until after the final report was issued. (This action was not required by the BCUC.) One previously scheduled presentation was still held ("Buyout on hold"; Kelly Gibney, personal interview, 12 September 1989).

162 Leiss, "The Management of Innovation," 26.

163 Salter, *Mandated Science*, 3–5, 8. For example, a large proportion of HWC's budget is allocated to AIDS research.

164 Mandated science is also referred to by others as "regulatory science" or "mission-oriented science."

165 Salter, *Mandated Science*, 1–4. Even science produced in more conventional settings can be altered by its use.

166 Ibid., 3–4, 9. This is not to imply that conventional science is a neutral process.

167 Ibid., 5–6.

168 Ibid., 6.

169 Ibid., 6–7.

170 Ibid., 7.

171 Even within science, the term "scientific uncertainty" has more than one meaning. Salter distinguished between four types: legitimate scientific uncertainty (with further resources, resolution is possible), practical indeterminism (resource constraints make resolution unlikely), methodological uncertainty (inherent limitations in scientific techniques, e.g., epidemiology, make resolution impossible), and uncertainty due to the tendency of scientific work to result in ever more complex and ambiguous conclusions (Salter, *Mandated Science*, 199–200).

172 Ibid., 8.

173 Ibid., 8–9.

174 Ibid., 188–9.

175 Ibid., 204–5, 190.

176 Ibid., 197, 193.

177 Ibid., 189, 195.

178 Ibid., 188.

179 Salter, *Mandated Science*, 175, 208–9, 7, 196.

180 Ibid., 1–5, 209.

181 Although appointed in mid-June 1989 as Manager, EMF Issues, B.C. Hydro, Kelly Gibney (formerly B.C. Hydro's Industrial Hygiene Supervisor) maintained a low profile until the BCUC report was issued (Gibney, telephone communication, 12 September 1989). B.C. Hydro

did not initiate any contacts with the media (Lorne March, telephone interview, 15 January 1990).

182  Erdreich and Sastre had little, if any, interaction with the public outside of the formal inquiry (Sastre).

183  Normally, B.C. Hydro did not further direct inquiries to B.C. MOH. Rather, B.C. MOH directed inquiries to B.C. Hydro (March, telephone interview, 15 January 1990).

184  Video depositions, becoming quite common in the U.S. with the small group of scientists and engineers who testify "regularly" on the PF E/MF health effects circuit, are limited for this same reason ("Florida Judge Restricts School Playground Use Based on EMF Concerns," TDHSR 7, 6:14–5).

185  Of course, even if the health effects were fully understood, reaching agreement on an appropriate societal level of control would be difficult since individual values (e.g., about fairness) differ (Rish and Morgan, "Regulating Possible Health Effects from AC Transmission Line Electromagnetic Fields," 1417). Value differences concerning such issues as large- or small-scale organization and the priority given to economic growth as a goal may never be resolved (Robert C. Mitchell, "Nuclear and Other Energy Sources," in Davies *et al.*, *Risk Communication*, 78).

186  Several hundred kilometres of high-voltage transmission lines would be built during 1988–93.

187  MWN 9, 6:3.

188  Covello, "Informing People About Risks From Chemicals, Radiation, and Other Toxic Substances," 12.

189  See R&R for several good recommendations about the management of PF E/MF health effects research.

See also United States, National Research Council, *Improving Risk Communication,* for a general discussion on how to improve risk communication, including a discussion of expert disagreement. See Morgan, *Electric and Magnetic Fields,* and OTA, *Biological Effects* (also by Morgan *et al.*) for examples of improved approaches to communicating about PF E/MF health effects. (There is still room for further improvement.) *Electric and Magnetic Fields* was the first publication intended for public consumption that attempted to explain the expert disagreement over PF E/MF health effects. Note that, in the brochure, Morgan explicitly states his and his colleagues' role in the controversy, including sources of funding for their research.

190  The U.S. National Institute for Occupational Safety and Health (NIOSH) recently commissioned a collection of expert reviews. See Bierbaum and Peters, eds., *Proceedings of the Scientific Workshop on the Health Effects of Electric and Magnetic Fields on Workers.*

The White House Office of Science and Technology Policy's Committee on Interagency Radiation Research and Policy Coordination

(CIRRPC) has completed a review of power line and VDT EMF health effects, but the report has not yet been released. As requested by the U.S. Congress, the U.S. National Academy of Sciences–National Research Council is expected to conduct a review of ELF health effects.

191 For example, the U.S. DOE sponsored research on "meta-analysis," a technique that combines data from studies regardless of merit and outcome (TDHSR 6, 8:11, 13). Another study focused on how measures of public health impact were estimated from epidemiological data ("1988 Contractors' Review Technical Summary (Part 8)," TDHSR 7, 7:12–13).

192 This presents a major barrier to conducting health effects studies as well as risk analysis. There are many scientists using many different types of exposures; this would not happen with a chemical agent (Gordon Hester, Project Manager, Energy Analysis Program, EPRI, personal communication, 2 December 1992).

193 "The distribution of scientific opinion on the probability that low-level exposure is hazardous [or risky] has never been formally elicited" (Florig, "Containing the Costs of the EMF Problem," 469).

194 See United States, Environmental Protection Agency, Office of Research and Development, "Evaluation of the Potential Carcinogenicity of Electromagnetic Fields."

195 United States, Environmental Protection Agency Science Advisory Board, Radiation Advisory Committee, Nonionizing Electric and Magnetic Fields Subcommittee, Final RAC/NIEMFS Report.

196 Robert McGoughy, Office of Research and Development, EPA, personal communication, 17 August 1992.

197 Advisory Group on Non-Ionizing Radiation, *Electromagnetic Fields and the Risk of Cancer,* 130–5.

198 MWN 9, 6:3; MWN 10, 4:2.

199 The residential study found an association between childhood leukemia and "calculated historical fields" (M. Feychting and A. Ahlbom, "Magnetic fields and cancer in people residing near Swedish high voltage power lines"). The occupational study found an association between chronic lymphocytic leukemia and measured magnetic fields (Floderus *et al.,* "Occupational exposure to electromagnetic fields in relation to leukemia and brain tumors: A case-control study").

200 MWN 12, 5:1.

201 If distribution lines are a more significant source, any risks would likely be perceived as more equally distributed among society. Morgan has predicted that pressure to control household wiring and appliances will likely be slower to build (Morgan *et al.,* "Power-line fields and human health," 68).

202 Proposals for managing research programs are not discussed here because sound recommendations have been made elsewhere and are in a few cases being incorporated into new research projects. In addition

to R&R, 38–9, see, e.g., OTA, *Biological Effects*, 81. Recently, the U.S. House of Representatives voted to change the lead agency for the federal PF E/MF research program from the U.S. DOE, originally designated by Congress, to the U.S. National Institutes of Environmental Health Sciences (NIEHS) because of NIEHS's greater scientific credibility (MWN 12, 3:3). Credibility of past research will continue to be a problem.

203 Ozawa and Susskind, "Mediating Science-Intensive Policy Disputes," 31.

204 Nancy Ellen Abrahms and R. Stephen Berry, "Mediation: A Better Alternative to Science Courts," *Bulletin of the Atomic Scientists* (April 1977): 50–3, cited in Ozawa and Susskind, "Mediating Science-Intensive Policy Disputes."

205 Mazur, *The Dynamics of Technical Controversy*, 37–42.

206 Marino, "We need a science court," vii-viii.

207 Ozawa and Susskind, "Mediating Science-Intensive Policy Disputes," 31.

208 TDHSR 6, 8:1.

209 U.S., NRC, *Improving Risk Communication*, 156.

210 Jasanoff, *Risk Management and Political Culture*, 73.

211 Wessel, *Science and Conscience*, 173–83. Other suggestions to help resolve expert disagreement include training scientists to be effective participants in the courts, and for a new profession of "Certified Public Scientist" to ensure objectivity as scientists engage more and more in public affairs (Nelkin, "Controversies and the Authority of Science," 291).

212 Ozawa and Susskind, "Mediating Science-Intensive Policy Disputes," 31.

CHAPTER SIX

1 "Alar®" is given as the first form of usage here to recognize the trademark held by Uniroyal; thereafter "Alar" is used, in recognition of the fact that the controversy made it a term in common use. As we shall explain more fully below, what was at issue was not only daminozide but also UDMH (unsymmetrical dimethylhydrazine); by 1985 UDMH was known to be a contaminant, a metabolite, and a degradation product of daminozide and to be produced in connection with daminozide in the following ways: as a contaminant in pure daminozide; as a product of hydrolysis in the formulated end product (Alar); as a product of hydrolysis in the digestive system of animals, including humans; and as a decomposition product of heating, e.g., in the making of applesauce.

2 Stockwin, "Apple Growers strike back," 32–4.

3 *Ottawa Citizen*, 19 March 1991, page A1; *Vancouver Sun*, 4 April 1991, page A5.

4 Citations to follow use the docket number from this collection in the following form: EPA D-123. We also had access to a collection of evaluation reports on studies of daminozide and UDMH done by the Food

Directorate, Health Protection Branch, Health and Welfare Canada between 1977 and 1989; we are very grateful to D.C. Kirkpatrick, then Director, Bureau of Chemical Safety, Food Directorate for making this collection available to us. We saw the very useful review article by L.M. Correia only after this chapter was written, but we have been able to draw upon it in making revisions.

5 See Appendix I at the end of this chapter for a description of the methodology used in constructing this case study.

6 Our interests here overlap one of Sheila Jasanoff's main concerns (*The Fifth Branch*, 150): "The cases discussed ... underscore a serious deficiency in the SAP advisory process: the absence of mechanisms for reconciling alternative constructions of science."

7 Harrison and Hoberg, *Risk, Science, and Politics*, ch. 4.

8 Jasanoff, "EPA's Regulation of Daminozide: Unscrambling the Message of Risk," 123, 122.

9 Classifying plant regulators as pesticides rather than food additives (possibly resulting in a less stringent standard for tolerances) is a somewhat arbitrary act. This was first done by specific legislation in the United States in 1959 (Correia, "'A' is for Alar," 879). The reader who is unfamiliar with what pesticides are and what they do may consult a source such as Koren, ch. 6.

10 EPA D-7270

11 It will become apparent to the reader that the authors have no training in toxicology. We have found a volume by Bruno Schiefer and his colleagues, with the charming title *You and Toxicology*, to be a very helpful introduction for non-experts. See also the essays by Robert Sielken and David Clayson in McColl, ed., *Environmental Health Risks*.

12 In a public presentation on Alar dated 4 September 1985, reviewing the regulatory history, Mr. R.A. Cardona, Uniroyal's Manager of Registration and Toxicology, listed only a single rat study done in 1966 as the sole basis of oncogenicity findings for the initial toxicological review (EPA D-640).

13 The HWC documents available to us cite four reviews prior to the first one we have, which is dated 18 August 1969 (three in 1967 and one on 8 August 1969), but we have not been able to obtain them.

14 W.H. Newsome, "Determination of Daminozide Residues on Foods and its Degradation to 1,1-Dimethylhydrazine by Cooking," was published in the spring of 1980. In a letter dated 23 March 1981, a scientist working for Uniroyal told the EPA that he thought the results of the Newsome study were "of questionable value" (EPA D-5542); by 1983, however, Uniroyal itself had generated data that supported Newsome's findings (EPA D-7203 [Draft Position Document 2/3/4], 12 September 1985, I-4).

15 EPA D-7203, Draft Position Document 2/3/4, 12 September 1985, I-4

16 Neither this calculation, nor the reviewer's alternate one – dividing the total amount of SADH (by weight) sold in Canada by the total Canadian population, to derive an average daily intake per person – would be regarded today as reflecting an acceptable methodology, and probably was not so regarded by his colleagues even at that time.

17 Given the entirely theoretical calculation of the average person's daily intake by that reviewer, as mentioned above, and the staff's subsequent recognition of the need for actual residue data, this is a surprising statement.

18 A staff review of the 1977 Toth study dated 15 August 1977 (EPA D-8879) says that the study makes Alar a "Rpar candidate." RPAR stands for "Rebuttable Presumption Against Registration," a procedure later called by the simpler designation of Special Review. See Correia, "'A' is for Alar," 876 note 131.

19 Harrison and Hoberg, *Risk, Science and Politics*, ch. 4.

20 EPA D-7222, unpaginated, Table 6–3 and nearby text. The occupational risks were estimated to be significantly lower and not to indicate unreasonable excess risk. ("Excess risk" means a risk that would not exist in the absence of any exposure to the particular substance being assessed.)

21 EPA D-7202, 07/18/84 (49 F.R. 29136).

22 EPA D-7204, 21–2.

23 See Jasanoff, "EPA's Regulation of Daminozide" and *The Fifth Branch*, 141–51 and 231.

24 EPA D-8349.

25 EPA D-7203 [Draft Position Document 2/3/4], 12 September 1985, II-30, 33.

26 For some reason that we cannot ascertain, the second of two Toth studies published in 1977, this one reporting on a feeding study of UDMH in water using hamsters, was much less frequently cited or reviewed by the regulatory agencies (for example, it is not even cited in the references in EPA D-7203). It was cited along with the others in the NRDC's legal petition against the EPA in 1986 (D-5444, 6).

27 The most important point for the reader to note is that *every* step in this process involves estimates, assumptions, and above all qualitative judgments, and is subject to challenge by other experts.

28 EPA D-7203, Tables 10 and 11. For simplicity we are ignoring the separate calculations for "average" and "upper bound (95 percent confidence limit)" for dietary exposure; the EPA calculated each separately and utilized the latter. The 95 percent confidence limit also appears in the EPA's extrapolation method in the dose-response assessment, and the EPA explains it as follows: "The cancer risks estimated by the Agency present the 95 percent upper bound risks of an individual

developing cancer over a lifetime of exposure ... . That is, there is a 95 percent certainty that the risks would be no greater than those estimated *and may in fact be as low as zero* [emphasis added]. Thus, the upper bound risk estimates represent conservative estimates of risk." The text goes on to explain that there are many uncertainties inherent in the estimates, and different factors could be responsible for risk being either underestimated or overestimated (or both in some respects, since risk is a composite of a number of independently calculated elements). EPA D-10806, "Daminozide Special Review Technical Support Document," May 1989, II-43.

29  *Science News,* 7 September 1985, p. 149; on the EDB controversy see Krimsky and Plough, *Environmental Hazards,* ch. 2.

30  EPA D-512, "Response of Uniroyal, Inc. to EPA's Notice of Special Review of Pesticide Products containing Daminozide" [undated], 15, 20.

31  Ibid., cover document, 1.

32  The narrative will be found in EPA D-7203, III-7 to 16; the detailed figures are in Appendix III.

33  Ibid., VI-5.

34  EPA D-5060 (SAP meeting 26/09/85), 97, 100.

35  Ibid., 104.

36  EPA D-5601: SAP, "Review of a set of scientific issues being considered by EPA in connection with the special review of daminozide," 4 October 1985. (Note that the Chairman has toned down considerably the remarks he made on the Toth studies during the hearing.) The transcript made at the hearing itself (EPA D-5062, 27 September 1985, 12–13) has wording that is slightly different from that of the formal report cited in the text. A full year later the EPA was still conducting internal correspondence on the laboratory audits of the Toth studies (EPA D-6960, 09/23/86).

37  Eliot Marshall, "Science advisers need advice," 20–22. The then head of the EPA, William Reilly, replied to the article with a letter referring to follow-up conflict-of-interest investigations on two of the eight SAP members by the Department of Justice and the Office of the Inspector General, both leading to the conclusion that "the facts do not merit prosecution." Reilly quotes from the Inspector General's report, which said that, while one of the scientists (Wilkinson) indeed had served as a consultant to Uniroyal, there was no conflict of interest because "the issues and matter concerning Alar handled by the SAP, while Wilkinson was a member, were different that [sic] the issue Wilkinson handled while he was a consultant to Uniroyal." (*Science,* vol. 250 [5 October 1990], 15.) Many other interested parties undoubtedly would regard this less-than-comforting information as a piece of legal hair-splitting. Jasanoff is a judicious observer of such matters and we cannot improve

upon her own observations: "When Congress established the SAP, it hoped to endow EPA's pesticide program with an advisory body of such integrity and expertise that its word would count as final on all issues of regulatory science. The SAP clearly did not live up to these expectations in the Alar controversy … . SAP's agreement with Uniroyal's reading of the Toth studies proved sufficiently questionable to provoke a backlash in favor of the alternative reading provided by the NRDC." *The Fifth Branch*, 149, 150.

38 Correia "'A' is for Alar," 874 note 98.

39 EPA D-661, 11 December 1985.

40 EPA D-5605; also D-5599, "Outline of Remarks" by EPA administrator Jack Moore at the daminozide press briefing.

41 EPA D-5381, letter from the NRDC dated 22 January 1986. Although the courts earlier had refused to overrule the EPA's handling of specific cases, one of the beneficial results of the court action was to require the EPA to place more abundant documentation – such as records of meetings between industry and regulators – in the public docket.

42 D-644 and D-10847 refer to 1,500 such letters received between fall 1983 and spring 1984.

43 A Seattle EPA official explained that the agency had not intended to announce the proposed cancellation at the end of August 1985, but rather planned to issue a public statement only after taking its proposed action to the SAP; however, there was a leak of an internal document to the newspaper *USA Today*, and the agency had to acknowledge that such a recommendation was being prepared. *Seattle Times*, 30 August 1985.

44 Recall than another senior EPA official was calling attention at the same time to the highest risk estimate made in the "Position Document" (one in a thousand – see note 24 above), which is a very high risk level indeed. There are some mixed messages here.

45 *The New York Times*, 30 August 1985, p. B4.

46 *The New York Times*, 14 January 1986, Sect. A, p. 15.

47 *The New York Times*, 5 May 1986, Sect. 3, p. 4.

48 "Sacred" commodities such as milk and apples have to be treated with special care, especially by government officials, as two episodes involving milk demonstrate. In the first one, the British Columbia public learned that a hormone called bovine somatotropin (BST), which occurs naturally in cows but which also can be enhanced artificially, the effect of which is to increase sharply their milk productivity, was being "tested" in a herd owned by a research institution, with the milk being incorporated in the general dairy "pool" in the Lower Mainland. Agriculture Canada officials were quoted as saying that the necessary scientific evaluation had been done before such authorization had been

given and the public had nothing to worry about. It didn't work. *By the very next day* the milk from this herd was being dumped as waste. ("Experimental herd's milk sold in B.C.," *Vancouver Sun*, 5 November 1988.) In the second, Health and Welfare Canada learned that minute amounts of dioxins, at the parts per trillion level, could leach into milk stored in waxed cardboard cartons (originating in the pulp out of which the cardboard was made). Although there was no scientific concern about health risk whatsoever at this level of contamination, HWC officials worked quietly with the pulp and paper industry to change their production processes so as to drive the dioxin levels below the limit of detection, in the course of this work even inventing the technology for detection of substances at the level of parts per quadrillion. See Health and Welfare Canada, Health Protection Branch (HPB), Bureau of Chemical Safety, "Health Hazard Assessment of Dioxins/ Furans in Milk packaged in Cardboard Containers," 10 November 1988, and HPB, "Issues: Dioxins and Furans," 28 November 1988.

49  There are few clean hands in health and environmental controversies. In 1988 a smaller California supermarket chain hired an independent firm to test both its apples and Safeway's for Alar residues, then took out newspaper ads to tell the public that these independent tests showed that Safeway's apples had alar residues while its own did not. *Supermarket News*, vol. 38 (8 February 1988), 2.

50  *The New York Times*, 26 July 1986, p. A4.

51  Lave, "Health and Safety Risk Analysis," 294.

52  The following section on the B.C. apple industry is based upon a course paper by Ms. Carolyn Liu (M.A. candidate, Department of Communication, Simon Fraser University) written in the spring of 1991.

53  *Vancouver Sun*, 30 August 1985, p. A3.

54  *Vancouver Sun*, 18 July 1986, p. A3. The president still tried to calm public fears even in making this announcement, saying that "an apple eater would need to consume 300,000 apples a day for life to be affected."

55  Telephone interview, April 1991.

56  For an account see Krimsky and Plough, *Environmental Hazards*, ch. 2, and Sharlin, "Macro-Risks, Micro-Risks and the Media."

57  *The New York Times*, 2 February 1989, p. A18. A few days later (5 February, p. A22) the *Sunday Times* published a long and balanced article on the chemical treatment of apple crops, citing the whole spectrum of opposing views, with no special prominence given to the NRDC or other environmental groups. It mentioned the fact that U.S. apple growers had about 100 registered products to choose from, and that on average a grower would use anywhere from 6 to 20 different chemicals each

season, and also cited an EPA official as noting that some of those chemicals protected the consumer from fungi and bacteria. Cf. Correia 869: "... [S]ome fruit and vegetable crops require a dozen or more pesticide treatments each year with six or more different active ingredients ..."

58  *The New York Times,* 17 March 1989, p. A16.

59  "How PR Firm executed the Alar scare," *The Wall Street Journal,* 3 October 1989.

60  Malcolm Tyrrell, "Assault on Alar," September 1990 (EPA D-12445).

61  Clorox: Martin Mittelstaedt, *The Globe and Mail,* 11 May 1991, p. A5. MSG: Bruce Ingersoll, *The Globe and Mail,* 21 October 1991, pp. B1, B4. No great public controversy about MSG followed the broadcast.

62  Agriculture Canada, Pesticides Directorate, Information Secretariat, "Daminozide" (June 1987).

63  On the other hand, the EPA had never set a separate tolerance for UDMH (Correia, "'A' is for Alar," 878 note 157).

64  Health and Welfare Canada, Health Protection Branch, "Alar (Daminozide)," *Issues,* 7 March 1989.

65  Transcript of CBC radio interview with L. Herwig-Wentell, Food Issues Committee, Consumers Association of Canada, 28 February 1989.

66  Tom Spears, *Toronto Star,* 1 March 1989. A selection of comments about the removal of apples from school lunch menus is in *The New York Times,* 6 March 1989, p. B10.

67  EPA D-10627.

68  In order: (1) EPA D-5245; (2) N.Y.: D-5370 to 73; Maine: D-5266, 5295; Massachusetts: D-5262, 5278, 5291, 5296, 5927; (3) D-5301 and D-5444; (4) D-7322; (5) HWC files; (6) D-9109; (7) D-10521 to 524; (8) D-10328, D-10320; (9) HWC files; (10) NRBC, *Intolerable Risk,* 36, 37; (11) EPA D-10804, 18 April 1989, 12, 10. See also p. 14: "In summary, the available data indicate that both Alar and UDMH produce significantly increased carcinogenic responses at multiple tissue sites in different experiments in both sexes of several strains and species (mouse and hamster) of animals. In addition, both uncommon vascular and common lung tumors were produced at a relatively high incidence and with an early onset (i.e., 9 to 12 months) in some studies. Furthermore, sufficient experimental data exist to implicate UDMH in the oncogenic response produced by Alar. That is, UDMH, the breakdown product and metabolite of Alar is mutagenic, produces similar tumors at similar organ sites as has been reported for Alar (as well as for other structurally-related hydrazine compounds), and is present as a residue on Alar treated foodstuffs that are consumed by humans. Finally, recently obtained metabolism data indicated that not only UDMH, but also dimethylnitrosamine was present in the urine of mini-pigs treated with Alar.

This finding is of potential interest because dimethylnitrosamine produces the same type of tumors in mice that are seen with Alar and UDMH"; (12) EPA D-11060; (13) D-10806 and 813 (press release); (14) D-11012; (15) D-11425, p. 27; (16) D-13042.

69 The quoted materials are from the "Executive Summary." The reader should note the claim that a risk assessment really couldn't be done because an "important study" was still incomplete: This was written twenty-one years after the chemical was registered for use on food crops! Also the concern that "public opinion rather than scientific fact" would influence events – after we have been told that a key part of the needed "scientific fact" is non-existent.

70 A major sub-theme in the entire risk assessment controversy is that, when test animals are fed very high doses of many substances, the excessive toxicity that is observed may be a function of the dose and not of the relative inherent toxicity of the substance itself. This theme is present in all the discussion of the Toth studies and recurs here. Uniroyal had objected vigorously, but to no avail, when the EPA ordered it to conduct new feeding studies using daminozide at the 80 ppm level – which, it claimed, represented concentrations that were up to a million times higher than were ever present in food products. Professor Bruce Ames of University of California, Berkeley, has been crusading against the worst-case estimates extrapolated from the use of MTDs in laboratory studies for years. For one of the original statements of these views, see Ames et al., "Ranking Possible Carcinogenic Hazards"; for one made in the context of the Alar debate, see Consumers' Research, April 1990, 32–4.

71 Compare #11 (in note 68 above), where a sixteen-member EPA in-house expert committee had concluded that UDMH is mutagenic.

CHAPTER SEVEN

1 The U.S. Department of Agriculture provided $15 million in payments to growers who would divert their unsaleable apples to other uses, including donations to low-income groups and prisons (Correia, "'A' is for Alar," 876).

2 Supermarket News, vol. 39 (26 June 1989), p. 1.

3 For the last two items see Pesticide and Toxic Chemical News, 12 and 20 December 1990.

4 Rosen, "Much Ado About Alar," 89–90. The special review for daminozide spanned ten years; for various fungicides (Dinocap, Captan, ethylene bisdithiocarbamates) four, nine, and over fifteen years, respectively; for pesticides containing cadmium, formerly used on lawns and turf, ten years (Correia, "'A' is for Alar," 880).

5  In Canada, Agriculture Canada constitutes the main regulatory authority, while Health and Welfare Canada constitutes the final *de facto* authority on health risk.

6  The FDA has been criticized repeatedly, for example by the U.S. General Accounting Office and in congressional hearings, for laxity in the discharge of its monitoring and enforcement activities (Correia, "'A' is for Alar," 868).

7  In early 1985 the EPA began running a series of workshops on risk assessment across the United States for invited participants. A model "Case Study on Risk Assessment" was developed for these workshops, using a hypothetical chemical whimsically named DNC ("dinitrochicken-wire"); a full hazard and exposure profile was given, based of course on invented data, and the participants were asked to arrive at a consensus on a quantitative risk assessment. The experience gained here undoubtedly was drawn upon later, when actual stakeholder negotiation exercises began to be undertaken in the "real world."

8  There are no hard and fast rules, obviously (for further discussion about an actual Canadian case, see chapter 8); if there is not unanimity, it is important that the dissenting stakeholders "stay at the table" if there are future rounds of negotiation. The U.S. "reg-neg" process operates under federal legislation according to more formal and different rules (Knaster and Harter, "The Clean Fuels Regulatory Negotiation," 20): "A consensus in this case means that each interest concurs in the recommended rule when considered as a whole; each interest, therefore, has a veto over the proposal. The agreement also provides that no one participating in the negotiations will do anything to inhibit its adoption or, to the extent the final rule is consistent with the recommended rule, challenge the rule in court. No rule that has been the subject of such a consensus has resulted in court action."

9  See generally Susskind and Cruikshank, "Breaking the Impasse," on which much of this list is based; the quotation is from p. 77.

10  British Columbia Roundtable, *Reaching Agreement, Volume 1*, 9.

11  Sadler, "Appendix 1," 79. Principled negotiation is also known as consensus-based or interest-based negotiation (Darling, *In Search of Consensus*, 23).

12  Fisher and Ury, *Getting to YES*, 11–13.

13  In one sense, multi-stakeholder negotiation is a sub-category of what is now known as "alternative dispute resolution" (ADR), a process that is applied to the entire range of individual and collective disputes, ranging from marital breakdown through commercial contracts to very large-scale negotiations among interested parties on land-use and resource-management issues. The annual conferences of the Society of Professionals in Dispute Resolution contain hundreds of diverse pres-

entations on this entire range of issues, and there are many relevant publications in the *Negotiation Journal.* See generally Cormick, "Strategic Issues in Structuring Multi-Party Public Disputes," and "Crafting the Language of Consensus"; Carpenter and Kennedy, *Managing Public Disputes*; Salter and Leiss, "Guide to Consultation and Consensus Building."

14 "Regulatory Negotiation" and "Negotiated Rule-making" are used interchangeably. See Pritzker and Dalton's *Negotiated Rulemaking Sourcebook* and Harter, "Federal Agencies and ADR," for material on numerous cases in the United States over the past ten years, conducted under the auspices of the EPA and many other agencies. The stakeholder meetings occur under the official aegis of the Federal Advisory Committee Act and the Negotiated Rulemaking Act of 1990 (an amendment to the Administrative Procedure Act) and at the EPA are managed through the Consensus and Dispute Resolution Program. As of October 1992, negotiated rule-making had been used at the EPA in all of the following areas:
- revision of the hazardous waste manifest;
- architectural and industrial maintenance coatings (emission of volatile organic compounds);
- disinfection by-products;
- national emission standards for coke oven batteries;
- oxygenated and reformulated fuels;
- recycling of lead-acid batteries;
- fugitive emissions from equipment leaks;
- asbestos in schools;
- underground injection of hazardous waste;
- woodburning stoves;
- farmworker protection standards;
- emergency pesticide exemptions;
- non-conformance penalties for heavy-duty trucks.

15 Pritzker and Dalton, *Negotiated Rulemaking Sourcebook*, 36–7.

16 Reg-neg was modelled on the practices of private sector organizations that write voluntary consensus standards, such as the standards developed by the American National Standards Institute or the Canadian Standards Association. Such standards are often adopted as regulations by governments and agencies (Pritzker, "Working Together for Better Regulations," 30). For a general description of the process see Siegler, "Regulatory Negotiations: A Practical Perspective."

17 Henry J. Perritt, "Analysis of Four Negotiated Rulemaking Efforts," cited in Cormick and Knaster, "Mediation and Scientific Issues," 7.

18 In the Grand Canyon dispute, after waiting since 1973 for compliance by the plant with an order under the Clean Air Act to install scrub-

bers, the EPA called together the plant owners and environmental groups, and an agreement was struck (*Newsweek*, 19 August 1991, p. 63). In the mining case, the company avoided lengthy litigation with environmental groups over its plans to construct a new mine on public land near the East Mojave National Scenic Area by agreeing to modify its extraction technology and to set up a trust fund under the control of those groups (*The Globe and Mail*, 27 December 1990, B6).

19 (1) In the mercury pollution case, costly and protracted litigation over damages to members of northern Ontario Native communities, stemming from pollution of rivers by pulp mills, was avoided through a negotiated settlement (Sigurdson, "Settling Environmental Disputes"). (2) In the "Height-of-the-Rockies" dispute, the B.C. Ministry of Forests sponsored a multi-stakeholder process that resulted, after ten years of controversy, in the designation of a Wilderness Area that had wide local support (B.C. Roundtable, *Reaching Agreement, Volume 1*, Appendix 3). (3) In a process that lasted almost two years, a national multi-stakeholder team, representing the entire range of interests in pesticides issues, reached agreement on a complex set of recommendations for a revised federal pest-management regulatory system (Canada, Agriculture Canada, Pesticides Registration Review, "Final Report"). (4) An agreement among all three levels of government called for the establishment of a nineteen-member multi-stakeholder group to oversee all activities in connection with the management of the Fraser River Basin (*Vancouver Sun*, 6 July 1992).

20 British Columbia. Commission on Resources and Environment (CORE), *Report on a Land Use Strategy*, 9, 22. CORE uses the term "shared decision making" to refer to consensus-building negotiation.

21 British Columbia Roundtable, *Reaching Agreement, Volume 2*, 10.

22 Ibid., 2–3.

23 Susskind and Cruikshank, *Breaking the Impasse*, 133.

24 Pritzker and Dalton, *Negotiated Rulemaking Sourcebook*.

25 Darling, *In Search of Consensus*, 26; Sadler, "Appendix 1," 80.

26 Susskind and Cruikshank, *Breaking the Impasse*; Flynn, "The Timber/Fish/Wildlife Agreement," 26–30; British Columbia Roundtable, *Reaching Agreement, Volume 1*, 21–8; *Volume 2*, 4.

27 Pritzker, "Working Together for Better Regulations"; Cormick, "Commentary II," 42.

28 Susskind and Cruikshank, *Breaking the Impasse* 21, 24, 31. "Success" is generally evaluated in terms of whether or not an agreement is reached or how well the objectives of each participating group were met (Flynn, "The Timber/Fish/Wildlife Agreement," 4).

29 This and the following paragraphs draw heavily upon Susskind and Cruikshank, *Breaking the Impasse*, 24–33.

30 Ibid., 28–30.
31 Buckle and Thomas-Buckle, "Placing Environmental Mediation in Context," 55, 69.
32 See especially Amy, *The Politics of Environmental Mediation*.
33 Negotiated approaches to consensus-building in environmental disputes have their intellectual roots in labour-management negotiations (Brock, "Mandated Mediation," 58).
34 Susskind and Cruikshank, *Breaking the Impasse*, 103–4
35 Gunton and Flynn, "Resolving Environmental Conflicts," 6–7; Gerald Cormick, one of the most accomplished facilitators in this business, has organized much of what has been descibed above into a set of recommendations for permanently institutionalizing dispute-resolution systems into society's established frameworks for decision-making (Cormick, "Commentary II," 41–2). See also Brock, "Mandated Mediation," for an expanded discussion of the conditions, features, and ingredients that contribute to successful development and operation. Brock also emphasizes the inherent difficulties in seeking to institutionalize alternative dispute-resolution systems (Ibid., 60–1).

CHAPTER EIGHT

1 Among other things, this chapter reports on the activities of a group known as the British Columbia Stakeholder Forum on Sapstain Control (BCSF), which played a key role in the events recounted here. It is important for the reader to note that neither the BCSF as a group, nor any of its individual members or associated organizations, have reviewed or endorsed the text of this chapter. The selection of materials for discussion, and the viewpoints expressed in this chapter, are solely the responsibility of this book's authors.
2 Deloitte Haskins & Sells (DHS), "An Economic Benefit Assessment of Anti-Sapstain Chemicals used in B.C. Sawmills."
3 PCP is still widely used as an oil-borne "heavy-duty" wood preservative in pressure-treatment plants for utility and telephone poles, railway ties, and similar uses. In the wood products industry, the chlorophenates used were mostly water-soluble sodium tetrachlorophenate (Na-TCP), with a small amount of sodium pentachlorophenate (Na-PCP). (See Jones, "Chlorophenols and their Impurities in the Canadian Environment," Figure 1.) In its "Discussion Document on Pentachlorophenol" (1987) and elsewhere, Agriculture Canada, perhaps reflecting common usage, used the term pentachlorophenol "to identify both penta and tetra and their sodium salts"; this has been a matter of concern to the industries that still make and use penta as a heavy-duty wood preservative.

4 DHS, "An Economic Benefit Assessment of Anti-Sapstain Chemicals used in B.C. Sawmills."

5 See generally Salter, *Mandated Science*, ch. 6.

6 Cf. Cedar, "An Annotated Chronology of Chlorophenol Incidents and Regulatory Action."

7 Canada. Agriculture Canada, "Discussion Document: Pentachlorophenol."

8 Salter, *Mandated Science*, ch. 6; McGee and Levy, "Herbicide Use in Forestry."

9 For a part of this history the interested reader should consult the series of case studies included in Harrison and Hoberg, *Risk, Science, and Politics.*

10 Doug Ward, *Vancouver Sun*, 26 September 1989.

11 DHS, "An Economic Benefit Assessment of Anti-Sapstain Chemicals used in B.C. Sawmills," 170.

12 The reader should recall (see note 3 above) that it was Agriculture Canada's practice to use "pentachlorophenol" or "PCP" to stand for the entire group of chlorophenate compounds.

13 See Appendix II, Document #1.

14 See Castrilli and Vigod, *Pesticides in Canada.*

15 The reader should note that, while the five federal agencies were not directly at the table, they maintained a keen interest in the proceedings of the BCSF throughout the process. The mechanism for doing so was to have the Chair of the BCSF serve as a "go-between," commuting between Vancouver and Ottawa regularly while the crucial series of six meetings was in progress. The Chair then briefed each side on what was happening at the other end.

16 CAPCO is the Canadian Association of Pesticides Control Officers.

17 Most concerns centre around the active ingredient in the formulated product, but there is also considerable annoyance about the failure of regulators to assess the properties of so-called "inert ingredients," such as emulsifiers, which are added in order to make the product work better. Koren (*Handbook of Environmental Health and Safety*, 242) says that, of the 1,200 inert ingredients used in pesticide formulations, 50 are known to be toxic but fully 900 are of unknown toxicity.

18 One of the outstanding features of the "Recommendations for a Revised Federal Pest Management Regulatory System" (Canada, Agriculture Canada, "Final Report," ix) is the proposal to change the existing legislation (the Pest Control Products Act) in order to create a Pest Management Promotion Office: "The mandate of the Pest Management Promotion Office is to support the integration of pest management with the broader goals of environmental sustainability,

including the role to set targets and establish workplans for the reduction of use of pesticides in all use sectors ... and to fund research, as appropriate." There is also a recommendation to create a permanent, national multi-stakeholder advisory council "to advise the Ministers of Agriculture and Health and Welfare on an ongoing basis ..." See generally Versteeg, "A Case Study in Multi-Stakeholder Consultation." As of the time of writing (June 1993), these recommendations were bogged down in the familiar terrain of protracted bureaucratic struggle.

19  For a superb recent discussion of risk/benefit approaches see Brunk *et al.*, *Value Assumptions in Risk Assessment*; DHS, "An Economic Benefit Assessment of Anti-Sapstain Chemicals used in B.C. Sawmills."

20  The alert reader will see, in the regulatory actions announced towards the end of "CAPCO Note 90–10" (Document #2, Appendix II), that Agriculture Canada had negotiated what is called a "voluntary product withdrawal" of PCP with its manufacturers. This is a common practice in North America. In the United States, the EPA followed the same route at the end of the highly public controversy over Alar. In both countries the legal structure under which the regulatory authorities operate make it extremely difficult to remove a product from the market, after it has been registered, against the wishes of the manufacturer.

21  We recognize that such assessments can and do change on the basis of new data (for both hazard profiles and exposure), new methodologies, and evolving community standards, among other things.

22  Witness the prevailing farce in large-scale environmental assessment in Canada – the Nechako River diversion in B.C., the Oldman River dam and Alpac pulp mill in Alberta, the Rafferty-Alameda dam in Saskatchewan, the decade-long Ontario Waste Management soap opera, and the determined effort by the government of Quebec to avoid a disinterested assessment of the Great Whale proposal.

CHAPTER NINE

1  "Cultural Theory and Risk Analysis," 95.
2  The best single summary statement of the need to find a proper balance between the responsibilities of institutions and individuals for appropriate risk decisions is the chapter entitled "Risk within Reason" (written with Richard Zeckhauser) in Viscusi, *Fatal Tradeoffs*. We would qualify what they say only in that uncertainties and periodic revisions in risk assessment (based on new information) render our risk management judgments inherently unstable.

3  In litigation in the United States, tobacco firms will go into court with dozens of lawyers, including junior lawyers in training for the next generation of lawsuits expected by the companies.

4  We have in mind the possibility that hundreds of different stakeholder representatives might be meeting concurrently in each nation, organized regionally and locally, with the type of party present being dependent on the particular issue at hand.

5  See Nelkin and Brown, *Workers at Risk*.

6  There will be almost as many exceptions to these generalizations as there are specific issues. As the case of Alar shows, regional governments (individually or collectively) may also exhibit a split between health protection and industrial promotion interests.

7  The weakening of organized labour in recent times, especially in the United States, where this process has been aided and abetted by both business and governments, is an unfortunate development in this context. If we are right in supposing that labour in particular occupies an intermediate point in the spectrum of positions on acceptable risk, then this undermining of organized labour's social role could turn out to be self-defeating for the business interests that have colluded in it, because in future negotiations on risk they will face a relatively higher proportion of the straightforward risk-averse positions of the public interest groups, who are increasingly adept in winning adherents to their cause in society at large.

8  See the Grand Canyon and East Mojave (California) negotiations referred to earlier (ch. 7, n. 18). We need not fear overmuch that the decision-making process will seize up (because some stakeholders might use the process for just such a purpose) if, as we suggest, the solution to many controversies should be sought in this venue. This is because there are "circuit breakers" available. In the United States, parties can and do go to court to assert their rights, and in any case the reg-neg outcomes are not binding on the government; in Canada, public bureaucracies have large zones of administrative discretion in which to manoeuvre.

9  For some time following the start of reg-neg processes in the United States, the NRDC expressed strong reservations about this approach. But the NRDC was at the table with thirty other parties at negotiations leading to an agreement under which volatile organic compound emissions from vehicle fuels will be reduced by 25 percent by the year 2000; the agreement was reached in August 1991 and the NRDC was among the signatories.

10  We are assuming that the interests of all potentially affected entities (including non-human entities, both animal and plant) are represented at the table and therefore that it is unnecessary for anyone to raise the

issue of the completeness of the set of stakeholders. Even those persons living far from the Pacific Northwest have heard by now of the spotted owl, which has replaced the snail-darter (a small fish found only in an ecosystem falling within the domain of the Tennessee Valley Authority) of an earlier era as an object of anti-environmentalist rage.

11 Natural Resources Defense Council, *Intolerable Risk*, 7–8.

12 There is a nice irony in one of the key pieces to the Alar puzzle that is relevant here. Throughout the 1970s Dr. Bela Toth of the Eppley Institute for Research in Cancer (University of Nebraska Medical Center) concentrated his research on the carcinogenic effects of a class of chemical compounds known as hydrazines; among his many published studies were the two (on UDMH in 1973 and SADH in 1977) that became focal points of the Alar risk-assessment controversy. Another of his studies, which did not become such a key part of the Alar folklore, noted that UDMH – always the centre of concern about Alar – is present at significant levels in tobacco, and that there are other naturally occurring and closely related hydrazines in some wild edible mushrooms (Toth, "The Large Bowel Carcinogenic Effects of Hydrazines and Related Compounds," 2429); see also Ames and Gold, "Environmental Pollution and Cancer," 165. Certainly the UDMH in tobacco would give rise to very extensive human exposure, as Toth noted.

13 No such stance has been adopted as a general rule. Few consumers who know that Alar is no longer used on apples could even name the myriad other chemicals still registered for use on that crop, much less the dietary risk numbers associated with them.

14 There is an instructive example in one of Bruce Ames's articles: "Historically, cases of cancer due to work place exposure resulted mainly from exposure to chemicals close to the toxic level. For example, I testified in 1981 in California that the EDB levels that workers were allowed to be exposed to were shockingly high (our calculations showed that the workers were allowed to breathe in a dose higher than the dose that gave half of the rats cancer). ... Despite the fact that the epidemiology on EDB in highly exposed workers does not show any significant effect, the uncertainties of our knowledge make it important to have strict rules about workers because the doses can get extremely high." Ames, "Six Common Errors relating to Environmental Pollution," 381.

15 EPA D-5291, letter dated 16 May 1986 from four faculty members at the Harvard School of Public Health: "Workers likely get exposed to even greater concentrations of daminozide [than do consumers]. However, EPA's analysis of occupational exposure to daminozide leaves much to be desired. Minimal worker exposures are assumed in risk calculations. Compliance with government regulations for applicators is taken for granted. Yet, farm labor conditions are notoriously poor and

enforcement of regulations is weak. Farm workers rarely receive health and safety training and sometimes cannot read English."

16 Occupational standards in the United States are generally set by a private agency, the American Council of Government and Industrial Hygienists (ACGIH), and ACGIH standards are often adopted by the provincial workers' compensation boards in Canada; the standard is expressed in terms of "Threshold Limit Value" (TLV), which is the upper limit of permitted exposure. The standard for UDMH was set in 1960 at 0.5 ppm (a recommendation was made in 1989 to lower the TLV to 0.01 ppm); a concurring OSHA guideline dates only from 1989. Thirty-three relevant scientific studies are cited (most of them published), dating from the period 1954–88, including of course the three Toth studies, but most of the rest were never cited by any party during the Alar controversy. ACGIH, *Documentation of the Threshold Limit Values and Biological Exposure Indices*, 491–4 (we are indebted to Dr. Chris Van Netten of the University of British Columbia for this information). On ACGIH see Salter, *Mandated Science*, ch. 3.

17 *Vancouver Sun*, 10 October 1991; 13, 14 and 21 February 1992.

18 We designate those public interest groups who hold this philosophy and who intervene in debates on health and environmental risks as surrogates for all citizens who, wittingly or not, wish to set risk standards for involuntary exposures generally much higher than those for voluntary activities, and we suggest that these groups assume responsibility for this stance on behalf of all such persons. This may be unfair, but there is much that is unfair about risk debates.

19 The book's authors have the benefit of hindsight in formulating the foregoing commentary. Obviously we are not suggesting that Uniroyal or any of the other parties ought to have known, or could have known, at the time when these events unfolded that their strategies were deficient; like the reconstruction of events in chapter 6, the commentary here is an interpretation for which the book's authors alone are responsible. In pressing these matters further here, we are motivated by the knowledge that the Alar dispute was very costly to many of the participants.

20 Another good case is provided by the struggle between Monsanto Corporation and the Government of Canada over the health risks associated with the herbicide Alachlor (discussed briefly in chapter 1). From the painstaking analysis of this case by Brunk, Haworth, and Lee it is hard not to draw the conclusion that both sides played elaborate games with their respective risk assessments.

21 Uniroyal funnelled much of its correspondence with the EPA, including the to-ing and fro-ing over the laboratory audits, through its law firm. Richard A. Merrill ("The Legal System's Response to Scientific Uncer-

tainty") has done a splendid analysis of legal challenges to agency risk assessment in the United States. Summarizing the results of one long-running episode, he writes (p. S425): "I do not know whether UF [urea formaldehyde] foam insulation poses a risk of human cancer. I am not sure that CPSC [Consumer Product Safety Commission] knows how serious the hazard is. I am morally certain that the Fifth Circuit [Court of Appeal] has no idea." See also D.L. Davis's more extensive discussion of risk assessment and judicial review, "The Shotgun Wedding of Science and Law" and T.O. McGarity's "Judicial Review of Scientific Rulemaking." The outcome of challenges to government-initiated risk assessments launched by lawyers in court and at quasi-judicial hearings is of special relevance to the negotiated-consensus approach to risk management advocated in this book. We have in mind the U.S. courtroom episodes discussed by Merrill, Davis, and McGarity, for example, in the well-known cases of formaldehyde, benzene, and others; the upcoming court test of the EPA's risk assessment of environmental tobacco smoke will be a long and disputatious one. In Canada such matters are not fought out in courtrooms but rather in official hearings that feature cross-examinations of experts by lawyers; two examples are the fight over lead contamination in Toronto in the early 1970s, heard before the Ontario Environmental Assessment Board (see Salter, *Mandated Science*, ch. 5), and Monsanto's challenge to the Canadian government's risk assessment of Alachlor, discussed briefly in chapter 1. We do not have time for a proper review of these proceedings here; suffice it to say that, once a good lawyer is finished exploiting the qualification of results, methodological subtleties, "reasonable doubts," and inescapable uncertainties in scientific risk assessments – especially if epidemiological studies are involved – usually there is not enough of the original edifice left to hang a decent guess on. Some of the destruction stems just from an adept lawyer's bag of tricks, to be sure, but not all of it does; the rest results from the inherent weaknesses in the structure of risk assessment itself. The point we wish to make here is this: Risk-promoters who are contemptuous of the doubts expressed by other parties about how good their risk estimates are, or who think that the untutored public's unreasonable fears are the only obstacle to our sensibly managing risks to life and safety, stand a good chance of having their bluff called when the parties assemble in court, a hearing room, or around a negotiating table. The lesson to be learned from this (as we said in chapter 1) is not that we can do without expert risk assessments; rather, it is that such assessments should be offered in a spirit of modesty and humility, rather than (as is too often the case) steeped in intellectual arrogance, when risk managers are facing others and negotiating acceptable risk.

22 The levels of risk that are likely to be the subject of negotiation rarely would approach those that are already experienced daily in occupations such as fishing, underground mining, tree falling, firefighting, and police work. Excess risks are screened out in many ways, for example when chemical manufacturers abandon work on new compounds with promising potential for industrial applications at an early stage of development, when preliminary toxicological findings point to a hazard profile that is likely to lead to an unacceptable level of risk.

23 A public inquiry may not even be appropriate to address the PF E/MF health effects issue, and may actually preclude implemention of recommendations for improvement such as those we made in chapter 5.

24 Ozawa and Susskind, "Mediating Science-Intensive Policy Disputes," 31–2.

25 See also, e.g., Cormick and Knaster, "Mediation and Scientific Issues," and Ozawa, *Recasting Science*.

26 United States, National Research Council, *Improving Risk Communication*, 12.

27 California EMF Consensus Group, *Issues and Recommendations for Interim Response and Policy Addressing Power Frequency Electric and Magnetic Fields (EMFs)*, Report Submitted to the Public Utilities Commission of the State of California, 20 March 1992.

28 Washington State, Department of Ecology, *Toward 2010: An Environmental Action Agenda*, Olympia, WA, July 1990, 1–2.

29 Ben Bonkowski, Senior Planner, Quality Control, Information Management & Comprehensive Planning, Washington State Department of Ecology, personal communication, 10 December 1992.

30 The Northeast Center for Comparative Risk at Vermont Law School recently completed an evaluation of the Washington 2010 process. We have not yet had the opportunity to review their report.

31 As discussed in chapter 5, some work has been done on re-evaluating the assumptions and adequacy of methodologies used to study PF E/MF health effects. With respect to mandated science in general, Salter suggests that epidemiological research should be given higher priority in the evaluation of risk "for intuitive reasons, and because of the particular type of information it provides about the human consequences." This would mean designing risk-assessment procedures "attuned to the methodological constraints of epidemiological research" (Salter, *Mandated Science*, 207).

32 A more subdued controversy over the pesticide Captan occurred in the early 1980s, both in the United States and in Canada, with very different results, largely (we believe) owing to the fact that at that time the more limited set of traditional stakeholders were the only players

around the table. See Salter, "Observations on the Politics of Risk Assessment: The Captan Case."

33 We wish to emphasize here an important point about each of the elements in the NRDC's strategy. First, with respect to their risk assessment: from the standpoint of multi-stakeholder negotiation it matters not in the slightest if some stakeholders think that another's so-called expert risk assessment is shoddily done. The only relevant question is: Does it obey in its construction and exposition the prevailing scientific rules of the game? There can be no doubt that the NRDC's report fulfilled this criterion, especially with the inclusion of its technical appendices. The only good way to have made a *scientific* case against it would have been in a forum established for that purpose, with all relevant parties present, but none existed. Second, with respect to the media strategy, we reiterate our earlier point that this was a perfectly legitimate attempt to obtain maximum public attention for the message that the NRDC had to deliver.

34 The power of the NRDC's case lay in its emphasis on children and its claim that the unique characteristics of childhood risk did not receive due consideration in the scientific assessment of health risk (in this case for pesticides). A distinguished expert panel has now supported this view (United States National Research Council, *Pesticides in the Diets of Infants and Children*, 359–60), but there is not a single mention of daminozide, UDMH, or the NRDC in this report.

35 Appendix 2, p. 308.

36 The article by Keeney and von Winterfeldt ("A Prescriptive Risk Framework for Individual Health and Safety Decisions") shows that we have not yet arrived at the "beginning of wisdom" in this regard – certainly not if what we seek is something by way of a prescription to communicate effectively to the non-expert citizen.

APPENDIX I

1 At present, the interaction between these fields and biological systems is largely unknown (Hauf, "Electric and magnetic fields," 176).

2 OTA, *Biological Effects*, 4; HWC, HPB, EHD, *Electric and Magnetic Fields and Your Health: A Report of the Working Group on Electric and Magnetic ELF Fields*, 2, 39.

3 In Europe, Japan, and New Zealand electric current alternates at 50 Hz.

4 AC current can be contrasted to the DC or direct current produced by batteries. DC does not change strength and direction over time. DC current is also used to transmit electric energy but is much less common than AC. In North America, there are five DC transmission lines.

5 OTA, *Electric Power Wheeling and Dealing: Technological Considerations for Increasing Competition*, 228.
6 The effects may be beneficial, adverse or negligible, depending on, e.g., frequency, wavelength, waveform, and intensity. With the exception of visible and audible radiation, humans possess no organ for specific perception of such fields.
7 Although technically ELF includes frequencies 30–300 Hz, some sources use "ELF" to refer to 0–300 Hz, 1–300 Hz, or 19–300 Hz.
8 BPA, *Electrical and Biological Effects of Transmission Lines: A Review*, June 1989, 12.
9 EPRI, *Electric and Magnetic Field Fundamentals: An EMF Health Effects Resource Paper*, EN.3012.9.89. The PF electric and magnetic fields may, however, produce synergistic effects.
10 Morgan, *Electric and Magnetic Fields from 60 Hertz Electric Power*, 5.
11 Bassett, "Premature alarm over electromagnetic fields," 38.
12 BPA, *Electrical and Biological Effects*, June 1989, 53–4.
13 P. Wong, "Electric and Magnetic Fields – what are they and how are they measured?" paper from B.C. Hydro, in co-operation with B.C. Ministry of Health, "Symposium on the Biological Effects of Electric and Magnetic Fields," Richmond, B.C., 20 October, 1988.
14 OTA, *Biological Effects*, 16.
15 Leonard Sagan, testimony from Subcommittee on Water and Power Resources, *Health Effects of Transmission Lines*, 112; Dan Bracken, "Properties and Effects of A.C. and D.C. Line Fields," in Ontario Hydro, *Health Effects of Electric and Magnetic Fields: Research, Communication, Regulation*. Ground currents arise because neutral (or grounded) wires of distribution lines are usually physically connected to earth. These ground connections provide alternate paths for distribution currents to return to local transformers or substations and leads to PF currents in water and gas plumbing (OTA, *Biological Effects*, 15).
16 Kelly Gibney, EMF Issues Manager, B.C. Hydro, personal communication. Power line electric fields near the ground are nearly vertical at all times. Power line magnetic fields on the ground are largely confined to planes parallel to the lines where, due to the phase difference of currents flowing in the individual line conductors, the horizontal and vertical components combine to give a total magnetic field which rotates at the PF (NYSPLP, 39). Phase refers to the relative timing with which the alternating current, voltage, or field is changing strength and direction.
17 Carstensen, *Biological Effects of Transmission Line Fields*, 19.
18 Hauf, "Electric and Magnetic Fields at Power Frequencies," 183.
19 Morgan, *Electric and Magnetic Fields*, 13–4.
20 Ibid., 14.

21 The remainder of the section PF E/MF *Interactions with Biological Systems* is excerpted, unless otherwise noted, from OTA, *Biological Effects*, 16–19.

22 Morgan, *Electric and Magnetic Fields*, 8.

23 Lee, "High-voltage Transmission Lines," 36; A.R. Sheppard and M. Eisenbud, *Biological Effects of Electric and Magnetic Fields of Extremely Low Frequency* (New York: New York University Press, 1977), cited in Rish and Morgan, "Regulating Possible Health Effects," 1417.

24 Sheppard and Eisenbud, cited in Rish and Morgan, "Regulating Possible Health Effects," 1417.

25 The "let-go" threshold is the current above which a person loses voluntary muscle control and cannot "let go" of a gripped contact. There is some concern that even 5 mA is too high because it is greater than the "let-go" threshold for some children and can result in a very unpleasant shock.

26 Florig, "Management options for power-frequency fields."

27 New York State, DOH, "New York State Power Lines Project."

28 Bracken, paper in Ontario Hydro, *Health Effects of Electric and Magnetic Fields*.

29 The section *Exposure Parameters* is excerpted, unless otherwise noted, from OTA, *Biological Effects*, 19–21.

30 Morgan, *Electric and Magnetic Fields*, 22.

31 OTA, *Biological Effects*, 76. With a chemical, dose is typically defined as the amount of chemical that enters into the body or, if the body is able to metabolize or get rid of the chemical, the rate at which the chemical enters the body.

32 Frequency windows are also associated with muscle contraction. Frequencies less than 20 Hz or greater than 200 Hz require a larger level of current to cause tetany than the "optimum frequencies" of 50/60 Hz (William Feero, "The Evolution of Electromagnetic Effects Issues," paper in Ontario Hydro, *Health Effects of Electric and Magnetic Fields*).

33 Moore, "Pursuing the science of EMF," 9.

34 Fitzgerald, Morgan, and Nair. "Special report – electromagnetic fields," 31–2.

35 Moore, "Pursuing the science of EMF," 6.

36 Shepard, "EMF and Human Health," 4.

37 Hauf, "Electric and Magnetic Fields at Power Frequencies," 183–4.

38 Moore, "Pursuing the science of EMF," 6.

39 Carstensen, *Biological Effects of Transmission Line Fields*, 48–9.

40 Sheppard, "Studies of Cells and Tissues Exposed to (ELF) Fields."

41 OTA, *Electric Power Wheeling and Dealing*, 233.

42 BPA, *Electrical and Biological Effects*, October 1985, 24.

43 Marino, "Are Power Lines Dangerous to Health? Probably So," 18.

44 NYSPLP, 52.

45 J.G. Wilson, "Review of *in vitro* systems with potential for use in teratogencity screening," *Journal of Environmental Pathology & Toxicology* 2 (1978): 149–67, cited in NYSPLP, 62.

46 Larry Anderson, "Studies of Laboratory Animals Exposed to ELF Fields," paper in Ontario Hydro, *Health Effects of Electric and Magnetic Fields*.

47 Carstensen, *Biological Effects of Transmission Line Fields*, 56.

48 Morgan *et al.*, "Controlling Exposure to Transmission Line Electromagnetic Fields," 84–5.

49 Kavet, "Biological Effects of Electric Fields," 2118; M.J. Free, W.T. Kaune, R.D. Phillips, and H.C. Cheng, "Endocrinological Effects of Strong 60-Hz Electric Fields on Rats," *Bioelectromagnetics* 2, 2 (1981): 105–22, cited in BPA, *Electrical and Biological Effects*, October 1985, 25.

50 R. Sander, J. Brinkmann, and B. Kuhne, "Laboratory Studies on Animals and Human Beings Exposed to 50-Hz Electric and Magnetic Fields," CIGRE, 1982 Session, 1–9 September, 36–01, cited in Anderson, paper in Ontario Hydro, *Health Effects of Electric and Magnetic Fields;* Kaune *et al.*, 1978, cited in ibid.; H.B. Graves, P.D. Long, and D. Poznaniak, "Biological Effects of 60 Hz Alternating Current Fields: A Cheshire Cat Phenomenon," in R.D. Phillips *et al.*, *Biological Effects of Extremely Low Frequency Electromagnetic Fields*, CONF-78 10 16, (Springfield, Virginia: NTIS, 1979), 184–97, cited in Ibid.; Stern, 1983, cited in Anderson, paper in Ontario Hydro, *Health Effects of Electric and Magnetic Fields;* U.S., BPA, DOE, *Electrical and Biological Effects*, June 1989, 28.

51 Moore, "Pursuing the science of EMF, 9.

52 BPA, *Electrical and Biological Effects*, October 1985, 32.

53 Morgan, *Electric and Magnetic Fields*, 10.

54 Carstensen, *Biological Effects of Transmission Line Fields*, 47.

55 TDHSR 2, 10:2.

56 TDHSR 1, 4:2–3.

57 Salter, *Mandated Science*, 30–1.

58 TDHSR 1, 4:3.

59 NYSPLP, 73. In particular, if the exposure measure is imprecise, the strength of association is weakened.

60 A statistically significant finding is one that, according to certain assumptions and based on a mathematical probability, has a low likelihood of being due to random sampling variation.

61 Carstensen, *Biological Effects of Transmission Line Fields*, 47.

62  BPA, *Electrical and Biological Effects*, June 1989, 3; OTA, *Biological Effects*,
    102. Epidemiology may measure effects on an absolute level (in terms
    of incidence rate, cumulative incidence, or prevalence) or a relative
    scale. Strictly speaking, attributable risk should be calculated only if
    the causation has been established.

63  Fitzgerald, Morgan, and Nair, "Special report – electromagnetic fields,"
    23.

64  BPA, *Electrical and Biological Effects*, June 1989, 39; OTA, *Biological
    Effects*, 102.

65  BPA, *Electrical and Biological Effects*, June 1989, 39; TDHSR 1, 4:3–4.

66  Salter, *Mandated Science*, 30–1.

67  Carstensen, *Biological Effects of Transmission Line Fields*, 47.

68  OTA, *Biological Effects*, 100.

69  Salter, *Mandated Science*, 30–1.

70  OTA, *Biological Effects*, 66.

71  Hill, "The Environment and Disease: Association or Causation?" 295–
    300. All epidemiological studies involve some level of statistical uncer-
    tainty, represented as "confidence intervals," a range of values from the
    lower to upper confidence limits. A 95 percent confidence interval (CI)
    means that one can be 95 percent sure that the actual value lies within
    that interval. An extremely wide CI including an RR of 1.0 suggests
    caution in its interpretation (Morgan, *Electric and Magnetic Fields*, 17;
    TDHSR 2, 5: 2; Fitzgerald *et al.*, "Special report – electromagnetic
    fields," 24).

72  TDHSR 3, 1:2, 11–2. Epidemiology has only begun to emerge as a
    sound methodology in the past three decades (OTA, *Biological Effects*,
    100). For example, Rothman, noting that the theoretical foundation for
    epidemiology lies in statistics, has suggested that some methods are not
    theoretically sound in biological applications although they make sense
    in other applications (ibid., 101).

73  Philip Cole, testimony from Subcommittee on Water and Power
    Resources, *Health Effects of Transmission Lines*, 122–3.

74  TDHSR 3, 1:2, 11–12.

# Bibliography

American Council of Government and Industrial Hygienists. *Documentation of the Threshold Limit Values and Biological Exposure Indices.* 6th edn. Cincinnati, OH: American Council of Government and Industrial Hygienists, 1991.

Ames, Bruce N. "Six Common Errors Relating to Environmental Pollution." *Regulatory Toxicology and Pharmacology* 7 (1987): 379–83.

Ames, Bruce N. and Lois Swirsky Gold. "Environmental Pollution and Cancer: Some Misconceptions." In *Phantom Risk*, eds. K. Foster, D. Bernstein, and P. Huber, 153–181.

Ames, Bruce N., R. Magaw, and L.S. Gold. "Ranking Possible Carcinogenic Hazards." *Science* 236 (17 April 1987): 271–80.

Amy, Douglas. *The Politics of Environmental Mediation.* New York: Columbia University Press, 1987.

"The Asbestos Removal Fiasco." Editorial, *Science* 247 (2 March 1990): 1017.

Australia. Centre for Behavioural Research in Cancer. "Health Warnings and Contents Labelling on Tobacco Products." Melbourne: Anti-Cancer Council of Victoria, 1992.

Bacow, Lawrence S., and Michael Wheeler. *Environmental Dispute Resolution.* New York: Plenum Press, 1984.

Badaracco, Joseph L., Jr. *Loading the Dice: A Five-Country Study of Vinyl Chloride Regulation.* Boston: Harvard Business School Press, 1985.

Bartlett, Robert V. *The Reserve Mining Controversy: Science, Technology, and Environmental Quality.* Bloomington: Indiana University Press, 1980.

Bassett, C. Andrew L. "Premature Alarm Over Electromagnetic Fields." *Issues in Science and Technology* 6, 3 (Spring 1990): 37–9.

Beck, Ulrich. *The Risk Society: Towards a New Modernity.* Translated by Mark Ritter. London: Sage Publications, 1992.

Bentkover, J.D., V.T. Covello, and J. Mumpower, eds. *Benefits Assessment: The State of the Art.* Dordrecht, Holland: D. Reidel, 1985.

Bettman, J.R., J.W. Payne, and R. Staelin. "Cognitive Considerations in Designing Effective Labels for Presenting Risk Information." *Journal of Public Policy and Marketing* 5 (1984): 1–28.

Bierbaum, P., and, J. Peters, eds. *Proceedings of the Scientific Workshop on the Health Effects of Electric and Magnetic Fields on Workers,* National Institutes of Occupational Safety and Health (NIOSH) publication no. 91–111. Cincinnati, OH: NIOSH, 1991.

Bingham, Gail. *Resolving Environmental Disputes: A Decade of Experience.* Washington, DC: The Conservation Foundation, 1986.

Bosso, Christopher J. *Pesticides and Politics.* Pittsburgh, PA.: University of Pittsburgh Press, 1987.

British Columbia. Commission on Resources and Environment (CORE). *Report on a Land Use Strategy for British Columbia.* Victoria, August 1992.

British Columbia Ministry of Health. *Selected Vital Statistics and Health Status Indicators, Annual Report 1992.* Victoria, B.C.: Ministry of Health, 1992.

British Columbia Roundtable on the Environment and the Economy Dispute Resolution Core Group. *Reaching Agreement.* Vol. 1, *Consensus Processes in British Columbia.* Victoria, 1991. Vol. 2, *Implementing Consensus Processes in British Columbia.* Victoria, 1992.

British Columbia Utilities Commission. "B. C. Hydro and Power Authority Proposed 230 kV Transmission Line Dunsmuir/Gold River: Inquiry Structure." 411A/17 Mimeo, n.d.; Order Number G-35–89. Mimeo, 12 June 1989; Order Number G-44–89. Mimeo, 27 July 1989; "Terms of Reference for Public Inquiry," 411A/16 Mimeo, n.d.

– "BC Hydro and Power Authority Proposed 230 kV Transmission Line Dunsmuir/Gold River." *Proceedings at Inquiry.* Courtenay, B. C., 11–14 July 1989. Vol. 1–6. Vancouver: Allwest Reporting Ltd., 1989.

– "British Columbia Hydro and Power Authority Proposed 230 kV Transmission Line Dunsmuir/Gold River." *Public Inquiry Report and Recommendations.* Vancouver, 26 July 1989.

Brock, Jonathon. "Mandated Mediation: A Contradiction in Terms: Lessons From Recent Attempts to Institutionalize Alternative Dispute Resolution Practices." *Villanova Environmental Law Journal* 2, 1 (1991): 57–87.

Brodeur, Paul. "Annals of Radiation." Parts 1, 2, 3. *The New Yorker,* 12, 19, 26 June 1989. Also published in book form as *Currents of Death: Power Lines, Computer Terminals, and the Attempt to Cover up Their Threat to Your Health.* New York: Simon and Schuster, 1989.

– "The Asbestos Industry on Trial." Parts 1, 2, 3, 4. *The New Yorker,* 10, 17, 24 June and 1 July 1985. Also published in book form as *Outrageous Misconduct: The Asbestos Industry on Trial.* New York: Pantheon Books, 1985.

Bronstein, J.M. "The Political Symbolism of Occupational Health Risks." In *The Social and Cultural Construction of Risk,* eds B.B. Johnson and V.T. Covello, 199–226.

Brown, M.S. "Communicating Information about Workplace Hazards: Effects on Worker Attitudes towards Risks." In *The Social and Cultural Construction of Risk*, eds B.B. Johnson and V.T. Covello, 251–74.

Brunk, Conrad, Lawrence Haworth, and Brenda Lee. *Value Assumptions in Risk Assessment*. Waterloo, ON: Wilfred Laurier University Press, 1991.

Buckle, Leonard G., and Suzanne R. Thomas-Buckle. "Placing Environmental Mediation in Context: Lessons From 'Failed' Mediations." *Environmental Impact Assessment Review* 6 (1986): 55–70.

Bulawka, A.O., W.G. Wisecup, L.A. Rosen, and W.E. Feero. "The U.S. Department of Energy 60-Hz Electric Fields Bioeffects Research." IEEE *Transactions on Power Apparatus and Systems* PAS-101 (November 1982): 4432–40.

Canada. Agriculture Canada. "Discussion Document on Anti-Sapstain Chemicals." Ottawa, Draft, n.d. (issued September 1989).

– "Discussion Document: Pentachlorophenol." Ottawa, 1987.

– Interdepartmental Working Group on Risk/Benefit Analysis. "Risk/Benefit Analysis in the Management of Toxic Chemicals." Ottawa: 1984.

– Pesticides Registration Review. "Final Report." Ottawa, December 1990.

– "Proceedings of the National Workshop on Risk/Benefit Analysis." Ottawa, 1985.

– "Report of the Alachlor Review Board." Ottawa, 1987.

Canada. Health and Welfare Canada. Drugs Directorate. "Guidelines for Preparing and Filing New Drug Submissions." Ottawa, April 1988.

– Environmental Health Directorate. *Electric and Magnetic Fields and Your Health: A Report of the Working Group on Electric and Magnetic ELF Fields.* 89-EHD-150. Ottawa: Minister of Supply and Services, 1990 (dated May 1989).

– Environmental Health Directorate. "Risk Assessment/Risk Management: A Handbook on Risk Management for use within the Bureau of Chemical Hazards." Ottawa, 1988.

– Health Protection Branch. *Risk Management in the Health Protection Branch.* Ottawa: Minister of Supply and Services, 1990.

Canada. Statistics Canada. *Accidents in Canada.* Ottawa: Ministry of Supply and Services Canada, 1989, 1991, 1992.

– *Occupational Injuries and Their Costs 1988–1990.* Ottawa: Ministry of Supply and Services Canada, 1992.

Canadian Nuclear Association. "Communications Plan within the Canadian Nuclear Association." 8 April 1987.

Canadian Public Health Association [CPHA], *Benefit Risk Cost Management of Prescription Drugs.* Ottawa: CPHA, 1993.

Canadian Safety Council. *Non-transport accident fatalities by place of occurrence.* Ottawa: Canadian Safety Council, 1989.

Canadian Standards Association. "Risk Analysis Requirements and Guidelines." CAN/CSA–Q634-91. Rexdale, ON, 1991.

Cannell, William, and Harry Otway. "Audience Perspectives in the Communication of Technological Risks." *Futures* (October 1988): 519–31.

Carpenter, David O., and Anders Ahlbom. "Powerlines and Cancer: Public Health and Policy Implications." *Forum for Applied Research and Public Policy* 3, 4 (Winter 1988): 96–101.

Carpenter, Susan L., and W.J.D. Kennedy. *Managing Public Disputes: A Practical Guide to Handling Conflict and Reaching Agreements.* San Francisco: Jossey-Bass Publishers, 1988.

Carstensen, Edwin L. *Biological Effects of Transmission Line Fields.* New York: Elsevier Science Publishing Co. Inc., 1987.

Castrilli, J.F., and Toby Vigod. *Pesticides in Canada: An Examination of Federal Law and Policy.* Study Paper, Protection of Life Series. Ottawa: Law Reform Commission of Canada, 1987.

Cedar, Frank. "An Annotated Chronology of Chlorophenol Incidents and Regulatory Action – A Canadian Perspective." In P.A. Jones, "Chlorophenols and their Impurities in the Canadian Environment, 1983 Supplement," Appendix 4.

Chociolko, Christina. "Expert Disagreement: A Regulator's Nightmare?" M.A. thesis, Simon Fraser University, 1991.

– "The Controversy Regarding Power Frequency Electric and Magnetic Fields and Human Health: Risk and Communication." Simon Fraser University, 1989.

Clayson, D.B. "Biological Basis of Carcinogenic Risk Assessment." In *Environmental Health Risks*, ed. S. McColl, 67–81.

Collins, Richard C. "Resolving Forest Management Planning Disputes: A Mediator's Perspective." *Resolve* 20 (1988): 1, 3–6.

Cormick, Gerald. "Commentary II." In *The Place of Negotiation in Environmental Assessment*, 39–43. Hull: Canadian Environmental Assessment Research Council, 1987.

– "Crafting the Language of Consensus." *Negotiation Journal* 7, 4 (October 1991): 363–8.

– "Strategic Issues in Structuring Multi-Party Public Disputes." *Negotiation Journal* 5, 2 (April 1989): 125–32.

Cormick, Gerald, and Alana Knaster. "Mediation and Scientific Issues." *Environment* 28, 10 (December 1986): 6–16.

Correia, L.M. "'A' is for Alar: EPA's Persistent Failure to Promptly Remove Hazardous Pesticides from the Food Supply." *Chemical Regulation Reporter* (14 August 1992): 868–80.

Covello, V.T. "Informing People About Risks From Chemicals, Radiation, and Other Toxic Substances: A Review of Obstacles to Public Understanding and Effective Risk Communication." In *Prospects and Problems in Risk Communication*, ed. W. Leiss, 1–49.

Covello, V.T., P.W. Brandt-Rauf, and H.H. Bendixen. "The Occupational Risk of Death from HIV Transmission in Health Care Workers." *Medical Science Research*, vol. 20 (1992): 689–90.

Covello, V.T., D.B. McCallum, and M.T. Pavlova, eds. *Effective Risk Communication*. New York: Plenum Press, 1989.

Covello, V.T., and J. Mumpower. "Risk Analysis and Risk Management: A Historical Perspective." In *Environmental Health Risks*, ed. S. McColl, 1–27.

Covello, V.T., D. von Winterfeldt, and Paul Slovic. "Risk Communication: A Review of the Literature." *Risk Abstracts* 3, 4 (1986): 171–82.

D'Agostino, Ralph, Jr. and Richard Wilson. "Asbestos: The Hazard, the Risk and Public Policy." In *Phantom Risk*, eds. K. Foster, D. Bernstein, and P. Huber, 183–210.

Darling, Craig R. *In Search of Consensus: An Evaluation of the Clayoquot Sound Sustainable Development Task Force Process*. Victoria: University of Victoria Institute for Dispute Resolution, 1991.

Davies, J. Clarence, V.T. Covello, and Frederick W. Allen, eds. *Risk Communication*. Washington, DC: The Conservation Foundation, 1987.

Davis, D.L. "The 'Shotgun Wedding' of Science and Law: Risk Assessment and Judicial Review." *Columbia Journal of Environmental Law* 10 (1985): 67–109.

Deloitte Haskins & Sells (DHS). "An Economic Benefit Assessment of Anti-Sapstain Chemicals used in B.C. Sawmills." In Canada. Agriculture Canada, "Discussion Document on Anti-Sapstain Chemicals," section 9.

DiFranza, Joseph R., *et al.* "RJR Nabisco's Cartoon Camel Promotes Camel Cigarettes to Children." *Journal of the American Medical Association* 266, 22 (11 December 1991): 3149–53.

Dorcey, Anthony H.J., and Christine L. Riek. "Negotiation-based Approaches to the Settlement of Environmental Disputes in Canada." In *The Place of Negotiation in Environmental Assessment*. 7–36. Hull: CEARC, 1987.

Ellis, Derek, ed. *Environments at Risk*. New York: Springer-Verlag, 1989.

Engelhardt, H. Tristam Jr., and Arthur L. Caplan, eds. *Scientific Controversies: Case Studies in the Resolution and Closure of Disputes in Science and Technology*. Cambridge: Cambridge University Press, 1987.

*Environmental Health Criteria 69: Magnetic Fields*. Geneva: World Health Organization, 1987.

Erdreich, Linda S., and Antonio Sastre. "Prepared Evidence and Report of Linda S. Erdreich and Antonio Sastre." Mimeo, 4 July 1989.

Feychting, M., and A. Ahlbom. *Magnetic fields and cancer in people residing near Swedish high voltage power lines*. IMM-rapport 6/92. Stockholm, Sweden: Karolinska Institute, 1992.

Fischer, G.W. *et al.* "What Risks are People Concerned About?" *Risk Analysis* 11 (1991): 303–14.

Fischer, Paul M., J.W. Richards, Jr., E.J. Berman, and D.M. Krugman. "Recall and Eye Tracking Study of Adolescents Viewing Tobacco Advertisements." *Journal of the American Medical Association* 261, 1 (6 January 1989): 84–9.

Fischer, Paul M., *et al.* "Brand Logo Recognition by Children aged 3 to 6 Years." *Journal of the American Medical Association* 266, 22 (11 December 1991): 3145–8.

Fischoff, Baruch, Paul Slovic, and Sarah Lichtenstein. "Lay Foibles and Expert Fables in Judgements About Risk." In: *Progress in Resource Management and Environmental Planning*, eds T. O'Riordan, and R. K. Turner. New York: John Wiley & Sons, 1981.

Fisher, Roger, and William Ury. *Getting to YES: Negotiating Agreement Without Giving In.* Markham, ON: Penguin Books, 1981.

Fitzgerald, Karen, M. Granger Morgan, and Indira Nair. "Special report – electromagnetic fields: the jury's still out." *IEEE Spectrum* (August 1990): 22–35.

Floderus, Birgitta, *et al. Occupational exposure to electromagnetic fields in relation to leukemia and brain tumors. A case-control study.* PM edition. Solna, Sweden: National Institute of Occupational Health, 1992.

Florig, H. Keith. "Containing the Costs of the EMF Problem." *Science* 257 (24 July 1992).

– "Management options for power-frequency fields." *Forum for Applied Research and Public Policy* 3, 4 (Winter 1988): 86–95.

Flynn, Sarah Grieg. "The Timber/Fish/Wildlife Agreement: A Case Study of Alternative Environmental Dispute Resolution." Report no. 103. Burnaby, B.C.: School of Resource and Environmental Management, Simon Fraser University, 1992.

Foster, Kenneth R., David E. Bernstein, and Peter W. Huber, eds. *Phantom Risk: Scientific Inference and the Law.* Cambridge, MA.: MIT Press, 1993.

Fraidenburg, Michael E. "The New Politics of Natural Resources: Negotiating a Shift Toward Privatization of Natural Resource Policy Making in Washington State." *The Northwest Environmental Journal* 4 (1989): 211–40.

Freeman, Michael. "The courts and electromagnetic fields." *Public Utilities Fortnightly* (19 July 1990): 20–2.

Freudenburg, W.R. "Perceived Risk, Real Risk: Social Science and the Art of Probabilistic Risk Assessment." *Science* 242 (7 October 1988): 44–50.

– "Heuristics, Biases, and the Not-so-General Publics: Expertise and Error in the Assessment of Risks." In *Social Theories of Risk,* eds S. Krimsky and D. Golding, 229–49.

Furby, Lita, Paul Slovic, B. Fischhoff, and R. Gregory. "Public Perceptions of Electric Power Transmission Lines." *Journal of Environmental Psychology* 8, 1 (1988): 19–43.

Golding, D., S. Krimsky, and A. Plough. "Evaluating Risk Communication: Narrative vs. Technical Presentations of Information About Radon." *Risk Analysis* 12 (1992): 27–35.

Gough, Janet D. *A Review of the Literature Pertaining to 'Perceived' Risk and 'Acceptable' Risk.* Information Paper No. 14. New Zealand: Centre for Resource Management, University of Canterbury and Lincoln University, 1990.

Graham, J.D., L.C. Green, and M.J. Roberts. *In Search of Safety: Chemicals and Cancer Risks.* Cambridge, MA.: Harvard University Press, 1988.

Gregory, Robin and Robert Mendelsohn. "Perceived Risk, Dread, and Benefits." *Risk Analysis* 13 (1993): 259–64.

Gregory, Robin, H. Kunreuther, D. Easterling, and K. Richards. "Incentives Policies to Site Hazardous Waste Facilities." *Risk Analysis* 11 (1991): 667–75.

Grima, A.P. "Environmental Risk Assessment and Community Impact Mitigation." In *Risk Perspectives on Environmental Impact Assessment,* eds A.P. Grima, C.D. Fowle, and R.E. Munn, 99–111. Toronto: Institute of Environmental Studies, University of Toronto, 1989.

Gunton, Thomas, and Sarah Flynn. "Resolving Environmental Conflicts: The Role of Mediation and Negotiation." *Environments* 21, 3 (1992): 1–6.

Harrison, Kathryn, and George Hoberg. *Risk, Science, and Politics: Regulating Toxic Chemicals in Canada and the United States.* Montreal: McGill-Queen's University Press, 1994.

– "Setting the Environmental Agenda in Canada and the United States: The Cases of Dioxin and Radon." *Canadian Journal of Political Science* 24, 1 (1991): 3–27.

Harter, Philip J. "Federal Agencies and ADR." In *ADR: Practice and Perspective.* Washington, DC: The Bureau of National Affairs, Inc., 1991.

– "Negotiating Regulations: A Cure for the Malaise." *The Georgetown Law Journal* 71, 1 (1982): 1–118.

Hattis, D., and D. Kennedy. "Assessing Risks From Health Hazards: An Imperfect Science." *Technology Review* 89 (May/June 1986): 60–69.

Hauf, R. "Electric and Magnetic Fields at Power Frequencies, with Particular Reference to 50 and 60 Hz." In *Nonionizing Radiation Protection,* ed. World Health Organization, 175–97. Copenhagen: World Health Organization Regional Publications, 1982.

Hester, Gordon. "Electric and Magnetic Fields: Managing an Uncertain Risk." *Environment* 34, 1 (January/February 1992): 7–11, 25–32.

Hill, A.B. "The Environment and Disease: Association or Causation?" *Proceedings of the Royal Society of Medicine* 58 (May 1965): 295–300.

Hoberg, George. "Risk, Science and Politics: Alachlor Regulation in Canada and the United States." *Canadian Journal of Political Science* 23, 2 (1990): 257–77.

- "Sleeping with an Elephant: The American Influence on Canadian Environmental Regulation." *Journal of Public Policy* 11, 1 (1991): 107–32.

Horisberger, B., and R. Dinkel, eds. *The Perception and Management of Drug Safety Risks.* Berlin: Springer-Verlag, 1989.

Inhaber, Herbert. "Is Risk Analysis necessary, sufficient, or both?" *Risk Abstracts,* 9 (1992): 1–3.

Janes, David E., Jr. "Background Information on High Voltage Fields." *Environmental Health Perspectives* 20 (October 1977): 141–7.

Jasanoff, Sheila. "EPA's Regulation of Daminozide: Unscrambling the Messages of Risk." *Science, Technology and Human Values* 12, 3/4 (Summer/Fall 1987): 116–24.

- *The Fifth Branch: Science Advisers as Policymakers.* Cambridge, MA.: Harvard University Press, 1990.

- *Risk Management and Political Culture.* New York: Russell Sage Foundation, 1986.

Johnson, B.B., and V.T. Covello, eds. *The Social and Cultural Construction of Risk: Essays on Risk Selection and Perception.* Dordrecht, Holland: D. Reidel, 1987.

Jones, P.A. "Chlorophenols and their Impurities in the Canadian Environment, 1983 Supplement." Ottawa: Environment Canada, Environmental Protection Service, March 1984.

Kabot, Robert, Jonathan Chary, William Bailey, and Antonio Sastre. *Background Report on Health Issues Associated with Exposure to Power Frequency Electric and Magnetic Fields.* Environmental Research Information Inc., 4 May 1988.

Kahneman, D., Paul Slovic, and A. Tversky, eds. *Judgment Under Uncertainty: Heuristics and Biases.* New York: Cambridge University Press, 1982.

Kasperson, Roger E. "The Social Amplification of Risk: Progess in Developing an Integrative Framework." In *Social Theories of Risk,* eds S. Krimsky and D. Golding, 153–78.

Kasperson, R., O. Renn, P. Slovic, H. Brown, *et al.* "The Social Amplification of Risk." *Risk Analysis* 8, 2 (1988): 177–87.

Kasperson, Roger E., and P.J.M. Stallen, eds. *Communicating Risks to the Public.* Boston: Kluwer Academic Publishers, 1991.

Kavet, Robert. "Biological Effects of Electric Fields: EPRI's Role." *IEEE Transactions on Power Apparatus and Systems* PAS-101 7 (July 1982): 2115–21.

Keeney, R.L., and D. von Winterfeldt. "A Prescriptive Risk Framework for Individual Health and Safety Decisions." *Risk Analysis* 11 (1991): 523–33.

Knaster, A.S., and P.J. Harter. "The Clean Fuels Regulatory Negotiation." *Intergovernmental Perspective* (Summer 1992): 20–22.

Koren, Herman. *Handbook of Environmental Health and Safety.* 2nd ed. Chelsea, MI: Lewis Publishers, 1991.

Kraus, N., T. Malmfors, and Paul Slovic. "Intuitive Toxicology: Expert and Lay Judgments of Chemical Risks." *Risk Analysis* 12 (1992): 215–32.

Krewski, Daniel. "Risk and Risk Management: Issues and Approaches." In *Environmental Health Risks*, ed. S. McColl, 29–51.

Krewski, Daniel, and P.L. Birkwood. "Risk Assessment and Risk Management." *Risk Abstracts* 4, 2 (1987): 53–61.

Krewski, Daniel, E. Somers, and P.L. Birkwood. "Risk Perception in a Decision Making Context." *Environmental Carcinogenesis Reviews* C5, 2 (1987): 175–209.

Krimsky, Sheldon, and D. Golding, eds. *Social Theories of Risk*. Westport, CT: Praeger, 1992.

Krimsky, S., and A. Plough. *Environmental Hazards: Communicating Risk as a Social Process*. Dover, MA.: Auburn House, 1988.

Lave, L.B. "Health and safety risk analyses: Information for Better Decisions." *Science* 236 (17 April 1987): 291–6.

– "The State-of-the-Art of Risk Assessment Approaches." In *Environmental Health Risks*, ed. S. McColl, 53–66.

Lee, Jack M., Jr. "High-Voltage Transmission Lines: The Ongoing Search for Biological Effects." *Public Utilities Fortnightly* 114 (20 December 1984): 33–42.

Lee, Kai N. "Defining Success in Environmental Dispute Resolution." *Resolve* (Spring 1982): 1, 3–6.

Leigh, J.P., "Estimates of the Probability of Job-related Death in 347 Occupations." *Journal of Occupational Medicine* 29 (1987): 510–19.

Leiss, William. *C.B. Macpherson: Dilemmas of Liberalism and Socialism*. Montréal: New World Perspectives, 1988.

– "Managing the Risks and Consequences of Innovation." In *Managing Technology*, eds L. Salter and D. Wolfe, Toronto: Garamond Press, 1990.

– "Multi-Stakeholder Negotiation in Environmental Controversies: The Case of Antisapstain Chemicals in the British Columbia Wood Products Industry." Waterloo, ON: Institute for Risk Research, University of Waterloo, 1992.

– "The Risk Management Process." Working Paper, Agriculture Canada. Ottawa, 1985.

– "A Typology of Risk Management Issues." *Risk Abstracts* 7, 3 (1990): 1–8.

Leiss, William, ed. *Prospects and Problems in Risk Communication*. Waterloo, ON: University of Waterloo Press, 1989.

Leiss, William, and Christina Chociolko. "Why is Risk Controversial?" *Risk Management* 40 (May 1993): 30–5.

Leiss, William, and Daniel Krewski. "Risk Communication: Theory and Practice." In *Prospects and Problems in Risk Communication*, ed. W. Leiss, 89–112.

Lind, N.C., J.S. Nathwani, and E. Siddall. *Managing Risks in the Public Interest.* Waterloo, ON.: University of Waterloo, Institute for Risk Research, 1991.

MacCrimmon, K.R., and D.A. Wehrung. *Taking Risks: The Management of Uncertainty.* New York: The Free Press, 1986.

McColl, R. Stephen, ed. *Environmental Health Risks: Assessment and Management.* Waterloo, ON.: University of Waterloo Press, 1987.

McColl, R. Stephen, and William Leiss. "Formaldehyde: A Case Study in Risk Assessment and Risk Management." A Report for the Bureau of Chemical Hazards, Environmental Health Directorate, Health and Welfare Canada. Ottawa, December 1988.

McDaniels, Timothy, M.S. Kamlet, and G.W. Fischer. "Risk Perception and the Value of Safety." *Risk Analysis* 12, 4 (1992): 495–503.

McGarity, Thomas O. "Judicial Review of Scientific Rulemaking." *Science, Technology and Human Values* 9 (1984): 97–106.

McGarity, Thomas O. "Substantive and Procedural Discretion in Administrative Resolution of Science Policy Questions: Regulating Carcinogens in EPA and OSHA." *Georgeown Law Journal* 67 (1979): 729–810.

McGee, A., and E. Levy. "Herbicide Use in Forestry: Communication and Information Gaps." *Journal of Environmental Management* 26 (1988): 111–26.

Manning, W.G., *et al. The Costs of Poor Health Habits.* Cambridge, MA.: Harvard University Press, 1991.

Marino, Andrew A. "Are Power Lines Dangerous to Health? Probably So." *Public Power* 45, 4 (July-August 1987): 18, 20.

– Editorial, "We Need a Science Court." *Journal of Bioelectricity* 4, 1 (1985): vii-viii.

– "Submission to the British Columbia Utilities Commission in the Matter of the Routing of the 230-kV B.C. Hydro Dunsmuir to Gold River Transmission Line." Mimeo, 3 July 1989.

Marino, Andrew A., and Robert O. Becker. "High Voltage Lines: Hazard at a Distance." *Environment* 20, 9 (November 1978): 6–15, 40.

Marshall, Eliot. "Science Advisers Need Advice." *Science* 245 (7 July 1989): 20–2.

Mayo, D.G., and R.D. Hollander, eds. *Acceptable Evidence: Science and Values in Risk Management.* New York: Oxford University Press, 1991.

Mazis, Michael B., D.J. Ringold, E.S. Perry, and D.W. Denman. "Perceived Age and Attractiveness of Models in Cigarette Advertisements." *Journal of Marketing* 56 (January 1992): 22–37.

Mazur, Allan, "The Dynamics of Technical Controversies." In *Scientific Controversies: Case Studies in the Resolution and Closure of Disputes in Science and Technology,* eds Engelhardt and Caplan, 265–82.

– *The Dynamics of Technical Controversy.* Washington, DC: Communications Press, Inc., 1981.

Meng, Ronald. "How Dangerous is Work in Canada? Estimates of Job-related Fatalities in 482 Occupations." *Journal of Occupational Medicine* 33 (1991): 510–19.

Merrill, Richard A. "The Legal System's Response to Scientific Uncertainty: The Role of Judicial Review." *Fundamental and Applied Toxicology* 4 (1984): S418-S425.

*Microwave News*, 6, 4 (July/August 1986) to 12, 6 (November/December 1992).

Milham, S., Jr. "Mortality from Leukemia in Workers Exposed to Electrical and Magnetic Fields." *New England Journal of Medicine* 307, 4 (22 July 1982): 249.

Mintz, M. *At any cost: Corporate greed, women and the Dalkon Shield.* New York: Pantheon, 1985.

Moore, Taylor. "Pursuing the Science of EMF." *EPRI Journal* (January/February 1990): 4–17.

Morgan, M. Granger. *Electric and Magnetic Fields from 60 Hertz Electric Power: What do we Know About Possible Health Risks?* Pittsburgh, PA: Department of Engineering and Public Policy, Carnegie Mellon University, 1989.

Morgan, M. Granger, H. Keith Florig, Indira Nair, and David Lincoln. "Power Line Fields and Human Health." *IEEE Spectrum* 22, 2 (February 1985): 62–8.

Morgan, M. Granger, H. Keith Florig, Indira Nair, and Gordon L. Hester. "Controlling Exposure to Transmission Line Electromagnetic Fields: A Regulatory Approach that is Compatible with the Available Science." *Public Utilities Fortnightly* (17 March 1988): 49–58.

– "Power-Frequency Fields: the Regulatory Dilemma." *Issues in Science and Technology* 3, 4 (Summer 1987): 81–91.

Morgan, M. Granger *et al.* "Powerline Frequency Electric and Magnetic Fields: A Pilot Study of Risk Perception." *Risk Analysis* 5, 2 (1985): 139–49.

Mossman, B.T., J. Bignon, M. Corn, A. Seaton, and J.B.L. Gee. "Asbestos: Scientific Developments and Implications for Public Policy." *Science* 247 (19 January 1990): 294–301.

Munro, I.C., and K.R. Solomon. "Mechanistic Factors in the Interpretation of Carcinogenic Risk Assessment." In *Environmental Health Risks,* ed. S. McColl, 83–94.

Natural Resources Defense Council. *Intolerable Risk: Pesticides in our Children's Food.* New York: NRDC, 1989.

Nelkin, Dorothy. "Controversies and the Authority of Science." In *Scientific Controversies: Case Studies in the Resolution and Closure of Disputes in Science and Technology,* eds Engelhardt and Caplan, 283–93.

Nelkin, D., and M.S. Brown. *Workers at Risk: Voices from the Workplace.* Chicago: University of Chicago Press, 1984.

New York State. Department of Health. *Biological Effects of Power Line Fields: New York State Power Lines Project Scientific Advisory Panel's Final Report.* Albany, 1 July 1987.

– "New York State Power Lines Project: Questions and Answers." Albany, July 1988.

Newsome, W.H. "Determination of Daminozide Residues on Foods and its Degradation to 1,1–Dimethylhydrazine by Cooking." *Agricultural and Food Chemistry* 28 (1980): 319–21.

"On the Process of Dispute Settlement." *Negotiation Journal* Special Issue 5, 2 (1989).

Ontario Hydro. *Electric and Magnetic Fields and Human Health Research.* Toronto, n.d.

– *Health Effects of Electric and Magnetic Fields: Research, Communication, Regulation.* Proceedings of the International Utility Symposium, Toronto, Ontario, 15–19 September 1986. Toronto: Ontario Hydro, 1986.

– "Information: Electric and Magnetic Fields." Toronto, n.d.

Ontario. Ministry of Health. Public Health Branch. Disease Control and Epidemiology Service. *Health Effects of Extremely Low Frequency Electromagnetic Fields: A Review of Clinical and Epidemiological Studies.* Toronto, 30 July 1987.

Otway, Harry. "Public Wisdom, Expert Fallibility: Toward a Contextual Theory of Risk." In *Social Theories of Risk,* eds S. Krimsky, and D. Golding, 215–28.

Otway, Harry, and Detlof von Winterfeldt. "Expert Judgement in Risk Analysis and Management: Process, Context, and Pitfalls." *Risk Analysis* 12, 1 (1992): 83–93.

Otway, Harry, and Brian Wynne. "Risk Communication: Paradigm and Paradox." *Risk Analysis* 9, 2 (1989): 141–5.

Ozawa, Connie P. *Recasting Science: Consensual Procedures in Public Policy Making.* Boulder, CO: Westview Press, 1991.

Ozawa, Connie P., and Lawrence Susskind. "Mediating Science-Intensive Policy Disputes." *Journal of Policy Analysis and Management* 5, 1 (1985): 23–9.

Peto, R. *et al.* "Mortality from Tobacco in Developed Countries: Indirect Estimation from National Vital Statistics." *The Lancet* 339 (23 May 1992): 1268–78.

Pierce, John P. "International Comparisons of Trends in Cigarette Smoking Prevalence." *American Journal of Public Health* 79, 2 (February 1989): 152–7.

Pierce, John P. *et al.* "Does Tobacco Advertising Target Young People to Start Smoking?" *Journal of the American Medical Association* 266, 22 (11 December 1991): 3154–8.

Pierce, John P. *et al.* "Trends in Cigarette Smoking in the United States: Educational Differences are Increasing" and "Projections to the Year

2000." *Journal of the American Medical Association* 261, 1 (6 January 1989): 56–65.

Pollay, Richard. "Propaganda, Puffing, and the Public Interest." *Public Relations Review* XVI (1990): 39–54.

Pollay, Richard, and A. Lavack. "The Targeting of Youths by Cigarette Marketers: Archival Evidence on Trial." In *Advances in Consumer Research*, eds L. McAllister and M. Rothschild, 20 (1993):266–71.

Pritzker, David M. "Working Together for Better Regulations." *Natural Resources and Environment* 5, 2 (1990): 29–31, 51–4.

Pritzker, D.M., and D.S. Dalton. *Negotiated Rulemaking Sourcebook*. Washington, DC: Administrative Conference of the United States, 1990.

Rayner, Steve. "Cultural Theory and Risk Analysis." In *Social Theories of Risk*, eds. S. Krimsky and D. Golding, 83–115.

Renn, Ortwin, and D. Levine. "Credibility and Trust in Risk Communication." In *Communicating Risks to the Public*, eds R. Kasperson and P. Stallen, 175–218.

Rest, K., S. Krimsky, and A. Plough. "Risk Communication and Community Right-to-Know: A Four Community Study of SARA Title III." The Center for Environmental Management, Tufts University, March 1991.

Riegert, Paul W. *From Arsenic to DDT: A History of Entomology in Western Canada*. Toronto: University of Toronto Press, 1980.

Rish, William R., and M. Granger Morgan. "Regulating Possible Health Effects from AC Transmission Line Electromagnetic Fields." *Proceedings of the IEEE* 67, 10 (October 1979): 1416–27.

"Risk Assessment of Pesticides." *Chemical and Engineering News*. 7 January 1991. Washington, DC: American Chemical Society.

Rohrman, B., P.M. Wiedemann, and H.U. Stegelmann. *Risk Communication: An Interdisciplinary Bibliography*. 4th edn. Vol. 2 of *Studies in Risk Communication*. Jülich, Germany: KFA Jülich GMBH, May 1990.

Rosen, J.D. "Much Ado About Alar." *Issues in Science and Technology* 7, 1 (Fall 1990): 85–90.

Ross, Randy. "Cancer Association With High Voltage Transmission Lines and Electric and Magnetic Fields of Extremely Low Frequency (ELF): A Review of Current Literature." Radiation Protection Service, B.C. Ministry of Health, Vancouver, 18 January 1988.

Roth, E. *et al.* "What do we know about making risk comparisons?" *Risk Analysis* 10 (1990): 375–88.

Rowell, Clark H. "Power Transmission Lines – A Future Scenario." *Public Utilities Fortnightly* (29 July 1976): 15–9.

Royal Society of Canada. *Tobacco, Nicotine, and Addiction*. Ottawa: Royal Society, 1989.

Sadler, Barry. "Appendix 1. Building Mediation into the Federal Environmental Assessment and Review Process." In *The Place of Negotiation in*

*Environmental Assessment.* 75–83. Hull: Canadian Environmental Assessment Research Council, 1987.

– "Institutionalizing Mediation in Federal Environmental Assessment: A Discussion Note." Federal Environmental Assessment Review Office, Ottawa, 15 November 1990.

Salter, Liora. *Mandated Science: Science and Scientists in the Making of Standards.* Boston: Kluwer Academic Publishers, 1988.

– "Observations on the Politics of Risk Assessment: The Captan Case." *Canadian Public Policy* 11 (1985): 64–76.

Salter, Liora, and William Leiss. "Guide to Consultation and Consensus Building." A Report for the Canadian Centre for Management Development, Ottawa, 1989.

Sandborn, Calvin. "The Democratization of Risk Decisions." Paper presented at the Global Conference on Ethics and Technology, University of Guelph, ON., October 1989.

Sandman, Peter. "Hazard versus Outrage in the Public Perception of Risk." In *Effective Risk Communication,* eds V.T. Covello, D.B. McCallum, and M.T. Pavlova, 45–9.

Savitz, David A., Neil E. Pearce, and Charles Poole. "Methodological Issues in the Epidemiology of Electromagnetic Fields and Cancer." *Epidemiologic Reviews* 11 (1989): 59–78.

Schiefer, H.B., "Antisapstain Chemicals: A Critical Evaluation." Saskatoon, Sask.: Toxicology Research Centre, University of Saskatchewan, 1990.

Schiefer, H.B., D.G. Irvine, and S.C. Buzik. *You and Toxicology.* Saskatoon, Sask.: Toxicology Research Centre, University of Saskatchewan, 1986.

Science Council of Canada. *Regulating the Regulators*: *Science, Values and Decisions.* Report No. 35. Ottawa: Minister of Supply and Services, 1982.

Sharlin, H.I. "Macro-Risks, Micro-Risks and the Media: The EDB Case." In *The Social and Cultural Construction of Risk,* eds B.B. Johnson and V.T. Covello, 183–97.

Shepard, Michael. "EMF and Human Health." *EPRI Journal* (October/November 1987): 1–15.

Shrader-Frechette, K.S. *Risk and Rationality: Philosophical Foundations for Populist Reforms.* Berkeley, CA: University of California Press, 1991.

Siegler, Ellen. "Regulatory Negotiations: A Practical Perspective." *Environmental Law Reporter* 22 (1992): 10647–54.

Sielken, R.L., Jr. "The Capabilities, Sensitivity, Pitfalls, and Future of Quantitative Risk Assessment." In *Environmental Health Risks,* ed. S. McColl, 95–131.

Sigurdson, S. Glenn. "Settling Environmental Disputes: Reflections on two Cases." *Canadian Environmental Mediation Newsletter* 2, 2. Toronto: Conflict Management Resources, York University, 1987.

Slesin, Louis. "Power Lines and Cancer: The Evidence Grows." *Technology Review* (October 1987): 54–9.
– "The Danger of Ignoring Non-ionizing Radiation." *Technology Review* (January 1989): 22–3.
Slovic, Paul. "Perception of Risk." *Science* 236, (17 April 1987): 280–6.
– "Perception of Risk: Reflections on the Psychometric Paradigm." In *Social Theories of Risk*, eds S. Krimsky, and D. Golding, 117–52.
Slovic, P., N. Kraus, and V.T. Covello. "What *Should* We Know About Making Risk Comparisons?" *Risk Analysis* 10 (1990): 389–92.
Slovic, Paul *et al.* "Risk Perception of Prescription Drugs: Report on a Survey in Sweden." In *The Perception and Management of Drug Safety Risks*, eds B. Horisberger and R. Dinkel.
Stanbury, W.T., and I. Vertinsky. "Guide to the Application of Cost-Benefit Analysis to Regulation." A Report to the Office of Privatization and Regulatory Affairs, Ottawa, 1988.
Stockwin, W. "Apple Growers Strike Back." *Farm Chemicals* (February 1991): 32–4.
Susskind, Lawrence E. "The Uses of Negotiation and Mediation in Environmental Impact Assessment." In *Integrated Impact Assessment,* eds F.A. Rossini and A.L. Porter, 154–167. Boulder, CO: Westview Press, 1983.
Susskind, Lawrence E., and Jeffrey Cruikshank. *Breaking the Impasse: Consensual Approaches to Resolving Public Disputes.* New York: Basic Books, 1987.
Susskind, Lawrence E., and Scott McCreary. "Techniques for Resolving Coastal Resource Management Disputes Through Negotiation." *American Planning Association Journal* (Summer 1985): 365–74.
Talcott, J.A., W.A. Thurber, A.F. Kantor *et al.* "Asbestos-associated Diseases in a Cohort of Cigarette-filter Workers." *New England Journal of Medicine* 321 (1989): 1220–3.
Torrance, George *et al.* "Risk-benefit and Quality-of-life Analyses of Prescription Drugs." Ottawa: Health and Welfare Canada, 1990.
Toth, Bela. "1,1–Dimethylhydrazine (Unsymmetrical) Carcinogenesis in Mice." *Journal of the National Cancer Institute* 50 (1973): 181–94.
– "The Large Bowel Carcinogenic Effects of Hydrazines and Related Compounds occurring in Nature and in the Environment." *Cancer* 40 (1977): 2427–31.
Toth, Bela *et al.* "Induction of Tumors in Mice with the Herbicide Succinic Acid 2,2–Dimethylhydrazide." *Cancer Research* 37 (October 1977): 3497–500.
"The Toxic Effect of Tobacco Vapors." A report in the *Journal of the American Medical Association* in 1891, reprinted in *Journal of the American Medical Association* 266, 22 (11 December 1991): front matter.
*Transmission/Distribution Health & Safety Report,* March 1983 to July 1989.

United Kingdom. National Radiological Protection Board. Advisory Group on Non-Ionizing Radiation. *Electromagnetic Fields and the Risk of Cancer.* NRPB Documents vol. 3, no. 1. Chilton, Didcot, Oxon, England: National Radiological Protection Board, 1992.

United States. Administrative Conference of the United States (ACUS). *Sourcebook: Federal Agency Use of Alternative Means of Dispute Resolution.* Washington, DC: Office of the Chairman, 1987.

United States. Congress. House Committee on Interior and Insular Affairs. Subcommittee on General Oversight and Investigations. *Electric Power Lines: Health and Public Policy Implications: Oversight Hearing.* 101st Cong., 2nd sess., 8 March 1990.

– Committee on Interior and Insular Affairs, Subcommittee on Water and Power Resources. *Health Effects of Transmission Lines: Oversight Hearing.* 100th Congress, 1st sess., 6 October 1987.

United States. Congress. Office of Technology Assessment. *Electric Power Wheeling and Dealing: Technological Considerations for Increasing Competition.* E-409. Washington, DC: U.S. Government Printing Office, April 1989.

– *Biological Effects of Power Frequency Electric and Magnetic Fields: Background Paper.* OTA-BP-E-53. Washington, DC: U.S. Government Printing Office, May 1989.

United States. Department of Energy. Bonneville Power Administration. *Electrical and Biological Effects of Transmission Lines: A Review.* Portland, June 1989 and October 1985.

United States. Department of Health, Education, and Welfare. National Cancer Institute. "Bioassay of Daminozide for Possible Carcinogenicity." *Carcinogenesis Technical Report Series* 83 (1978).

United States. Environmental Protection Agency. "Case Study on Risk Assessment." Part I. Workshop on Risk Assessment, 17–8 March 1985.

– Office of Research and Development. "Evaluation of the Potential Carcinogenicity of Electromagnetic Fields." External Review Draft, EPA/600/6–90/005B .Washington, DC, October 1990.

– Science Advisory Board. Radiation Advisory Committee. Nonionizing Electric and Magnetic Fields Subcommittee. "Final RAC/NIEMFS Report." September 1991.

United States. National Research Council. *Improving Risk Communication.* Washington, DC: National Academy Press, 1989.

– *Pesticides in the Diets of Infants and Children.* Washington, DC: National Academy Press, 1993.

– *Risk Assessment in the Federal Government: Managing the Process.* Washington, DC: National Academy Press, 1983.

– *Toxicity Testing.* Washington, DC: National Academy Press, 1984.

United States. National Science Foundation. "Risk Assessment and Risk Assessment Methods." Washington, DC, January 1985.

Versteeg, Hajo. "A Case Study in Multi-Stakeholder Consultation: The Corporate History of the Federal Pesticide Registration Review." Ottawa: Canadian Centre for Management Development, 1992.

Versteeg, Hajo. "The Conflict between Law and Science." Paper presented to the Canadian Institute for the Administration of Justice, Halifax, NS, October 1988.

Vertinsky, I.B., and D.A. Wehrung. *Risk Perception and Drug Safety Evaluation.* Ottawa: Health Protection Branch, Health and Welfare Canada, 1989.

Victor, Peter. "Techniques for Assessment and Analysis in the Management of Toxic Chemicals." In *Proceedings of the National Workshop on Risk-Benefit Analysis.* Ottawa: Agriculture Canada, 1985.

Viscusi, W.K. *Fatal Tradeoffs: Public and Private Responsibilities for Risk.* New York: Oxford University Press, 1992.

– *Smoking: Making the Risky Decision.* New York: Oxford University Press, 1992.

Warner, Kenneth E. "Effects of the Antismoking Campaign: An Update" and "Smoking and Health: A 25-Year Perspective." *American Journal of Public Health* 79, 2 (January 1989): 141–51.

Weiss, John. "The Power Line Controversy: Legal Responses to Potential Electromagnetic Field Health Hazards." *Columbia Journal of Environmental Law* 15 (1990): 359–88.

Wells, Jennifer. "The Fault Line." *The Globe and Mail Report on Business Magazine.* December 1992, 33–52.

Wessel, Milton, R. *Science and Conscience.* New York: Columbia University Press, 1980.

Wigle, Donald T. "Illness and Death in Canada by Smoking: An Epidemiological Perspective." Laboratory Centre for Disease Control, Health Protection Branch, Health and Welfare Canada, August 1989.

Wilson, R., and E. A. C. Crouch. "Risk Assessment and Comparisons: An Introduction." *Science* 236 (17 April 1987): 267–71.

World Health Organization. *Extremely Low Frequency (ELF) Fields.* Environmental Health Criteria 35. Geneva: World Health Organization, 1984.

Wynne, Brian. "Risk and Social Learning: Reification to Engagement." In *Social Theories of Risk,* eds S. Krimsky and D. Golding, 275–300.

Zeckhauser, R.J., and W.K. Viscusi. "Risk within Reason." *Science* 248 (1990): 559–64.

# Index

68, 73, 204, 257, 265, 278. *See also* Acceptable risk; and the following entries
Risk assessment (risk analysis, risk estimation), 7, 20–1, 28, 29–30, 32, 35, 37, 38–9, 41, 42, 46–8, 57, 144–6, 263–5, 364n.7, 373n.21, 375n.33; and Alachlor, 18; and antisapstains, 226, 227, 251, 252; and daminozide and UDMH, 161–6, 169, 173, 183–4, 188–93, 268–70; and EMF, 91, 95, 108–9, 133–4, 147–8; and formaldehyde, 48–9; and intuitive judgment, 8, 30, 38, 58, 59, 65, 68, 70, 71, 72; and pathology, 19, 21, 167; and qualitative judgment, 39; and smoking, 74; and uncertainty, 7, 9, 30, 46, 47, 52, 137, 139, 142–4, 277, 279, 319n.8, 353n.171; and under-assessment, 10, 52–4, 258, 259, 260
Risk/benefit analysis, 18, 40, 170–4, 187, 191, 324n.34
Risk/benefit trade-offs, 19, 23, 33, 34, 39, 42, 44, 45, 50, 51, 56–73, 58–60, 171, 203, 204, 210, 250–1, 253, 256–7, 270, 277
Risk communication, 34–8, 46, 65, 69, 73, 101, 198, 354n.189
Risk comparisons, 33, 34, 71, 74, 233–5
Risk constituencies, 259–62
Risk management, 27–50, 58, 262–71, 309–15

Risk, occupational, 59, 61–2, 77, 326n.10, 374n.22; and antisapstains, 221, 233, 242, 249, 259, 260, 261, 266; and cadmium, 54–5; and daminozide and UDMH, 202, 203; and EDB, 371n.14; and EMF, 86–8, 90, 93, 97–9, 114, 118; and farmworkers, 200–1, 203, 206, 266, 327n.14, 371n.15; and formaldehyde, 50, 54, 64, 259; and mining, 54, 61–2, 257; and tobacco, 330n.46
Risk perception, 21, 30–2, 37, 46, 47, 59, 65, 66, 73, 104, 146, 176, 179
Risk-averse behaviour, 4, 10, 16, 20, 57, 157, 262, 264, 265, 266, 267, 268, 270
Risk-promoters, 259, 264, 268–71, 373n.21
Risk-taking behaviour, 4, 9, 11–16, 20, 52, 54, 58
RNA, and ELF experiments, 84, 331n.10
Robertson, Herb, 131
Ross, Randy, 115
Royal Society of Canada, 73, 329n.42

SADH. *See* Alar
Safety factors, 33, 162, 189, 192
Safeway, 175, 178
Salter, Liora, 140–4
Sandborn, Calvin, 240, 242
Sandman, Peter, 69, 198
Sastre, Antonio, 114, 115, 116ff., 125, 138, 139, 140. 146, 349n.73
Savitz, David, 96, 97, 104, 108, 117, 119, 126, 127, 138, 140

Schiefer, H.B., 236–43
Science, 21–2, 29, 38, 40, 54, 55, 58, 116–17, 119–20, 125–7, 138–44, 146, 155; and EMF, 90–2, 127; "mandated science," 17, 140–4, 374n.31; and peer review, 38, 39, 150, 201; and policy, 45–7, 140–4; and research funding, 120, 124–7, 130–1; science court, 149–50; scientific audit, 167, 268, 359n.36; scientific consensus-finding conference, 151, 272, 273; scientific controversy, 90–1, 97, 99, 119–23, 129–30, 167, 172–3, 201, 271–2; scientific panels, 150
Sexually transmitted diseases, risks of, 56–7
Shannon, Elizabeth, 107, 110
Shrader-Frechette, K. S., 9, 323n.26
"60 Minutes," 154, 180, 181, 182, 183, 197
Skelly, Bob, 115
Slovic, Paul, 10, 27, 32, 66, 70
Smith, Neptune, 112, 115
Smoking. *See* Tobacco
Socio-Economic Impact Analysis, 41
Solomon, K.R., 236–43
Somers, Emmanuel, 42
Stakeholders, 206–8, 229–55, 259–65, 272, 370n.10
Streep, Meryl, 180, 181
Susskind and Cruikshank, 213, 215–16, 273
Suzuki, David, 137
Swanson, Milt, 112, 115
Sweden, 148